The Case for Qualia

The Case for Qualia

edited by Edmond Wright

A Bradford Book
The MIT Press
Cambridge, Massachusetts
London, England

© 2008 Massachusetts Institute of Technology

MIT Press books may be purchased at special quantity discounts for business or sales promotional use. For information, please e-mail special_sales@mitpress.mit.edu or write to Special Sales Department, The MIT Press, 55 Hayward Street, Cambridge, MA 02142.

This book was set in Stone Sans and Stone Serif by The MIT Press and was printed and bound in the United States of America.

Library of Congress Cataloging-in-Publication Data

The case for qualia / Edmond Wright, editor.
    p. cm.
Includes bibliographical references and index.
ISBN 978-0-262-23266-1 (hardcover : alk. paper)—ISBN 978-0-262-73188-1 (pbk. : alk. paper)
1. Knowledge, Theory of. 2. Qualia. 3. Philosophy of mind. I. Wright, Edmond Leo, 1927–.
BD161.C353   2008
111—dc22   2007031242

10 9 8 7 6 5 4 3 2 1

For Anna and Bob,
Oliver and Mieko

Contents

Acknowledgments

I should like to thank the following for the stimulation and pleasure of sharing philosophical thoughts with them: Louis Allix, Harold Brown, Barry Brummett, Mark Crooks, Terry Eagleton, Judy Feldmann (for her meticulous copyediting), James Giles, Ernst von Glasersfeld, Jonathan Harrison, Robert Kirk, Jonathan Lowe, Graham Dunstan Martin, Barry Maund, Moreland Perkins, Matjaž Potrč, Calvin Schrag, Philip Smith, and John Smythies. Finally, and not least, thanks are due to all the contributors to this volume.

Introduction

Over ten years ago I edited a volume (Wright 1993) that put forward arguments for what was then called "new representationalism," which in effect was a collection in support of indirect realism. Indirect realism is the view that regards qualia, sensory experiences, as the evidence for our objectivizing of the real outside us. In that volume a number of the contributors complained of the failure of opponents of qualia to address the answers to the objections that had been made, admittedly to sense-datum theory as it was then characterized. At the present time there remains a strong sense of complacency about the dismissal of that theory, a mood which is suspect, particularly because sense-datum theory was centrally presented as mired in inconsistency over its purported belief in the copying in the brain of external entities, which led to its being shelved as a myth. Michael Tye, for example, feels that he has no need to rehearse any of the old objections to the theory "for a host of familiar reasons" (Tye 2000: 45–46). Austen Clark regards the very use of the term itself now as "infamous" (Clark 2000: 3). A recent review of a book by John Hyman (Hyman 2007; Mulhall 2007) takes it for granted that no one at all these days holds to a belief in qualia.

"Complacency" is, however, not the right word here; it would be if no one had voiced any objections to the myth claim since the supposed demolition of so-called "sense-data" long ago by Ryle, Austin, Pitcher, Armstrong, and the like (Austin 1962; Ryle 1966; Armstrong 1966; Pitcher 1971). When considering opponents of the notion of qualia from the last half of the twentieth century, it is revealing to look at their indexes and their lists of references and see how many publications of the following list of philosophers and psychologists they include: Virgil C. Aldrich, Ned Block, Harold Brown, David Chalmers, Arthur W. Collins, Paul Fitzgerald, John Foster, A. Campbell Garnett, Richard Gregory, C. L. Hardin, Jonathan Harrison, John Heffner, Emmett L. Holman, Frank Jackson, O. R. Jones, James S. Kelly, Charles Landesman, Michael Lockwood, E. J. Lowe, D. L.

C. MacClachlan, J. L. Mackie, Maurice Mandelbaum, J. B. Maund, C. W. K. Mundle, Robert Oakes, Christopher Peacocke, John Pennycuick, Moreland Perkins, H. H. Price (still publishing in 1964), Howard Robinson, William Robinson, Wilfrid Sellars (loyal here to his father Roy Wood Sellars, who was himself still publishing in 1970), Sidney Shoemaker, John R. Smythies, Andrew Ward, and myself (a representative list of publications is given in the references section of this introduction). On the cover of the most recent collection of essays on perception (Gendler and Hawthorne 2006) the explanatory text speaks of the "decades of neglect" of the topic of the philosophy of perception; however, it ignores the question of "Who has neglected whom?"

Our opponents have been very selective. Block, Hardin, Peacocke, and Jackson have received attention: Block for his "population of China" and "inverted Earth" counterexamples, and his consideration of orgasm; Hardin for his work on color; Peacocke for his "scenario" concept, his queries about nonconceptual sensing, double vision, and perspective effects; Jackson for his "knowledge argument" (inevitably weakened by the apostasy of its proponent); and David Chalmers for his zombie argument. Michael Tye and Daniel Dennett have addressed a number of empirical issues (Tye 1995a,b, 2000, 2006; Dennett 1991, 2006), but in all they have relied on two assumptions, the alleged nonphysical nature of qualia, and a division into given entities, these together providing them with immediately accessible refutations. Pro-qualia views that patently did not construe qualia from the point of view of sense-datum theory were ignored; perhaps, to use the phrase in favor, they were too "freakish"—the "qualia freak" often rears her ugly head in qualiaphobe writings, but who the freak is and what characterizes the failures of her freakishness are never specified.

One of the odder symptoms of this blindness is Michael Tye's decision to call his own theory "representationalism" (introduced in Tye 1994; specifically called "representationalism" in Tye 1995b: 45–68; some philosophers refer to it as "representationism"; see Howard Robinson's comment on this oddity, this vol.: 227–233). The "new representationalisms" put forward in the 1993 collection all espoused qualia even if they did not include pictorial resemblance and the neural copying of entities in the brain. The term "representationalism" was kept to precisely because it was the general term of choice to name the threads of argument that had developed from sense-datum theory through to that time. Since Peter Hare had warned me (pers. comm.) that "representationalism" (and "representative theory" which was sometimes used instead) was not the best term for my own view (which rejects pictorial reproduction), I had had doubts about continuing with it; nevertheless, it was the term widely used in the journals and current books, so to have thrown it aside might have confused the readership—the contributors were, after all, *new* representationalists.

But with an ahistoric confidence Tye decided to use the term for a theory that is wholly dismissive of the old representationalism. This might have been acceptable if he had shown himself aware of the irony of what he was doing (I have been unable to discover any awareness of it in his writings), but to make this attribution as if it were an original designation with no sense of its being a misnomer is surely a sign that he not only had not read the qualiaphile arguments that continued from the Austin–Ryle days to the 1990s, but also, if he had, he considered them to be not worth mention. The effect of this sequestration of the term, which has spread rapidly in the journals, has forced me—willingly—to abandon the term entirely, as Hare advised, and other qualiaphiles have done the same. It also brought me to realize that it was the unthinking commitment to the entity-as-such, the *Ding an Sich*, that was in need of analysis, particularly as, from my point of view, it is a regulative idea and not a reality, that is, an idea in which it is vital to perform a commitment *without believing in it*.

The Non-epistemic

Another such transfer has been the shift of term from "non-epistemic" to "nonconceptual." We shall leave the question of the term "nonconceptual" aside for a while as its use needs to be explained in contrast to that of "non-epistemic." To describe sensation as "non-epistemic" is the proposal that sensory experiences do not carry "information" about entities, but are merely evidence, "natural signs" which can be interpreted according to the motivations of the observer, human or animal (Reid 1970 [1764]: 218; Grice 1967: 39). This implies that sensations are not *symbols*, which are part of the human communication process; they are "semantically inert." The key place given to this feature in any current theory of perception is revealed by the fact that, in the most recent collection on perception, the editors claim that "it is common ground" among all the contributors to reject the "semantic inertness" of sensations (Gendler and Hawthorne 2006: 6).

To explain this "inertness" with an illustration: one might discover by careful testing that the ceiling over my head was warmer than that over the rest of the room, but no one would say, except metaphorically, that there was "information" about me in the ceiling. Evidence, yes, but not information. Michael Tye believes that tree rings, for example, contain information in a nonmetaphorical sense: "Before any human noticed rings inside trees, the number of rings represented the age of the tree, just as it does now" (Tye 1995b: 100). We do not ask who is selecting what parts of the "rings" to count as rings, nor what is to count as a "year," when we know that years are all different from each other in length of time. If Tye protests that such minimal differences "do not matter," he has given his argument away, for "to matter" is to have relation to human desires and fears, human intentions, and thus human selections from that real. Human observers are required to extract indications from the bare evidence, from the Heraclitean real, and those indications are endless. Just how far are we to trace the causal chain? I have just seen a ringdove take off from a birch tree branch—the branch is still swinging—does that constitute *information* about the dove, or mere *evidence* that I am at liberty to interpret? The degree of swing no doubt also relates to the force of the breeze that is blowing, so it is also evidence about the placing of other trees and the houses in the area, about the present (and past) meteorological air-pressures over East Anglia, as well as to the degree of fatigue in the fibers of the branch, the strength of the dove, what induced it to move, and so on, ad infinitum. Human interest is manifestly relevant in determining for what purposes the evidence shall be interpreted. To pick out one of these effects and say it is "representing" its cause is to believe that our words match the world in "what matters," which is, frankly, an occult belief—very reassuring, no doubt, but misguided to say the least. This applies even to synthetic measures and gauges, even to the speedometer that Fred Dretske is fond of using as illustration (Dretske 1997: 13–14), for the moving needle is also registering the degree of friction on its axle, the density of the air inside the gauge, the setting it received in the factory, and so on, ad infinitum.

It is plain that to avoid this error one must keep sensation and perception on a different level, where we can distinguish blank evidence from its interpretation, for it is dangerous to equate the two. There is a fair analogy here with keeping separate the states of the phosphor cells on a television screen or the minibulbs on a "Movitype" screen from what our current motivations induce us to perceive there (R. W. Sellars 1916: 237; J. B. Maund is the philosopher who has made a special point of making this distinction clear [see Maund 1975]). They are what I have called the "field-determinate" level (sensing/the phosphor cells) and the "object-determinate" level (the perception/the object or person taken to be recognized on the screen [Wright 1990: 71–72]). This allows for the possibility of some neurophysiologist in the future being able to give a precise description of at least a part of the neural matrix or raster, and, significantly, without any necessary reference to what is being perceived by the subject—just as an electronics expert could give a detailed list of the states of the phosphor cells on the television screen without any reference to "what" was being shown (cartoon, recording, live show, interference, etc.). The bare evidence is thus in principle not in the least "ineffable" as some qualiaphobes have immediately assumed (anyone still chary of the television analogy must see how the metaphor can be shorn of its objectionable aspects; see Wright 2005: 96–102). There is the *evolutionary advantage* in this approach, in that it allows for learning in perception and the adaptable fine-tuning of what is learned (and perhaps for the complete replacement of the former "objectivity"). There is a particular advantage here for human beings, for one person can update another by means of language, often surprisingly, about what one "sees"—or, to phrase it differently, one can render a former "transparency" opaque by replacing it with a new one. On top of that, it may be not a new "one" entity, but a revealing of two entities, or three-and-a-half where "one" was perceived before. Fred Dretske seems to know before anyone has looked that "twenty-seven children" are to be perceived by someone; one can fairly ask "How do you know?" (Dretske 1981: 147). It is the speckled hen problem in another form, for the answer to how many speckles are seen depends on who is looking—a poultry expert or a child?—and thus on what they consider to be a speckle and what not—and even experts can disagree. It is a curious form of reification to be certain that not only does every region of the real lend itself to counting, but that in a doubtful case it has already provided a specific number of them to a favored philosopher-knower. It is as if nobody ever learned anything, as if everything were already known, and no one need tell anyone else what they have learned that was different from what other people said they knew.

It is instructive here to place in contrast these rival statements from the world of psychology. A psychologist of the early part of the last century who was committed to a "stimulus–response" approach, R. S. Woodworth, formulated what he called a "perceptual-reaction" theory, in which the brain reacts to given separate sensory items; the view is not far removed from that of James J. Gibson, who also conceives of "invariants" in the real as already logically discrete before perception has taken place (Gibson 1968: 320). Thus one finds Woodworth in 1947 denying that "there can ever be seeing without looking or hearing without seeing" (Woodworth 1947: 120), which one can take as an anticipation of Gilbert Harman and Michael Tye's "transparency" proposal (Harman 1990; Tye 2000). On the other hand, someone who investigates autism, B. Hermelin, asserts the contrary of her child-subjects: "Although they can hear and see, they cannot listen and look" (Hermelin 1976: 137). In case you might think that, since this was said of autistic subjects, it cannot be applied to normal ones, consider this not uncommon occurrence: one can be gazing fixedly out of a railway compartment window, but be lost, as we say, "in a brown study," such that one is attending to some inward thought with such intensity that, though one's eyes are open, as with Lady Macbeth, "their sense is shut," taking nothing in perceptually of what was to be seen through that window. The trope in the idiom is revealing: one is "*studying* something within" to the degree that one's visual field suffers the metaphorical equivalent of a "brown-out," all distinction lost even though color, as sensory awareness, is still present, though out of conscious recognition. Motivation, is, as always, sovereign in perception, and can withdraw attention from current sensation even as the latter is still operating—non-epistemically. When Michael Tye discusses such a situation, he weakens his case by assuming that all before the person's eyes has *already* been sorted in past history into familiar objects (Tye 2000: 182).

As far as I can judge, Arthur W. Collins was the first to use the term "non-epistemic," though he wrote it without the hyphen (Collins 1967: 455). He stressed the fact that we need "auxiliary information" from the memory to interpret what arrives at our sensory organs (ibid.: 456), much as when hearing a joke we need clues to the rival meanings. He was far from being the first to examine the notion. One can find immediate predecessors, of whom I mention three: (1) H. H. Price described bare sensation as "ineffective," meaning that, before anyone has attended to some portion of the field, however subliminally, that sensation can have no effect on knowledge or action (Price 1961 [1932]: 150); (2) Geoffrey Warnock is notable for a careful analysis of the process of noticing and attending, in which he was led to distinguish a level of plain sensing from those occasions on which we notice something. He confines his inquiry to seeing, and concludes: "One who sees . . . need not know anything at all. . . . there must be a sense in which seeing does not involve the acquired abilities to identify, recognize, name, describe, and so on" (Warnock 1955–56: 211, 218); and (3) A. Campbell Garnett: "the still more sophisticated usage [of the word 'sensation'] has been developed which distinguishes between the perceptual process and the item that appears or is presented as its object or content, calling the former 'sensing' and the latter the sense quale, the sense-datum, and so forth, whether it is actually perceived or not" (Garnett 1965: 42). One's only quarrel here is that Garnett should not have used the phrase "*perceptual* process" for sensing alone. It is the picking out of an "item" that is the perceptual move; sensation is prior as it is from the sensation-fields that "items" are picked.

Garnett's use of the word "quale" for the item perceived, making it equivalent to "sense datum," provides the opportunity to clear up an ambiguity. The word "quale" (derived from Latin *qualis*, "of such a kind") is pluralized as "qualia." Garnett's use of the singular is obviously for any *entity* singled out from the field, some*thing* perceived, and the plural "qualia" would be for a number of such items. In such a use it is without doubt the same as "datum" for the sense-datum theorists. C. D Broad, for example, carefully pointed out that in his view a sense datum, a "sensum" as he preferred to call it, was indeed something cognized and not merely sensed: "A sensum is not something that exists in isolation; it is a differentiated part of a bigger and more enduring whole, viz., of a sense-*field* which is itself a mere cross-section of a sense-*history*" (Broad 1923: 195). As this makes clear, the "datum," as its name implies, was for Broad an *epistemic* item, something perceived in the sense of being "differentiated," that is, selected from a larger whole, the sense-field proper, in order to guide the actions of the animal or human being in the service of their needs. That larger whole could contain both (a) other items before they were cognized (which would not then be the focus of attention); and (b) regions never attended to, each of which would be being non-epistemically sensed. One must add that, even for an item attended to, there are always sensory features that are given no significance, which entails that non-epistemic sensing can remain within a supposedly certain identification as well as outside it. This must be the case; otherwise, no one could ever correct another about a percept, his or her take on some problematic region of the real. "Qualia" as used in the title of this book therefore applies generally to *all the sensory experiences across the differing sense-modalities*, that is all the "sense-fields," and *not to perceived items*. It is of these fields that it is claimed that they have a non-epistemic character.

The debate about the separation of sensing and perceiving is fraught with ethical implications, for it is widely believed that to hold to the idea that we have only evidence to go on leaves us with no firm ground for objectivity, and hence truth, a place where only unsteady relativists dare venture. All those in the Gendler and Hawthorne collection, for example, are mindful of what they consider to be the danger of, as they would say, putting the world beyond a "veil of perception." The old sense-datum theorists are generally regarded as having not only become trapped in epistemological contradictions because of this move, but also imprudently opened the door to relativism. As a result, there are and have been many philosophers and psychologists who with determined seriousness question any attempt to detach sensation from perception, and busy themselves with avoiding being characterized as an "indirect realist," as it is taken to be canonical that indirection can only hide or distort what is real, thus setting truth and knowledge at terrible risk.

The History of the Notion of the Non-epistemic

History, however, reveals a repeated resurfacing of this distinction, which can be traced back quite far. D. W. Hamlyn, in his history of the theories of the relation of sensation to perception, mentions Empedocles as noting that "in order to perceive things we have sometimes to concentrate and pay attention" (Hamlyn 1961: 7), which implies that something must provide a field over which that act of attention can move. Carneades claimed that "in no particular case is any sense-impression self-evidently true to the object it purports to represent" (Long 1986: 95). Hamlyn himself, however, is profoundly unhappy with the distinction, noting that Aristotle made an "uneasy compromise" between "special sensibles" which "involved no judgement," claiming that it is "we who judge rather than the senses" (Hamlyn 1961: 26). Hamlyn also quotes Epicurus as one who considered sensing as such to be non-epistemic, *alogos*, "unconnected with reason or judgement." The idea recurs in the work of St. Augustine, who denied that truth and falsity could be properties of sense-impressions alone (*De quantitate animae*, 23).

The sixth-century Indian Buddhist sage Dinnaga believed that the visual field was made up of infinitesimal points and that these are to be distinguished from the entities we pick out from the field (Matilal 1986: 365–367). We might fitly take as analogy the phosphor cells on a television screen mentioned above, each of which is evidence of an undefined multiplicity of causes, but which for the human subject (not the neurophysiologist), cannot be interpreted without memory-guided human selection *across* the sense-field. We do not investigate each point in turn in order to project a useful gestalt. What neither Dinnaga nor Vasabandhu, another Buddhist philosopher, inquired into was the place of human motivation in the perceptual process. Pain or pleasure enforces the placing in memory of what at first appears to be salient, and lodges it there attended with the concomitants of fear and desire. Vasabandhu did speak of a multitude of phenomenalistic atoms being shaped into a "conglomerate" (ibid.: 360–362); what he did not explore was the *motivation* that drives our brain to shape these memories. The nearest he got to it was his reflecting on

Descartes's demon situation, comparable to Jonathan Harrison's "brain in a vat," for what was presupposed in that thought experiment, though few today even take it into consideration, is the threat to one's desires (Harrison 1985). Dinnaga further noted the obvious fact that one person's correction of another might be of the very singularity of "the" entity in question—that perhaps the new perceiving might reveal a number of entities with different criteria of identification where one was considered to exist before. As he puts it, against Russell, Husserl, and Tye simultaneously, "Even 'this' can be a case of mistaken identity" (Matilal 1986: 332). One can add that, since non-epistemic evidence remains uninterpreted within the epistemic, as we have just seen, all "thises," whether of object, self, or other person, retain a unmeasured measure of "mistaken identity."

Thomas Hobbes noted that when one is reading, only the immediate portion of the line one is concentrating on is perceived, even though all the page is still before one's eyes as part of one's sight, which has the obvious implication that what we here call "the rest of the page" is not only unread but not even at that moment a part of our interpretation of the visual field (Hobbes 1839: 393). It would be relatively straightforward to set up a psychological experiment on a computer screen in which the "rest of the page" was slowly transformed into French while what the eye was moving its attention over remained in the original readable English, which would be an empirical proof of non-epistemic sensing, as well as the "non-transparency" of the French text. Notice that Hobbes was not arguing that the whole field was as clear as a "snapshot," as Alva Noë seems to suggest qualiaphiles believe (thus still holding to the ancient pictorial objection; see this vol.: 342–345), but that there is an unclear but obviously sensed peripheral region around the fovea as it moves in the eye's saccades (Noë 2006: 421; it is not that the detail is "strictly unseen," as Noë claims, but that the peripheral field is *seen* but is *not sensorily or perceptually detailed*).

Nicolas Malebranche made a distinction between *sensation*, which was "confused," having "no clear idea" of objects, a matter of *voir* alone, and *illumination*, in which, through sensation, the mind was able to perceive "the essences of things," a matter of *regarder*—which anticipates Hermelin's remark about seeing and looking (Malebranche 1992 [1674]: 69). His noticing that there are some persons for whom colors are different for the right and left eye (quoted in Yolton 1984: 46) is also an indirect admission of non-epistemicity, since the difficulty of exploring this as useful evidence would not be obvious to the persons concerned. There is no doubt that it could be: take Daniel Dennett's claim that, once the cry of the osprey has been taught to someone, then a Wittgensteinian point is reached when teaching has been completed, so that the public word-use has been finally cleared up for the pupil and no disagreements can ensue (Dennett 1985: 39). He forgets that in a case where, say, the pupil was under age ten and could hear sound-waves up to 20KHz, there might be a circumstance (say in a heavy rainstorm) where the pupil could hear the osprey but the teacher could not. Before that moment, since neither teacher nor pupil was aware of this difference, it lay within the non-epistemic, outside the "illumination" of perception, the cry of the osprey thus being the reverse of "transparent" (on this question of fine differences between person and person, see also Block 2003: 28–29; on a case of human sensitivity to ultraviolet light, see Matthen 2005: 34–35). Similarly for Malebranche's example: the person with a difference in response to red in his two eyes might more readily notice an oncoming red traffic-light with his right eye than with his left (though not necessarily be aware of this difference). Malebranche also acknowledged both the importance of motivation in perception and the value of a non-epistemic field in allowing for flexibility in selection from it, for he argued that, although sensations have no truth-value, revealing nothing about the objects in our environment, they do "alert us to that which is useful and dangerous" (quoted in Yolton 1984: 45, 53).

Robert Boyle can be said to refer indirectly to the non-epistemic. When he was considering the fact that people often have mistaken notions about the world around them, he said that it was much "fitter" to think of words as being constantly altered to things, rather than believing words to be wholly successful in matching what is outside us, and added that we too often accommodate ourselves to "forms of words" when our understanding is limited—as he put it, "when the things themselves were not known, or well understood, *if at all thought on*" (Boyle 1979 [1666]: 58; my emphasis). This is an admission that not only can the familiar object be doubtfully identified, but that experience *within a percept* can still be can be outside knowledge. Boyle is, of course, well known for denying that color bears no resemblance to what causes it, and he was the first to cite the experience of phosphenes: he observed that coughing in the dark produced the sight of "very vivid, but immediately disappearing flames"—it would be hard for the ordinary person to attribute any meaning whatever to such undoubtedly real sensations (Boyle 1964 [1664]: 13). He was also intrigued by Aristotle's remark that the eye sees both light and darkness, that the brain produces a "positive" sensation when the eye is deprived of light altogether (Boyle 1979 [1666]: 229). To an infant, darkness could hardly be more non-epistemic; hence, perhaps, in some cases, the intensifying of the fear of it.

At a first superficial reading of his *Essay on Human Understanding* John Locke might be said to be one who held to the theory of the semantic inertness of sensation because he seemed to place such an emphasis on the separation of "sensation" and "reflection," the latter being the mind's operations upon the "ideas" it received through the senses. However, a close look at his description of the process reveals an early blurring of the two, which could fairly be described as an inconsistency. He begins with the mind as a blank sheet, a "white paper," but what comes to be written on it removes that blankness entirely: notice that he speaks of the "ideas" of "*yellow, white, heat, cold, soft, hard, bitter, sweet*" as if they were indeed *semantically* recognized at this initial stage (*Essay*, II, i, 3; his emphasis). But no infant ("without speech") has such words or "ideas" even though it senses perfectly well. Further Locke refers to "material things" as the "objects of sensation," and assures us that "*External objects furnish the minds with the* ideas *of sensible qualities*" without inquiring into how the mind comes to select such portions of its fields as "material things" (ibid., II, 1, 4, 5; his emphasis on the word "ideas"). If he had said, instead, "the external real furnishes the mind with sensible qualities," it would have been acceptable, for the infant can have the sensation of yellow without having any knowledge of it; we would say "without any idea of it," not employing Locke's own dubious meaning for the term. This might be said to be an early example of the suspect attempt to smuggle epistemic elements into the notion of sensing. Another way the inconsistency shows itself can perhaps be found in his use of "I know not what" for the real: if the real is outside knowledge, it is no surprise that the "involuntary" sensory fields are "white paper" to start with, as they are just as much "I know not what," being as real as what causes them. One can add that, since they are "involuntary," they are outside motivation—something that motivation, the will, works on, quite distinct from itself.

One odd absence in the eighteenth century of a consideration of the non-epistemic is that in the works of the would-be arch-skeptic David Hume. His discussion of sense-impressions, as he calls sensory experience, never touches the question, except indirectly. He was much taken up with the fragmentariness of our perception of objects (as some philosophers today still are; see Noë 2006) and is led to regard their continuance out of sight as a product of imagination, which does contain an valuable insight. Nonetheless, he did not make the move to consider the possibility that more than one individual's imagination was in *play* in a mutual projection. This, ironically, was probably because, as he said himself, he could not resist breaking away from his abstruse inquiries and seeking human company: "I dine, I play a game of backgammon, I converse, and am merry with my friends; and when after three of four hours' amusement, I wou'd return to these speculations, they appear so cold, and strain'd, and ridiculous, that I cannot find it in my heart to enter into them any farther" (*Treatise of Human Nature*, Bk. I, section 7). It is not without significance that mutuality, especially when heightened by play, wit, and humor, should reconcile him to everyday existence in the world. His skeptical mask was difficult to wear when intersubjectivity forced itself on him. A pity that he never stood back and inquired as to why and how this came about, and whether the structure of play, wit, and humor could have anything to do with it.

Bishop George Berkeley and Cardinal Giacinto Gerdil, unsurprisingly perhaps given their clerical profession, were both aware of the danger of leaving perception without epistemic support (Berkeley 1972 [1713]; Gerdil 1748). One might say (mistakenly) that, although they were nearer to the qualia camp in that they considered sensation to be a spiritual matter, part of the "mind," they veered toward modern transparency theory in asserting a given objectivity for all external entities, the only difference being that God supplied that objectivity without any need for materiality. I have argued elsewhere that this lodging of an ideal objectivity in God is an understandable acknowledgment—though through a mythical misrepresentation—of the needful faith on which all language is based (Wright 2005: 111–120, 194–195). We can now connect Berkeley and Gerdil with David Chalmers's entertaining of the notion of an "Edenic perception," which is also an indirect acknowledgment of that real faith, although Chalmers does not see it as such (Chalmers 2006: 75–125). Chalmers, believing that he has found a way to escape relativism, cannot resist introducing the notion of "complete endorsement" of an identification (ibid.: 120), but without seeing that *to endorse* is to enter upon a pact of faith with others, and faith must include the acceptance of inevitable risk. As regards the non-epistemic, Berkeley did concede that sensing was "altogether passive" in the sense of being outside one's volition (Berkeley 1972 [1713]: 228). It could be argued that there was also an indirect acknowledgment that sensing is not mental in Philonous's curious remark that sensations, because of their "passivity," could be called *"external objects"* (ibid.: 229).

John Yolton, who is outstanding in his historical investigations into the philosophy of perception in the seventeenth and eighteenth centuries, introduces us to Zachary Mayne, who wrote a book on sense and the imagination in 1728, which Yolton describes as "a sophisticated analysis," "one of the more important essays on ideas and awareness" in that century (Yolton 1984: 109–113). Mayne is worth mentioning here for two observations that he made. First, he describes sensation as "a bare Representation of some corporeal Phenomenon or external appearance as *Colour, Sound, Taste, Odeur,* etc." (Mayne 1728: 9), from which the mind has to get at the meaning or significance, which clearly places sensing as "semantically inert," with understanding being what contributes the knowing through an interpretation of the evidence. The word "representation" cannot therefore imply that there exists some given copying of external entities or properties. Indeed, he strongly disapproved of Locke's equation of the sensory "phantasm" with the "idea" (in the sense of some rational understanding): as he puts it, "to have an *Idea* [i.e., sense impression] cannot be the same thing with an Act of *Understanding*" (ibid.: 70). Second, he noted the tendency of common sense to accept habitual interpretations, so that an apparently objective identification is likely to be the product of what "people fancy they understand" (ibid.: 14). In view of the fact that all human beings have to behave *as if* they are identifying some "entity" in the same way (they could not get a rough overlap of their understandings otherwise), his use of the word "fancy" is not out of place. They turn a necessary act, which has the character of a regulative idea, something imagined for the nonce, into an actual delusion—nothing is easier than *to believe* what you should only be *assuming* when the "entity" is apparently before you in the form that you understand it! What such a blinkered approach neglects, of course, is the sensory and perceptual perspectives of others. Mayne is firmly an indirect realist for he insists that, whether one is observing something external or entertaining a mental image, one is still confronting an "appearance" (ibid.: 146).

Condillac is noteworthy for his elaborate thought experiment of a "statue" (for which we might currently read "robot") which was given elements of mind in stages until it reached the human one. The imaginary chronological advance can readily be translated into what is prior in the act of knowing. Condillac places sensing first, but denies it any epistemological value until pain and pleasure have enforced selections from the fields. For him non-epistemic sensing is the first requirement; the implication is that no learning and no adaptation of that learning could take place unless there was the flexibility to move the selections about on those fields at the behest of motivation. Not even the "I" is given, but in time the self–world division gets established: "From the moment I realise this it seems my modes of being cease to belong to me. I make then into collections outside me. I form them into objects of which I am aware"

(Condillac 1930 [1754]: 231). Of that within the sense-fields which gives neither pleasure nor pain, "they are part of a confused mass of which it has no knowledge"; there would be no *attention* on any portion (ibid.: 220, 61). He is unusual in giving motivation a dominant initial place in the course of a being's learning to cope in the world: "Thus it is that pleasure and pain are the sole principle[s] which, determining all the operations of its soul, will gradually raise it to all the knowledge of which it is capable" (ibid.: ch. II, sect. 4).

Thomas Reid is interesting because of his determined attempts to deny the implications of his own argument. Having admitted the profound difference of sensation from what causes it (he even entertained the thought of tasting with our fingers, smelling with our ears, and hearing with the nose; see Reid 1970 [1764]: 216–217), he is content to say that "Sensation, taken by itself, implies neither the conception nor belief of any external object. It supposes a sentient being, and a certain manner in which that being is effected; but it supposes no more. Perception implies an immediate conviction and belief of something external—something different both from the mind that perceives and from the act of perception" (Reid 1941 [1785]: 155), which would plainly appear to be a Lockean separation of "sensation" and "reflection," non-epistemic and epistemic. He was fearful, however, of the skeptic's attack (as are many in the Gendler and Hawthorne volume), defending his belief in an external world of objects. He admitted that nature presents us only with natural signs, whereas humans can employ "artificial" signs like "articulate sounds" or "writing" (here anticipating Grice 1967: 39), but he is sure that we can interpret nature's signs as correctly as our own. We pass safely from the "appearance" to the "conception" in three ways: "by original principles of our constitution, by custom, and by reasoning" (Reid 1970 [1764]: 218). The first rests on the experiences of pain and pleasure, and the interests which spring from them, which makes us guide our actions by "prudence" (ibid.: 208–209); the second confirms them by repeated success, resulting in "common sense"; and the third works by inquiry into and dependence on the first two. He could not see, of course, how, with such a firmly Cartesian commitment to the singularity of the self, he might be tripped by Descartes's demon or "brain-in-a-vat" arguments, but he does indirectly betray a sense of how people together maintain their differing sensings and perceivings in harness, how they manage to update each other, for he alludes to "taking" belief "on *trust* and without suspicion" (ibid.: 207). He also cannot help using the metaphor of "a kind of drama," where "nature is the actor" and "we are the spectators." It does not occur to him that the structure of drama might contain a clue as to how agents beset by otherness from each other might overcome it (and all threats of relativism and solipsism) by the *performance* of a *perfect* perception that enables them, ideally, to facilitate the updating of each other's *imperfect* ones.

Kant, of course, made an outright statement of the non-epistemic–epistemic distinction: "Thoughts without content are empty, intuitions without concepts are blind" (*Critique of Pure Reason*, A51/B75). In saying that "intuitions" (Kant's term for sensory impressions) are "blind," Kant is using a hyperbolical metaphor: he does not mean that they cease to be experienced, only that no knowledge can be derived from them if no perception is active. One has to bear in mind Boyle and Warnock's point, that it is not the case that someone's identification of and observation of some region of the real can take in "all" the significance of all the evidence available, as if there were a quantifiable amount to be discovered. A most vivid "intuition" may be "blind" in an endless number of respects. What to Dr. Watson is just a depression in the ground is for Sherlock Holmes an indication that a lame woman of nine stone or so, wearing shoes purchased at Harrod's within the last three months, has just passed by. And Dr. Watson may have keener eyesight than Holmes, and a more vivid sense of color—though these availed him not. A short-sighted entomologist may be able to pick out confidently the camouflaged moth on the bark of a tree that is "invisible" to his sharp-eyed student. Frank Jackson's Mary, just out of the black-and-white room, may be having her first experience of red and *not know it* because the red was on a small Dretskean cuff-link in an open drawer, and, though she was looking into that drawer, she was so amazed at the *greenness* of a tie next to the cuff-link, that she had not noticed the red of the latter (this is where the knowledge argument falls apart—for to sense is not to know).

Kant did not escape inconsistency, however, and for the same reason as many another philosopher, the same antiskeptical desire to retain epistemic contact with the singular external object, for elsewhere he did tie intuition to it: "In whatever manner and by whatever means a mode of knowledge may relate to objects, *intuition* is that through which it is in immediate relation to them" (*CPR*, A19/B33). Here we find again a claim to a real perfect perception, when all that is required is a mutual postulate that there is such a thing. He even clung to the notion of given discrete singularities in the *noumenon* where things resided in absolutely pure ontological singularity, the *Dinge an Sich*—he could not refrain from the addition of that "*an Sich*," forgetting that they can only be "as such" to someone. It matches John McDowell's "thus-and-so" and "that shade" exactly, as he himself agrees (McDowell 1994: 9, 56–57). Both are *believing* in the real existence of a singularity that is really only the product of a mutually *hypothesized* regulative idea; none of this casts any doubt over the existence of what each person's "singularity" *is being selected from* (see this vol.: 352). To develop Dinnaga's dictum: even "that shade" can be a case of mistaken identity.

Ludwig Feuerbach had a more perspicuous metaphor for our sensings: "The senses give us riddles, but they do not give us the solution, understanding" (Feuerbach 1903–11: II, 144). A riddle has at its core a non-epistemic element, not necessarily singular (for puns and riddles permit of an accommodating degree of fudging the notion of "one"), over which rival epistemic interpretations strive for motivational supremacy according to the salience of the rival contextual clues that the joker has placed in the context (see Wright 2005: ch. 1). This can be regarded not as an analogy for learning, but as an actual example of its structure, although the outcome is usually taken as irrelevant to any immediate conscious concerns (though not perhaps to deep-seated unconscious ones). The whole point of a joke is in its rivalry of motivations, for in a good joke the contrast between the motivational associations of the two meanings involved points to the key pressures of desire and fear on our perceptions. What a joke brings to uncomfortable or consoling notice is how non-epistemic the most familiar of perceptions can become.

George Henry Lewes has a claim upon our attention not merely because he was George Eliot's husband. It might have interested Richard Rorty to learn that he was an empiricist opposed to the idea of the mind producing a "mirroring of things"; Lewes says that wants to "discredit the old idea that the Senses directly apprehend—or mirror—external things" (Rorty 1980: 390; Lewes 1874: I, 122). He sees "sensation proper" as "a passive affection of the organism, whereas "Mind is the secondary and completing stage of Reaction" (Lewes 1874: I, 74–75). He attributes this "completion" to the operation of motivation, through what he terms "the Law of Interest": "It has long been observed that we only *see* what interests us, only know what is sufficiently like former experiences to become, so to speak, incorporated with them—assimilated by them. The satisfaction of desire is that which both impels and quiets mental movement" (ibid.: I, 121; his emphasis). This does not imply, *pace* Noë (2006), that we cease to sense what we do not perceive, only that the unperceived remains within the non-epistemic, whether that non-epistemic is a background to what is attended to or is inside it. Another way of saying this is that a percept cannot be wholly defined by the agent's own view of her intention.

Notice that Lewes differs from the contributors to the Gendler and Hawthorne volume in not neglecting the part played by motivation in the impulse to perceive. They are too bemused by the *noun* "mind" to see that semantically its more important use is as a *verb*—"Mind the two steps down as you go out!" In fact, if you look at their extremely detailed index (for a book of 530 pages on perception) you will find only two references to "motivation" (and neither of those has anything to say about its relation to perception), six to "pain" (again with no account of its embedding memories that are attended with fear), two to "desire" (again merely passing allusions), none to "fear," and none to "pleasure." Another recent example is Mohan Matthen's (2005) book *Seeing, Doing, and Knowing,* which has no references at all to any of them, nor to "intention." The determination of most qualiaphobes to avoid relativism leads them to steer clear of the examination of the place in "perceptual experience" of pain and pleasure, fear and desire, because "common sense" is taken to have already sorted out those troublesome "subjective" *matters* and consigned them to impersonal, third-person "objectivity." They forget what "to matter" means. It is not only their tendency to rigidify tradition and to further scholastic intricacy that makes them remind one of monks (see Howard Robinson's remarks on their treatment of Ned Block's argument concerning orgasm, this vol.: 232–233; Block 2003: 11–13).

The great psychologist Hermann von Helmholtz is remarkable in the keenness of his investigation of visual optics. In his discussion of "the facts of perception" he makes a clear distinction between the non-epistemic and the epistemic: "The assumption of every nativist theory—that ready-made representations of objects are elicited through our organic mechanism—appears much more audacious and doubtful than the assumption of the empiricist theory, which is that only the non-understood material of sensations originates from external influences, while all representations are formed from it in accordance with the laws of thought" (Helmholtz 1868: 175–176). As a good empiricist he gives several examples of how the non-epistemic can invade our mundane take on the real. He says that we are "not in the habit of observing our sensations accurately" for we are "wont to disregard all those parts of sensations that are of no importance so far as external objects are concerned" (ibid.):

(1) The vitreous humor of most people's eyes contain floating wisps of semitransparent tissue, called "floaters" or *mouches volantes* (I have indeed myself occasionally mistaken them for flies). These can be noticed when the eyes move rapidly as they shift suddenly across the field of vision, but

many people do not notice them at all. (A friend of mine who became ill and somewhat depressed noticed them for the first time and attributed them to her illness, having never observed them before although they had been present throughout her life.)

(2) When the fixation point of the two eyes rests upon an object, a great deal of the background is taken up with double images (test it for yourself now with a finger close to your eyes). So for most of the time your vision consists of a confused overlay which you never normally notice (cf. Lowe, this vol.: 61–65).

(3) Double images are not the same, as a careful comparison, say, of the two images of a finger observed in a squint. One sees farther round the right-hand side with the right eye and the left-hand side with the left eye. (Gilbert Ryle and George Pitcher both assume that the images are identical; see Ryle 1966: 207; Pitcher 1971: 41.) The truth is that the two fields as wholes are different *at every point*, and it is this which enables the brain to create the sensory phenomenon of stereoscopic shape and depth.

(4) Normally, says Helmholtz, we are "unskilled" in separating our sensing from our perceiving. However, if, while standing, you bend your head down and look behind you at a landscape, you will discover that the prospect, upside-down, provides an impression profoundly different from the normal. As Helmholtz says, "the colours lose their associations with near and far objects, and confront us now purely in their own peculiar differences." The non-epistemic temporarily becomes detached from the epistemic (a fact denied by Harman [1990]).

(5) Afterimages of what you last looked at briefly continue, so that whatever you are looking at still contains a faint record of the previous look. This can have definite effects, as when a butcher places green paper under his meat, for the afterimage of green being red makes the meat look redder; the customer, of course, is not aware of this (Helmholtz 1868: 176–180).

It is therefore no surprise to find Helmholtz, like R. L. Gregory (Gregory 1993), treating objects as hypothetical choices from the sense-fields, "unconscious conclusions" as he called them, though he did not inquire into the intersubjective parameter of such hypotheses.

To make mutual sense out of this "confusion" of nature, Helmholtz says that we must "start with the *assumption* of her intelligibility, and draw consequences in conformity with this assumption, until irrefutable facts show the limitations of this method" (quoted in James 1977: 115). Like Helmholtz, James preferred to see the "flux of sensations" as blank evidence for this assumption to work upon, as not in itself containing any given "information":

Sensations are forced upon us, coming we know not whence. Over their nature, order and quantity we have as good as no control. *They* are neither true nor false; they simply *are*. It is only what we say about them, only the names we give them, our theories of their source and nature and remote relations, that may be true or not. . . . What we say about reality thus depends on the perspective into which we throw it. The *that* of it is its own; but the *what* depends on the *which*; and the which depends on us. Both the sensational and the relational parts of reality are dumb; they say absolutely nothing about themselves. We it is who have to speak for them. (James 1977: 451, 452)

The "Thing" he regards as a "conceptual instrument" which we by a process of "triangulation" are forever adjusting (ibid.: 423, 60). There is a risk in entering such a triangulation, for the evidence may be misinterpreted, and the person we trust may have had a different interpretation from the start. This is the kind of risk that those who pride themselves on refuting the skeptic are not facing up to, namely, that trust has to be faith, reaching beyond such painful discoveries of cross-purposes to retain, perhaps through some sacrifice, one's commitment to the other. James quotes Helmholtz again: "Hier gilt nur der eine Rath: vertraue und handle!" ("There is only one worthwhile piece of advice: have faith and act!")

Roy Wood Sellars was much taken with the need to adjust our percepts, seeing our perceptual traffic with the sensory as a continual "from–to" of adjustment by feedback of the flux's responses to our tentative selections from it. Even so, Sellars professes himself unhappy with the notion that, before the "configurational wholes" are selected, the field itself is in an "anoetic" state (Sellars 1932: 88), his term for the "non-epistemic." Yet he still wants to maintain an intuition–judgment distinction (1965: 236), with the intuition "simpler" than the perception. It is because of this that "artists are able to disturb inferential elements" (1916: 18) since they are more responsive to unnoticed sensory features. Two years earlier he had defined his point more exactly in saying that he did not believe that there was a "chaos" of sensations but a "patterned field" controlled by "the stimuli coming to the organism" (1930: 268). However, the patterned field does not contain any given information. If he is to allow for shifts in attention over the field to improve reference, as he insists, he cannot in the same breath believe that there is already a set of given singular selections awaiting choice.

It is not that, as he puts it, "it is *as though* we were directly aware of a thing" (Sellars 1965: 237, his emphasis); but the part of our body that is our sensings is certainly part of *existence*. It is true that it is only "as though" we are aware of a *singular* thing, but mutually negotiated, tentative choice is from something that undoubtedly exists, the sense-field (quite apart from our would-be objective percepts), and what that sense-field as a whole is caused by undoubtedly exists, as a portion of the real continuum. To put it another way, we are all making our *differing* choices from real existence, but the supposed singularity that lies across all those choices is a convenient, even pragmatically necessary, but nevertheless unreal hypothesis. There is no veil of perception, because the "veil" is part of the real. To use James's words, both sensing and what it is caused by "simply *are*," regardless of what we are perceiving and regardless of whether the cause is external to the body or internal (as is the case with phosphenes, afterimages, dreams, hallucinations, migraine "fortification" patterns, and the like). Perception remains merely viable—until the next item of feedback, or someone else's correction of our choice, which, right or wrong, will still prove that another can invade our supposedly private world and suggest to us that what we perceived from what we sensed was incorrect. Since that can include the self as a major choice, redirecting our motivation, solipsism is an impossibility. Perception is a *choice*, because motivation energizes the whole perceptual process.

The Nonconceptual

"Nonconceptual" is a term that Gareth Evans introduced to characterize the "information" that he believes awaits the observer in the world, whether or not that observer has recognized its presence (Evans 1982: 156, 226–229). He was convinced that "informational states" existed within sensory pre-sentations, regarding it as a given that there must be some access to the external world if reference was to be confirmable. Of late this idea has been seized upon by many philosophers of perception (see the representative collection edited by York H. Gunther: Gunther 2003), and it is easy to see why it has been so popular since, in building on information that was waiting to be picked up and conceptualized, it provided a firm bridge to the external across the mire of subjectivity, thus escaping in one move the threat of skepticism. It is obvious, then, that *it cannot be equated with the non-epistemic*. Evans showed himself sensitive to the danger of adopting a pro-qualia approach that would seem to place the external out of reach, using the familiar antipictorial argument: "inner states cannot intelligibly be regarded as objects of an internal gaze" (Evans 1982.: 231. This is similar to John McDowell's "mysterious" ploy [see McDowell 1994: 139]).

What is central to Evans's definition of the nonconceptual is the ability of an observer (and animal observers can here be included) to discern discrete objects, already singular, that await the selection process. Discrimination of the object is taken to be the vital element, so that we can in future recognize it, be able to provide some description of it, and so on. The representation of that information he defines as follows: "We can speak of a certain bit of information being of, or perhaps from, an object, in a sense resembling the way in which we speak of a photograph being of an object" (Evans 1982: 124). What is occluded here is how and why "an object" is discriminated in the first place. Again there is no whisper of the place of motivation, nor how it is known beforehand that the real does consist of discretely singular entities that are the same for all observers. Nor does he ask whether that "discrimination" serves any purposes, nor whose purposes. The whole book takes for granted that *singular* entities preexist their sorting from the real apart from human choice. He actually uses the phrase "take to be" when speaking of "information": "We *take* ourselves *to be* informed, in whatever way, of the existence of such-and-such an object" (Evans 1982: 121, my emphases). But "to take to be" is *to assume, to accept something* as if *it were something else*, which is a clue to what actually happens, namely, that each of us "takes an object" to exist in a perfect singularity apart from us just in order to bring, via this strictly fictive mutual act, our *differing* "referents" into some kind of rough convergence, and why?—so that a speaker can update a hearer and adjust the boundaries of his or her "referent" closer to those of the speaker.

Thus whenever Evans speaks of "nonconceptual content" it is always in terms of discrete singular entities awaiting perception. "Information" about entities is already there in the sensations. Instead of evidence to be interpreted à la Sherlock Holmes, we have semantically defined regions that already carry the knowledge waiting to be absorbed. Even in the version Christopher Peacocke presents, entities may have disappeared but identifiable parts of space still linger; he produces the notion of a "scenario" content, in which, before any perception has taken place, there are already marked out, point by point, spatial features of the world (Peacocke 1992: 67–84). Thus he is able to claim that there is "content" in the visual array and that it is representational before anyone has interpreted it. But spatial features of the world are knowledge, not evidence. One has to *learn* how the distribution of features in one's sense-fields matches external space; it is not a given (the same can be said of Austen Clark's notion of "feature-placing," which exists when learning has gone on but not before; his term "sensory reference" is paradoxical in the absence of learning, and even with it is only viable; see Clark 2000: 74–80). Peacocke does commit himself now to what he calls the "autonomy thesis" being realizable, that is, "nonconceptual states could exist in the absence of conceptual states" (Peacocke 2003: 320). He is thinking here of animals that are able to act in the world, but lack the ability human beings have of being aware of self and being able to recombine concepts (such as recombining "That's green," "That's square," and "That's in the dark" into "That's a green square in the dark"; ibid.: 321), However, such a state, even in an animal, is well on the way up the path of learning. The reasons for this are that the content has already been acquired; motivation has embedded sensory features in the memory and marked them with fear or desire, so a measure of representation has been achieved. It was certainly not there before the learning, and the learning has not erased what the "fine-grain" of the sensory might yet yield up, for there is no end to learning—for there is no end to what we purpose (only death brings desire to an end). The conclusion is clear; the nonconceptual is not the non-epistemic, for the latter is wholly without content. Indeed, the term "nonconceptual content" does not avail anything to those who want to load the sensory with meaning. It is a perfectly harmless term if one merely wants to characterize what perceptual state a rat is in and one wants to deny it an egocentric node and the ability to recombine concepts; however, if one wants to hang confirmatory news of the external on it, something to which truth conditions are applicable, something that will save one from the relativist pit, then, unfortunately, "nonconceptual content" becomes an oxymoron.

Incidentally, it is worth pointing out that what was true of the Gendler and Hawthorne collection is even more applicable to the Gunther one, for not a single reference can be found in the index to "motivation," "pleasure," "desire," or "fear"—there are five references to pain, but they are all concerned with its representational properties, none with its power to embed perceptions and suffuse them with fear. This is a clue to the entity's being a notion believed in, not, sensibly, merely "taken for granted"; and to the failure to keep in mind "mind" as a verb. As Lewes said, "we only *see* what interests us" (Lewes 1874: I, 121), though one has to unpack that "we" and that "us."

The Essays

Qualiaphiles, of course, are just as concerned to find a satisfactory account of knowledge. If their opponents are to be credited with anything, it must be that, as far as the debate has gone on over the last fifty years, they are faced with the especial difficulty of establishing philosophical contact with the real when they hold that our access to it appears to be second-hand—and, worse, hidden behind a screen of sensations that contain no information. They are the ones, it is confidently claimed, who are in an ethical dilemma, seemingly purveying a view that slides easily into relativism and solipsism.

So several supporters of qualia have undertaken defenses of the indirect realist position, as is evidenced by a goodly proportion of the contributions in this volume. For that reason, they have been grouped under the title of "defenses."

It will become plain at once that supporters of qualia do not agree about the nature of them. The reader may find it useful to employ the criterion of belief in non-epistemicity as a way of distinguishing the various positions taken by the contributors. Harold Brown, for example, takes it as generally agreed that "normal perception" is caused by "physical items" (45). However, were the reader to take the word "items" to mean countable entities perceivable by the human eye (whether assisted or not by instruments such as microscopes, etc.), then non-epistemicity would be ruled out; but Brown acknowledges that our objectifying is not a matter of a given response to entities, even if the whole field is traceable to some overall external cause (48). On the one hand, Jonathan Lowe holds to the qualia experiences being of "private objects," but his discussion of illusion makes it plain that he does not hold to an automatic registration of external things; on the other, William Robinson regards the tying of sensory experiences to identifiable properties as an acceptable premise. I suggest that the reader use this criterion as a guide through the arguments that follow, for it will be a direct sign of whether or not the writer makes a sharp distinction between sensation and perception, on which distinction hangs a great deal, both epistemologically and metaphysically.

Harold Brown argues that an indirect causal link is no bar to knowledge. He makes an analogy with science, in which many examples can be found of well-founded theories being based on evidence that is far from direct. He points out that direct arguments make appeal to analyses of everyday concepts, which "everyone can happily concede embody direct realism," but adds: "But we should no more expect a correct account of perception from conceptual analysis than expect to establish relativity theory or the principles of statistics in this manner" (this vol.: 45). He supports his case with a new argument from illusion, one resistant to the familiar objections, such as those proposed by J. L. Austin (1962). He leaves aside the ontological questions concerned with what constitutes the "items" observed in "normal perception," but stresses the fact that what we sense and perceive is numerically distinct from what the causes may be. He is in search of an argument to the best explanation, given the insights afforded by science. Following C. L. Hardin (1988), he gives a detailed account of the transmission of sensory and neural impulses, and concludes that the resulting experience, though bearing similarities to the input, is far from being numerically identical with it. He instances the fact that many different combinations of wavelengths can result in the same color (see Hardin in this vol.: 143). Furthermore, indirect realism can attribute a credible ontological status to the appearance per se.

E. J. Lowe unabashedly describes his theory as a sense-datum theory, as he has a right to, having published a book making a thoroughgoing statement of his position (Lowe 1996), even though opponents have assumed that no one holds to such a theory nowadays because of "all the familiar reasons." In that book he carefully distinguishes between accounts of what we perceive and accounts of the way in which we refer to our sensations, an "oblique" form of reference, which a sophisticated observer can use. So in 1996 he had already produced an argument that questions the claim that we are always faced with an immediate relation to the items perceived. He also then insisted that any causal relation between the external and the inner presentation could only be via "sensuous features" and *not* between external object and perceived item (1996: 115). In his essay here he mentions that there is a tendency to turn one's back on sense-datum theory because one "doesn't like the questions that it raises" (this vol.: 70). Like Brown, his central concern is the question of illusion, as presented in the typical cases of double vision and hallucination.

William S. Robinson is openly a dualist, entirely opposed to a physicalist explanation of the sensory. In his recent book (W. S. Robinson 2004) he defends a form of qualia realism, the belief that phenomenal experiences have an ontological existence that no form of materialism is able to explain. He there presents many convincing examples of stubborn facts in sensory experience that the physicalist must account for if she is to sustain her metaphysical beliefs. As he puts it, there is a "basic question" that she must answer, namely, how, for example, "does color come into a full accounting of what normally happens when a person sees a red apple?" (ibid.: 8). A full explanation, he believes, must accept that qualia as events are real but nonmaterial, a view he calls "qualia event realism." He is prepared to claim that a full account of qualia will largely decide the issue of consciousness itself (ibid.: 33), that directing research on the "explanatory gap" will reduce the "puzzlement" about the relation between our experiences and our brains. To ignore the existence of that gap, as some materialists do, is to reduce materialism to an empty shell "whose only virtue is that it cannot be shown to be self-contradictory" (ibid.: 250). In his essay here he sets out to refute the claim that sensory experiences can be equated with judgments (thus following in the non-epistemic tradition), and therefore denies that qualitative events are representational. He uses a thought experiment to establish the fact that a physicalist version of representationalism is unable to explain the intrinsicality of qualitative events.

Terence Horgan and George Graham are qualia realists, in the sense that they consider the character of "what it is like" for a human being to be essential to consciousness. In the first part of their essay they define the term "qualia," taking it beyond the use as confined to direct sensory experience. They borrow Ned Block's distinction between "access-consciousness" and "phenomenal consciousness" (Block 1995): A state is A-conscious if it is ready to be used for the direct rational control of thought and action, so it is plain that it can make use of phenomenal consciousness. The non-epistemic view, of course, allows for the separation of the two, that is, for sensing to go on apart from cognitive engagement (notice that this is not illustrated by the situation in which one becomes aware that a dog has been barking for a while unnoticed, but one in which a *novel and unrecognized* noise has been going on unnoticed). Horgan and Graham, on the other hand, take phenomenal consciousness to be "inseparably intentional or representational"; that is, qualitative experiences possess intentionality (they allow that there might be counterexamples, but feel sure that such would not disturb their argument). Their definition, however, contrasts with that of the modern representationalist, for she sees the phenomenal as "exhaustively, non-intrinsically, intentional," whereas they see it as "intrinsically intentional," constituting a "phenomenal intentionality." They conceive of qualia as "multidimensional," for they include within their definition the phenomenology of agency, the what-it-is-likeness of apparently voluntarily controlling one's apparent body, that of conative and cognitive phenomenology, that of "attitude content" (e.g., hoping or fearing that something is or might be the case), and that of "self-modification or self-attribution" (when one experiences a thought or sensation as one's own). These inclusions mark out an interesting extension of the term qualia. The second part of the essay is taken up with three other considerations in favor of qualia realism.

Like Horgan and Graham, Matjaž Potrč sees qualia both as real and as "intertwined with intentional content." He regards qualia as "what holds the experiential world together," using the metaphor of cement for the purpose. Here he can be said to be close to Horgan and Graham in regarding qualia as omnipresent in conscious states, and not only in the form of sensory experience. He draws attention to what he calls the "sharpening up" of intentional content that qualia enable us to perform. Here he pays tribute to the part qualia play in learning, as he puts it, in the "dynamic" aspects of cognition, but he is concerned to retain the "preliminary existence" of what that cognition is in search of. Here we see the determination to avoid the "veil-of-sensation" accusation, coupled with the conviction that real existence is what the dynamic process wrestles with. He concludes by stressing the importance of context as contributing to the process, in that a holistic awareness must underlie it, since interpretation cannot gain a hold without placing an experience against such a context. Here he is bearing witness to the richness of memory in the performance of our actual perceiving.

Robert J. Howell, like myself, is someone for whom the existence of qualia does not imply the falsity of materialism. Indeed, his article sets out to reconcile subjective experiences such as qualia with a physicalist ontology. He calls his approach "subjective physicalism." His version of physicalism is one in which it is asserted that all things, properties, and facts are physical, but within which "no objective theory, including physics, can completely describe the world" (this vol.: 126). He claims that his argument shows that dualism is not the only outcome of such an approach and that it does not therefore lead to the problem of nomological danglers such as epiphenomenalism implies. The key assertion with regard to the subjective is that these states "must be undergone in order to be fully grasped" (cf. Edelman and Tononi 2000: 12–13; and in this volume, W. S. Robinson: 78, and Wright: 347). This does not imply that they are not physical, only that they are "not identical with any property mentioned in a completed physics." The bulk of his argument is taken up with rendering that position credible and avoiding the dualist conclusion.

The second group of articles really falls under a subheading of the first, since they are, in various ways, scientific defenses of the existence of qualia. C. L. Hardin is well known for his clear and painstaking exploration of the scientific evidence for the characterization of colors as qualia. His book *Color for Philosophers* is a classic of its kind; it won the 1986 Johnsonian Prize for Philosophy. His essay is an argument that sets out to show that colors are not properties of physical objects, but are "two removes from the occurrent bases of the dispositions to see them" (this vol.: 143), and central to the proof of this is not only the fact that the causes of color are many and varied, but the degree to which individuals vary in their sensory responses. Different spectral power distributions (SPDs) can produce the same color (the phenomenon of metamerism) and the mode of illumination is a key factor. The contrast between one region and another will produce anomalous effects if surroundings are changed; "even black is a contrast color." He mentions an interesting situation in which an increase of light will actually make black blacker. This recalls Locke's observation that black was a "positive" state of sensation, one produced by the entire absence of input (one wonders what those for whom qualia are "transparent," allowing access through to what causes them, have made of this; Locke, *Essay*, II, viii, 2). He cites many more interesting examples that challenge the mundane view. He also carefully considers the objections that have been made to the apparent qualia-favoring consequences of these facts, noting that often an appeal is made to the experiences of a "normal" observer when it is questionable whether there is such a person. What undermines the commonsense view are the well-documented differences between persons, of which he gives a scientific account (in the present writer's view this is a conclusive proof of the non-epistemic, since no propositional agreement can capture these hidden differences in advance of test). He concludes that "phenomenology must be the arbiter of adequacy" in the investigation of these matters, and does not rule out the hope that much more will become clear "with plenty of time and good science."

Isabelle Peschard and Michel Bitbol's essay can fitly be linked with that of Hardin's, for what they say of heat, temperature, and phenomenal concepts allies itself firmly with his investigation of color. Just as he resists the reduction of color to spectral power distributions, they resist the reduction of the sensory experiences of heat (and cold) to molecular kinetic energy. To take the latter as key cause, of course, facilitates the attempt to turn discourse about sensations into a scientific description of neural activity. The possibility of such a reduction is what they set about to refute, endeavoring to show that the phenomenal cannot be removed from science by such means. There is no straightforward relation between temperature and heat sensation. It is worth, they believe, going back to Locke's citing of the experiment in which the two hands are placed in cold and hot water respectively and then moved to a bowl of lukewarm water (Locke, *Essay*, II, viii, 21); it establishes the "perspectival" nature of our sensing without losing contact with the world. They claim, against my own argument (Wright 2005: 84), that even the experience of peripheral vision is not without some representational element; this, then, constitutes a rejection of the possibility of the non-epistemic, and they believe that it gives them access to the external across the veil of perception. They go on to argue that heat sensations are recognitional and not functional, so that they can claim that they have not yielded up a qualia-realist stance. It is in this last section that they are nearest to Hardin's position, and it is interesting to compare the facts that establish a similar philosophical contention.

Riccardo Manzotti's way of countering the relativist attack is to assert that qualia are to be defended by a thoroughgoing rejection of the traditional dichotomy between phenomenalism and representationalism. He presents a realist view of qualia that is capable of explaining illusions, dreams, afterimages, phosphenes, and so on without yielding up their intentional aspect. He is determined to link the external object, which he takes as given, with the internal presentation. He notes that his fellow-countryman, Galileo, was among the first scientists to make the sharp distinction between the internal sensation and the outer cause, but acknowledges the apparent challenge to the materialist scientist posed by this hypothesis, since it regarded as real something that appears obstinately beyond scientific description. Manzotti takes the view that the explanatory gap only exists because of a refusal to see perception as a Whiteheadian process in which sensation and cause cannot be detached from each other. The color of, say, a red ball, is not to be lodged either on the surface of the ball nor in the neural structures in the brain that are the end-point of the process, but in the process as a whole. The process is "partially outside the brain and partially inside it," thus collapsing the distinction between sensation and perception. By this device he claims to have escaped both dualism and naive realism, as well as Daniel Dennett's dismissal of what he takes to be generally accepted criteria of qualia (that they are ineffable, intrinsic, private, and directly apprehensible). He concludes with an examination of difficult cases, such as hallucination, by tracing their causal histories to past experiences.

John R. Smythies, the psychologist, has been a stalwart of the belief in qualia, from his first endeavor in the field, *Analysis of Perception*, published (astonishingly) in 1956. He has not become an apostate to the cause, as did his colleague Lord Brain, and like our contemporary Frank Jackson, but has held to the notion of qualia over all these years, arguing tenaciously for their inclusion in a materialist science. His latest contribution here is a robust attack on direct realism (dealing, for example, with one of the "familiar objections," the vicious regress of homunculi). He also presents the notion of perception not being a reproduction of what is "out there" as perfectly plausible from a scientific point of view. He also has a section on the "binding problem," that is, how the brain unifies the deliverances of the different sense modalities (see O'Dea, this vol.), and provides significant evidence from the recovery of brain-damaged patients.

But, since attack proverbially is the best form of defense, there are also numerous detailed criticisms of opposing views, both representationalist and tough-minded-physicalist, and these have been grouped under the heading of "attacks."

The first, that of Mark Crooks, is an attack on eliminativism, the thesis that there are no qualia whatsoever. This is a summary way of dealing with the imaginary danger that adhering to the notion of qualia inescapably leads to either dualism or relativism. Instead of interpreting perception as wholly definitive of qualia, as the transparency thesis has it (as we shall see in a moment), the supporters of this view, notably Daniel C. Dennett, Paul M. Churchland, and Patricia S. Churchland, hold that sensing, in being reducible to neural architecture, neither has nor requires any phenomenological aspect. Qualia do not exist within this theory, being only the outcome of a folk interpretation of the actual case. The whole problem of how Locke's "sensation" and "reflection" are to be related is thus rendered unreal in a theory that, by definition, is materialistic, so one need not concern oneself with issues such as how a visual field registers the nature of external or internal entities, which are, of course, believed in without question. The metaphysical dilemma thus evaporates. Were it a cogent argument, all defenses of qualia could be regarded as ingenious scholastic constructions devoid of any purchase on the world. It is important, then that a refutation of this "neurophilosophy," as Patricia Churchland calls it, is carried through, and this is what Mark Crooks has undertaken here. The core of his argument relies on showing how the eliminativists surreptitiously retain a commitment to qualia while apparently rejecting the notion. In defining the perception of a distinct sensation (such as the tartness of lemon juice), Paul Churchland, for example, in a covert operation that he is not aware he is performing, "confounds a percept with its cause." This can be seen to be the result of providing a premise that is actually no more than a convenient act of legislation that identifies "object" with "percept," which, naturally, escapes the problem of having to explain how something that uses an indirect path to external existence can have as its product reliable knowledge. Crooks presents a number of other examples of what he calls "misleading fallacies of equivocation" (this vol.: 206). Patricia Churchland is accused of relying on a questionable philosophy of science to support her claims of intertheoretic identification that would allow her desired reductions to go through. He claims to show, for example, that "The Churchlands have inconsistently retained logical empiricism's claim of identification of cross-theoretic properties while concurrently rejecting the premises on which those claims are based" (this vol.: 211–212).

Crooks concludes that few, if any, intertheoretic identities (of percepts with neural architecture) are admitted by the eliminativists, and those that are are no more than "misidentified psychophysical correspondences."

There is a particular target for attack that qualiaphiles have come to prefer: the currently popular claim that qualia can be fully accounted for by the "transparency thesis." This is specifically described by those attacking it, as will be seen, but, in brief, it is the theory that phenomenal experience is fully explicable in terms of what human beings detect by its means. For example, if one looks at the superb greenness of a lagoon beside the holiday atoll, there is no way one can detach that greenness from the reality of the lagoon. The "intentionality," as its proponents are fond of saying, wholly explicates the sensory experience, exhausting all that can be said of it: hence, there is no way in which the sensory can be separated from its import. If it fully accounted for this, then there are no qualia, no "sense-data," no awkward danglers that smack of the occult that can tempt the unwise into dualism, relativism, and the rest. It is another attempt to bridge the imaginary space between our perceptions and the knowledge we impute to them. What could be plainer than the fact that we "look through" our sensations to unmistakable singular entities to the point in the argument where sensations can drop out of consideration altogether as supposed screens between us and the things and persons around us, which are all visibly "thus-and-so"?

Howard Robinson, a dualist like his namesake, roundly turns on Frank Jackson for his abandonment of the qualia cause, taking up the knowledge argument where Jackson left off. Jackson declared his apostasy precisely because he saw the transparency argument as providing a ready confirmation of direct access to knowledge of external things. Robinson argues that representationalism fails as an account of experience as a whole, particularly because it is unable to provide a satisfying explanation of hallucination. He mentions phosphenes, which, being the result of a direct stimulus to the brain, do not of themselves "represent" anything. I might add here that in childhood, I was mystified by the strange patterns I saw in the dark when I was coughing (see Boyle 1964 [1664]: 12) and then could gain no knowledge of them whatever. In addition, the experience of hallucinations remains stubbornly real, with the result that tough-minded physicalists cannot dismiss them as imaginary. He regards it as implausible that one should attempt to deny that hallucinations resemble veridical experiences in their phenomenology. It is worth appending the note here that M. J. M. Martin, who is one of Robinson's targets, leaves out of his account altogether the fact that hallucinations can be so chaotic as to be unobjectifiable, and thus nonrepresentational (as in hypnagogic visions). Robinson also considers Michael Tye's discussion of Ned Block's argument about orgasm (Block 1995; Tye 1995b) and concludes that it commits him to a "radically reductive account if the experience itself."

Torin Alter is also concerned to defend the knowledge argument from its recent attackers. The most recent form of attack has been to claim that there are cases in which acquaintance with the nature of the phenomenal has been achieved without actual experience of that phenomenon. They opponents bring forward as evidence Hume's "missing shade of blue" and various thought experiments in which "RoboMarys" and "Swamp Marys" have knowledge of the phenomenal without actually having had the experience. Alter examines with patient care these various claims, and produces counterarguments to show that it is not a priori deducibility of phenomena that is arrived at but dispositional states. These, in effect, amount to a smuggling of the existence of qualia as a concealed premise into an account that was ostensibly meant to be free of them. The proponents of this view already know what it is like to see color before they make their deduction. Alter actually accuses Dennett's "RoboMary" of "cheating."

Barry Maund sets about an attack on the "strong intentionalists," who argue that there is no need for a strong account of qualia since all their character can be explained in terms of their intentional content. If he is right, then the intentionalism–transparency route to external knowledge can be shown not to achieve the breakthrough it is in search of, that what they have won has not the reliability they claim, and that they will be forced to accept that, in attacking a straw man, they have been blindly avoiding more intractable problems. Maund is careful at the outset to define qualia and show that, although the sensory phenomena and the subjective awareness of them are the most obvious candidates, there are also more subtle "feels" that are undoubtedly a part of our consciousness, such as those that accompany our ordinary understanding (even of something as mundane as one's response to the query "Would you like a cup of tea?"), which ought not to be omitted from consideration. Maund takes a firm line on the non-epistemicity of sensations, emphasizing their "intrinsic, non-intentional features." The supporters of the transparency theory (Harman, Tye, Byrne, Crane) discount the possibility of the non-epistemic entirely, confining the phenomenal, that is, sensation, completely within intentional bounds. Maund points out that the transparency theorists operate with altogether too narrow a definition of qualia, ignoring empirical facts that appear to demonstrate non-intentional characteristics (such as the blind regaining sight; and hypnagogic and hypnopompic imagery).

However, the central weakness of the notion of transparency is that it is forced to try to explain the phenomenal in terms of the "physical qualities of physical bodies." The theorists of transparency, aware of this, do attempt such a reduction, for example, in the reduction of surface color to spectral reflectance, but as Hardin, Thompson, Maund, and others have pointed out, such a reduction has been shown to be flawed. They have tried to refute this objection, but their response rests overmuch on an idealized view of a "normal" observer (see Hardin, in this vol.: 145–148). Maund concludes with a refutation of Tim Crane's version of transparency, which, he believes, ignores obvious features of phenomenal experience.

A similar criticism is that of Amy Kind, for she too regards the case for transparency as employing an insufficiently broad definition of qualia. A closer investigation of the phenomenology of our sensory experience reveals aspects that cannot be explained merely by detailing the recognizable, intentional features of everyday things and persons. She examines first what she calls some "exotic" cases, but then shows how the deliverances of that inquiry are just as applicable to the entities of mundane perception. There are two camps of opponents to qualia, those physicalists who are convinced that qualia cannot exist since they are not explicable in any current neurophysiological science, and the representationalists for whom all sensory experience can be lodged within conscious perception. The state of the argument appears to be that the latter believe that their case is plausible, even proven, and thus the ball is in the qualiaphile court to provide an answer to these strong objections. Kind sees the phenomenological data as proving the contrary, that qualia do exist, and not only in the exotic cases (that of blurry images and phosphenes, which are obviously not "transparent" in any direct way). A mundane example is that of attending to a pain, which (as Maund also points out) cannot be reduced to the idea that it specifies its location (one can add here what V. S. Ramachandran and Sandra Blakeslee have documented, that it is not uncommon in injured patients for pains to be felt in a different part of the body from the actual damage; Ramachandran and Blakeslee 1999: ch. 2). The thesis also is revealed as inadequate to explain the phenomenology of emotions and moods. She concludes by denying outright the claim that we can never be aware of the sensory features of our experience apart from what we are been taught is "objectively" before us. One wonders, indeed, how any teaching and learning could go one if everything were "transparent" in the manner described.

John O'Dea takes up an unusual contention of Michael Tye, that the binding problem (i.e., the means by which the mind fits together the inputs from the different sense modalities), results in it being correct to deny that there is a specifically visual experience as distinct from a tactile or auditory or gustatory one. Watching a TV advertisement, for example, you are subjected to a succession of sounds (words, music, noises of various kinds) which are deliberately, more often than not, synesthetically bound together with the changes in the images with which you are presented, with the result that you cannot help but link them (think of Walt Disney's *Fantasia*). Tye asks how an explanation of the unity of consciousness is to be achieved if, as qualiaphiles maintain, there is a stubborn uniqueness about each modality that marks it off from all the others. He proposes instead an "experienced togetherness" in which there are no such sense-specific experiences. O'Dea, using an example from H. P. Grice, argues that this view leaves out the fact that the intentional contents are differently presented in different sense-modalities. He cites experiments that show that the projected unities can often be mistaken: a notable instance is that of the ventriloquist's performance, where the puppet's jaw movements and its "body-language" induce us to attribute the source of sound to the puppet and not the ventriloquist. One can also instance those psychological experiments in which a subject is fooled into thinking a false hand within her visual range that is being touched is her own hand. O'Dea also notes that the form of binding varies: in the case of a blue pebble, the blue invests the whole shape of the pebble (an "*inter*modal" blending, a binding of sensory elements to each other) whereas in the case of us dropping the pebble and hearing a click as it hits another, there is a mere coinciding of sight and sound (an "*intra*modal" blending, a binding of modalities to one object). These bindings are "psychological facts" about the act of perception rather than facts about the object perceived, which implies the falsity of transparency.

Martine Nida-Rümelin argues that the transparency thesis fails in different ways for our experiences of color and shape. In her view, "phenomenal character" (the term she prefers to "qualia") is "an intrinsic property of the experiencing subject" (this vol.: 309). She concedes that there is an intimate relation between phenomenal character and content. In order to refer to sensory experiences we often use the content as a convenient mode of reference (on this point, see Maund 1976: 62), but this does not imply that there are not "cases of misrepresentation" (which must be the case if learning is to be possible), nor does it exclude the possibility that "there are experiences with phenomenal character but without representational content," the existence of latter being enough to overturn representationalism (see the discussion on the non-epistemic above). Colors may appear to be properties of objects, "but it is doubtful that they also appear to be *objective* in any more substantial sense" (this vol.: 314). It is plain that a judgment about the color of something can be *both* a judgment about the object *and* a judgment about one' s visual experience. Neither the concept of being blue nor the concept of a blueness experience is more fundamental than the other. To use the term "introspection"—or Block's term, "mental paint" (though the latter is probably just a mischievous challenge)—skews a proper understanding of the process. Nida-Rümelin argues that a transparency statement cannot avoid a reference to phenomenal character, however much it would prefer to conceal the fact. Finally, she claims that it is impossible to carry through a direct reduction of phenomenal character to a material base without begging the question of the subject of experience, and this is noticeably absent from the transparency thesis.

Diana Raffman has a similar aim to that of Nida-Rümelin, that is, to show how proponents of the transparency thesis cannot escape covert reliance on the phenomenal quality of sensory experiences when they try to equate "outer" qualities with "inner," with the result that inner qualities disappear into outer ones. They believe that this support of what is supposed to be naive common sense (though many a layperson has doubts about the directness of his or her sensory experiences) would banish at one go the problem of the reliability of what passes for knowledge, as well as getting rid of the troublesome apparent resistance of the phenomenal to scientific explanation. She begins with the concession that awareness of content can infuse phenomenal experience, but denies that definition of the content "exhausts that awareness." It is vital that the would-be materialist does justice to our intuitions about the sensory, in particular, by explaining how one could be aware of content without having access through the sensory fields: "*How content gets fixed, and how one gains awareness of that content, are two different questions*" (this vol.: 326). One answer that is given is that experiencing external color, say, red, consists in tokening a mental predicate "RED." Raffman believes that one cannot equate a conceptual representation with a perceptual one, though one can, if one chooses, talk of the first as a "representation," but that would not capture the sensory feature, only classify it. She draws attention to what is missing in this account by having the reader imagine she presents an actual example of red within her text. What this makes clear is that the tokening of a word cannot "constitute a *look*." This makes plain that the representationalist's argument includes a covert stipulation about "a (hitherto unknown) kind of mental representational vehicle that has all and only the properties that his theory requires" (this vol.: 330). She traces this stipulation in the arguments of both Michael Tye and Gilbert Harman. She concludes with a section in which she deals with some possible objections to her case. The problem of how a "word-picture" could be effective without awareness of intrinsic phenomenal properties has not been solved.

In the final essay, my own attack on the transparency thesis comes from another quarter, providing an ethical criticism of its beliefs (for an extended treatment, see Wright 2005). I regard the discovery and constant adjustment of objectivity as an endless intersubjective process, in which the sensory fields provide evidence that is fundamentally corrigible, though they themselves are brute at the level of registration of input. The fields covary with the inputs at the sensory organs in a "structurally isomorphic" manner. Just as the laser beams moving over the surface of the disc inside a DVD-player can covary in subtle ways with the states of the phosphor cells on the TV screen and the vibrations that issue from the stereo loudspeakers and yet bear no direct similarity to them, so too our sensory experience covaries, not necessarily exactly, with the inputs, but *bears no direct resemblance to them*. This implies, for example, that there is no "pictorial" similarity between our experience of color and the causes that affect our eye, and that, by the same token, external surfaces are not colored with the phenomenal colors that we sense—although there is a principled covariance. These fields provide evidential access to the real—in particular, to the features that affect our creaturely life, and these, initially as a result of pain and pleasure, become embedded in memory as unitary gestalts. They are honed to greater success there by subsequent encounters, remaining able to track change in those encounters, and, most importantly, are tabbed in memory with fear and desire. This is why I call in philosophy for the word "mind" to be seen first as a *verb*—as in "Mind the thorns on the rose-bush by the door!," and not as a noun, as in "the philosophy of mind." This emphasis on its meaning as a verb makes motivation a key issue in the philosophy of consciousness. Such a process, with which evolution has provided our animal ancestors, has, by further evolution, received an enhancement as a result of the development of language, which essentially enables updatings of percepts to be proposed among species members. Such updatings necessarily involve trust between agents about what is to be considered "an" object, for the hypothesis of there being a "common," singular entity is a necessary mutual ploy to get a rough coordination of understandings. Consequently, the nature of that trust becomes critical, since it is attended with unavoidable risk. To imagine that the *singularity* of a current objectification, mutual by the very mode of its creation and maintenance, already exists as a given in the real is thus an act of undue complacency. Indeed, since it ignores the risk inherent in a proper faith between agents, it can thus be said that such complacency partakes of superstition. However, this is what is implied in any philosophy of perception that assumes a singularity of entities without realizing the ethical responsibility of that strictly false assumption, and transparency theory, in *believing* the assumption, even though that assumption is still a practically necessary, mutual, regulative idea, is thus open to that criticism.

As I noted at the beginning of this introduction, the existence of qualia has for many years been regarded as an eccentric notion, a relic of early Enlightenment "natural philosophy," a Galilean misconception that unfortunately led to "infamous" relativistic, even occult, conclusions. Notoriously, this notion has been presented as comical, half-baked fantasy by Daniel Dennett (2006: 77–102). It is no surprise that such defenses of qualia that appeared were automatically ignored for it was taken as read that no professional philosopher would so imperil his reputation—or career—by espousing a belief in them. That some psychologists and neurophysiologists (John Smythies, Lord Brain, R. L. Gregory) still showed signs of tinkering with the idea only betrayed their philosophical amateurishness. The older philosophers who favored qualia, like Wilfrid Sellars, Jonathan Harrison, Virgil C. Aldrich, and J. L. Mackie, were given respectful but unenthusiastic hearings (see, as representative, the response to Sellars's Carus Lectures, in the *Monist* of January 1981). The earlier volume I edited (Wright 1993) met with the same indifference: I do not know of a single philosophical journal that ran a review of it in spite of the fact that it contained essays by reputable philosophers and psychologists.

From my own point of view the motivation for this neglect is traceable to an irrational source, from which spring the accusations of solipsism and relativism that are deemed to provide powerful refutation of a qualia-based theory. I also regard the belief that to countenance the existence of qualia is reactionary and unscientific, tempting one too easy to fall in with Dennett's mockery, as equally insecure. However, it may come to be argued that this is an unfair ad hominem attack, one ignoring in its turn the positions taken up by the other side. But mine is not the only novel objection in this volume. Whether or not the counterarguments here are cogent, there does seem to have been a hubris-like overconfidence among the qualiaphobes, together, one might claim, with a certain professional insularity, as evidenced in the refusal to encounter the qualiaphile objections, except in those limited cases mentioned at the outset. It is to be hoped that, from this time forth, the philosophical conversation about sensation and perception can be conducted in a less myopic, less dismissive manner, with the objections here presented not thoughtlessly overlooked; otherwise, the qualiaphobe could fitly be likened to the cartoon cat who has run off the edge of a cliff but hasn't yet fallen, *because it hasn't looked down.*

References

Aldrich, Virgil C. 1980. Mirrors, pictures, words, perceptions. *Philosophy* 55: 39–56.

Armstrong, D. M. 1966. *Perception and the Physical World*. London: Routledge and Kegan Paul.

Austin, J. L. 1962. *Sense and Sensibilia*. London and Oxford: Oxford University Press.

Berkeley, G. 1972 [1713]. *Three Dialogues between Hylas and Philonous*. In *A New Theory of Vision and Other Writings*, ed. G. J. Warnock, 197–303. London: Collins Fontana.

Block, N. 1980. Are absent qualia impossible? *Philosophical Review* 89, 2: 257–274.

Block, N. 1995. On a confusion about a function of consciousness. *Behavioral and Brain Sciences* 18: 227–247.

Block, N. 2003. Mental paint. In *Reflections and Replies: Essays on the Philosophy of Tyler Burge*, ed. Martin Hahn and Bjørn Ramberg. Cambridge, Mass.: MIT Press/A Bradford Book. Available at http://www.nyu.edu/gsas/dept/philo/faculty/block/papers/mentalpaint.pdf/.

Boyle, R. 1964 [1664]. *Experiments and Considerations Touching Colours*. Facsimile edition. Ed. M. B. Hall. New York: Johnson Reprint Corporation.

Boyle, R. 1979 [1666]. *Selected Philosophical Papers of Robert Boyle*. Manchester: Manchester University Press.

Brain, W. R. 1951. *Mind, Perception, and Science*. Oxford: Blackwell Scientific.

Broad, C. D. 1923. *The Mind and Its Place in Nature*. London: Kegan Paul, Trench, Trubner.

Brown, H. 1987. *Observation and Objectivity*. New York: Oxford University Press.

Chalmers, D. 2006. Perception and the Fall from Eden. In *Perceptual Experience*, ed. T. S. Gendler and J. Hawthorne, 49–125. Oxford: Clarendon Press.

Clark, A. 2000. *A Theory of Sentience*. Oxford: Oxford University Press.

Collins, A. W. 1967. The epistemological status of the concept of perception. *Philosophical Review* 76: 436–459.

Condillac, E. B. de 1930 [1754]. *Condillac's Treatise on the Sensations*. London: Favil Press.

Dennett, D. C. 1985. Quining qualia. Medford, Mass.: Center for Cognitive Studies, Tufts University.

Dennett, D. C. 1991. *Consciousness Explained*. London: Penguin Books.

Dennett, D. C. 2006. *Sweet Dreams: Philosophical Obstacles to a Science of Consciousness*. Cambridge, Mass.: MIT Press/A Bradford Book.

Dretske, F. 1981. *Knowledge and the Flow of Information*. Oxford: Basil Blackwell.

Dretske, Fred. 1997. *Naturalizing the Mind*. Cambridge, Mass.: MIT Press/A Bradford Book.

Edelman, G. M., and G. Tononi. 2000. *Consciousness: How Matter Becomes Imagination*. London: Allen Lane, Penguin Press.

Evans, G. 1982. *The Varieties of Reference*. Oxford: Clarendon.

Feuerbach. L. 1903–11. *Sämtliche Werke*, 13 vols. Ed. W. Bolin and F. Jodl. Stuttgart: Fromann Verlag.

Fitzgerald, P. 1979. Review of F. Jackson, *Perception. International Philosophical Quarterly* 19, 1: 103–113.

Foster, J. 1982. *The Case for Idealism*. London: Routledge and Kegan Paul.

Gadamer, H.-G. 1975. *Truth and Method*. London: Sheed and Ward.

Garnett, A. C. 1965. *The Perceptual Process*. London: George Allen and Unwin.

Gendler, T. S., and J. Hawthorne, eds. 2006. *Perceptual Experience*. Oxford: Clarendon Press.

Gerdil, G. S. 1748. *Défense du Sentiment du P. Malebranche sur la nature et l'origine des idées, contre l'examen de M. Locke*. Turin: L'Imprimerie Royale.

Gibson, J. J. 1968. *The Senses Considered as Perceptual Systems*. London: George Allen and Unwin.

Gregory, R. L. 1993. Hypothesis and illusion: Explorations in perception and science. In *New Representationalisms: Essays in the Philosophy of Perception*, ed. E. L. Wright, 232–262. Aldershot: Avebury.

Grice, H. P. 1967. Meaning. In *Philosophical Logic*, ed. P. F. Strawson, 39–48. Oxford: Oxford University Press.

Gunther, Y. H., ed. 2003. *Essays on Nonconceptual Content*. Cambridge, Mass.: MIT Press/A Bradford Book.

Hamlyn, D. W. 1961. *Sensation and Perception*. London: Routledge and Kegan Paul.

Hardin, C. L. 1988. *Color for Philosophers*. Indianapolis, Ind.: Hackett.

Harman, G. 1990. The intrinsic quality of experience. In *Philosophical Perspectives 4: Action Theory and the Philosophy of Mind*, ed. J. Tomberlin, 31–52. Atascadero, Calif.: Ridgeview.

Harrison, J. 1976. Direct perception and the sense-datum theory. In *Contemporary British Philosophy: 4th Series, Personal Statements*. London: George Allen and Unwin.

Harrison, J. 1985. *A Philosopher's Nightmare*. Nottingham: Department of Philosophy, University of Nottingham.

Heffner, J. 1981. The causal theory of visual perception: Its scientific basis and philosophical implications. *International Philosophical Quarterly* 21, 3: 303–332.

Helmholtz, H. von. 1868. *Helmholtz on Perception: Its Physiology and Development*. Ed. R. M. Warren and R. P. Warren. New York: John Wiley.

Helmholtz, H. von. 1962. *Treatise on Physiological Optics*, 3 vols. Trans. J. P. C. Southall. New York: Dover.

Hermelin, B. 1976. Coding and the sense modalities. In *Early Childhood Autism*, ed. L. Wing, 135–168. Oxford: Pergamon Press.

Hobbes, T. 1839. *Elements of Philosophy, The First Section: Concerning Body*. Trans. Sir Bart W. Molesworth. London: John Bohn.

Holman, E. L. 1979. The problem of theory-laden perception. *Philosophical Studies* 35: 91–99.

Hyman, J. 2007. *The Objective Eye: Form and Reality in the Theory of Art*. Chicago: Chicago University Press.

Jackson, F. 1977. *Perception*. Cambridge: Cambridge University Press.

Jones, O. R. 1972. After-images. *American Philosophical Quarterly* 9: 150–158.

James, W. 1977. *The Writings of William James: A Comprehensive Edition*. Ed. J. J. McDermott. Chicago: University of Chicago Press.

Kelly, J. S. 1989. On neutralizing introspection: The data of sensuous awareness. *Southern Journal of Philosophy* 27, 1: 29–53.

Landesman, C. 1989. *Color and Consciousness: An Essay in Metaphysics*. Philadelphia: Temple University Press.

Lewes, G. H. 1874. *Problems of Life and Mind*, 4 vols. London: Trübner.

Long, A. A. 1986. *Hellenistic Philosophy: Stoics, Epicureans, Sceptics*. London: Duckworth.

Lockwood, M. 1989. *Mind, Brain, and the Quantum: The Compound "I."* Oxford: Basil Blackwell.

Lowe, E. J. 1996. *Subjects of Experience*. Cambridge: Cambridge University Press.

MacClachlan, D. L. C. 1989. *Philosophy of Perception*. Englewood Cliffs, N.J.: Prentice-Hall.

Mackie, J. L. 1976. *Problems from Locke*. Oxford: Clarendon Press.

Malebranche, N. 1992 [1674]. *Philosophical Reflections*. Ed. S. Nadler. Indianapolis, Ind.: Hackett.

Mandelbaum, M. 1966. *Philosophy, Science, and Sense Perception: Historical and Critical Studies*. Baltimore: The Johns Hopkins University Press.

Matilal, B. 1986. *Perception: An Essay on Classical Indian Theories of Knowledge*. Oxford: Clarendon Press.

Matthen, M. 2005. *Seeing, Doing, and Knowing: A Philosophical Theory of Sense Perception*. Oxford: Clarendon Press.

Maund, J. B. 1975. The Representative Theory of Perception. *Canadian Journal of Philosophy* 5: 41–55.

Maund, J. B. 1976. The non-sensuous epistemic account of perception. *American Philosophical Quarterly* 13, 1: 57–62.

Maund, J. B. 1995. *Colours: Their Nature and Representation*. Cambridge: Cambridge University Press.

Mayne, Z. 1728. *Two Dissertations Concerning Sense and the Imagination*. London: J. Tonson.

McDowell, J. 1994. *Mind and World*. Cambridge, Mass.: Harvard University Press.

Mulhall, S. 2007. Because it's pink. *London Review of Books* 29, 2: 26–27.

Mundle, C. W. K. 1971. *Perception: Facts and Theories*. Oxford: Oxford University Press.

Noë, A. 2006. Experience without the head. In *Perceptual Experience*, ed. T. S. Gendler and J. Hawthorne, 411–433. Oxford: Clarendon Press.

Oakes, R. 1982. Seeing our own faces: a paradigm for indirect realism. *Philosophy and Phenomenological Research* 42, 3: 442–449.

Peacocke, C. 1983. *Sense and Content: Experience, Thought, and Their Relations*. Oxford: Clarendon Press.

Peacocke, C. 1992. *A Study of Concepts*. Cambridge, Mass.: MIT Press/A Bradford Book.

Peacocke, C. 2003. Nonconceptual content: kinds, rationales, relations. In *Essays on Nonconceptual Content*, ed. Y. H. Gunther, 309–322. Cambridge, Mass.: MIT Press/A Bradford Book.

Pennycuick, J. 1971. *In Contact with the Physical World*. London: George Allen and Unwin.

Perkins, M. 1983. *Sensing the World*. Indianapolis, Ind.: Hackett.

Pitcher, G. 1971. *A Theory of Perception*. Princeton, N.J.: Princeton University Press.

Price, H. H. 1961 [1932]. *Perception*. London: Methuen.

Price, H. H. 1964. Appearing and appearances. *American Philosophical Quarterly* 1, 1: 3–19.

Ramachandran, V. S., and S. Blakeslee. 1999. *Phantoms in the Brain: Human Nature and the Architecture of Mind*. London: Fourth Estate.

Reid, T. 1970 [1764]. *An Inquiry into the Human Mind*. Ed. T. Duggan. Chicago: Chicago University Press.

Reid, T. 1941 [1785]. *Essays in the Intellectual Powers of Man*. Ed. A. D. Woozley. London: Macmillan.

Robinson, H. 1994. *Perception*. London and New York: Routledge.

Robinson, W. S. 2004. *Understanding Phenomenal Consciousness*. Cambridge: Cambridge University Press.

Rorty, R. 1980. *Philosophy and the Mirror of Nature*. Oxford: Basil Blackwell.

Ryle, G. 1966. *The Concept of Mind*. Harmondsworth: Penguin.

Sellars, R. W. 1916. *Critical Realism: A Study of the Nature and Conditions of Knowledge*. Chicago: Rand McNally.

Sellars, R. W. 1930. Realism, naturalism, and humanism. In *Contemporary American Philosophy*, vol. 2, ed. G. P. Adams and W. P. Montague, 261–285. London: George Allen and Unwin.

Sellars, R. W. 1932. *The Philosophy of Physical Realism*. New York: Macmillan.

Sellars, R. W. 1965. The aim of critical realism. In *Perception and the Physical World*, ed. R. J. Hirst, 235–244. New York: Macmillan.

Sellars, W. 1981. The lever of Archimedes; Naturalism and process; Is consciousness physical? The Carus Lectures. *Monist* 64, 1: 3–90.

Shoemaker, S. 1994. Phenomenal character. *Noûs* 28, 1: 21–38.

Smythies, J. R. 1956. *Analysis of Perception*. London: Routledge and Kegan Paul.

Tye, M. 1994. Qualia, content, and the inverted spectrum. *Noûs* 38, 2: 159–183.

Tye, M. 1995a. Blindsight, orgasm, and representational overlap. *Behavioural and Brain Sciences* 18: 268–269.

Tye, M. 1995b. *Ten Problems of Consciousness: A Representational Theory of the Phenomenal Mind*. Cambridge, Mass.: MIT Press/A Bradford Book.

Tye, M. 2000. *Consciousness, Color, and Content*. Cambridge, Mass.: MIT Press/A Bradford Book.

Tye, M. 2006. Nonconceptual content, richness, and fineness of grain. In *Perceptual Experience*, ed. T. S. Gendler and J. Hawthorne, 504–530. Oxford: Clarendon Press.

Ward, A. 1976. Direct and indirect realism. *American Philosophical Quarterly* 13, 4: 287–294.

Warnock, G. J. 1955–56. Seeing. *Proceedings of the Aristotelian Society* 55: 201–218.

Woodworth, R. S. 1947. Reinforcement of perception. *American Journal of Psychology* 60: 119–224.

Wright, E. L. 1990. New representationalism. *Journal for the Theory of Social Behaviour* 20, 1: 65–92.

Wright, E. L., ed. 1993. *New Representationalisms: Essays in the Philosophy of Perception*. Aldershot: Avebury.

Wright, E. L. 2005. *Narrative, Perception, Language, and Faith*. Basingstoke: Palgrave Macmillan.

Yolton, J. 1984. *Perceptual Acquaintance from Descartes to Reid*. Oxford: Basil Blackwell.

I Philosophical Defenses

1   The Case for Indirect Realism

Harold I. Brown

There is a troubling gap between the current philosophical and scientific literatures on perception. In the philosophical literature (as in everyday life), direct realism is the default position, and philosophical "defenses" of this view largely consist of replies to arguments against direct realism. (Le Morvan 2004 provides a recent review.) When direct arguments are given they typically consist of analyses of everyday concepts which, we can happily concede, embody direct realism. But we should no more expect a correct account of perception from conceptual analysis than expect to establish relativity theory or the principles of statistics in this manner. Many proponents of indirect realism recognize that the main evidence for their position comes from empirical considerations. I develop this approach in section 1, beginning with illusions. Illusions provide initial support for the thesis that we perceive qualia and, I argue, illusions should push philosophers to examine the scientific literature on perception; doing so enhances this support. It is also commonly held that indirect realism undermines our ability to learn about the world. I reply to that objection in section 2.

1   Illusions Redux

I assume throughout this essay that normal perception is caused by physical items that act on a perceiver's sense organs. This is an assumption only in the sense that I will not argue for it here. It is not particularly controversial and is accepted by both direct and indirect realists. This assumption does eliminate phenomenalism from the discussion, but phenomenalism is hardly in play at present, although phenomenalism was the default view in Anglo-American philosophy for much of the twentieth century. I also want to introduce some terminology. I use *item* as an ontologically neutral term involving no commitments about whether I am discussing an enduring object, process, event, and so forth. I describe items that cause a particular instance of perception as an *external arrangement*, where "external" implies only that these items exist apart from a particular sense organ. My hand is external with respect to vision and my eyes are external with respect to touch. I refer to the immediate items of perceptual awareness as a *perceptual display*. In this terminology, the central question of section 1 is whether a given perceptual display is numerically identical with the external arrangement that causes it. I use *illusion* broadly to describe any qualitative mismatch between a perceptual display and the external arrangement that causes it. Describing something as an illusion does not imply that anyone is deceived by it. Let us examine some illusions.

Consider a class of illusions known as *subjective contours*; two examples are given in figure 1.1. In these illusions the perceptual display includes lines that do not correspond to any lines in the external arrangement. We can be confident of this because we can draw that arrangement ourselves and thus know that these contours are not included. Although the external arrangement plays a causal role in generating our awareness of these lines, our visual system also plays a causal role. We have, then, cases in which the perceptual display is qualitatively different from the external arrangement. But, as Leibniz taught us, qualitative difference implies numerical difference. It is not yet clear how far we should push this familiar point. A minimal proposal is that our visual system adds something to the perceptual display, but that other aspects of that display are numerically identical with the external arrangement. Let us explore some other cases.

In some cases we can establish a one–one mapping between areas in a perceptual display and areas in an external arrangement. In such cases it may seem reasonable to assume that the properties of the external area, A, determine the properties of the corresponding area, A^*, in the perceptual display, but this is not true for colors. The color we see at A^* often depends on both A and the surrounding area. In such cases we can leave A untouched, make changes in other parts of the external arrangement, and find that the color of A^* changes. This phenomenon is familiar to scientists

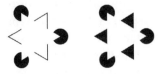

Figure 1.1
Subjective contours.

who study vision. "When two target patches return the same spectrum to the eye but are surrounded by regions that return different distributions of wavelengths, the sensations of color elicited by the two targets are no longer the same" (Purves and Lotto 2003: 99, henceforth P&L). Artists are also familiar with this phenomenon. For example, impressionists "never presented, let us say, green by itself. Instead of using green mixed mechanically from yellow and blue, they applied yellow and blue unmixed in small dots, so that they became mixed only in our perception" (Albers 1975: 33). Albers adds that such optical mixing provides the basis for:

photomechanical reproduction techniques, the 3- and 4-color processes for paintings, and the halftone process for black-and-white pictures. In the first case, 3 or 4 color plates subdivided into tiny printing dots mix to innumerable color shades and tints. In the second case, a plate for black also subdivided by a screen in tiny dots mixes with the white paper in just as innumerable tones of white–grey–black. (Ibid.)

Properties of the external arrangement determine the properties of the light that reaches our eyes, but somewhere between the impinging of light on our retinae and our awareness of a perceptual display, the brain integrates information arriving from various parts of an external arrangement to produce the colors that we see.

An example from early color movies provides another twist:

technicolor motion pictures were using only two component hues to make colors that should have been trichromatic. One color was put on each side of the film, and the film had only two sides. It was the blues that were cheated. The colors used were a slightly bluish red and a slightly bluish green, which will mix to give good reds and greens, poor yellows and very poor blues. What did the audiences, unused in those days to colored movies, say? That the American flag was beautiful, that the (bluish-green) skies were lovely. But the heroine never wore a pure blue dress (whatever she had on in the studio) because dresses, unlike the sky or the flag's field, can be any color and obey the laws of color mixture without this kind of cerebral mediation. (Boring 1946: 100)

In this case information stored in the brain as a result of previous experience enters into the perceptual display.

Seeing black provides a further variation on this theme. Phenomenologically black is on a par with other colors. When a display includes black areas, nothing in my experience indicates that my perception of black is brought about in a different way from my perception of other colors. My crayon set includes a black crayon that I use in the same manner as any other color. Yet the external conditions that produce black are different from those for other colors.

A painter or dyer, who never enquired into their causes, hath the ideas of white and black, and other colours, as clearly, perfectly, and distinctly in his understanding, and perhaps more distinctly, than the philosopher, who hath busied himself in considering their natures, and thinks he knows how far either of them is in its cause positive or privative; and the idea of black is no less positive in his mind, than that of white, however the cause of that colour in the external object may be only a privation. (Locke 1984: 133)

A full account of the conditions that lead to seeing black is complex (see Hardin 1988: 22–24, henceforth H), but we can focus on one case: black occurs in a perceptual display when a portion of an external arrangement does not reflect any light to our eyes. The appearance of black in this display results from internal construction.

A final example takes us to another sense and to further variations on our theme. Several years ago, when I had aluminum siding put on my house, the contractor assured me that aluminum is a good insulator because it reflects both heat in the summer and cold in the winter. (I refrained from asking if it saved electricity by reflecting the dark.) If the contractor's claim seems absurd, it is because we recognize that felt heat and cold are not on a par either ontologically or causally. An item feels warm to my hand when there is heat flow from that item to my hand; it feels cold when heat flows in the reverse direction. Yet this flow of heat from my hand to another item is incorporated into the perceptual display as a property on a par with warmth and color; its special causal conditions are not apparent to introspection. This phenomenal status of cold was recognized by Aristotle who treated hot and cold as a pair of mutually incompatible qualities; neither was considered a privation of the other. This is an accurate reflection of how these qualities appear in perceptual displays in spite of the differences that we now recognize.

I am now ready to formulate a new argument from illusions in two steps. *First*, in normal perception the perceptual display we are aware of is caused by an external arrangement and (let us grant) there is a one–one mapping between areas of the display and areas on the surface of its external cause. But there are often substantial qualitative differences between properties of these corresponding areas, and qualitative difference implies numerical difference. To this extent the perceptual display is not wholly numerically identical with the external arrangement that causes it. One might maintain that the perceptual display is a heterogeneous compound of elements of the external arrangement and elements generated by our perceptual system. But given the coherent integration of the various elements of the perceptual display, we get a more intelligible picture if we consider the entire perceptual display to be a brain-construct that is numerically distinct from the external arrangement involved in its causation.

Note that this is an argument to the best explanation, as should be expected in an empirically based inquiry. The argument provides *initial grounds* for holding that perceptual displays are numerically distinct from the external arrangements that cause them. The *second step* is to conclude that these examples should lead us to ask how features of a perceptual display are generated. This question takes us to the relevant science—especially physiology and physics. Before pursuing these considerations I want to make three observations on the argument thus far.

First, at a minimum our examples show that we cannot decide whether elements of a perceptual display are identical to their external cause just by examining the perceptual display.

Second, causal interactions regularly produce effects that are qualitatively different from their causes. When Descartes heats a ball of wax the wax gets warm, but its color, shape, odor, and other properties also change; these new properties need not mirror any properties of the heat or the heating agent. (See Brown 1992 for more examples and further discussion.) To be sure, even in complex causal interactions some of the outcomes may mirror some of the inputs. Sound-recording systems that begin with a voice and run through the steps required to produce a CD and play it back through a set of speakers are explicitly designed to produce an output that is as close a copy as possible of the initiating cause—although this is qualitative, not numerical, identity. This returns us to the first point: we cannot decide if we have any form of identity just by examining the output.

Third, note two differences between the present argument from illusion and the traditional version. First, I do not treat perceptual displays as atomistic sense-data. Perceptual displays are the complex perceptual fields that we normally take them to be. The conclusion that perceptual displays are numerically distinct from their external causes does not require that these displays be any less rich in detail than their causes. Second, one defect of the traditional argument is that it moves directly from the result that some items in a perceptual display do not exist without the perceiver to the conclusion that none do. Berkeley pointed out this defect: "it must be confessed this method of arguing doth not so much prove that there is no extension or colour in an outward object, as that we do not know by sense which is the true extension or colour of the object" (1948: 47). The present argument works differently. It is an argument to the best explanation that has the double purpose of providing initial grounds for holding that perceptual displays are numerically distinct from their external causes, and directing us to scientific accounts of the generation of perceptual displays for further insight. I will now pursue this *second step* in the case of vision.

An external arrangement plays a causal role in vision when light that has interacted with or been emitted by that arrangement interacts with a functioning visual system; any information about the arrangement that we derive from vision is carried by the light. Extraction of this information begins at the retina and proceeds up the visual system. A full account of the current understanding of these processes cannot be given here; it would require (at least) accounts of the external arrangement and of light from physics, of the interaction of light with the retina, and of the neural processes that follow. I will sketch some key features of the process that begins when light arrives at the retina, then look even more briefly at what physics tells us about the external arrangements with which vision brings us into contact—whether directly or indirectly.

A normal human retina has four types of receptor cells. These cell types divide, first, into rods and cones. Rods respond primarily to the amount of light (number of photons) impinging on them, although the wavelength of that light also plays a role. All photons of a given wavelength carry the same amount of energy, but the number of photons required to generate a particular output signal from a rod varies with this energy.[1] The rods' sensitivity peaks in the green and drops off as we move toward both the red and blue ends of the spectrum (Livingstone 2002: 42, henceforth Lvg). For a given wavelength the frequency of the output is determined by the number of photons absorbed. This output always has the same properties; only the frequency varies. The physical measure of the amount of incoming light is known as "luminance" (H 33; P&L 237). Thus while both luminance and wavelength play a role in determining the output frequency, there is no way of distinguishing their relative roles in this output. Rods play a role in determining how bright an item appears in dim light—such as moonlight and starlight; in typical indoor lighting and in daylight rods become saturated and cease to contribute (P&L 22). Moreover, rods contribute only to the achromatic colors (black, white, and gray) but makes no contribution to color vision, which depends solely on the cones.

There are three types of cones, which are commonly labeled long, middle, and short (henceforth L, M, and S) to indicate the relative wavelength of the portion of the spectrum in which they have their maximal response. Each type of cone responds to a large portion of the spectrum, but responds differently within its range. As in the case of rods, this difference lies in the number of photons required to elicit a particular output; outputs vary only in their frequency. Here too there is no way to determine the relative contributions of the amount of light absorbed and its wavelength just from the output. To understand how color perception comes about we must move up the processing stream.

In the retina, four cell layers are involved in processing the output of rods and cones, but I will pass over three of these (horizontal, bipolar, and amicrine cells; cf. H 13, Lvg 25, P&L 26) and consider the last layer before an impulse leaves the retina: the retinal ganglion cells. Some of these cells are connected to rods, and several rods provide input to a single ganglion cell. This multiple connection enhances the ability of the ganglion cells to respond to dim light, but yields low-acuity vision since information about the locations of the individual rods on the retina is lost. Fewer cones are connected to a single ganglion cell—which is why cones provide information only in brighter light and yield high-acuity vision. In the fovea—the small portion of the retina where vision is sharpest—there is often a one–one connection between a cone and a ganglion cell. (There are no rods in the fovea.) Cones also provide luminance information (see below). The distinction between color and luminance is generated in the retinal ganglion cells and kept distinct for a substantial part of the subsequent processing: "The areas of our brain that process information about color are located several inches away from the areas that analyze luminance—they are as anatomically distinct as vision is from hearing. From the earliest stages of visual processing, in our eyes, color and luminance are analyzed separately" (Lvg 38).

Given three cone types we might expect color information to be a function of three variables, but the retinal ganglion cells transform this into a function of two chromatic variables and an achromatic luminance signal. One type of ganglion cell yields L − (S + M) while another yields S − (L + M). This gives two distinct channels. The first channel gives a value on an axis running from red to green, the second on an axis running from yellow to cyan. A third type of ganglion cell adds inputs from the three cone types, giving a luminance signal (Lvg 88–90). Labeling the three signals that leave the retina A, B, and C, we have three equations:

$A = L − (S + M)$

$B = S − (L + M)$

$C = L + M + S.$

Since these equations can be solved for L, M, and S, none of the original information from the cones is lost. But nothing in the individual signals leaving the retina can be mapped onto colors; these are constructed at a later processing stage. People who lack two of the cone types are completely color blind, even if they have cones of the third type (Lvg 34–35).

Another basic division begins in the retina, processes two different types of information, and keeps them anatomically distinct for much of the subsequent neural processing. There are both large and small retinal ganglion cells. Both types receive input from rods and cones, but the system that begins with the large ganglion cells "is responsible for our perception of motion, space, position, depth (three-dimensionality), figure/ground segregation, and the overall organization of the visual scene" (Lvg 50). The system involving the small cells "is responsible for our ability to recognize objects, including faces, in color and in complex detail" (Lvg 50; cf. P&L 27–30). In addition, the system beginning with the large ganglion cells is color blind, but more sensitive to differences in contrast (Lvg 50). Signals from the ganglion cells go to the next stage in processing after the retina, a structure in the thalamus called "the lateral geniculate nucleus" (lgn). The large and small retinal ganglion cells project to different portions of the lgn (Lvg 49–50; P&L 27). Amid all this disassembly of the inputs to our visual system, the overall topography of the retina is retained in the lgn and at the next processing stage—the primary visual cortex (P&L 31). However, this topography breaks down at higher visual processing levels (P&L 33). For example, information deriving from the large retinal ganglion cells eventually arrives in the parietal lobe; information from the small ganglion cells arrives at the temporal lobe (Lvg 64). Meanwhile, inputs from other parts of the brain are added. For example, in the primary visual cortex only about 10 percent of input is from the lgn (P&L 37). Integration of all this information eventually occurs in producing a perceptual display, but this integration occurs in the brain only after massive disassembly: "the eye begins from the moment its receptors absorb light to transform and reorganize the optical information that comes to it from the world" (H 10).

I have mentioned only a small part of what is known about visual processing in the retina and upstream, but it is enough to return us to our original question: Is there any reason to believe that the perceptual display resulting from this process is—even in part—*numerically* identical with the external arrangement that played a role at an early stage of this process? The very complexity of the process leaves the claim of numerical identity beyond the reach of plausibility. We can compare this process of disassembling input, extracting and transmitting information, and then constructing a final output to simpler systems that carry out similar procedures, such as faxes and email. In these cases we arrive at an output that is—in certain respects—qualitatively identical to the input, but clearly not numerically identical. Moreover, qualitative identity is limited by the transmission medium. A fax machine may transmit the text of a message without transmitting the texture or color of the original paper. Visual processing in the brain is much more complex, and the visual system is optimized for transmitting certain types of information rather than others. For example, a given color in a perceptual display may be generated by a large number of different combinations of surface properties of objects and ambient light. Even if we focus on the light that arrives at the retina, many different combinations of wavelengths can result in the same color in the perceptual display (see Hardin, this vol.: 143–144). Much information is lost in the service of providing a biologically useful outcome, while other features are added. There is no reason for holding that this outcome is, somehow, numerically identical with one contributor to the causal process that produced it. This conclusion would hold even if there were qualitative identity between an external arrangement and a perceptual display.

Some reflections on the account of the world that we get from physics will underline the qualitative differences between properties of a perceptual display and the external arrangement that entered into its causal history. We can find examples without plumbing the depths of quantum theory and its interpretation. Consider a familiar illusion that was not mentioned above: a stick that is partially submerged in water and that looks bent although it is actually straight. In this case the illusion is generated by the physics of light, rather than by features of our perceptual system, but this does not eliminate the fact that the visual display is qualitatively different from the external arrangement. In addition, the familiar color circle, in which red merges into blue, is an artifact of our color-vision system: the stimulus is part of a linear wavelength spectrum. Nor is there any basis for the existence of primary or complementary colors in the physical properties of light or the objects that reflect, transmit, or emit that light; these also arise because of the way our visual system processes incoming light (cf. H 37; Lvg 85–86).

There is a standard direct-realist response to the issues raised by illusions: we directly perceive external arrangements, but do not always perceive them as they actually are. But this is a verbal response; we have already encountered two reasons why it will not do. First, illusions are cases in which perceptual displays are qualitatively different from the relevant external arrangements, and qualitative difference implies numerical difference. Second, the way visual displays are generated makes it much more plausible that these displays are internal to the brain, not located at some distance from the brain. Similar accounts apply for the other senses. In addition, when a subjective contour, a specific color, or other item occurs in a perceptual display but not in its external cause, this item has *some ontological status*. Indirect realism gives an account of this status; the standard direct realist response just evades the matter. More than a quip is needed to resolve this issue.

2 Epistemological Considerations

Indirect realism holds that perception is a triadic relation both causally and epistemically. It is causally triadic in that an external arrangement acting on our senses initiates a process that generates a perceptual display. Perception is epistemically triadic since our knowledge of external arrangements is based on evidence provided by perceptual displays. A long tradition holds that such epistemic intermediaries block our ability to learn about external items; I will argue that this is not correct. However, even if indirect realism has unpleasant epistemological consequences, it does not follow that it is false. Rather, it follows that we should explore our actual situation and seek to understand its epistemic opportunities and limitations.

Note also that, given the existence of illusions, direct realism faces the same basic epistemic problem as indirect realism: we must still figure out which of the features that appear in perception characterize external arrangements—as Berkeley notes in the passage quoted above. Direct realists must rely for this purpose on the same hypothetico-deductive strategy that indirect realists have invoked since Boyle and Locke (cf. Brown 1992).

I will approach my main concern by exploring some epistemic lessons we can learn from contemporary observational physics. One lesson has already been noted: a significant fraction of the properties that occur in perceptual displays do not characterize the external arrangements involved in causing these displays. In addition, the world is full of items we cannot detect with our unaided senses—for example, electrons, neutrinos, quarks, and the fields through which they interact. Yet physicists are able to learn a great deal about these items. Their research provides a model of indirect empirical study of items in the physical world. Key features of these studies provide general lessons that transfer to the epistemology of indirect realism.

Consider a relatively simple example: using a Geiger counter to detect local radioactivity. Since we have no sense that responds to radioactivity our only choice is to study it by means of instruments. Ignoring many details, we may say a Geiger counter is a device that is affected by radio-activity and emits an electrical signal as its output. That signal is typically run through an amplifier and speaker so that we hear a series of clicks whose frequency is an indicator of the intensity of local radioactivity. The electrical signal can also be channeled to an oscilloscope to give a visible output. In either case there is no qualitative match between properties of the output and properties of the radiation; radioactivity does not have a characteristic sound or shape. Still, the output provides information about the intensity of radioactivity in the environment that can guide behavior and further research. Such research follows a standard pattern: we test hypotheses about items we cannot detect with our unaided senses by introducing a device, or chain of devices, that yields an output we can detect; this output can be compared with predictions from our hypotheses. When hypotheses pass such tests we derive further predictions to be tested using the same, or additional, instruments. Indirect realism adds a step to the causal chain: the instrument is an external arrangement that plays the usual role in generating a perceptual display. The properties of this perceptual display need not be numerically or qualitatively identical with properties of the instrument for us to make use of that display as a guide to those properties (and thus to those aspects of the world that affect the instrument). The same holds for perception of any external arrangement.

Another feature of both empirical research in science and everyday perception is crucial to this process: we are not passive observers relying on momentary glimpses for information about the world. Scientists interact with items over time and are often able to examine them under different observational conditions. The items being studied also have multiple properties that can be detected in various ways using different instruments. This enhances our ability to test, modify, and replace hypotheses about external arrangements. In a similar way, when it sounds as if my car has an exhaust leak I can look for a crack in the exhaust system and feel around for leaking exhaust. To be sure, in everyday perception we rarely formulate and evaluate hypotheses or seek out new evidence. In part this is because much of the work has been done by evolution which has tuned our perceptual systems to respond to a small set of biologically relevant items in our environment. We are also social creatures who can learn from our ancestors and avoid repeating all of their errors for ourselves. But even in an everyday context our perceptual systems sometimes misreport and sometimes give unclear reports that lead to further study. There is, again, a parallel with empirical research in science. The use of instruments depends on established background beliefs that are built into our instruments; in familiar cases we accept their output without reflection. But when anomalies arise we sometimes reconsider the operation of our instruments and the beliefs at the basis of their construction. Sometimes this examination includes a reconsideration of prior beliefs about the operation of our senses. (See Brown 1985, 1987 for detailed examples.)

Advocates of direct realism will reply that this entire process must be anchored in direct perception of external items. But this claim confuses two different points. First, we can agree that we must perceive something directly at some stage; indirect realists hold that we directly perceive perceptual displays that arise through the same general types of causal processes as instrumental outputs. Second, indirect realists agree that perceptual displays are causally anchored in external arrangements and carry information about those arrangements as a result. But this does not require either numerical or qualitative identity between the perceptual display and the external arrangement (cf. Wright 1993).

I want to press this last point with a hypothetical example. Consider the fraternal twins Pat and Terry. Each has a genetic mutation that permits detection of radioactivity in the environment by providing an element in a perceptual display that most of us do not experience. In Pat's case the additional element is visual; in Terry's case it is auditory. As a result, Pat and Terry do not need instruments to detect radioactivity. But neither twin automatically achieves a better understanding of radioactivity than the rest of us. If they wish to understand the items that cause their percepts they must go through the same process of formulating and testing hypotheses as all of us must do to determine, say, the external cause of some specific color.[2]

But, some will reply, we would have a better grasp of the nature of external arrangements if the causal chains were shorter, or if our perceptual displays were qualitatively identical to items in those arrangements. Yet we must use indirect detection to study items for which we have no evolved detectors. Removing these links will not improve our knowledge; it will eliminate it. So a shorter, simpler chain does not always yield an improved epistemic outcome. This point extends to practical situations. Unaided perception is not much help in discovering radioactivity or toxic wastes in our environment. The study of items we cannot sense has also deepened our understanding of the world and provided major practical outcomes, including the germ theory of disease which led to antibiotics, and quantum mechanics which provided the basis for inventing transistors. Moreover, sight, hearing, and smell allow us to detect items at a distance, and thus depend on indirect detection by means of causal chains.

Returning to the claim that our epistemic grasp of external arrangements would be improved by qualitative identity between arrangement and display, direct realists owe us an account of how such identity comes about. The Aristotelian version of direct realism takes up this challenge, holding that perception makes us immediately aware of properties of physical objects because the undistorted forms of those objects are instantiated in our minds. Although this view fails because it does not account for illusions and will not stand up to the scientific evidence, it has the virtue of proposing an account. Contemporary direct realists owe us as much.

3 Conclusion

I have argued that illusions support an indirect-realist theory of perception; this support is strengthened by considering the processes that yield visual perception. I have also argued against the view that devastating epistemological consequences follow from indirect realism. This view is an illusion. Moreover, current versions of direct realism do not do any better in this respect. Nor do they provide a significant account of illusions or an account of the means by which direct perception of the world beyond our skins comes about that accords with contemporary scientific results. On balance, direct realism has little to recommend it, while indirect realism faces these issues and integrates smoothly with our contemporary understanding of the physical and physiological processes involved in perception.

Notes

1. Since rods fire spontaneously, giving a base rate, we are discussing differences from that base rate. Describing light in terms of its wavelength is common practice in the literature on vision. I use "frequency" only for the frequency of neural outputs.

2. Cf. "But how would we describe a rainbow if we were blind? We are blind when we measure the infrared reflection coefficient of sodium chloride, or when we talk about the frequency of waves that are coming from some galaxy that we can't see" (Feynman, Leighton, and Sands 1964, vol. II: 20–11).

References

Albers, J. 1975. *Interaction of Color*, revised edition. New Haven: Yale University Press.

Berkeley, G. 1948. *Principles of Human Knowledge*. In *The Works of George Berkeley Bishop of Cloyne*, vol. 2. Ed. A. Luce and T. Jessop. London: Thomas Nelson.

Boring, E. 1946. The perception of objects. *American Journal of Physics* 14: 99–107.

Brown, H. 1985. Galileo on the telescope and the eye. *Journal of the History of Ideas* 46: 487–501.

Brown, H. 1987. *Observation and Objectivity*. New York: Oxford University Press.

Brown, H. 1992. Direct realism, indirect realism, and epistemology. *Philosophy and Phenomenological Research* 52: 341–363.

Feynman, R., R. Leighton, and M. Sands. 1964. *The Feynman Lectures on Physics*. Reading, Pennsylvania: Addison-Wesley.

Hardin, C. 1988. *Color for Philosophers*. Indianapolis, Ind.: Hackett.

Le Morvan, P. 2004. Arguments against direct realism and how to counter them. *American Philosophical Quarterly* 41: 221–234.

Livingstone, M. 2002. *Vision and Art: The Biology of Seeing*. New York: Abrams.

Locke, J. 1984. *An Essay Concerning Human Understanding*. Ed. P. Nidditch. Oxford: Clarendon Press.

Purves, D., and R. Lotto. 2003. *Why We See What We Do: An Empirical Theory of Vision*. Sunderland, Mass.: Sinauer.

Wright, E. 1993. More qualia trouble for functionalism: The Smythies TV-hood analogy. *Synthese* 97: 365–382.

2 Illusions and Hallucinations as Evidence for Sense Data

E. J. Lowe

The term *quale*, as it is used in contemporary philosophy of perception, is difficult to define to everyone's satisfaction, and—partly for that very reason—I shall avoid explicit use of the word in this essay, despite the fact that the essay is intended as a contribution to a volume entitled *The Case for Qualia*. I assume, however, that all parties to current debate in the philosophy of perception will agree that, if any theory of perception is committed to the existence of sensory qualia, the *sense-datum* theory certainly is—and hence that by defending a version of that theory, as I intend to here, I am defending their existence. At the very end of the paper, I shall explain that point more fully.

In recent times, sense data have found able defenders in philosophers such as Frank Jackson (1977) and Howard Robinson (1994). However, I believe that I have some new points to make in their favor and, in any case, my own version of the sense-datum theory (Lowe 1981) has some distinctive features. By *sense data* I mean *private mental objects* which, I contend, we perceive *directly* whenever we perceive ordinary public objects, and by perceiving which we perceive those public objects only *indirectly*. By a *public* object I mean one that can be perceived by more than one person—so that this class includes not only *material* objects, such as tables and trees, but also what might be called *phenomenal* objects, such as rainbows, reflections, and shadows. By a *private* object I mean one that can be perceived *directly* by only one person. I shall not attempt here to define what *indirect* perception is (for that see Lowe 1981: 332; Lowe 1986: 278). However, plenty of uncontentious examples of indirect perception may be provided by way of illustration: for instance, I see my face indirectly by seeing its reflection in a mirror, and I see the Prime Minister indirectly by seeing an image of him on a television screen during a "live" broadcast. In these cases, one public object (my face, the Prime Minister) is perceived indirectly by perceiving another public object (a mirror reflection, a television image). My claim, however, is that *all* public objects are perceived only indirectly, ultimately by perceiving sense data, which are themselves perceived directly. By *direct* perception, I simply mean perception that does not involve any *in*directness, in the sense just illustrated. I do *not* mean, then, what Norman Malcolm does when, discussing G. E. Moore's notion, he offers the following definition: "*A directly* perceives *x* if and only if *A*'s assertion that he perceives *x* could not be mistaken" (Malcolm 1963: 89). Accordingly, I do not claim that we have incorrigible knowledge of our own sense data.

In this essay, as its title proclaims, I want to concentrate on the evidence for sense data that is provided by illusions and hallucinations. For present purposes, the following rough-and-ready characterizations of these phenomena will suffice. An *illusion* occurs when a person *does* perceive an "external," public object, but has an experience rather like that of perceiving a public object with properties different from those of the object that he actually perceives. A *hallucination* occurs when a person does *not* in fact perceive an "external," public object of a certain kind and yet has an experience rather like that of perceiving just such an object. Note that these characterizations carry no implication that the subject of an illusion or hallucination is in any way *deceived* by it. At most, illusions and hallucinations involve *misleading* experiences: the subject need not actually be *misled* by them. Note also that I said that the foregoing characterizations are only *rough-and-ready*: as Edmond Wright has pointed out to me, some hallucinatory experiences do not seem to be of *objects* at all—for example, the hypnagogic imagery experienced just before sleep.

Judicious sense-datum theorists will be extremely cautious in their appeal to illusions, at least if they adopt my version of the theory. It will not do to appeal to the round plate that "looks elliptical" when held at an oblique angle to the line of sight. This is because, on my theory, sense data are *not* invoked as objects that, supposedly, *actually* possess the properties that public objects *appear* to possess. Unlike Jackson (1977: 88), I do not adhere to what George Pitcher calls "Assumption A": "if something, *x*, looks *F* to someone . . . then where *x* is not in fact *F*, something else, *y*, different from *x* really *is F* and is being seen by that person" (Pitcher 1971: 32). Again, it will not do to appeal to the straight stick that "looks bent" when it is half-immersed in water. For this illusion can be accounted for without reference to *private* objects of any sort, since it may be explained by reference to an optical (refractive) image that is perfectly *public*.

The sort of illusion I *would* appeal to is one like that of double vision. Even J. L. Austin, the arch-scourge of sense-datum theories, was a little uneasy about this, going so far as to say that "double vision is a quite *exceptional* case, so that we may have to stretch our ordinary usage to accommodate it" and speaking of it as "a rather baffling anomaly" (Austin 1962: 90–91). From this it appears that Austin was thinking only of double vision occasioned by ocular (or other medical) disorder, or by pressing one eyeball, as Hume famously relates doing in the *Treatise* (Hume 1978: 210–211). In fact, double vision is far from being abnormal: one's own nose "looks double" most of the time—although, of course, one may not notice this. The best way to draw someone's attention to the phenomenon is to tell him to hold up his finger some ten inches in front of his nose and focus his eyes on distant objects—preferably on a plain background, such as a white wall—while still attending to his finger. The finger will then "look double." I urge readers to perform this experiment for themselves before proceeding, to remind themselves of the vividness of the illusion.

How does this illusion help the sense-datum theorist? It does so, I believe, because I think we have to say that, when my finger thus "looks double," I see *two private mental objects*—call them "visual images," if you will—by seeing each of which I see my finger only *indirectly*. No other account, I believe, satisfactorily explains the basis of the illusion.

At this point I anticipate an objection of the following kind. It is the task of *science*, it may be said, not of *philosophy*, to explain such phenomena as double vision. Philosophy should only *describe*. As Wittgenstein puts it: "[W]e may not advance any kind of theory. There must not be anything hypothetical in our considerations. We must do away with all *explanation*, and description alone must take its place" (Wittgenstein 1958: 109). However, one cannot wholly separate description and explanation, any more than one can wholly separate observation and theory. How we should describe what we see during the double-vision experience cannot be entirely divorced from an explanation of how that experience arises and why it has the features that we feel constrained to ascribe to it. We cannot simply shift the entire burden of "explanation" here on to the sciences of psychology and physiology. For *what is it* that we should ask them to explain? Why the finger "looks double"? Yes, but what exactly do we *mean* by saying that the finger "looks double"? As I think will soon become clear, once we attempt to answer this question, we find that we cannot entirely divorce the task of describing the phenomenon of double vision from that of explaining it.

So, then, what *do* we mean by saying that the finger "looks double"? One thing that seems clear is that we do *not* simply mean (*contra* Armstrong

1961: 80–93) that we are in some degree *inclined to believe*—or *would be* inclined to believe, if we didn't have reason to believe otherwise—that the finger *is* "double," that is, that there are *two* fingers there. Nor even do we simply mean that there is *some visual evidence tending to support*, however inconclusively, the proposition that there are two fingers there. In short, "looks" is not being used here merely in an *epistemic* sense (for which see Jackson 1977: 30–31).What I should say that we mean is something like this: that seeing one's finger in these circumstances is an experience some-what similar to the experience of *seeing two fingers*, held side-by-side in front of one's nose, when one focuses one's eyes on them. In other words, we are alluding to a certain *resemblance* between two experiences. But resemblance, of course, is always and only resemblance *in some respect*. So, in what respect do the two experiences resemble each other? I want to say in the following respect: in each case, one sees *two* visually very similar objects of some sort. "Visually similar in what respect?" you may ask. And I answer: in respect of color and shape. In both cases I see two elongated pinkish objects of some sort. But if that is so then it surely follows that, in the double vision case, at least one of these objects is *not my finger*— indeed, on grounds of symmetry, *neither* is. They cannot *both* be my finger: for they are two and thus numerically distinct, whereas my finger is one. And from this it takes but little argument to show that I must, on this occasion at least, be seeing my finger only *indirectly* by seeing two private mental objects of some sort. We may notice here how an inquiry into *what* one sees in double vision slides naturally into a partial *explanation* of the illusion, thus overriding the spurious dichotomy between description and explanation, while at the same time avoiding illegitimate trespass into the proper territory of psychology and physiology.

Very well: when my finger "looks double," I want to say that I see *two* elongated pinkish objects of some sort. I *want* to say this, but *should* I? What, however, could I at all plausibly say instead? It may be suggested that rather than say that I see two elongated pinkish objects, I should say that I see just *one* elongated pinkish object—namely, *my finger*—but that I see it *twice*, once with my right eye and once with my left. As Pitcher (1971: 41) notices, however, the trouble with this is that even when I see my finger "singly," I *still* see it twice, once with each eye (assuming that I have both open). Unfortunately, Pitcher then goes on rather lamely to remark that "In reply to this, the direct realist could say that the difference between normal and double vision is simply this: in double vision it looks to the perceiver as if there are two [fingers]" (1971: 42). But this, of course, just takes us back to where we started from: the finger "looks double." That is uncontentious, but we want to understand what it *means* to say this and what the basis of the illusion consists in.

Equally unsatisfactory is C. W. K. Mundle's position. He remarks that "[Double vision is] simply a consequence of the fact that we have two eyes in different places. It would be baffling if creatures with two such eyes . . . did not experience double vision" (Mundle 1971: 83). This doesn't help, again because we are currently concerned with what double vision *is*, that is, with what it *means* to say that something "looks double"—and, plainly, it simply *doesn't* mean that it is seen from two different places at once by the same percipient. (Apart from anything else, as already remarked, even objects that are seen "singly" are normally seen from two different places at once.) If anyone should still be in doubt about this, then he stands in need of D. J. O'Connor's reminder that double vision may occur even in certain disorders of *monocular* vision (O'Connor 1976: 85).

For the same reason, it doesn't help when Mundle goes on to say: "Moreover, when, with eyes focused on finger-tip, I see a steeple in two widely different directions, these two directions need to be specified by saying, not merely 'one from each eye,' but also 'one relative to the direction in which each eye is looking'" (Mundle 1971: 83). The basic trouble with all such accounts of double vision that make essential reference to our eyes and their number, position, or orientation is the fact that it is a purely contingent matter that we see *with our eyes* at all—at least if by "eye" is meant a certain physiologically identified part of the human body, rather than *by definition* "organ of sight." It seems perfectly conceivable that someone *without* eyes (in the purely physiological sense) should be made to experience the double vision phenomenon, by tampering suitably with his cerebral processes. Physiology can tell us under what conditions double vision is normally experienced in human beings—for example, how the retinal images in the two eyes are situated when this phenomenon occurs—but it cannot tell us what double vision *is*, in the sense of what it *means* to say that something is seen "double."

Let us return, then, to our earlier question: what *should* I say, when my finger "looks double," if not that I see two elongated pinkish objects of some sort? Pitcher has another suggestion, slightly better than his previous one. The direct realist, he suggests, may say that the finger "as seen by one eye looks to the perceiver to be displaced from the (very same) [finger] as seen by the other eye, thus making it look to him as though there were two [fingers]" (Pitcher 1971: 42). To the extent that this account makes reference to the percipient's *eyes*, it is unacceptable for the reason stated just a moment ago. But perhaps the direct realist can still make something of Pitcher's suggestion, as follows. Maybe he can say that although I see only *one* elongated pinkish object—my finger—and see it *directly*, I nevertheless seem to see it in two different places at once, because it appears to be displaced *both* slightly to the right *and* slightly to the left of its true position, which is directly in front of my nose. However, I don't think that this will do. To see why, we first need to ask how "appear" is being used here. The answer, surely, is that it is being used in some sort of *epistemic* sense. For, clearly, in saying that my finger *appears* or *looks* to be in two different places at once, I can't be taken to mean—as the *non*-epistemic sense of "appear" or "look" would imply—that seeing the finger in these circumstances is an experience somewhat similar to that of actually *seeing the finger in two different places at once*. This is because, quite obviously, *there can be no such experience* as the latter. There can be no such experience simply because there is no possible situation for it to be an experience *of*, as a finger cannot be in two different places at once.

Now, in saying that my finger *appears* to be situated slightly to the *right* of my nose, I think I am implying that there is visual evidence tending to support—although by no means *conclusively*, of course—the proposition that my finger *is* situated slightly to the right of my nose. Similarly, in saying that my finger *appears* to be situated slightly to the *left* of my nose, I am implying that there is visual evidence tending to support the proposition that my finger *is* situated slightly to the left of my nose. Of course, I can't accept either proposition, because they are mutually conflicting. But what is the nature of the visual evidence in question? I feel bound to answer that it consists in the fact that I *see something fingerlike*—elongated and pinkish—in each direction, both to the right and to the left of the center of my field of vision. That is, I see two elongated pinkish objects of some sort, each of which is suggestive of the presence of my finger in a certain place.

We may reinforce this conclusion by the following consideration. When is it, quite generally, that we speak of things "appearing"—in the *epistemic* sense—to be in places in which they are not? Is it not precisely when we perceive them *indirectly*, by perceiving *other things* that actually occupy the places in question? For instance, a man may *appear* to be standing directly ahead of me because that is where a mirror-image of him is actually located. (I trust that it won't be objected here that mirror-images are *not locatable*. The fact that no solid objects possessing their shape need be found in the positions that they are said to occupy is indicative only of their not being *material* objects.) If I don't know that the mirror-image *is* only a mirror-image, I might well be led to believe that *the man* is standing directly ahead of me. What I *do* see tends to support this belief. But why shouldn't we analyze the double vision case in much the same way, as involving two differently situated elongated pinkish objects, both of which *are* seen by me, but neither of which is my finger? How else, indeed, *can* we analyze it?

The final blow to all attempts to avoid talking about *two* elongated pinkish objects in the double vision illusion seems to me to be this. Even if a way were found to "translate" the statement "I see two elongated pinkish objects," as it is naturally deployed in the double vision case, into something implying that I see *only my finger*, much more formidable problems of translation would soon arise. For instance, if I tilt my head from side to side while I hold my finger still, I shall naturally report what I see in something like the following way: "I see two elongated pinkish objects *and as one of them moves upward the other moves downward*." The problem, as Jackson succinctly puts it, is that "[W]hen we talk about things looking double to us, we talk not just of their looking double, but also of the differences and relations between the images. The sense datum theorist has no difficulty with this fact. He interprets all this talk at face value" (Jackson 1977: 100). At this stage, the direct realist may change his tack altogether. He may concede, at last, that in some sense I do indeed "see two elongated pinkish objects." But, he may ask, need it also be conceded that two such objects *exist*? Taking a leaf out of Elizabeth Anscombe's book (Anscombe 1981), he may contend that these are merely "intentional" objects. In one sense of "see," he may say, "I see an *X*" does not entail "There is an *X* that I see," any more than "I want an *X*" entails "There is an *X* that I want."

In order to assess the merits of this proposal, I think it will be helpful to look first at how the notion of an "intentional" object might be appealed to in cases of *hallucination*. We shall return to the double vision illusion later. Consider, then, that most hackneyed of examples, *Macbeth's dagger*. In one sense, it will be said, Macbeth *saw a dagger*—and yet there was no dagger that he saw. But was there *anything* that he saw? The sense-datum theorist will say "Yes—there was a *private mental object* that he saw." And here it is worth reminding ourselves, as Jackson (1977: 50) also points out, that it is *not* "true by definition" that in a visual hallucination there is nothing at all that is seen (*contra* Hamlyn 1961: 175). The most that is "true by definition" is that there is no "*external,*" *public object* of an appropriate sort that is seen—for example, no *dagger*, nor indeed any other public object that is mistakable for a dagger (as in a case of illusion).

Now, with what plausibility could it be maintained, against the sense-datum theorist, that there was in fact *nothing at all* that Macbeth saw?

Anscombe, I think, would maintain precisely this. She claims: "While there must be an intentional object of seeing, there need not always be a material object. That is to say 'X saw A' where 'saw' is used materially, implies some proposition 'X saw—' where 'saw' is used intentionally; but the converse does not hold" (Anscombe 1981: 17). I should say that this is, in fact, the very reverse of the truth. First of all, I believe that there may be something that a person sees even though there is *no* description of that thing such that he sees it "under that description." For instance, suppose that against a black backdrop I place a white card cut in the outline of a sitting cat and a black cat comes and sits exactly in front of the card, so that the card's outline coincides with that of the cat as seen from a certain direction. Then I ask someone to look in that direction. Does he see the cat? In one sense—what Anscombe calls the "material" sense—I think that he *does*: but *not* in the "intentional" sense, contrary to Anscombe's claim. He sees the cat in the material sense, I should say, because the cat's presence is partly responsible for the character of his visual experience at the time. However, he does *not* see the cat in the intentional sense, because he cannot visually discriminate the cat from its background under *any* description.

I also think that Anscombe is wrong in supposing that there may be an "intentional" object of seeing where there is no "material" object (where "material," in this context, just means *real* or *existent*, not necessarily solid and tangible because *made of matter*). Perhaps it will help to recall Macbeth's exact words in the play:

Is this a dagger which I see before me,
The handle toward my hand? Come, let me clutch thee:
I have thee not, and yet I see thee still.
Art thou not, fatal vision, sensible
To feeling as to sight? or art thou but
A dagger of the mind, a false creation,
Proceeding from the heat-oppressed brain.
(*Macbeth*, act 2, scene 1)

To *what* is Macbeth referring by means of the demonstrative pronoun "this," when he asks "Is this a dagger which I see before me?" Roderick Chisholm would say: *nothing*. He claims that "When the victim of a hallucination uses a demonstrative term, saying, 'That is a rat,' the term 'that' may seem to indicate, or purport to indicate, but actually it indicates nothing" (Chisholm 1957: 163–164). This seems to me implausible. The whole burden of Macbeth's speech is that he is sure that he is confronted with *something*, but doesn't know what it is—a real dagger or "a false creation, proceeding from the heat-oppressed brain." Interestingly, it would appear that Austin (1962: 32) could be enlisted on our side in this debate: but then, he doesn't allow that there *is* a sense of "see" in which what is seen may not exist (Austin 1962: 94).

Perhaps it will be urged that Macbeth's assurance that he is confronted with *something* does not guarantee a reference for his use of the word "this." No, indeed. But if we consider him to be mistaken on this score then we are, I think, claiming much more than that he is merely a victim of hallucination. To be under a hallucination does not, as such, imply the possession of any false belief. Hallucination is at most indicative of sensory, not cognitive, disorder—although, of course, cognitive disorder may sometimes be associated with it. In short, we must be careful to distinguish between hallucination and *delusion*, which does involve cognitive disorder (cf. Austin 1962: 23).

Another point that I would make, when it is urged that hallucinatory objects are "purely intentional," is this. As was indicated earlier, we are sometimes invited to compare "see" with intentional verbs like "want" and "seek." I may seek a unicorn, even though there is, of course, no unicorn that I seek. Analogously, it may be said, Macbeth sees *something* (he knows not what), although there is in fact nothing that he sees. The trouble with this purported analogy is as follows. When I say that I want or seek an *X*, in the "purely intentional" sense, I am not in the slightest degree tempted to suppose that there must be an *X* that I want or seek. I never confuse the "intentional" object of my wanting or seeking with a "material" object (in Anscombe's special sense of "material"). But just such a confusion must be attributed to Macbeth, by the present account of hallucination. For Macbeth is sure that there *is* something that he sees—that is, that his seeing has a material object—and is only unsure as to its nature. Yet if Macbeth saw only a "purely intentional" something, why should he be in this state of confusion? The fact is that it is highly misleading to compare "seeing an *X*" with "wanting an *X*." When I "see an *X*" despite the fact that there is no *X* that I see, there is, I suggest, always *something*, say a *Y*, that I see *as* an *X*. For example, I may "see a man" inasmuch as I see a scarecrow *as* a man (cf. O'Connor 1976: 91). "Wanting an *X*" does not have this feature. The difference is that "wanting" can take a "purely intentional" object, but "seeing" cannot: there must always be a "material" object of seeing.

With this we may return to the double vision illusion. The proposal we have to consider is that in the *intentional* sense of "see," I do indeed "see two elongated pinkish objects," but that in the *material* sense I see *only my finger*. I urged a moment ago that when I "see an X" despite the fact that there is no X that I see, there is always *something*, say a Y, that I see *as* an X. But it is very hard to see how the direct realist can square this principle with the foregoing proposal. For, since he contends that *my finger* is, in this case, the only (relevant) *material* object of my seeing and yet that, in the intentional sense, I see *two* elongated pinkish objects, it seems that he must say that in this case I see my finger *as* a pair of objects or, more precisely, as *two* fingers. However, it makes no clear sense to speak of seeing *one* thing "as two," in the way in which it makes sense, say, to speak of seeing a scarecrow "as a man." I can see a scarecrow "as a man," inasmuch as I see it "under a certain description," namely, under the description "a man." But one cannot see *one* finger under the description "two fingers," for the very simple reason that "two fingers" is not a description under which *one* finger can possibly fall. As H. H. Price (1950: 57) aptly puts it, "'doubleness' is not a quality at all." Thus, the proposal now under consideration seems to be fatally flawed.

Another difficulty with that proposal is the following. When I see a scarecrow "as a man" and then learn that it is in fact a scarecrow, I am able to refer to the scarecrow demonstratively and say, truly, "*That* is really a scarecrow." But according to the foregoing proposal, it seems, *each* of the two elongated pinkish objects that I see—allegedly only in the "intentional" sense of "see"—is in fact *my finger*, seen under a certain description. So I ought to be able to refer demonstratively to the *right-hand* elongated pinkish object and say, truly, "*That* is really my finger." By the same token, I ought to be able to refer demonstratively to the *left-hand* elongated pinkish object and also say, truly, "*This* is really my finger." But now I have allegedly asserted two true identity statements, each identifying just *one* of the two elongated pinkish objects with the *same* thing, namely, *my finger*. However, "*That* is really my finger" and "*This* is really my finger" surely jointly entail, by the laws of identity, "*That* is really *this*." But *that* and *this* are *two*, not one. Notice that the case is quite different from one such as the following. I see the head of a tiger protruding from behind one side of a rock and the tail of a tiger protruding from behind the opposite side of the rock: then, pointing first at the head and then at the tail I proclaim, truly, "*That* tiger is *this* tiger."

No affront to the laws of identity is implied here, because I was at no time committed to the claim that "that" and "this" denoted two *different* things of any sort. In the double-vision case, by contrast, I surely *am* entitled to say, as I attend to each of the two elongated pinkish objects in turn, that *that* one and *this* one are distinct: for how else could I be entitled to say, as the present proposal concedes that I am, that I see *two* elongated pinkish objects? Note, in this connection, that these elongated pinkish objects are not even *qualitatively* identical: as Edmond Wright has reminded me, on inspection it is clear that they are subtly different.

I must now conclude my discussion of the double vision illusion. I hope I have managed to show, as conclusively as anything is ever shown in philosophy, that appeal to the "intentional" sense of "see" does nothing to explain away my belief that I see *two* elongated pinkish objects of some sort, in the *material* sense of "see." Appeal to the "intentional" sense of "see" cannot explain this away, any more than it can explain away Macbeth's conviction that he really is confronted with *something*, he knows not what. But if I *am* thus confronted with two real objects in the double vision illusion, they must clearly be *private mental objects*, just as Macbeth must in fact be confronted with a private mental object. They are *private* because, plainly, no one else can see directly *the very same two objects* that I see, and they are *mental* because they clearly depend for their existence on *my mind*, inasmuch as they wouldn't exist if I, as their observer, were not a conscious being. Although, being a philosopher who believes in the sense-datum theory, I can see each of these objects *as* a private mental object—a sense datum—I can, in another and more usual frame of mind, also see each of them *as* a finger. This, indeed, is precisely why it can seem to me that I see *two* fingers, even though only one finger exists to be seen: I can seem to see two because I can see *each* of the private mental objects *as* a different finger. The case is entirely parallel to one such as the following. I may "see two men," in the "intentional" sense of "see," where only one man exists to be seen, because I can see, in the *material* sense of "see," two different mirror-images of the same man, each of which I see *as* a different man.

Of course, I fully anticipate that some who cannot fault my reasoning so far will still stubbornly resist my conclusion—that at least sometimes we see "external," public objects only indirectly by seeing private mental objects—on the grounds that they find the very notion of a private mental object intolerable. They may well do so for reasons of a broadly "Wittgensteinian" kind. For instance, they may contend that it is impossible for anyone to learn how to *describe* a putatively private mental object, because we can only be taught vocabulary apt for describing *public* objects, where the correct use of the vocabulary is subject to an objective checking procedure. However, I myself have in fact used only such vocabulary in describing the sense data involved in the double vision illusion: I described them as being "elongated" and "pinkish," both of which adjectives can be used equally well to describe *public* objects. It is true that no one other than myself can check whether I have *correctly* used that vocabulary to describe the sense data that *I* see. Even so, that my use is not arbitrary is confirmed by the fact that *other people* performing the double vision experiment are happy to describe what *they* see in very similar terms.

Here it may be objected that it is simply *nonsensical* to suppose that the adjectives "elongated" and "pinkish" could literally apply, in exactly the same sense, to two things as radically different from one another as a *finger* and a *private mental object*. But why so? If the thought is that something can *literally* be elongated and pinkish only if it is a *public* object, then I fail to see why we should suppose that to be true. It won't do to urge, for instance, that only public objects can intelligibly be described by color-terms on the grounds that only such objects can be emitters, reflectors, or transmitters of *light*. For it is no part of the *meaning* of a color-term that it applies only to such objects. After all, people used such terms comprehendingly long before theories of the emission, reflection, and transmission of light were developed by scientists, and children today use those terms comprehendingly despite having no knowledge of those theories.

Other critics may object that, even if the notion of a private mental object—a sense datum—is not incoherent, the belief that such objects exist raises unanswerable questions, such as "Where are sense data *located*, if at all?," "How are sense data related *causally* to events and processes in the brain?," and "How do we *perceive* sense data?" (see, e.g., Chisholm 1976: 51; Armstrong 1979). I don't dispute that these and similar questions need to be answered by the sense-datum theorist, although I shall not attempt to answer them here. Some of them may indeed be difficult questions to answer. But it would be intellectually irresponsible to turn one's back on the sense-datum theory just because one doesn't like the questions that it raises. If arguments like that based on the double vision illusion provide compelling reasons for believing in the existence of sense data, as I think they do, then the intellectually responsible thing to do is to face the questions squarely and try to answer them as best we can. We may, as a result, have to revise some of our ontological beliefs quite radically. But that has happened before in the intellectual history of humanity and there is no reason to suppose that it won't ever happen again. Thus, I see questions such those just raised as presenting a challenge rather than a threat.

And what, finally, about *qualia*? Well, I take it that the *elongatedness* and the *pinkishness* of the two sense data that are distinctively present in the double vision illusion are examples, par excellence, of visual qualia.

Other visual qualia are just further items like this—*particularized qualities* of visual sense data that are discriminable features of one's conscious visual experience—and likewise for other sensory modes of perception such as audition and olfaction. The double vision illusion provides an existence proof of such entities, whose incorporation into our ontology is accordingly mandatory.

References

Anscombe, G. E. M. 1981. The intentionality of sensation: A grammatical feature. In her *Metaphysics and the Philosophy of Mind*. Oxford: Blackwell.

Armstrong, D. M. 1961. *Perception and the Physical World*. London: Routledge and Kegan Paul.

Armstrong, D. M. 1979. Perception, sense data, and causality. In *Perception and Identity*, ed. G. F. Macdonald. London: Macmillan.

Austin, J. L. 1962. *Sense and Sensibilia*. Ed. G. J. Warnock. Oxford: Oxford University Press.

Chisholm, R. M. 1957. *Perceiving: A Philosophical Study*. Ithaca, N.Y.: Cornell University Press.

Chisholm, R. M. 1976. *Person and Object*. London: George Allen and Unwin.

Hamlyn, D. W. 1961. *Sensation and Perception*. London: Routledge and Kegan Paul.

Hume, D. 1978 [1739–40]. *A Treatise of Human Nature*. Ed. L. A. Selby-Bigge and P. H. Nidditch. Oxford: Clarendon Press.

Jackson, F. 1977. *Perception*. Cambridge: Cambridge University Press.

Lowe, E. J. 1981. Indirect perception and sense data. *Philosophical Quarterly* 31: 330–342.

Lowe, E. J. 1986. What do we see directly? *American Philosophical Quarterly* 23: 277–285.

Malcolm, N. 1963. Direct perception. In his *Knowledge and Certainty*. Ithaca, N.Y.: Cornell University Press.

Mundle, C. W. K. 1971. *Perception: Facts and Theories*. Oxford: Oxford University Press.

O'Connor, D. J. 1976. The status of sense data. In *Impressions of Empiricism*, ed. G. Vesey. London: Macmillan.

Pitcher, G. 1971. *A Theory of Perception*. Princeton, N.J.: Princeton University Press.

Price, H. H. 1950. *Perception*, 2nd edn. London: Methuen.

Robinson, H. 1994. *Perception*. London: Routledge.

Wittgenstein, L. 1958. *Philosophical Investigations*, 2nd edn. Trans G. E. M. Anscombe. Oxford: Blackwell.

3 Experience and Representation

William S. Robinson

Sitting down to dinner with my friends, I see the food on my plate and the wine in the wineglass. As I begin to eat, I taste and smell the food and the wine. I feel my fork, and I hear what my friends are saying.

Philosophers have a way of summarizing a myriad of humdrum facts of the kind just noted. They say that our ordinary, perceptual experience presents or, more frequently, represents items in the world to us. We do not infer a world from our experience; instead, the representation of objects in the world just is the nature of experience. We can, of course, make some inferences from our experiences. Seeing that a tomato is greenish, for example, we infer that it will not taste as sweet now as it will if we leave it to ripen for a few days. But neither the presence of the tomato nor its greenish character is in this way inferred from anything; these matters are represented in the experience we have when we look at the tomato in daylight.

One cannot object to such talk of representation, so long as it remains a summary way of encapsulating the obvious facts just described. However, as we shall see, the idea of representation has been invoked in the service of attempts to give an accounting of experience that will be compatible with physicalist principles. The primary aim of this paper is to show that there is a tension between this use of the idea of representation and physicalism.

To pursue this aim, it is necessary to have a clear understanding of just what kinds of occurrences we are talking about when we refer to "experiences," "episodes of qualitative consciousness," "qualitatively conscious events," "conscious occurrences," or "qualitative events"—that is, events in which we say that "phenomenal qualities," "phenomenal properties" or "qualia" occur. Achieving this understanding is a delicate matter, for we must be careful not to beg questions against representationalism. Thus, a secondary aim of this paper is to establish a way of talking about experiences that will be as neutral as possible with respect to divergent views about their proper analysis. I shall begin with this secondary task.

1   What Are We Talking About?

I shall focus on occurrences in which something looks, tastes, smells, sounds, or feels a certain way. Examples of the kind I have in mind are cases in which something looks red, tastes bitter, smells oregano-ish, sounds squeaky, or feels warm. In these cases, red is the way something looks, bitter is the way it tastes, oregano-ish is the way it smells, squeaky is the way it sounds, and warm is the way it feels. These ways things may look, taste, smell, and so on are *phenomenal qualities*, also known as *qualia*.

I believe it will be generally accepted that if something looks, tastes, smells, etc. some way to an entity, *E*, then *E* is conscious. But we must be careful to mean these verbs in their ordinary "thick" sense, and not in a metaphorical or attenuated or "thin" sense. The distinction can be illustrated by thermostats. Someone might very well say that the room feels cold to the thermostat—after all, its coil has just contracted to the point where it has turned on the furnace. If the thermostat has been set too high, someone might even say "The thermostat thinks it's cold in here." But most people think that thermostats do not think at all, and most people think that thermostats are not the kind of entities to which anything feels any way whatsoever. This shows that "feels" and "thinks," when applied to thermostats, are weak metaphors in which there is exceedingly little overlap among the properties of target and source. Similarly, no one supposes that smoke smells in some way to a smoke detector, or that acids must taste in some way to pieces of litmus paper.

It is important to avoid thinking of "phenomenal qualities" as *defined by* reference to our talk about how things look, taste, etc. Instead, I mean to fix the reference of "phenomenal qualities" by calling attention to certain paradigmatic events. The full extension of the term is then to be determined by taking cases that are like these paradigmatic cases, and making explicit some limits that will shortly be introduced. Already, however, we can see that color words in general can indicate ways things look, taste words can indicate ways things taste, and so on.

Things can look broken or taste spoiled, but *broken* and *spoiled* are not phenomenal qualities. We can give a general rule that will exclude these and many other cases by noting that things can be broken or spoiled without looking broken or tasting (or smelling) spoiled even under normal conditions of vision or taste (or smell). By contrast, a thing cannot be red without looking red to normal observers under normal conditions, or be sweet without tasting sweet under normal conditions. In general:

(A)   If "*F*" denotes a phenomenal quality then, in our world, things are *F* only if they look (taste, etc.) *F* to normal observers in normal conditions.

The inclusion of "in our world" is required by reflection on the possibility of a world in which normal conditions are different from the normal conditions in our world, or the normal observers are different from the normal observers in our world. In such worlds, it might be that red things, for example, ripe strawberries, look different, that is, do not look red to normal observers in normal conditions. However, in our world, the red things just are those that look red to normal observers in normal conditions. In contrast, it is not true that the broken things are just those that look broken to normal observers in normal conditions. Squeaky hinges just are those that sound squeaky to normal hearers when the hinge is moved, but it is not true that spoiled food just is food that tastes or smells spoiled to those with normal taste and smell.

Our discussion picks out some clear cases in which things look, taste, etc. a certain way (in the thick, i.e., the ordinary sense of these verbs) and gives an indication of how to extend the list of examples. It is not claimed that a necessary and sufficient condition for the intended class of cases has been provided, but such a condition is not required for our discussion to proceed. From the indications that have been provided we can identify a considerable list of phenomenal qualities, and we can know that if something looks, tastes, etc. *F* to an entity, *E* (where "*F*" denotes a phenomenal quality), then *E* is a conscious entity. Let us call occasions on which something looks, tastes, etc. to some entity "qualitative events." We may then ask some questions in a general form, by phrasing them as questions about qualitative events; and we can ask other general questions by referring to the phenomenal qualities that are picked out by the predicates that may follow "looks," "tastes," and so on.

2   Learning Words for Phenomenal Qualities

Accepting (A) does not imply (as Chisholm [1957: 50] seems to think) that we cannot apply color-words, taste-words, and so on to things without first being able to apply "looks *F*," "tastes *F*," and so on (where "*F*" denotes a phenomenal quality). On the contrary, what we learn in the nursery is how to classify blocks, crayons, and so forth by color-words. We have learned our color-words when our responses to instructions such as "Give me the red crayon" or "Tell me what color this is" match the responses of our linguistic community.

In the normal course of development, we encounter surprises. The thing we recently called "blue," when the lighting was bad, we now say is green, even though we believe that it has not been painted, dyed, or heated in the intervening time, but merely moved into good light. The first bite of peach after eating honey may have tasted tart, unlike further bites of the same peach. In such cases, we learn to say that the green thing "looked blue" and that the peach "tasted tart" at first, and we learn some generalizations about how things look, taste, etc. under various conditions.

Although surprise is typical in learning "looks F," "tastes F," and so on, there is no implication in adult speech that if a thing looks F it is not really F. On the contrary, things normally look the way they are (which is evidently required by (A)) and only sometimes look otherwise. Further, if pressed to describe, say, the sound of some musical instrument that is not ready to hand, one might say, with no sort of oddity, that it sounds rather like a 'cello. This description is surely elliptical for "sounds similar to the way a 'cello normally sounds," and thus it implies that there is a way that a 'cello normally sounds.

3   Qualitative Events and Judgments

A deflationary view of qualitative events assimilates them to occasions on which judgments are made. For example, "This looks blue" may be held to be equivalent to something like "I see that this is blue," said, perhaps, with less than full confidence. In this strong form, the deflationary view is easily rejected. It is not remotely paradoxical to affirm that something looks green but is not green, but it would be Moore-paradoxical to say something tantamount to "I tentatively affirm that this is green but it is not green."

A more subtle deflationary view is that cases in which things are said to look, taste, etc. a certain way are cases in which one recognizes that one would classify a thing in that way were it not for knowing some fact that implies that it isn't that way. For example, one might declare that a certain wine is sweet, were one not mindful of just having sucked on a lemon; so one says instead that it *tastes* sweet, but may or may not *be* sweet. Now, it is true that we use "looks," "tastes," and similar verbs in such cases; the question is only whether the stated view gives a complete description of what occurs when something looks, tastes, etc., a certain way. The answer is negative. Sometimes, doubts are recognized not to be well founded. A thing may look a certain way when we have doubts, and it may continue to look that way when our doubts are resolved. It may be that, in some context, we would have been unlikely to say that something looks a certain way if we were not suspicious that it doesn't look the way it is, but that does not show that rejecting the way it looks as veridical is part of the meaning of "looks." If we are reluctant to rely on our judgments about wine if we taste it immediately after having sucked on a lemon, that is because the way it tastes just then may not be the way it tastes later on. If we clear our palates and subsequently find that the wine consistently tastes medium dry and fruity, we may judge that that is the way it really tastes. If we express this judgment, we cannot sensibly be supposed to be hedging our bets.

4 Gibbons's Objection

John Gibbons (2005) has offered an interesting argument that, if successful, would block the kind of introduction of qualia I have given. This argument turns on rejecting a consequence of my approach, namely, that something might look, taste, etc. a certain way to one person, and look, taste, etc. a different way to another person. Let us call this scenario "differential seeming." According to Gibbons, differential seeming is not coherent, and so any view that appears to allow it must be rejected.

The argument is this. Let us suppose that Jane and John are cognitively normal and that each has had a normal upbringing in a family of native English speakers. Then they have both learned standard color words, for example, "red" and "green," and they are able to apply these terms correctly and effortlessly to objects they have never seen before. Their color judgments agree with each other and with those of all normal English speakers. Further, they have learned words such as "looks" and "seems" in the same way, and their respective usage is standard, that is, they apply these words in the same kinds of situations as other English speakers, and in a way that agrees with judgments of similarly placed, normal speakers of English.

Let us suppose that Jane and John are standing next to each other, looking at the same object, and both say that it looks red. Very plausibly, they mean the same thing by their words, and are speaking correctly. Without begging any questions, we may suppose that they are not lying, and are not intending irony or metaphor. In that case, they say the same thing, they mean what they say, and what they say is true. But that is to say that the object looks red to both, and that implies that the object looks the same way to both. So, it is false that it looks different to them. Since the case evidently generalizes, it is incoherent to suppose that it could be generally the case that things look different to them.

The premises of this argument, however, do not entail its conclusion. That is because "looks red" can be understood as "looks the way red things normally look." Jane and John have both learned to apply "looks red" when something looks the way red things normally look (whether they take the surrounding circumstances to be normal, or not). If that is the way they use the term, then they use it the same way as each other and the same way as other English speakers. If competent English speakers agree that the object looks red, then what each of them says is true. These facts are compatible with difference in the phenomenal qualities in their experiences, just so long as the way this object looks to each of them is the same way that red objects normally look to each of them.

5 Taking Stock So Far

There are qualitative events, that is, there are occurrences in which something looks, tastes, smells, sounds, or feels a certain way to someone. Phenomenal qualities are ways in which things look, taste, etc., subject to the qualification indicated in (A). Qualitative events require consciousness, that is, if something looks, tastes, etc. F to someone (in the thick, i.e., the ordinary, nonmetaphorical sense of these verbs) then that someone is conscious, and the occurrence of something's looking, tasting, etc. some way to that person is an episode in the history of that person's consciousness. Qualitative events are not reducible to judgments or tendencies to hold judgments—although, of course, we can judge that we are having a qualitative event of one kind or another, and we can judge that a thing is of a certain kind with various degrees of confidence.

I have approached these matters with some care because I want it to be clear that proponents of many different views can agree with what has been said so far. Die-hard deflationists will perhaps not be convinced, but all others can, I believe, agree with what has been said up to this point, and should be able to consider questions phrased in terms of qualitative events and phenomenal qualities without feeling that questions have been begged against their views. In particular, the representationalists against whom I will argue in the remainder of this paper are not deflationists, and can consistently regard their view as a proposal for analyzing qualitative events.

6 Representationalism

Representationalism holds that qualitative events are representational. Phenomenal qualities are actually physical properties of physical things, for example, molecular surface structures, molecules of various kinds, vibrations in the air, thermal vibrations, variations in spatial frequencies, and so forth. Qualitative events are nothing other than representations of such qualities.[1]

In considering this view, it is crucial to avoid thinking that representation is accomplished *by means of* qualitative events that have a phenomenal quality in some sense other than that they represent qualities. The point of representationalism is to *deny* that qualitative events have any intrinsic qualitative nature of their own. Instead, they are events in us that represent properties without having them. Analogously, the word "red" represents a certain color, but not by means of being itself written in red ink.

An important alleged advantage of representationalism is that it is supposed to allow us to account for all our qualitative events without having to introduce any special, problematic qualities or bearers of such qualities. That is to say, it claims not to introduce anything that is not *physical*.

It will help to remind ourselves why philosophers have thought that something nonphysical might be required in accounting for our qualitative events. One useful kind of case (but not the only one) involves afterimaging. For example, after reading an announcement printed on bright red paper, one might turn one's eyes to an ordinary piece of white paper and notice that it looks somewhat green. In such a case, there is nothing green before one's eyes. There is no part of one's brain that is green, either, and it hardly makes sense to say that an activation state of the neurons in some part of one's brain is green. In short, nothing in the inventory of physical things that are present in the indicated situation is green. But green seems to be involved in *some* way, and one way of recognizing this involvement would be to suppose that there is *something* that actually *is* green. If one does say this, then whatever it is that is green will have to be something that is not in the standard inventory of physical things.

Representationalists give a different account of the indicated situation. It contains nothing that is green, but it does contain something that *represents* green or, more fully, that represents the paper as being green. What does the representing is neural events, which are straightforwardly physical events. What is represented are physical properties—in our case, certain sets of combinations of reflectance percentages at various wavelengths, or sets of molecular structures that underlie those reflectance percentages. Many surfaces do have such properties, and representations of things as green are normally correct representations. But it is built into the concept of representation that misrepresentation is possible, and in the case described in the preceding paragraph the paper is misrepresented by the experience as being green.

An obvious question to ask is *how* neural events can represent the physical properties of surfaces (or molecules of various types in food or air, or vibrations, etc.). The importance of this question is this. If representationalism is to live up to its leading motivation, namely, consonance with a physicalist account of the world, including our qualitative events, then it must be able to say what representation consists in, and it must do this in a way that uses only those resources that are available from a physicalist point of view. It will not do to say that representation is a special, *sui generis* relation that cannot be composed out of relations found elsewhere in the physical sciences. Such a view might claim to avoid the introduction of nonphysical *entities*, but the price would be the introduction of a nonphysical relational property, and the resulting view would not be a kind of physicalism on accepted understandings of "physicalism."

The argument I will soon offer is designed to show that representationalism is unable give a satisfactory account of the relation of representation without departing from "physicalism" in the accepted sense. But it is far from obvious that this is the case, and representationalists do put forward what appear to be physicalist accounts of representation. There are several such accounts; fortunately, it will not be necessary examine them all in detail. Instead, I will discuss one leading idea and then briefly mention some variations on its theme. The argument to come will apply to all these variants.

The leading idea in physicalist accounts of representation is *tracking*. (This is Tye's [1995] term.) Neural events track physical properties if they systematically covary with those physical properties in normal conditions. A class of events in the auditory system, for example, is such that in normal conditions one of them will occur only if the eardrum is vibrated at a certain frequency, another will occur only if the eardrum is vibrated at a different frequency, and so on. If these conditions hold, events of each of these types represent the frequency that is its cause in normal conditions. Evidently, this account allows for misrepresentation. If one has an event of one of these types in abnormal conditions, for example, through disease, one will have a neural event that represents a certain frequency even though nothing of that frequency is currently affecting one's eardrum.

The idea of tracking may be supplemented in various ways. Normal covariation may be too strong a requirement; perhaps it is enough for representation if normal covariation occurs in some special learning period (Dretske 1981). Or it may be that representation is achieved if the circumstances under which covariation occurs are those that made the system of covarying states evolutionarily viable, even if those circumstances are not normal (Millikan 1984). Representation may require that the tracking events feed into a larger system that can react in specific ways to represented properties (Tye 1995). It may be required that the larger system has developed under pressure of natural selection (Dretske 1995).

These views all retain a central feature of tracking, namely, dependence of representation on a causal relation between representing events and represented properties. The argument to come depends only on this causal relation and that is why we will be able to proceed without examining the further details of these accounts of representation.

7   Planet X

Planet X is just like Earth with only the following three exceptions and whatever follows from them. (1) The sun around which Planet X revolves emits light of a composition that is slightly different from that of our Sun. Consequently, if you took a $blue_{24}$ object (i.e., an object of a certain shade of blue) to Planet X and looked at it in Planet X's ordinary daylight, it would look $blue_{27}$ to you (where $blue_{27}$ is a somewhat different shade of blue). (2) There are no $blue_{27}$ objects on Planet X. (3) There are no cows on Planet X, but there are robots that look just like our cows. If you were not informed of this difference and you went to Planet X and looked out on certain fields, you would naturally take it that you were looking at some cows. But Planet X-ers know all about their robots and have never heard of cows. When they look out on those same fields, they naturally take it that they're looking at some of their robots.

Since Planet X-ers would have different beliefs about what they were looking at on such occasions, we should not think that their brains are duplicates of ours. But (by hypothesis) their physiology is exactly ours and their psychology, whether sensitive, affective, or cognitive, is exactly ours. The differences in their beliefs are consequences of their different education. If you had been in their shoes, you would believe as they do.

On these assumptions, it is highly plausible to hold that

(1)   Robots look to Planet X-ers just the way cows look to us, apart from a very slight difference in color (due to the small difference in the sunlight).

and

(2)   In whatever sense our visual experience represents cows to us, Planet X-ers' visual experience represents robots to them.

Since the way cows and robots look to their respective viewers is virtually the same in each case, but what is represented is different, the way cows and robots look is not sufficient to determine what is represented. When this is the case, I shall speak of "extrinsic" representation.

Definition 1:   Extrinsic representation = *df*. representation in which the way things look, taste, etc. is not by itself sufficient to determine what is represented.

Since Planet X-ers' physiology and psychology are exactly ours, and since $blue_{24}$ objects look $blue_{27}$ to us when we are on Planet X, it is also highly plausible to hold that

(3) $Blue_{24}$ objects look to Planet X-ers just the way $blue_{27}$ objects look to us.

But it is not plausible to affirm a parallel to (2), that is, it is not plausible that

(2')   In whatever sense our qualitative events when we look at $blue_{27}$ objects in normal conditions on Earth represent $blue_{27}$ to us, Planet X-ers' qualitative events when looking at $blue_{24}$ objects in normal conditions on Planet X represent $blue_{24}$ to them.

Instead, it is highly plausible to hold that

(4)   In whatever sense our qualitative events when we look at $blue_{27}$ objects in normal conditions on Earth represent $blue_{27}$ to us, Planet X-ers' qualitative events when looking at $blue_{24}$ objects in normal conditions on Planet X represent $blue_{27}$ to them.

The argument for (4) is this.

1. $Blue_{24}$ objects look to X-ers in normal conditions on Planet X exactly like $blue_{27}$ objects look to us in normal conditions on Earth.
2. The color that a qualitative event represents an object as having is the color that the object looks to have.

So,

3. The color that X-ers' qualitative events represent objects as having, when they look at $blue_{24}$ objects in normal conditions on Planet X, is the

same color that we represent objects as having when we look at blue$_{27}$ objects in normal conditions on Earth—namely, blue$_{27}$.

I will shortly consider an objection to (4) and to this argument for it, but let us first develop the view that grows out of accepting (4) and rejecting (2'). We can begin this project by noting that if (4) is right, then

(5)   Qualitative events represent colors (and by parallel reasoning, phenomenal qualities in general) *intrinsically*

where "intrinsic representation" is given as follows.

Definition 2:   Intrinsic representation =*df.* representation in which the way things look, taste, etc. is sufficient by itself to determine what is represented.

A further premise that we need is:

(6)   Physicalism can account for extrinsic representation, but offers no hope of accounting for intrinsic representation.

Behind latter part of (6) is the fact that present physicalist accounts depend on causation of qualitative events by what they are held to represent and, providing we accept (4), there can be cases where the qualitative events are the same but the causes, and thus what is represented, are different. Therefore, the way things look, taste, etc. is, according to causal accounts, not sufficient to determine what is represented, that is, the representation is extrinsic and not intrinsic.

It is always possible to imagine that some as yet unheard of idea will come to the rescue. Many first-rate physicalist philosophers, however, have given the most serious kind of consideration to the representation relation, and all have given accounts that plausibly succeed in providing extrinsic representation while failing to suggest how intrinsic representation could work. That physicalism offers no hope of accounting for intrinsic representation thus seems to be a precise description of our situation.

From (5) and (6) it follows that

(7)   Physicalism offers no hope of accounting for the way in which qualitative events represent phenomenal qualities.

Further, since representationalism is supposed to be a species of physicalism,

(8)   Representationalism offers no hope of accounting for the way in which qualitative events represent phenomenal qualities.

8 Two Objections

(O1) The light received by the eyes of Planet X-ers when they look at
$blue_{24}$ objects is the same as the light received on Earth by our eyes when
we look at $blue_{27}$ objects. All that the foregoing argument shows is that
what is represented is the color of the light.

The facts noted in this objection are correct, and their application in a
causal explanation is also correct. It is, indeed, implicit in the description
of the case that $blue_{24}$ objects look $blue_{27}$ to X-ers because the light they
receive (because of the different composition of their sunlight) is the same
as the light we receive on Earth from $blue_{27}$ objects, and their physiological
and psychological constitution is the same as ours.

These facts do not undercut the argument, however. To sustain the
objection, one would have to hold that what we represent when something looks a certain way to us is some property of light. But it is not the
case that the light looks blue, or red, etc. to us. Nor does our experience
represent the salivary solution in our mouths as tasting in some way to us.

This response can be reinforced by considering a variant of our thought
experiment. Suppose, for purposes of this paragraph only, that the constitution of X-ers is not quite like ours. They differ in just one small respect,
namely, their intraoptic fluid is not quite optically neutral and has the
effect of making $blue_{24}$ objects (objects that would look $blue_{24}$ to you on
Earth, but would look $blue_{27}$ to you on Planet X) look $blue_{24}$ to them. In this
scenario, the strategy of the objection would require us to say that X-ers
were representing a condition of their retinas, and, by parity of reasoning,
that our visual qualitative events represent conditions of our retinas. But
it is not plausible to affirm that what is represented to us when something
looks a certain way to us is a condition of our retinas. One could, of course,
stipulate that whenever something looks blue to us we are representing* a
certain condition of our retinas. This is equivalent to *defining* "representation*" in terms of one of the causal conditions of our qualitative events.
But one cannot define, or stipulate, what it is that our qualitative events
represent. Representation is supposed to be a natural relation that is found
in, or is part of the analysis of, episodes of something's looking a certain
way to us. If it is not true that x looks a certain way to us, then our relation
to x cannot be the correct analysis of such episodes.

(O2) Assumption (3) of the foregoing argument is that $blue_{24}$ objects will
look to X-ers the way that $blue_{27}$ objects look to us. But this assumption
begs the question. Since it is normally $blue_{24}$ objects that cause things to

look a certain way to X-ers, the way they look to X-ers is $blue_{24}$. They will look $blue_{27}$ to us if we visit Planet X, but they don't look that way to X-ers.

This extreme version of externalism is a logical possibility, but it is not a view that physicalists can adopt. The reason is that it attributes a causal power to sheer normalcy, and that is not a causal power that can be found anywhere in our sciences.

To explain "sheer normalcy" we may contrast it with normalcy effects that work through a mechanism. For example, other things being equal, erosion will occur faster in locales that normally have higher rainfall. The connection is that higher rainfall means more water, and thus more time for dissolving and more friction effects from rushing water.

The possibility suggested in (O2) is not like this. $Blue_{24}$ objects have no chemical effects on the operation of the senses. There aren't any more of them on Planet X than there are here. The laws of nature on Planet X, and the physiological and psychological constitution of its residents, are just as they are here. If certain objects look different to X-ers than they would to us if we visited Planet X, that would be an effect of sheer normalcy, that is, an effect of the normalcy of their sunlight *per se*, without any intervening mechanism by which that normalcy could have its effect. Such effects are not encountered in science, and it is not plausible that they could be added in any extension of science that would be recognizable as a development of science as we know it.

The two objections to which I have just responded seem to me to be the critical ones. If this is right, and if the responses are adequate, then the conclusion in (8) stands. One can, of course, still hold that qualitative events represent. What I believe one cannot do is to consistently claim that any view on the present scene gives an adequate account of representation that can fairly be claimed to be a physicalist account. To the extent that representationalism is motivated by the desire to save physicalism, it is a failure.

9   Qualitative Event Realism

Representationalism was introduced as a response to the question of how green gets into the situation in which a piece of white paper looks green to us. I want to close with a very brief indication of a qualia-realist alternative that I believe to offer a better account. Since not every qualia realist will agree with all I am going to say, I will use a special term, "qualitative event realism" (QER) to refer to the particular view I will be applying here.[2]

According to QER, a thing's looking green to someone is an episode of consciousness of a certain kind. Green enters the situation as a property of such episodes. If something looks red or blue, that is a different kind of conscious episode. When things taste, smell, sound, or feel a certain way to us, we are likewise having episodes of consciousness of various kinds. These episodes are caused by neural events, but the properties in virtue of which episodes of consciousness are similar and different are not properties of neurons or their activation states.

Representationalists sometimes attempt to criticize qualia realism by pointing out that it is *things* that look *F*; it is not our consciousness of things that looks *F* (where *F* is a phenomenal quality). This is correct, but it is no objection to QER. For QER also recognizes that the way things look to us (and sound to us) has a spatial character. This spatial character causally depends on our having spatially separated eyes (and ears) and on our ability to move and to reach for things, but the spatiality of the way things look and sound is not arrived at by conscious inference. Instead, distance of things is immediately there in the way things look and sound. Something's looking two feet away and something's looking five feet away are different kinds of conscious episodes, not one kind of conscious episode that is inferentially associated with different beliefs. This fact is often described by saying that we "look through" our experience to the objects. From the point of view of QER, this description is an understandable mistake, but a mistake nonetheless. The correct description is that the distance is in our qualitative events, just as are color and shape. When we look at the paper (i.e., in our example) the character of our qualitative event is not green in our heads plus rectangular shape in our heads, plus an opinion about distance; its character is rectangular green over *there*. Such events are typically surrounded by automatic expectations, for example, that the paper will feel a certain way if we pick it up, and that it will sound a certain way if we crumple it. They are also surrounded by beliefs, for example, that the paper was made from trees, and that it will be useless if it gets wet. The fact that distance is already in our qualitative events permits a seamless transition between the ways things look and our beliefs about their nonphenomenal qualities and their nonphenomenal relations to things in three-dimensional space.

Notes

1. An alternative possibility for a representationalist view would hold that nothing actually has phenomenal qualities: things are represented *as F* in qualitative events,

but nothing ever actually *is* F. Since there can be no tracking of properties that nothing has, it will be quite evident that the argument given in the text defeats this alternative view.

2. See Robinson 2004 for a full discussion of qualitative event realism.

References

Chisholm, R. M. 1957. *Perceiving: A Philosophical Study*. Ithaca: Cornell University Press.

Dretske, F. I. 1981. *Knowledge and the Flow of Information*. Cambridge, Mass.: MIT Press/A Bradford Book.

Dretske, F. I. 1995. *Naturalizing the Mind*. Cambridge, Mass.: MIT Press/A Bradford Book.

Gibbons, J. 2005. Qualia: They're not what they seem. *Philosophical Studies* 126: 397–428.

Millikan, R. G. 1984. *Language, Thought, and Other Biological Categories: New Foundations for Realism*. Cambridge, Mass.: MIT Press/A Bradford Book.

Robinson, W. S. 2004. *Understanding Phenomenal Consciousness*. Cambridge: Cambridge University Press.

Tye, M. 1995. *Ten Problems of Consciousness: A Representational Theory of the Phenomenal Mind*. Cambridge, Mass.: MIT Press/A Bradford Book.

4   Qualia Realism, Its Phenomenal Contents and Discontents

George Graham and Terence Horgan

Qualia realism, roughly, is the thesis that qualia are real. They are a ubiquitous part of the conscious face of existence. The opposite view is qualia antirealism, the thesis that qualia are absent from the conscious face of existence. In our judgment, qualia antirealism is a kind of nihilism or eliminativism about consciousness. If there are no qualia, no phenomenal qualities to human mental states, then, we believe, there would be no full-fledged conscious mental states at all. Humans would be nonconscious zombies. Although humans might still undergo mental states, namely, states with some kind of intentionality, and although human neural cognitive architecture might render some of these nonphenomenal mental states directly accessible and readily describable, such mere "access consciousness" is no real consciousness at all. Zombies are not truly conscious, not even if they have functional architecture that reliably enables them to form (nonconscious) second-order beliefs about possessing certain first-order intentional states (states that are themselves nonconscious).

Here is how the following essay is organized. It is divided into two main sections. In the first, we describe what qualia are and outline the form of qualia realism that we favor. In the second section, we offer three arguments for qualia realism. While our first argument is an argument for the full picture of qualia that we favor, each of the second and third arguments can be adjusted to possess more narrow scope than that offered by our full picture and to apply, for example, only to sensory qualia. We don't describe such possible adjustments here, although we do intend to be cordial to qualia realists whose conceptions of the nature of qualia may be somewhat more limited or restricted than ours.

1   Qualia and Qualia Realism

Qualia realism is a thesis about what there is, about a range of properties that are part of the world, namely, that part in conscious heads. Simply put, it is the thesis that conscious states of mind, such as conscious sensations, feelings, perceptions, and, more controversially, beliefs and thoughts as well, have characters or qualities that consist of something it is like for conscious subjects to be in such states. These qualities are what we designate by "qualia." Though there is need for clarification, elaboration, and eventually a second statement of qualia realism, as a first pass we state qualia realism thus:

(QR)   For every conscious mental state, there is something it is like for the subject to be in that state or to undergo such an experience.

The expression "something it is like" (and similarly, the expression "what it is like") has been used in a variety of ways in the philosophy of mind. Sometimes it means "something it feels like" (or "what it feels like") and so is restricted in application to sensory states and the like. We mean to use the expression more broadly, as will be evident and explained below.

The term "conscious," as employed in QR, means "conscious rather than nonconscious or unconscious." On some views of what it means to be conscious, many mental states that are conscious as opposed to non-conscious are said to lack qualia—that is, there is nothing it is like to be in such a state. However, according to qualia realism, as we understand this doctrine, *genuinely* conscious mental states have a distinctive and proprietary qualitative character, a "what-it's-likeness." To use the influential terminology of Ned Block (1995), all "access conscious" mental states are, on our view, "phenomenally conscious" as well.[1] Indeed, being phenomenally conscious is what *makes* the states "access conscious." (If there were a cognitive agent who somehow could reliably form spontaneous beliefs about possessing certain first-order states that happen not to be phenomenally conscious themselves, then those first-order states would not thereby qualify as *conscious*, even though their presence would be immediately accessible to the cognitive system.)

Tim Crane (2001: 170) notes: "[T]here is not a clear consensus [among philosophers] about how the term 'qualia' should be understood." Dennett (2005: 78) makes the same observation but in the form of an antirealist complaint that "philosophers have endowed the term ['qualia'] with a variety of ill-considered associations and special powers [though without an] agreed upon definition." Its use has "persisted . . . in spite of its incoherence" (78). He adds: "The philosophers' concept of qualia is a mess" (87).

We certainly don't want our concept of qualia to be a mess. So, here are six comments, each aimed at clarifying and elaborating on what we mean by referring to qualia as the what-it's-likenesses of experience.

First, we think of qualia as, to use a popular term of art in contemporary philosophy of mind, *narrow*, in this sense: they are not constituted by anything "outside the head" or in the external environment of the conscious person. No doubt, occurrences of qualia or conscious mental states are caused by external events, and, if one assumes that they are causally potent, qualia possess causal or dispositional powers. However, no objects or occurrences in the external world are constitutive of qualia—that is, figure in the individuation conditions of qualia. This means that physical duplicates of you can be expected to have the same qualia as you. The phenomenal aspects of experience supervene locally on bottom-level aspects of the brain and central nervous system.

Second, we also conceive of the something-it-is-like (or phenomenal or qualitative) character of experience as *inseparably* intentional or representational. The phenomenal content of conscious experience *represents* the world or self as being various ways. It possesses intentionality.[2]

The term "representationalism" has come into use as a label for a package of philosophical views about phenomenal consciousness espoused by philosophers like Michael Tye (1995), Fred Dretske (1995), Gilbert Harman (1990), and a number of others. We ourselves are not representationalists, in the relevant sense—even though, like them, we are committed to the proposition that conscious experience represents both world and self. Representationalists, by contrast, are committed to two additional propositions: first, that the phenomenology of experience can be exhaustively analyzed, without nonrepresentational residue, in terms of its representational or intentional features; and second, that mental intentionality itself can be analyzed in other terms—for example, in terms of causal covariation, or asymmetric counterfactual dependence, or evolutionary proper function, or operant-conditioning driven "recruitment" of internal states as "control switches," and so on. On such accounts, intentionality is not intrinsic, but rather is constitutively determined by an internal state's "long-armed functional role," which is a role that takes account of causal-explanatory connections between occurrences of the internal state and circumstances or objects in the wider ambient environment. It should also be noted, in order to distinguish our claim of intentionality from that made by representationalists, that being *inseparably* intentional (our claim) is not the same as being *exhaustively, non-intrinsically,* intentional (their claim). If I read a magazine story about a city, the vehicles of representationality are ink blots on the page. The blots represent the city for me and other readers, but they don't intrinsically represent anything. I must interpret them as about a city. A city is represented via the blots. What are presented are blots; what is represented is a city. Not so with the qualitative or phenomenal content of conscious mental states. Phenomenal content is not just intentional, we claim, but intrinsically intentional. Since phenomenal character is also self-presenting to the experiencing subject, it therein wears its intentional content on its subjectively manifest sleeve, that is, intrinsically. Suppose, for example, that I am thinking of a city. A city-thought immediately presents itself to me, that is, without needing to be "read" or interpreted by me. (Whether or not my city-thought successfully *refers* to some real city does depend constitutively on whether or not I am suitably related, within my larger ambient environment, to such a city. But the city-ish *intentionality* of my thought, the thought's *purporting* to refer to a real city, is intrinsic.)

So, third, we think that one rich and distinctive aspect of conscious experience is that it is intrinsic, and in a self-presenting way. The what-it's-likeness of conscious experience is not just intentional, but *intrinsic*. Our view is that representationalism about phenomenology leaves out the intrinsic character of conscious experience (see Graham and Horgan 2000, 2005).

Fourth, we believe that the most fundamental, nonderivative sort of intentionality is fully constituted by phenomenology. The representationality of a magazine's ink blots derives from how those blots are interpreted, whereas the intentionality of a conscious thought derives from nothing at all. It is inherent in the thought. This means that such fundamental intentionality is intrinsic (given the third claim above) and narrow (given the first claim above). With John Tienson, we call this fundamental, intrinsic and narrow intentionality *phenomenal intentionality* (see Horgan and Tienson 2002; Horgan, Tienson, and Graham 2005).[3]

It should be mentioned that, for us, phenomenal intentionality is not just an epistemic phenomenon. It is a metaphysical phenomenon. Consider one of the more famous thought experiments regarding qualia. Frank Jackson's (1982) Mary is raised in a black-and-white room in which she learns all the cognitive-representational and causal-functional facts about color vision. When she ventures outside that room for the first time, she learns (upon perceiving a ripe red tomato) a new fact about color vision, something she was not able to infer from her knowledge of the cognitive-representational and causal-functional aspects of color vision. "This is what it is like to see red," she might think to herself. "I didn't know what this was like before."

Some critics of Jackson (1982) deny that Mary learns a new "robust fact" when she ventures forth from her monochromatic chamber—that is, a fact involving some new property instantiated by colored objects and/or by her color-experiences. What Mary acquires, some say, is merely a new way of referring to certain scientifically describable properties instantiated by external objects, and/or certain scientifically describable properties instantiated by herself or by internal states of her visual system, about which she already knew (see Tye 1995). What she acquires as her new mode of reference is a "phenomenal concept." This is a new concept about an old item (e.g., a physical or functional property) and therein a new capacity for referring to previously known robust facts about color vision. Beliefs deploying these newly acquired concepts are about "new facts" but only in the anodyne sense of "fact," as involving no new ontology but only the newly acquired capacity to deploy phenomenal concepts—a capacity that is supposedly just a matter of being able to color-classify things directly on the basis of one's visual experiences, without reliance on collateral information. Our view, by contrast to such critics, is that when Mary has her first exposure to something experienced as red, she acquires not merely the ability to make color-judgments directly on the basis of visual experience (and thus the ability to deploy anodyne, "recognitional," color concepts whose deployment just consists in the new visual-classificatory capacity); she also learns the *intrinsic basis in* color experience of such recognitional capacities (see Graham and Horgan 2000, 2005). This experiential basis is something that she did not know before; and it is a substantial piece of new knowledge, not just the deployment of a new recognitional or classificatory skill. "Red color experience is like this," and other such statements that Mary, then, might make using phenomenal concepts come to identify, for her, an interesting and exciting new fact about red color vision—namely, what the visual experience of red is like. (Whether it also is an ontologically robust fact, involving a new and different property over and above the properties she already knew about, is a vexing question. We ourselves know of no philosophical or scientific defense of a negative answer to that question that we find theoretically compelling, or that avoids telling objections [see Graham and Horgan 2002; Horgan and Tienson 2001].)

Fifth: We claim that phenomenal intentionality has different aspects or dimensions. It is multidimensional rather than single-dimensional. Among the different aspects are the following (see Horgan and Tienson 2002: 520–533; Horgan, Tienson, and Graham 2003; Graham 2004: 89–105).

In the first place, there is the phenomenology of *perceptual experience*: the what-it's-like of being perceptually presented with a world of apparent objects, apparently instantiating a rich range of properties and relations.

Second, there is the phenomenology of *agency*: the what-it's-like of apparently *voluntarily controlling* one's apparent body as one apparently moves around in, and apparently interacts with, apparent objects in one's apparent environment. Third, there is *conative and cognitive* phenomenology: the what-it's-like of undergoing various occurrent propositional attitudes, including conative attitudes like occurrent wishes or desires and cognitive attitudes like occurrent thoughts. There are phenomenologically distinguishable aspects of conative and cognitive phenomenology, notably (i) the phenomenology of *attitude type* and (ii) the phenomenology of *attitude content*. The former is illustrated by the subjectively manifest difference between, for instance, *occurrently hoping* that the U.S. military will withdraw from Iraq and *occurrently fearing* that it will withdraw—where the content remains the same while the attitude-type varies. The phenomenology of content is illustrated by the subjectively manifest difference between occurrently fearing that the military will withdraw and occurrently fearing that it will not withdraw—where the attitude-type remains the same while the content varies.

Yet another aspect (a fourth) of the multidimensionality to which we refer is the phenomenology of *self-modification* or *self-attribution*: the what-it's-likeness of experiencing feelings, thoughts, and sensations as one's own, or as modifying oneself, or as states of oneself. What do we mean by this? What we refer to as the phenomenology of self-attribution can be illustrated by noting that there are phenomenologically distinguishable aspects of self-attributive phenomenology, notably (i) the phenomenology of *subjectivity* and (ii) the phenomenology of mental *agency*. The difference between these two aspects is introspectively evident in, say, the difference between experiencing an advertising jingle running through your head (occurring as in your stream of consciousness but without your experiencing personal authorship or control over the course or character of the jingle) and experiencing yourself as mentally composing a jingle (where the jingle appears as under your authorship). Just how explicit or introspectively salient the phenomenology of self-modification is (in either mode or aspect) depends on the conscious subject's focus of attention and conceptual sophistication. Some conscious experiences possess the phenomenology of self-modification vividly, as when you experience a pain (as) in your tooth (which would be an instance of the phenomenology of subjectivity); others fail to possess it vividly; still others possess it in various atypical and abnormal manners.[4] (See Stephens and Graham 2000, 2007.)

Finally, sixth: Conscious mental states need not possess a proprietary and distinctive "feel." Sensory, perceptual and emotional experiences typically possess such a feel or feel-quality, as in, for example, experiencing a sharp, stabbing pain, wherein the what-it's-likeness of the state is identical with what it feels like to undergo it. But in cases in which a conscious mental state does not possess a special sensory or sensory-imagistic "feel," it still possesses a what-it's-likeness (insofar as it is self-presentationally immediate). It still consists of a quale. Or so we claim. To illustrate: Galen Strawson has coined the expression "understanding-experience" to refer to the conscious experience of immediately comprehending the meaning of an utterance (Strawson 1994: 5–13). An understanding-experience, unlike a pain, does not possess a distinctive and proprietary feel, yet the utterance's meaning is as immediately evident or self-presented within experience as the sound of the words. Just compare, for instance, what it's like to understand an utterance, say, in your mother tongue, with what it's like to fail to comprehend an utterance in an alien tongue. Barry Dainton (2000: 12) puts Strawson's sort of linguistic note nicely. He writes that in hearing someone speak in his own language, "I do not hear [the] words as mere *sounds* at all"; "I hear meaningful words and sentences." He adds: "Meaning is as much a phenomenal feature of what I hear as the timbre and pitch of . . . voice."[5]

Those are six comments: six statements concerning just how we understand qualia and what we mean by qualia realism. So, let's restate QR with added details now drawn from those statements:

(QR*)   For every conscious mental state, there is something it is like to be in the conscious state or to undergo the conscious state. This phenomenal character is inseparably intentional as well as narrow and intrinsic. It may be spoken of as a state's "phenomenal intentionality." It is multidimensional, insofar as it includes various types of phenomenology, and it needs not consist of a distinctive and proprietary sensory feel (although it may).

QR* is complex. At the risk of multiplying complexity beyond descriptive necessity, two further comments are in order.

First, as part of our assumption of intrinsicness, we assume that for many properties and relations—including various sorts of spatiotemporal-location properties, shape-properties, size-properties, artifact-properties, and personhood-involving properties—successful mental reference to such properties and relations is wholly constituted by conscious experience or phenomenology alone. Even systematically *nonveridical* phenomenology, as would be the case of the experience of a high-tech brain-in-a-vat that mistakenly believes it is embodied and moving about in the external world, provides *reference-constituting direct or experiential acquaintance* with such properties and relations. It makes no difference to such acquaintance with such properties—and hence it makes no difference to mental *reference* to such properties—whether or not the properties are ever actually instantiated in one's surrounding environment (see Horgan, Tienson, and Graham 2005).

Second, the constitution of the self-presented or intrinsic character of phenomenally intentional states is affected by cognitive development and conceptual maturation. There are, for example, two loosely distinguishable ways in which concepts are embedded in phenomenal intentionality. On the one hand is conceptually thick phenomenal intentionality—the kind possessed by full-fledged, occurrently conscious, human mental states as in thoughts of retirement, intentions to write books, deliberations about marriage proposals, hopes for military withdrawals, and the like. This kind of intentionality requires considerable cognitive sophistication and cultural and linguistic scaffolding, and it is plausible that the conscious mental lives of nonhuman animals (absent special training, as in the case of sign-language-trained chimps) possess none of it. On the other hand is conceptually thin intentionality—the kind possessed, for instance, by the perceptual experiences of nonhuman animals and human infants in perceiving predators or recognizing a mother's voice. Cultural and linguistic scaffolding is not required for this sort of intentionality.

So, why favor qualia realism? Why believe that qualia of the sort described in QR* are real?

2 Qualia Realism Defended

Before we offer three arguments for qualia realism, something should be said about different ways of arguing for the position.

The most direct means of arguing for qualia realism is through an argument from introspection. Introspective argumentation is direct because our access to qualia, epistemically, is introspective. However, the relationship between introspection and qualia is a controversial one. There are two general types of controversy associated with the relationship, namely, (i) internal family disagreements among realists and (ii) disputes between realists and antirealists. Qualia realists sometimes challenge each other's descriptions of the deliverances of introspective evidence. Some realists, for example, say that qualia are sensory only; others (including ourselves) are much more generous in qualia-talk. Qualia antirealists (depending on their type) sometimes challenge realists to defend the reliability of introspection to decide questions about the real properties of conscious mental states.

Of our three arguments for qualia realism, only the first is essentially of the introspective sort. For purposes of that first argument (below) here is what we mean by referring to introspection. We take it that persons are introspectively aware of an experience or mental state when they notice or attend to it for the purpose of forming a non-inferential judgment or belief about it. This does not mean that one engages in two activities or processes, undergoing a mental state and attending to it, the way one inserts a thermometer into a hot loaf of baking bread and then reads its gauge. Introspection or introspective attention is a specific *way* of being in a first-order conscious state—not a distinct, perception-like, state that is intentionally directed toward the first-order state. It is a *manner of undergoing* the first-order state-type, namely, the introspectively attentive manner. One can feel pain, and one can do it attentively or with introspective concentration—that is, for example, focusing on where in one's body it feels most severe or whether the sensation is affected by the movement of one's limbs. We have conscious mental states, we can direct our attention to them, and we can form (second-order) beliefs and judgments about them.

Our first argument for qualia realism of the QR* sort we favor is *the argument from introspection*. It goes, very roughly, like this: Attend to your experience or stream of consciousness. Here is a general question about it: Do you find that there is something it is like for you to undergo experience, some quality or qualities that conscious mental states possess? For example, if you are having a visual experience, is it as if you see a bright red, round patch of paint on a wall before you? Is that what it is like? Or is it like something else entirely? We assume that each and every person will answer this general question in the affirmative. Yes, there is something it is like to undergo conscious experience.

Keep attending. Is the what-it's-likeness of conscious experience narrow, intrinsic, inseparably intentional and multidimensional, as QR* describes it? In answering this question consider the following. When you examine your own experience, does its manifest character hold good even if you are hallucinating or dreaming, and thus even if the experience is not veridical? It does, doesn't it? (Suppose, for example, you are not in front of a painted wall, but only dream of being so situated. Presumably, a direct appearance as of being in front of a painted wall would still be occurring, and would still have just the same intentional content, even in such dreamy circumstances.[6]) This means that qualia, conceived as the what-it's-likeness of experience, are not constituted by features of the external world but are narrow. Also, when you examine your own experience, isn't the content self-presented? You are not acquainted with the content indirectly via inference from something else, say, observations of your bodily movements. (You don't take yourself to perceive a painted wall because you appear to yourself to be reaching for a paint brush.) This shows that qualia are intrinsic. Also, we claim, experience is inseparably representational; as introspection reveals, it's *as if* you see through experience to something outside of it (e.g., a painted wall). Experiential contents are as of something (as of, e.g., paint on a wall before you). There is no significant distinction to be drawn (within the experience) between the character of your experience and the character of that aspect of the environment that is perceived. As for the multidimensionality of phenomenology, this, too, we take to be evident on introspection.

Consider, for just one brief example, the phenomenology of agency. As we are writing this chapter, each of us has sensed himself struggling to get the arguments right, thinking the problems through. When we stop for a break, sometimes it seems to require real effort to return to the task, as more and more cognitive resources need to be devoted to responding to criticisms and counterexamples (see Bayne and Levy 2006).

The argument from introspection, so tersely sketched above, has been offered by us elsewhere in different ways and for different purposes (see Horgan and Tienson 2002; Horgan, Tienson, and Graham 2003). It has not escaped criticism.

One criticism is that the deliverances of introspection seem to differ from person to person (judging from third-person introspective reports) and some persons fail to notice, or seem not to notice, any what-it's-likeness to nonsensory experiences (such as those of conscious propositional attitudes). The two of us claim to notice a what-it's-likeness of such experiences, and we are not alone.[7] However, other philosophers claim not (see Georgalis 2006; see also Wright 1996).

This criticism raises a Big Topic: What is introspection, what does it do, how does it work? And it is similar to a criticism that has been leveled against representationalism. This is that some persons, on introspection, report mental states that are nonrepresentational or devoid of intentional structure (diffuse moods, for example). Who's to say who is right? If we claim that introspection delivers one verdict (that phenomenal consciousness is representational or that it includes a phenomenology of nonsensory, non-emotional states), and another says that it expresses a contrary verdict, what is a theorist supposed to do with the evidence of introspection? Such issues are too complex to address here, so we need some warrant for qualia realism that does not presuppose that such questions about introspection have been adjudicated.

Besides which, the argument from introspection, sketched above, is apt to be regarded as question-begging against antirealists, who maintain that there are no qualia—period—and hence one never discerns qualia introspectively in sensory experience or otherwise. So, we turn next, very briefly, to two other arguments for qualia-realism, neither of which can be charged with question-begging or with presupposing that we know precisely how introspection works. Each makes appeal to data that even the antirealist should be willing to acknowledge (unlike the deliverances of introspection, which antirealists tend to regard as confabulation). In each case, our pro-qualia reasoning will take the form of an inference to the best explanation.

One is the *argument from suitably determinate conscious attitude-content* (see also Horgan, Tienson, and Graham 2006). It goes like this: Humans routinely believe of their own first-order beliefs, thoughts, and other intentional mental states, and believe with great confidence, that these states have determinate content; and they form equally confident higher-order beliefs about what the specific content is of these first-order mental states.[8] That people hold such higher-order beliefs, and hold them with great confidence, is an empirical datum.

Now ask: What best explains these higher-order beliefs, as well as the extreme confidence with which they are held? All else equal, the best explanation will be one that vindicates the beliefs, rather than debunks them. After all, it is virtually impossible, psychologically, *not* to form such beliefs—which would make it especially worrisome if they should turn out to be massively or categorically false. However, in addition, the best explanation will also have the following feature, all else equal: it will vindicate as epistemically appropriate the extreme confidence with which those second-order beliefs are held—rather than treating such confidence as epistemically rash and excessive.

What kind of explanation could fill this compound bill? Certainly there are philosophers, in recent and current philosophy of mind, who believe that there is a way to secure determinate mental intentionality without appeal to phenomenology. Various nonphenomenological approaches on the current menu—most of them strongly externalist in spirit—include (i) causal theories of content that find the necessary connection in the causal antecedents of the state; (ii) covariational theories that find the connection in certain kinds of systematic correlations between occurrences of an internal state and occurrences of an external state of affairs; (iii) teleosemantic theories that look to environmentally situated proper functions that certain internal states possess in virtue of evolutionary design; and

(iv) learning-based theories that invoke internal adaptational changes in the creature's own history. (See Stich and Warfield 1994 for a representative sample of such theories. See also Adams 2003.)

But the big trouble with such approaches is the looming epistemic possibility that they will fail to ground suitably *determinate* mental intentionality, and instead will end up rendering human mental states radically indeterminate in intentional content. Philosophical arguments to the effect that such nonphenomenological resources cannot escape radical indeterminacy are well known, and have been propounded by some philosophical heavy-hitters: for example, Quine's (1960) global-interpretationist arguments for the radical indeterminacy of translation and mental content; Putnam's (e.g., 1981) model-theoretic argument against any privileged unique assignment of content to sentences and thoughts; and Kripke's (1982) rendering of Wittgenstein on meaning and private language. Furthermore, potential susceptibility to radical content-indeterminacy is not merely a *bare* epistemic possibility in light of the lately mentioned approaches to mental content; on the contrary, it is an all-too-genuine possibility. And this, in turn, has the following epistemological consequence: even if some nonphenomenological account of mental content happens to be correct, and even if it happens to deliver determinate content and fend off the indeterminacy worry, nevertheless people's current extremely confident higher-order beliefs about content determinacy would then be vastly *too* confident, from an epistemological point of view. Obviously a potentially bewildering array of causal or externalistic relations would be relevant to the nonphenomenological account of content determinacy. It's hard to see how the presence of such relations (especially since their role in content determination would be unknown to typical subjects) could warrant the confidence that we persons have in what our mental states are about.

Is there, then, a different kind of account of what constitutes or is responsible for suitable determinacy in conscious content—an account that not only vindicates the well-nigh-unavoidable belief in determinate mental content, but also vindicates the overwhelmingly high confidence that typically attaches to such belief? We claim that when one surveys the theoretical possibilities for what may be called a *conscious-content determinator*—that is, for something that confers determinate content, and does so in a way that underwrites people's enormous confidence about the content of their own first-order intentional mental states—one and only one candidate truly fits the bill. This is phenomenal intentional content, which is self-presented to the subject in the way that only phenomenal character can be. My conscious belief is that of a crooked picture, say, and not that of a chair; this is the content that presents itself to me as experiencing subject. It is the content with which I am experientially acquainted, and which I confidently report when I say what I'm thinking.

If this proposal is right, then not only do intentional mental states really possess determinate content—and normally the very content that the experiencing agent attributes to them, when forming second-order beliefs about their content—but the experiencing agent is enormously well justified in attributing this specific content to them. The source of this exceptional justification is the self-presentational nature of phenomenal consciousness: self-presentation closes the otherwise ubiquitous "epistemic gap" between appearance and reality. Thus, qualia realism evidently provides the best explanation of the target-datum, namely, people's enormously high confidence in the content determinacy of their own mental states, and in their beliefs about what that content is.[9]

A third argument for qualia realism is the *argument from the inconceivability of radical error about one's current conscious mentality*. It goes like this. People have little trouble conceiving of possible scenarios in which their mental life is the just the same as in actuality, but in which their world-directed beliefs and other externally directed mental states are radically nonveridical in content. As potential knowing agents, we may be epistemically cut off from the world (as Descartes warned). One may, for example, be a brain in a vat, mentally representing a putative world in which one seems to oneself to be moving about, when one is not moving at all. Or one may be undergoing systematically nonveridical experiences caused by an Evil Demon. Such hypothetical possibilities grip the epistemic imagination as intelligible and coherent.

What, however, about conceiving of possible scenarios in which one's mental life is just the same as in actuality, but in which one's beliefs about one's current mental life (these would be second-order beliefs since they are directed at one's first-order mentality) are radically nonveridical in content? Can one successfully conceive of a scenario in which one's second-order beliefs about the content of one's own conscious occurrent mental states are radically mistaken? Suppose, for instance, that you believe of yourself that you are currently having a conscious visual experience as of a round, red sphere positioned on a flat red surface. Can you successfully conceive of a scenario in which (i) your conscious mental life is just the same as it currently is, but (ii) you are *not* having (as you believe you are having) a conscious visual experience as of a round, red sphere positioned on a flat red surface? The answer, we submit, is no. External world skepticism can get a psychological grip on one's epistemic imagination, but analogous internal world skepticism grains no epistemic traction.

Our "can you" question can be put another way, a third-person way that focuses on what persons *say* about their experience, rather than a first-person way that appeals to one's own introspective take on one's own mental life. If people are *asked* whether or not they can conceive of the sort of the internal world skeptical scenario just described, what will they say? The answer, we predict, is that they will say "No"—and this will be a robust result, across the vast majority of subjects in a well-conducted survey. Thus, the data to be explained can be characterized, in Dennett's terminology, as "heterophenomenological," that is, as about people's self-monitoring *reports* or judgments.[10]

Now, the psychological or imaginative inability to conceive of such a nonveridicality scenario—or, at the very least, the predicted robust pattern of *reports* of such inconceivability—is a datum that calls out for explanation. And, we claim, for those who deny qualia realism, this is a daunting task—a task not typically appreciated. Suppose, for example, that one holds that there are no qualia. One is a qualia antirealist. Suppose furthermore that for a (first-order) mental state to be conscious (for the antirealist) just is for that state to belong to the class C of mental states within the cognitive agent, such that the agent's neural cognitive architecture has the causal capacity, in normal circumstances, to non-inferentially generate reliable second-order beliefs or judgments about the presence of, and the contents of, the mental states in C. Well then, why shouldn't it be possible to conceive of *abnormal* circumstances in which the architecture generates radically nonveridical second-order beliefs? Shouldn't there be some suitable analogue, for such beliefs, of abnormal circumstances (e.g., being an envatted brain) in which one's normally reliable perceptual systems generate radically nonveridical perceptual experiences?

If one supposes that there are no qualia, that is, no features of one's mental life that are both intrinsic and self-presenting, what's to explain the difficulty we have in imagining that those beliefs are radically false? By contrast, qualia realism can provide the needed explanation of that datum. Here it is: People are unable to conceive that they are mistaken in their beliefs about the current character of their conscious experience because (i) it is *phenomenal* character; (ii) it thus is intrinsic and self-presenting; and (iii) it functions in the relevant second-order belief as a self-presenting, content-determining, *mode of presentation* of the first-order psychological state that the belief is about. The phenomenal character of the first-order state is a constitutive or indispensable element in the second-order belief.

So, there is no epistemic space between the experience (say, an experience of a red sphere on a flat red surface) and what is believed about what is being experienced (say, that one is having an experience of a red sphere on a flat red surface). Conscious mentality possesses qualia, and qualia are self-presenting modes of presentation. Qualia wear their content on their introspectively manifest sleeve, in such a way that what you introspect about the content of your first-order mental states is, essentially, how they are (see Horgan, Tienson, and Graham 2006, for more detailed discussion of this and related points). Qualia realism thus provides an explanation for the data here that are in need of explanation; by contrast, antirealism seems not to possess an explanation. Remember: This is data that can be conceived as heterophenomenological to avoid, if one wishes, the kind of direct appeal to introspection that antirealists like Dennett consider question-begging against themselves. (Persons would judge, we predict, that they cannot doubt their own beliefs about the conscious content of their own first-order occurrent mental states.)

"Please give me the argument, based on premises that we can all accept," Dennett (2005: 113) has pleaded of realists (specifically, of us) that in effect qualia are real. Well, we think that we have done just that with the argument from inconceivability.

We conclude: Qualia realism is true. Or at least, given the three arguments we have offered, one has excellent reason to believe that qualia do exist.

Notes

1. Over the years in philosophy of mind, there have been many philosophers who are "separatists," in this sense: they maintain that only some, but not all, access-conscious mental states are also phenomenally conscious. For example, some have held that qualia accrue only to *sensory* experiential states likes tastes, pains, and visual color-experiences (and perhaps also to mental images of such states), and not to states like access-conscious thoughts. Qualia realism, as we are characterizing it in this paper, is thoroughly nonseparatist. We do acknowledge for the record, however, that one could be both separatist about qualia and a realist about whatever qualia one recognizes (e.g., sensory qualia). Also, we use the locution "phenomenally conscious" to pick out those mental states that possess qualia and since, for us, states that possess qualia include nonsensory states, we do not restrict the class of the phenomenal to the class of the sensory experiential states.

2. Aren't there counterexamples (such as diffuse moods, under one construal) to the claim that consciousness is inseparably intentional? We cannot examine the

possibility of such counterexamples here. (See e.g. Graham, Horgan, and Tienson 2007). We shall say simply that if there are counterexamples, they are few and far between and do not affect the main points of this essay, which is not devoted to defending the essential or inseparable intentionality or representationality of phenomenal consciousness, but to defending the reality of qualia (even if construed somewhat more narrowly or more restrictively than we do).

3. Here is a good place to acknowledge our debt to John Tienson for co-development of some of the ideas used in this essay, that of phenomenal intentionality foremost. We should also mention that we are not alone in using the phrase "phenomenal intentionality." A number of other philosophers, including Brian Loar, Colin McGinn, and Uriah Kriegel, use the phrase. We don't have space here to compare and contrast such uses with ours.

4. Can conscious states occur in which the subject of consciousness is not aware of itself as modified in any way whatsoever? And: Can conscious states occur without a subject, period? (These could be qualia without a minded creature, full stop.) We take no stand on such questions here. For discussion of the first, see Kriegel 2004. For discussion of the second question, see Kennedy and Graham 2007.

5. Dainton's and Strawson's point has to be understood in a proper way. They are not claiming that another's speech (in one's own language) lacks auditory qualities (or else it would not be heard). They are claiming that the speech sounds as heard are inherently infused with comprehensibility.

6. The phenomenally constituted intentionality of the experience would be a matter of *purporting* to refer to a wall. Whether the experience *actually* refers to any object—and if so, which object—constitutively depends not just on the experience's intrinsic phenomenal character, but also partly on matters externalistic.

7. The list of those who agree with us that occurrent tokens of conscious attitudes possess introspectively accessible qualia or phenomenal features (that are distinctive of and proprietary to them) includes Flanagan (1992), Goldman (1993), Strawson (1994), and Pitt (2004), among others.

8. Assumption of content determinacy is important for purposes of psychological explanation. Actions are explained, in part, by reference to beliefs and desires with specific contents rather than others.

9. One short note about the notion of content determinacy being deployed in the second argument: What might, on occasion or depending on the case, be determinate phenomenologically is that the content is (in certain respects) indeterminate. Suppose I form a mental picture of a tiger. No specific number of stripes may be represented in the experience.

10. Dennett asks: "[I]s there some privileged subset [of activity] that anchors qualia?" (2005: 100). He answers no, dismissing qualia on grounds that without

an anchor, without tell-tale evidence of their presence, there is no good reason to believe that they exist. Just what Dennett has in mind as anchor or test is restrictive, for he does not permit anything introspective or first-personal to count as evidence. He writes that first-person (in his terms, autophenomenological) evidence "will either collapse into heterophenomenlogy" (third-person evidence), "or else manifest an unacceptable bias in its initial assumptions" (2005: 56). Here, in the body of the essay, we are arguing that there are certain third-person data that are best explained by assuming that qualia realism is true.

References

Adams, F. 2003. Thoughts and their contents: Naturalized semantics. In *The Blackwell Guide to the Philosophy of Mind*, ed. S. Stich and T. Warfield, 143–171. Malden, Mass.: Blackwell.

Bayne, T., and N. Levy. 2006. The feeling of doing: Deconstructing the phenomenology of agency. In *Disorders of Volition*, ed. N. Sebanz and W. Prinz, 49–68. Cambridge, Mass.: MIT Press/A Bradford Book.

Block, N. 1995. On a confusion about a function of consciousness. *Behavioral and Brain Sciences* 18: 227–247.

Crane, T. 2001. The origins of qualia. In *History of the Mind–Body Problem*, ed. T. Crane and S. Patterson, 169–194. London: Routledge.

Dainton, B. 2000. *Stream of Consciousness: Unity and Continuity in Conscious Experience*. London: Routledge.

Dennett, D. 2005. *Sweet Dreams: Philosophical Obstacles to a Science of Consciousness*. Cambridge, Mass.: MIT Press/A Bradford Book.

Dretske, F. 1995. *Naturalizing the Mind*. Cambridge, Mass.: MIT Press/A Bradford Book.

Flanagan, O. 1992. *Consciousness Reconsidered*. Cambridge: Mass.: MIT Press/A Bradford Book.

Georgalis, N. 2006. *The Primacy of the Subjective: Foundations for a Unified Theory of Mind and Language*. Cambridge, Mass.: MIT Press/A Bradford Book.

Goldman, A. 1993. Consciousness, folk psychology, and cognitive science. *Consciousness and Cognition* 2: 364–382.

Goldman, A. 2006. *Simulating Minds: The Philosophy, Psychology, and Neuroscience of Mindreading*. Oxford: Oxford University Press.

Graham, G. 2004. Self-ascription: Thought insertion. In *Philosophy of Psychiatry: A Companion*, ed. J. Radden, 89–105. Oxford: Oxford University Press.

Graham, G., and T. Horgan. 2000. Mary Mary, quite contrary. *Philosophical Studies* 99: 59–87.

Graham, G., and T. Horgan. 2002. Sensations and brain processes. In *Consciousness Evolving*, ed. J. Fetzer, 63–86. Amsterdam: John Benjamins.

Graham, G., and T. Horgan. 2005. Mary Mary *au contraire*: A reply to Raffman. *Philosophical Studies* 122: 203–212.

Graham, G., T. Horgan, and J. Tienson. 2007. Consciousness and intentionality. In *The Blackwell Companion to Consciousness*, ed. S. Scheider and M. Velmans. Malden, Mass.: Blackwell.

Harman, G. 1990. The intrinsic quality of experience. In *Philosophical Perspectives 4: Action Theory and the Philosophy of Mind*, ed. J. Tomberlin, 31–52. Atascdero, Calif.: Ridgeview.

Horgan, T., and J. Tienson. 2001. Deconstructing new wave materialism. In *Physicalism and Its Discontents*, ed. C. Gillett and B. Loewer, 307–318. Cambridge: Cambridge University Press.

Horgan, T., and J. Tienson. 2002. The phenomenology of intentionality and the intentionality of phenomenology. In *Philosophy of Mind: Classical and Contemporary Readings*, ed. D. Chalmers, 520–533. Oxford: Oxford University Press.

Horgan, T., J. Tienson, and G. Graham. 2003. The phenomenology of first person agency. In *Physicalism and Mental Causation: The Metaphysics of Mind and Action*, ed. S. Walter and H.-D. Heckmann, 323–340. Exeter: Imprint Academic.

Horgan, T., J. Tienson, and G. Graham. 2005. Phenomenal intentionality and the brain in a vat. In *The Externalist Challenge: New Studies in Cognition and Intentionality*, ed. R. Schantz, 297–317. Berlin, New York: de Gruyter.

Horgan, T., J. Tienson, and G. Graham. 2006. Internal-world skepticism and the self-presentational nature of phenomenology. In *Consciousness and Self-Representation*, ed. U. Kriegel and K. Williford, 41–61. Cambridge, Mass.: MIT Press/A Bradford Book.

Jackson, F. 1982. Epiphenomenal qualia. *Philosophical Quarterly* 32: 27–36.

Kennedy, R., and G. Graham. 2007. Extreme self-denial. In *Cartographies of the Mind*, ed. M. Marrafa, M. DeCaro, and F. Ferretti. Dordrecht: Springer.

Kriegel, U. 2004. Consciousness and self-consciousness. *Monist* 87: 185–209.

Kripke, S. 1982. *Wittgenstein on Rules and Private Language*. Cambridge, Mass.: Harvard University Press.

Pitt, D. 2004. The phenomenology of cognition, or What it is like to think that *p*. *Philosophy and Phenomenological Research* 69: 1–36.

Putnam, H. 1981. *Reason, Truth, and History*. Cambridge: Cambridge University Press.

Quine, W. V. O. 1960. *Word and Object*. Cambridge, Mass.: MIT Press.

Raffman, D. 2005. Even zombies can be surprised: A reply to Graham and Horgan. *Philosophical Studies* 122: 189–202.

Stephens, G. L., and G. Graham. 2000. *When Self-Consciousness Breaks: Alien Voices and Inserted Thoughts*. Cambridge, Mass.: MIT Press/A Bradford Book.

Stephens, G. L., and G. Graham. 2007. Philosophical psychopathology and self-consciousness. In *The Blackwell Companion to Consciousness*, ed. S. Schneider and M. Vellmans. Malden, Mass.: Blackwell.

Stich, S., and T. Warfield, eds. 1994. *Mental Representation: A Reader*. Oxford: Blackwell.

Strawson, G. 1994. *Mental Reality*. Cambridge, Mass.: MIT Press/A Bradford Book.

Tye, M. 1995. *Ten Problems of Consciousness: A Representational Theory of the Phenomenal Mind*. Cambridge, Mass.: MIT Press/A Bradford Book.

Wright, E. 1996. What it isn't like. *American Philosophical Quarterly* 23: 23–45.

5   The World of Qualia

Matjaž Potrč

1   Qualia May Well Be the Cement of the Experiential World

What is the role of qualia? The relation of qualia to the physical world remains unclear. In the following, our considerations will be limited to the *experiential* world, and it will be argued that qualia may well be whatever helps to hold such a world together. The experiential world, consisting of conscious experiences, is made up of intentional contents and total cognitive states (TCSs)[1] involving these contents. One question, then, is how several TCSs come together. An often proposed answer is that this succeeds by the involvement of inferential rules in transitions between cognitive states. For a striking example, just tell a child that she is brave and that whoever is brave deserves chocolate, but that she, despite of being brave, will not get it. The child will vehemently protest, thereby displaying her tacit mastery of inferential reasoning.

Sharpening Qualia

Here is a plausible-sounding thesis to start with:

(S)   Qualia sharpen up intentional content.

The thesis is plausible if we consider examples of qualitative or phenomenological experiences.[2] These experiences aim at something specific, and they tie the smelling, tasting, hearing, seeing, or one's acting, to a precise moment in time, to a certain place, and above all to the unique specificity of subjective experience. In this manner we can talk about sharpening as exercised by qualitative experiences.

The following picture offers itself as an illustration. Let us suppose that you entertain the content concerning the cat, the intentional content "cat." Now imagine again that you add to this content the qualitative feeling or the phenomenological experiential specificity that goes along with the content "cat." It certainly seems that in such a case of adding the quale to the intentional content, the content gets *sharpened up*. The content that was somehow undetermined becomes specific, and it obtains a quality that wasn't previously there. You may grasp what this sharpening means if you compare the difference between the qualitative feel related to your thinking about the cat with the qualitative feeling of thinking about a spider. The quality of your experience will change from one case to the other, in stark contrast to the supposed situation where there may be content without any quality. Notice also that qualitative sharpening proceeds along the change in propositional attitude: the qualitative feel related to your being angry at the cat is different from your qualitative experience of desiring a cat or just thinking about it.

Original Intertwinedness

The above thesis S seems plausible, for it is built on the mentioned cases of qualia and on their characteristic sharpening of things along several involved parameters. The rest of this short exercise, however, will try to show that S is misguided. Sharpening, according to S, as specifying parameters such as time and space, is actually just a caricature used against atomism (items such as contents are treated in the manner of isolated building blocks) and separatism (qualia are separate from intentional content, not connected with it). The disputed point is that S presupposes a piecemeal atomistic tinkering, according to which there is first an intentional content that exists in an independent and detached manner, and then there are qualia that are added to this content and that exercise an effect on it, such as sharpening the previously indeterminate content. This picture is disputed by the qualitative intentionality (QI) and the intentionality of qualia (IQ) theses:

Qualitative intentionality   Mental states of the sort commonly cited as paradigmatically intentional (e.g., cognitive states such as beliefs, and conative states such as desires), when conscious, have qualitative character that is inseparable from their intentional content.

The intentionality of qualia   Mental states of the sort commonly cited as paradigmatically qualitative (e.g., sensory-experiential states such as color-experience, itches and smells) have intentional content that is inseparable from their qualitative character. (Horgan and Tienson 2002: 521)[3]

According to this, intentional states *already* have qualia constitutively built into them in order to be able to function at all. And similarly, each qualitative feel is constitutively intentionally directed (at the contextual background space of the subject[4]).

The claim here is not just that the conjunction of these, QI & IQ, is right in respect to the thesis S and that it trumps it. The claim is also that the lesson of QI & IQ needs to be extended along several consecutive steps until it encompasses the whole of the world. The (QI & IQ)-inspired and generalized claim is that of *original intertwinedness*:

(OI)   In the experiential world, several dimensions (intentionality, qualia, context, background) are originally intertwined from the very start.

The context and the background may offer separate steps for us to gradually reach the ultimate full state of the OI thesis that involves the world. But in doing so we provisionally continue to assume that each of the involved steps adds something to the supposedly previously existing detached state, which is actually in contrast to the spirit of the OI thesis.

Dynamical Cognition and Morphological Content

We began our exercise with the thesis of QI & IQ, expanding it to the broader OI thesis of original intertwinedness. This is a shift from local intertwining to holistically inclined overall intertwining. The cognitive model we would like to have is holistic and dynamical, allowing for efficiency of non-explicit strata.

There is such a model available, the dynamical cognition (DC) model (Horgan and Tienson 1996). DC is proposed with the intent to improve some insufficiencies of classical cognitive models, such as the language of thought (LOT; Fodor 1975). Classical LOT presumes the efficiency of general exceptionless rules in guiding cognitive transitions, thereby offering the allegedly only available way to get the needed syntactic structure. The DC model opposes this, claiming that it is perfectly possible to reach the desired syntactical structure using nonclassical multidimensional dynamics, inspired by connectionist cognitive models. The road to this direction is paved by the shortcomings of those general exceptionless rules used by the classical cognitive models, exhibited by the frame problem. The frame problem arises when one tries to achieve relevance on the basis of cognitive processing guided by general exceptionless rules. The reasoning from here goes like this: But the actually existing cognitive systems do achieve relevant behavior in an effortless manner, on a massive scale. Thus, these cognitive systems must be guided in ways other than by general exceptionless rules. A connectionism-inspired model offers such a proposal via its dynamical landscape, where the positioning of TCSs succeeds not in accordance with an algorithm, but in agreement with the activity of forces that are effective in the virtual dynamical multidimensional landscape of the cognitive system. Such a system may well achieve a syntactical structure, but not on the basis of exceptionless general rules; rather, it achieves such structure on the basis of dynamical forces that position representations or TCSs within the landscape.

There is a kind of content active in such positioning that is inherent to subtle transitions operating in dynamical systems, so-called *morphological content* (MC). This is not the occurrent content, but the content residing in the memory of the landscape; it is "in the weights" of the system, to use the connectionist expression. The name "morphological content" comes from the shape of the landscape. Examples of MC include content inherent in the process of *getting* a joke (as opposed to explicit content of a pun) and the specific accent coloring my English talk. MC has something to do with the background of one's cognitive system.

DC and MC naturally invite a more integrated picture of qualia than is the case for classicism, with its leanings toward separatism. If exceptionless general rules guide transitions of representations, qualia are left over as something additional to the picture. If DC and MC deliver the picture of cognition, then the very positioning of TCSs seems to be more inherently tied to the dynamics of the cognitive system and to its background. MC is not identical to qualia. But on the other hand, the positioning of cognitive content within the dynamical landscape involving DC seems to have some affinity with the quality that comes along inherently with a certain representational intentional state. It is somehow natural to presume that qualia are effects of the contents' positioning. This also explains their intertwinedness with the intentional content, and further with the cognitive background. This idea leads naturally to the picture of OI: several dimensions are there from the very start. The cognitive background may then be seen as the context of qualia.

This also gives an answer in the direction of the argument here pursued and soon to be spelled out. QI & IQ already introduces the intertwinedness of qualia and intentional contents. But they may still be treated atomistically. Because of the inadequacy of cognitive classicism, it is plausible to appropriate a DC- and MC-inspired view. This picture involves holism and naturally underscores the OI thesis. It is further plausible to suppose that transitions in the dynamical background landscape of the cognitive system also support qualia, for some certain quality must be inherent to the positioning of TCSs. In the experiential world, though, this quality may then have the role of cement: qualia stemming from background cognitive transitions are what holds the experiences (TCSs with their content) together.

The World Is Already There

We now shift from talk of the cognitive system to talk of the world. If the world is interpreted in a narrow sense, these two systems may be in agreement. The point of the OI thesis is that your experiences, including your qualitative experiences, include the background, that is the world—from the very start.

Our experiences do not present to us contents, or even context, as completely separated from the background or from the world. The richness of the world is already there, with all its dynamics and intertwinedness. The background has earlier been recognized as the world (the experiential being-in-the-world) and as that which enables intentional directedness (Searle 1983).

The result of the discussion up until now is that the OI thesis should be taken as broadly as possible. The background, or the world, is already there, and it involves qualia in a constitutive manner. The background as the world is thus *already* sharp: once it is there, it does not come without qualia. This is the hermeneutic circle: our experiences are enabled by the preliminary existence of the horizon on the basis of which they succeed. And yet the background imposes its qualitative features on each particular occasion of experience.

The Experiential World Is Brain-in-a-Vat Compatible

As we talk about the background as the world, the plausible-sounding hypothesis is indeed that we are aiming at the *experiential* world. Such an experiential world is compatible with the world of the brain in a vat (BIV). A BIV, we will recall, has all the experiences one might wish for. She experiences all the intentional contents, qualities, and the background in an irreducibly intertwined manner, along the guidelines of OI. She experiences her body and her actions. The BIV has the whole world indeed. You can understand this easily by noticing that BIV has the world, experiences the world, just in the same manner as you do—if it is plausible that you have difficulties demonstrating that you are *not* a BIV. The setting of the BIV is a counterfactual scenario figuring a possible situation of your brain being separated from your body and constantly fed a private movie show to its neural inputs, featuring exactly the situation you find yourself in at this very moment. The experiential world of the BIV includes the background with all the sharp qualia, just in the same manner as does your actual experiential world. Narrowness of phenomenology means that the experiential world does not depend on the external world (Horgan and Tienson 2002). Yes, we are correct to notice that none of the BIV's statements about her world are true. But there is still lot that a BIV may know about her experiences.

Qualia Are the Cement of the Experiential World

It would be a much too pretentious thing to say something definitive here about the nature of the mind- and language-independent world. This is why again I would like to stress that the discussion is limited to the experiential world.

Our very first hypothesis about qualia, S, was that they are in the business of sharpening up things. And indeed, qualia do provide a feeling of situatedness in our world. Qualia, according to the generalized OI thesis, involve relevance in the rich holistic world; they involve the simultaneous existence of the world.[5]

Now if the expanded or generalized thesis OI is right, then the following may hold as well:

(C)   Qualia are the *cement* of the experiential world.

This thesis bets that qualia are not in the background accidentally, but *constitutively* so. They hold the experiential world together, first because they are inherent to the intentional acts. But besides this, transitions between TCSs are enabled by the shape of the background suitable for the DC and MC models of cognition. In the experiential world, qualia inherent to the background hold items together. This fact is not sufficiently appreciated. In discussions involving the experiential world, it tends to be screened off by a misguided understanding that only causality can fulfill the cement-providing role.

Dynamical Cognition and the Language of Thought

Remember the child who protested because she was denied the deserved chocolate, thereby exposing her mastery of inferential reasoning? Inferential transitions between TCSs were proposed as basic by the classical LOT cognitive model. The role of qualia is not easy to come by according to such a picture; it gets somehow screened off, and this is understandable given that propositional inferential roles are placed at the center of attention.

One does not need to abandon inferential relations between TCSs though; one can even retain a version of LOT, and also get a clearer account of qualia into the picture. This may be achieved by appropriating DC. In opposition to the classical model of cognition this picture does not postulate general exceptionless inferential rules supporting transitions between

TCSs. Transitions between representations are enabled by their positioning within the dynamical cognitive background. On examination, it will come to one's attention that the forces operating in this background may well have something to do with qualia—at least, they do not exclude them so readily from the picture as does classical LOT. Classical models of mind build on the almost exclusive role of propositional-style inferences for TCS transitions. This focus tends to separate qualia from the mentioned transitions and, before this, from any involvement with a single intentional content.

In order to oppose separatism—the view that qualia are separated from or are just additions to TCSs—one is invited to proceed along the already indicated two steps. First, one affirms the intertwinedness of TCSs and of qualia on both counts: TCSs are inherently qualitative, and qualia are inherently directed, perhaps at the experiential space. Second, one has to introduce the DC model, with the hope that it supports the picture of intertwining.

1. Qualitative intentionality and intentional quality theses (QI & IQ)
2. Dynamical cognition and morphological content theses (DC & MC)

The first premise affirms the inherent intertwinedness of TCSs with qualitative experiences. Traditionally, TCSs have been treated in an isolated and atomistic manner as intentional states and as their contents. So, the content of the TCS figuring the cat on the mat is the intentional state figuring a cat on the mat. Premise 1 now affirms the inherent involvement of qualia in intentional contents, and the inherent intentional directedness of qualia, or its directedness at the intentional space.

The second premise states the precondition, in the cognitive model, of the intertwinedness of TCSs (content-endowed intentional states) with qualia or qualitative states. In order to counter separatism between intentional states and qualia, a dynamical model of cognition needs to support transitions between TCSs. DC builds on a rich multidimensional cognitive background, with the recognition of a kind of content that operates on the landscape of the background—of the MC.

Notice that the very expression "intentional content" tends to be understood in an atomist and separatist manner: as coming in a lonely desperate search for a hook-up with other items of its kin, and as unrelated in this to qualia. The expression TCS, on the other hand, is best understood as involving both intentional content and qualia—for this is what a cognitive state upholds in its totality.

One affirms the intertwinedness of intentional contents with qualia (premise 1) and their support from the part of the dynamical picture of cognition involving MC that inhabits its dynamical multidimensional space (premise 2). This then shows qualia—coming along with the positioning of TCSs—figuring as whatever holds the totality of TCSs together, as the cement of the experiential world. Therefore:

Qualia could be the cement of the experiential world.

Some words are in order to summarize what supports the premises. Although the intertwinedness thesis gives more plausible place to qualia than separatism, this can be further improved by the involvement of holistic DC together with MC. The QI & IQ thesis can still be understood in an atomistic manner. Only through the (DC & MC)-supported intertwinedness thesis (which involves Quinean and isotropic properties of a system) is one led to the conclusion that qualia could be the cohesive support of experiences. Bringing both theses (QI *and* DC) together allows for a new account of the role of qualia: the holistic background makes it plausible that qualia could act as the cement of experiential world.

If qualia would exist separate from intentional content, they would have no cohesive force. Being entangled with it, as thesis QI & IQ claims, makes them candidates for the cement of the experiential world. Qualia are inherent in TCS transitions that succeed as supported by the DC & MC. In the *experiential* world, qualia—and not the background itself—hold together both single TCSs and transitions between these. Here is summary of the proposed reasoning: If one takes seriously QI & IQ, and if one also accepts the holistic, MC-inspired picture of DC, then it follows that qualia could well be the cement of the experiential world.

Why is the conclusion so weak? We started with the OI thesis as opposed to the S thesis. This sounds sensible, for sharpening is already phenomenologically supported, and everybody thinks that the experiential world is intertwined with content. The argument underpins the reasoning that there are many dimensions to the experiential world. First, QI & IQ accounts for individual experiences; then the relation between experiences—providing an answer to the question of how these experiences may be linked and intertwined—is settled by DC & MC. The conclusion now asks what holds this experiential world together, what is the glue of OI; and an acceptable answer is that perhaps qualitative experiences hold the experiential world together. As this is just a working hypothesis, it is stated in a weak form. Here follows discussion of some mechanisms that would allow qualia to play the indicated role.

2   Qualitative Cement

A general theory about the possibility of qualia being the cement of the experiential world can be further spelled out by considering the QI thesis and the phenomenon of infallibility as the epistemic consequence of qualia's nature. We will now look at the question of whether qualia's cohesive role for experiences has been noticed. The answer is that others have indeed acknowledged this role for qualia, both in cases of intentional states and knowledge.

Qualitative Intentionality as Cement

The qualitative intentionality thesis, QI, was introduced by Brentano (1981) in roughly the following way. Suppose that I think about a cat. In this case, I am directed at the intentional content (or at the intentional object) cat.

I → cat
(Intentional relation)

Now, at the same time as I am intentionally directed at the cat (notice by the way that this relation may perfectly well be narrow), I am also reflexively directed at my own act of experience. I can now say that I am reflexively directed at my act of directedness toward an object or content. Let us use the sign "@" for this kind of reflexive pointing back to the act of directedness:

@
I → cat
(Intentional relation)

The reflexive act of being directed at the act of intentional directedness may be called *awareness*. This inner awareness, or consciousness, according to Brentano's understanding, is not just contingently there in the act of intentional directedness; it is substantially and constitutively there.

This would then be a case of the QI thesis, if @ is to be understood as the quale or phenomenological state (i.e., it is the reflexive awareness or consciousness). But we wish to claim something in addition to this, namely that if @ is really a kind of quale, it plays the role of *cement* in this case, namely the role of *holding* a specific intentional cognitive act *together*—not only making it compact, but enabling it. The reflexive @ has then a cohesive function in respect to a specific experience of intentional directedness.

This reflexive quality as the cement of the intentional act is empha-
sized by Brentano. Consciousness, in this sense, is the precondition for
specific experiences. In Brentano talk, there is a twofold energy to psychical phenomena:

> Each act, whilst directed towards an object is at the same time and besides this
> directed toward itself. Being presented with a "primary object," e.g., a sound, we
> are aware of being presented with something. A psychological phenomenon as such
> always includes the consciousness of itself as the "secondary object of perception."
> As certain as it is that no consciousness ever is without an intentional relation, so
> it is certain for Brentano that the consciousness also, besides its object of primary
> relation, has itself as a secondary object. This secondary inner perception is a true,
> self-referential, evident perception in the strict sense. (Baumgartner 1996: 32)

The reflexive act of consciousness or "inner perception" plays the role of
cement for the intentional act: without it, this act would not hold together,
it would not be real.

It should be noticed that the very positioning of the question—Do
intentional states have qualia holding them together?—is superseded if
we counter the separatist inclination and instead talk of the TCSs of a
cognitive system. For such cognitive states will typically include both the
intentional content *and* qualia from the very start, according to the OI
thesis.

We have just taken reflexive consciousness to equal or involve qualitative "what-it's-like" experiences. This needs some arguing. Let us look
again at the phenomenon of qualitative intentionality. First, there is an
intentional relation here, directedness at a content or at an object. And
together with this, there comes awareness or reflexive consciousness. This
means that consciousness, besides to being directed at content or at an
object, is also directed at itself. Now according to the QI thesis, the entire
act of intentional directedness is qualitative; it comes endowed with the
what-it's-like quality of experiences. But where does this quality come
from? On the one hand, it certainly is influenced by the involved content
or object. The thought about the cat will probably have a quality distinct
from that of a thought involving a spider. But quality cannot arrive at the
content exclusively from a direct intentional relation. For all that we know,
such a relation could well be causal or covariational, in which case there is
no experiential quality tied to it. On the other hand, reflexive consciousness or awareness is a good candidate for the habitat of qualia. As I think
about the cat, the quality that accompanies the intentional directedness
has its source in my awareness or in my reflexive consciousness involving
such direction. In fact, it presents the quality of my being directed toward

the content. Qualia are then inherent in reflexive consciousness, for this is the appropriate place to put them in the overall intentional act. But are qualia also involved with awareness or reflexive consciousness? In order to answer this question, we will have to look at the nature of awareness or reflexive consciousness. The reflexive consciousness that comes with my cat-related thought—and this is the kind of setting that we deal with—does not center on myself. If it would, then we would have another thought, one having myself and not the cat as its object. Reflexive consciousness or inner awareness goes together with the cat-related thought by being built into its experience, peripherally, and is constitutive of its quality. But what is actually built into intentional experiences and peripheral to them in the sense that it is not their focus but still constitutive of them? In the experiential dimension, this could only be qualia. So, for intentional acts, the role of reflexive consciousness or intentional awareness is identical to, or necessarily involves, qualia. States of reflexive consciousness or qualia are built into the intentional relation and yet they are peripheral: the focus is not on them. It is hard to see what other role inner awareness or reflexive consciousness proper to the intentional states could have other than that of qualitative or what-it's-like experiences.

The role of reflexive consciousness or qualia as cement in the overall intentional act or TCS is rather easy to establish. Just why would inner awareness or consciousness be inherent to an intentional act? In the *experiential* world, states of reflexive consciousness or qualia hold the act together. For without the support of experiential quality, the intentional relation (of causal or covariational nature) would be just a kind of free-floating orphan, an objective item without any caring ownership. Such a thing may perhaps happen in the physical world, but not in the experiential world. In this experiential world, qualitative cement is needed for intentional relations to be sustained.

Qualitative Infallibility

The thesis of QI and its implication of qualia's role as cement look plausible. We now wish to find out whether the QI thesis may be strengthened or used in some other area. A step in this direction is offered by the *qualitative infallibility* thesis, which claims that reflexive phenomenological or qualitative experiences are epistemically infallible. Notice by the way that this is still compatible with the BIV scenario.

The point of the *qualitative infallibility* thesis is epistemic. It strengthens the role of qualitative experiences as *cement*. Historically, this is again Brentano's thesis, which he understood to follow from the thesis of qualitative intentionality as cement. The qualitatively underpinned conscious experience is undeniably real.

What we *can* say is that the person who thinks is real and the very act of thinking is a reality that the person is directly aware of. When an intentional phenomenon occurs to us, we (in inner awareness) know that it occurs; and in knowing this we grasp its essential nature. "Whenever we judge we know what it *is* to judge" (Baumgartner 1996: 33).

In this way, the epistemic cement of qualia follows from the cement proper of single intentional acts. Consciousness or qualia, though, through their reflexivity, do not hold just individual intentional acts together; they also underlie the cohesion of their knowledge. Because knowing that *p* is more demanding than just entertaining *p*, cohesion in the case of knowledge has to be firmer. In accordance with this, knowledge may be understood as following from the evidential basis of qualia (Chisholm 1966), that is, ultimately from the reflexive nature of qualia.

Recent discussion has tried to spell out how features of inner awareness provide *cement* or epistemic infallibility. Let us call the sign "@" such as it appears in the former subsection the phenomenon of inner awareness. Then,

(1)   Inner awareness is *built in* in that it is a component of experience itself (if this is the case, then higher-order theories of consciousness miss the point).

(2)   Inner awareness is *peripheral*, and only occasionally focal, as compared to awareness of intentional content.

(3)   Inner awareness is *constitutive* of qualia, so the "what-it's-like" experience of smelling flowers or the respective quality is constituted by the inner awareness of the same (Horgan and Kriegel 2007).

Epistemically, though, inner awareness enables the infallible character of experiences: we cannot fail to know this kind of experience, once we entertain them. This is in counterdistinction to the epistemically fallible knowledge directed at intentional objects or contents, such as cats: you can never be really certain about cats, if these become separated from their perceived qualities.

Toward a Generalized Theory of the Experiential World

Our wide theme is the experiential world, with consciousness as its cement. We have just tackled the theses of the role of qualia as cement in self-reflexive intentional acts, and in infallible knowledge. By discussing holism and some background, a basis may be laid for a general theory about how the experiential world is linked together. The underlying question is how to understand the experiential world, and how to spell out the OI thesis.

Contextual Qualia

Our experiences gain in clarity as they are considered in context. Qualia are curious in this respect. On the one hand, the nature of the context that they provide experience is much too large to be able to impinge on specific cases, at least in an explicit and direct manner. The context of qualia is the whole holistic background of the subject, or the subject's entire experiential world. But somehow, such a background is able to make itself felt in extremely specific situations, providing the real individual situatedness of conscious experiences. A clue to how to understand this disparity between the much too wide and the most individual and specific in qualia is reached by pointing out the holistic nature of the background to which qualia are linked. The positioning of TCSs within the cognitive background does not involve awareness of much of the content stored there, but it does involve an awareness of the transitions' qualitative aspects, of the occurrent TCSs' positioning. In the experiential world, qualia's role is to hold TCSs together. Holism and the background specify the context of qualia.

Holism

Holism is opposed to atomism. Often, individual contents tend to be specified in an atomistic manner, with rules for mastering transitions between them. In this case, any inherent relation to qualia is not forthcoming. If they enter the scene in such a setting, qualia are there only as something that is being added. Holism on the other hand is closer to the notion of background. The experiential world is holistic and not atomistic in that several contents tend to be brought together in it in an intertwined manner, in accordance with the OI thesis.

Holism underlies the DC model, a complex and rich multidimensional system. Quinean and isotropic characteristics underpin holism, which is an important issue for a proper understanding of the intertwinedness of the experiential world. Fodor (1983) uses an analogy between higher human cognition and scientific confirmation to illustrate the holistic approach.

The dynamics of beliefs and TCS positioning is hard to account for using only atomistic and inferential approaches guided by general rules. On the other hand, this may not be an insurmountable task for a Quinean isotropic holistic DC system. In DC, the positioning of TCSs is linked to the holistic background. Qualia then acts in such a background, making use of the Quinean and isotropic features in the holistic setting of higher cognition. Again, by their reflexive awareness, qualia play the role of cement in the *experiential* world.

The Background

States of reflexive consciousness or qualia hold experiences together through a holistic setting. But just what is the holistic space underlying this qualitative positioning of experiences? It may be called the background. The general-rules-governed model (such as classical LOT) centers on transitions between occurrent TCSs. But it is plausible to believe that these transitions get supported by some underlying space that, in allowing positioning, is not occurrent itself. Such an underlying space is a natural part of a holistic system. The holistic background consists of everything the cognitive system has stored that sits somewhere in the back of its memory. This wide background knowledge enables transitions between TCSs without becoming occurrent itself. It merely enables the positioning of TCSs, by providing an awareness of their itinerary in the experiential space. One is aware of transitions taking place within the multidimensional background not by being aware of specific contents residing in the background, but of the *quality* that is proper to the passage. In the experiential space, each occurrent TCS has to appear within such a background, and qualia are thus intertwined with each TCS. During the process, one becomes aware of this quality. In the experiential space, qualia also enable the positioning of TCSs.

One name for the background is *being-in-the-world*. If we assume the world is holistic and thereby Quinean and isotropic, quality comes from the positioning of TCSs within a rich and dynamical multidimensional landscape. The reflexive nature of qualitative awareness enables transitions within such a landscape and plays the role of cement. Notice again that we are dealing with the *experiential* world, not the physical world. In such a world qualia provide support for innumerable experiences, acting as the cement that holds them together and enables them to be lived as one's own.[6]

Notes

1. "[I]ntentional state types . . . are total cognitive states, a single TCS sometimes comprising several individual cognitive states that can be instantiated simultane-

ously (perhaps in various different cognitive subsystems)" (Horgan and Tienson 1996: 21).

2. "Qualia are precisely what permit the disambiguation of presentations" (Wright 1991: 84). The important question is "sharpening up for whom." The purpose of such sharpening up is to make our criteria more precise across our communication group. And this means that an "object" or "person" can be "sharper" for one person than another. (See Wright 2005: chapter 4.)

3. In these passages I have substituted the expressions "qualia" and "qualitative" for "phenomenology." Horgan and Tienson (2002) thus talk about the phenomenology of intentionality and the intentionality of phenomenology.

4. In what follows, more will be said about the *space* of the background world that determines the contextual nature of qualia. Brentano affirmed the necessary link between sensations (qualia) and the experiential space (see Potrč 2002), and only reluctantly tackled the holistic or monistic nature of the world (see the final chapter of Brentano 1981).

5. "Qualia are . . . as real as what they are varying proportionately with, the equally real, non-sensory input" (Wright 2005: 100).

6. For their help in preparing this chapter, I thank Vojko Strahovnik and Edmond Wright, as well as Judy Feldmann for copyediting. The inspiring influence of Terry Horgan and Wilhelm Baumgartner is also acknowledged.

References

Baumgartner, W. 1996. On the origins of phenomenology: Franz Brentano. In *Phenomenology and Cognitive Science*, ed. E. Baumgartner, 25–35. Dettelbach: Röll.

Brentano, F. 1981. *The Theory of Categories*. The Hague: Nijhoff.

Chisholm, R. 1966. *Theory of Knowledge*. Englewood Cliffs, N.J.: Prentice-Hall.

Fodor, J. 1975. *The Language of Thought*. New York: Thomas Y. Crowell.

Fodor, J. 1983. *The Modularity of Mind*. Cambridge, Mass.: MIT Press/A Bradford Book.

Horgan, T. 1991. Metaphysical realism and psychologistic semantics. *Erkenntnis* 34: 297–322.

Horgan, T., and U. Kriegel. 2007. Phenomenal epistemology: What is consciousness that we may know it so well? *Philosophical Issues*, in press.

Horgan, T., and M. Potrč, eds. 2002. *Vagueness: from Epistemicism to Transvaluationism*. Dettelbach: Roell.

Horgan, T., and M. Potrč. 2008. Particularist semantic normativity. In *Challenging Moral Particularism*, ed. M. Lance, M. Potrč, and V. Strahovnik, 123–139. New York: Routledge.

Horgan, T., and J. Tienson. 1996. *Connectionism and the Philosophy of Psychology*. Cambridge, Mass.: MIT Press/A Bradford Book.

Horgan T., and J. Tienson. 2002. The intentionality of phenomenology and the phenomenology of intentionality. In *Philosophy of Mind: Classical and Contemporary Readings*, ed. D. Chalmers, 520–533. Oxford: Oxford University Press.

Potrč, M. 1999. Morphological content. In *Connectionism and the Philosophy of Psychology*, ed. M. Potrč, 133–149. Dettelbach: Röll.

Potrč, M. 2002. Intentionality of phenomenology in Brentano. In *Origins: The Common Sources of the Analytic and Phenomenological Traditions*, ed. T. Horgan, J. Tienson, and M. Potrč, 231–267. Memphis: The Southern Journal of Philosophy Supplement.

Searle, J. 1983. *Intentionality: An Essay in the Philosophy of Mind*. Cambridge: Cambridge University Press.

Wright, E. 1991. Potrč on content. *Acta Analytica* 7: 79–86.

Wright, E. 2005. *Narrative, Perception, Language, and Faith*. New York: Palgrave Macmillan.

6 Subjective Physicalism

Robert J. Howell

The debates about qualia and consciousness are puzzling in part because the majority of philosophers agree about the majority of facts. In particular, most agree with the following four theses:

(a) The world is a world of physical things.

(b) The physical sciences tell the complete causal story about the world.

(c) There is such a thing as conscious experience.

(d) The nature of consciousness is not fully captured by descriptions in the physical sciences.

As a background for debate, these four theses represent quite a bit of agreement. One might think, in fact, that the remaining issue—as to whether or not physicalism is true—is more or less terminological. As usual, however, things are not quite so simple.

One can, of course, define "physicalism" in any way one wishes, but the real question is whether theses (a) through (d)—and (d) in particular—can be acknowledged by a monistic metaphysics. A monistic metaphysics is roughly characterized by the stance that there is one fundamental type of thing that explains everything that happens and that accounts for everything that exists. A closer look at this notion reveals several places that could engender disagreement over the consistency of qualia with physicalism. In particular it is difficult to explain the notion of a "fundamental type," and it is unclear what sense of "accounting" or "explanation" is assumed in the definition of monism. All of these notions allow both metaphysical and epistemological interpretations, and reading them in different ways generates different views on the mind–body problem. Since monism is a metaphysical position about the nature of the world, we must take care to avoid allowing epistemological elements to cloud the waters. This is easier said than done, and the failure to do this effectively explains much of the disagreement among qualia theorists.

In this essay I present and defend a version of physicalism according to which all things, properties, and facts are physical, but no objective theory—including physics—can completely describe the world. In particular, some physical states are subjective, in that those states must be undergone in order to be fully grasped. Subjective physicalism can be developed in two ways, involving either of the following two claims:

(1) There are two ways of grasping some physical properties: objectively, via physical descriptions, and subjectively, via conscious experiences. There are no properties, however, that physical descriptions leave out.

(2) Some physical properties can be grasped only subjectively. The properties that underwrite conscious experiences (e.g. qualia) are physical, but they are not identical with any property mentioned in a completed physics.

Call a view that accepts (1) *inclusive subjective physicalism*, and a view that accepts (2) *exclusive subjective physicalism*. According to inclusive subjective physicalism, a complete physics will refer to every property and event that there is, but there are ways of understanding those things that the theoretical descriptions of physics will not impart. According to exclusive subjective physicalism, on the other hand, physical descriptions will actually leave something out, because the nature of some properties simply cannot be fully captured by theoretical objective descriptions. I have developed inclusive subjective physicalism elsewhere, but here I want to argue that exclusive subjective physicalism is also a view of great promise.[1] In particular I wish to show not only that it deserves its status as a monistic position, but that it can avoid some of the problems that befall the dualistic position that it resembles. For the remainder of this essay, therefore, I will be defending the view that embraces the second thesis above, and for simplicity I will call that view subjective physicalism.

I will present the view in several stages. First, I will explain the operative notions of subjective and objective, explaining why no objective description of the world can be complete. Next, I will propose a plausible understanding of physicalism that allows that everything can be physical even if no objective description of the world can be complete. I will then explain and motivate the basic position of exclusive subjective physicalism, comparing it to a couple of positions with which it could easily be confused. Finally, I will explain how subjective physicalism deals with the threat of epiphenomenalism, and suggest that it is in a better position to evade it than property dualism.

Subjective and Objective: The Real Lesson of the Knowledge Argument

Frank Jackson's knowledge argument and Thomas Nagel's arguments in "What Is It Like to Be a Bat?" clearly promote the same intuition: there is something about minds that cannot be fully understood from "the outside" (Nagel 1979a; Jackson 1982, 1986). Nevertheless, at least as they are typically understood, Nagel and Jackson disagree about the ontological import of their insights. Nagel appears reticent when it comes to the implications for physicalism whereas Jackson targets physicalism directly. Despite the fact that I think Jackson's argument is more straightforward in many ways, I share Nagel's reluctance to draw the ontological conclusion. The knowledge argument is best directed not at physicalism but at the claim that the world can be fully described by objective theories. That is, in essence, the conclusion of what I call the *knowledge argument against objectivism* (Howell 2007).

This slightly modified version of Jackson's argument goes as follows. Mary is a brilliant scientist who has lived her life in a black-and-white room. During her prolonged imprisonment she was taught all of physics, neuroscience, and biology through black-and-white computer screens. In fact, she eventually gained all the information about the world that could possibly be conveyed to her through such screens and monitors. At that point she had all the objective information about the world. Nevertheless, when she left the room to be presented with a red rose by her captor, she saw the red of the rose and learned something new—she learned what it is like to see red. Thus, not all information is objective information.

The most obvious modification of Jackson's argument is that it is now an argument against the claim that all information is *objective*.[2] This is a conclusion that is not, on the face of it, ontological. This version of the argument discourages the thought that something nonphysical is needed to take up the slack left by physical explanations of the world (Lewis 1999c; Churchland 1985). Mary's ignorance stems from the fact that there are aspects of the world that can be completely grasped only by occupying particular conscious states. In other words, the knowledge argument shows that the problem with physical theories stems more from their approach to their subject matter, than with the subject matter itself. The problem with physical theory is that it is objective, and if dualism is presented as objective in the same sense, then it is as vulnerable to the knowledge argument as physicalism.

Too often "objective" is used as a synonym of "real," thus leaving "subjective" a mark of ontological deficiency. The sense of "objective" and "subjective" employed by subjective physicalism, however, applies primarily to theories, and can be captured by the following necessary condition for theory objectivity:

Necessary condition for theory objectivity   An objective theory cannot require that one enter any token state of determinate type T in order to fully understand states of type T.[3]

In the case at hand, an objective theory of a particular type of experience cannot require that one have a token of that type of experience in order to have a complete understanding of that type of experience. Given that Mary while imprisoned can learn about the world outside of her room only by objective theories, and that she also learns all any true objective theory can convey, then the fact that she still fails to understand something about the world shows that there are some token states that must be entered in order to be fully understood. This does not show that they are not physical; it just shows that a complete grasp of them cannot be gained solely by objective theories.[4]

I have defended this version of the knowledge argument elsewhere, but the basic idea is this: all of the physicalist responses to Jackson's argument that grant that Mary has an "aha"-moment upon leaving the room must maintain that her epistemic achievement is a result of her becoming "hooked up" to the world of colors in a way that she had previously only read about (Howell 2007). By itself, however, being hooked up to a process one had previously only read about is not sufficient for an epistemic gain— I could have read about the effect a salt pill has on my blood, but learn nothing by actually taking it. The only plausible "hooked-up" response, therefore, must entail that the objectivity constraint is violated—it must require that there is some epistemic gain that Mary can make only in virtue of undergoing the state that she now knows about. There is, therefore, something that objective descriptions leave out.

It is important to realize that, although this entails that there is a sense in which physics is incomplete, the incompleteness is not necessarily ontological. So far, this knowledge argument only makes a point about understanding and the descriptive potential of theories, where descriptive potential is determined in part by the theories' ability to provide information. Showing that the falsity of physicalism does not follow straightforwardly from the incompleteness of the objective, however, requires a definition of physicalism that is ontological and untainted by epistemic elements.

Metaphysical Physicalism

The intelligibility of subjective physicalism depends on a strictly metaphysical construal of physicalism, free of epistemic elements. A thesis about the completeness of objective representations of the world should not entail by itself that the furniture of the world includes something other than the physical. Nevertheless, some definitions of physicalism might have that result.[5]

I therefore propose a supervenience definition of physicalism: physicalism is true if and only if everything metaphysically supervenes on the physical. Supervenience definitions capture the sense in which everything is completely metaphysically grounded in the physical, which is what is required by the basic monistic thrust of physicalism.[6] The supervenience thesis I prefer is:

(SVP) Any metaphysically possible world that is a physical duplicate of our world is either a duplicate of our world *simpliciter* or it contains a duplicate of our world as a proper part.[7]

SVP captures the sense in which physicalism is a contingent thesis. Intuitively, physicalism is a claim about our world that is not falsified in virtue of strange goings on in other worlds—if there are ghostly worlds, a physicalist thesis about our world should not thereby be falsified (Lewis 1999b; Jackson 1998; Chalmers 1996). On the other hand, we cannot completely ignore worlds with furniture different from ours.[8] Doing so ignores alien entities or properties that could problematize actual world connections in ways that physicalism should disallow (Hawthorne 2002). (Physicalism would intuitively be false, for example, if beliefs were necessitated by brain states only in worlds where there were no ghosts—physicalism should demand a closer relation than that.) This definition avoids both of these problems.

Implicit in SVP is a distinction between a broad sense of "physical" and a narrow sense. The former, which is what is being defined by the supervenience thesis, applies to anything that is physicalistically respectable. The latter, which appears within the thesis itself, applies to a narrower group of properties on which all the others supervene. I propose a negative definition of "physical" in its narrow sense,[9] according to which phenomenality and intentionality are excluded from being basic. If a physical thing has a phenomenal property (there is something that it is like to have that property) or an intentional property (a property in virtue of which the thing represents something else), that property had better be metaphysically grounded in some property or properties that are not intentional or phenomenal. For this reason, I offer a negative definition of the narrow that is similar to that offered by Crook and Gillet (2001):

(NIP)   Something is physical iff it is fundamental, contingent, and is not phenomenal or intentional.[10]

The resulting notion of physicalism is strictly metaphysical. Roughly speaking, physicalism is true if and only if everything is metaphysically grounded in the fundamental features of the world, which are themselves nonmental.

Subjective Physicalism

Subjective physicalism maintains that the world is completely metaphysically grounded in the physical, in that everything supervenes on things, properties, and states that are not fundamentally intentional or phenomenal. Nevertheless, some of those supervening states and properties cannot be exhaustively described by an objective theory since they cannot be fully grasped except by an agent that is undergoing them. Physicalism is therefore true, despite the fact that physics—or any other objective science, for that matter—cannot provide a complete understanding of the world.[11]

Subjective physicalism thus insists that minds—at least in this world—are fully physical. Many things can be said about the constitution of minds, the functional complexity required, and the various processes and interactions that make minds work. All of these features of minds can be fully described from "the outside." Minds are unique, however, in that the outside take is not the only one. This doesn't mean that a new fundamental *type* of property appears from the inside. The property one experiences is physical because it is necessitated by the physical properties described by physics. Once the outside is fixed, the inside comes along as just another aspect of the physical. Just as one cannot make a dome that doesn't offer perspective to the inside that one cannot get from without, God could not make a physical mind like ours without there being something that it is like to enjoy certain of its states.

The commitments of subjective physicalism can perhaps best be highlighted by contrasting it with other, somewhat similar positions in recent literature.[12] It holds a great deal in common, for example, with the hypothesis that qualia are physical but ineffable (Byrne 2002; Hellie 2004). According to the ineffability theory (IT), qualia cannot be captured by physical description because they are ultimately indescribable. According to Byrne, for example, "the content of perception, although it can be remembered and believed, cannot be (entirely) expressed in language, and is in this sense ineffable" (Byrne 2002). Hellie (2004) advances a similar thesis involving "inexpressible concepts" that underlie phenomenal knowledge. The general idea is that phenomenal content is encoded in such a way that it is not as amenable to communication as typical propositional content.

There are several ways in which subjective physicalism is distinct from IT. In the first place, IT fails to provide a complete analysis of the intuitions behind the knowledge argument since it doesn't specify the source of the ineffability. There are many reasons something could be inexpressible. Kant's *noumena* is ineffable, because it is a condition of our experience that things be represented according to the categories implemented by our understanding. It seems likely that some mathematical truths are inexpressible. It also seems likely that there are restrictions on the nature of our human concepts such that in principle reality outstrips them. None of these sources of ineffability seems to be relevant to the puzzling nature of qualitative experience. Most important, what is interesting about these cases is the source of their inexpressibility, rather than the fact that they are ineffable.

According to subjective physicalism, the source of ineffability is that there are aspects of the world one cannot fully understand without occupying particular subjective states. This understanding, therefore, cannot be conveyed without putting someone else in that subjective state. This ineffability is a consequence of the peculiarity of these aspects of the world, however; it is not the *explanation* of their peculiarity. It is the necessarily experiential nature of qualitative states that makes them intractable for an objective description of the world.

Furthermore, although it does seem to be the case that the information we get by occupying subjective states is ineffable, that seems to be a contingent matter. Consider the following possibility. Some people can sight-read music and can "hear" the music in their heads much as we do when we have an annoying jingle repeating in our minds. This is probably a result of the sheet music allowing them to vivify memory traces, or something else similarly based on experience of the notes.[13] Still, we can imagine someone born with the innate ability to hear the sounds internally upon reading sheet music. It seems no less imaginable that there be individuals capable of sight-reading neuroscience: individuals hard-wired such that when confronted with descriptions or depictions of brain states, the corresponding subjective states are vivified in their mental theaters, much as sounds are for sight-readers. If we were all neuro-sight-readers it seems that subjective experiences would be expressible, because they could be conveyed intersubjectively. The manner in which they would be conveyed seems unusual to us, but they seem to be communicated nonetheless.[14] In such a case, subjective physicalism would still be true—a completely objective theory would be leaving something out—while IT would not hold.

Subjective physicalism is also similar to views employing phenomenal concepts to explain the peculiarity of subjective knowledge (Loar 1997; Papineau 2002). Accounts of phenomenal concepts themselves vary, but the general picture is that phenomenal concepts employ physically explicable modes of presentation of conscious states that are not the same as the modes of presentation employed by concepts used in scientific categorization. It is furthermore at least implicitly presupposed that phenomenal concepts can be employed with respect to an experience only by the individual having that particular experience.[15]

Strictly speaking, the phenomenal concept strategy is consistent with subjective physicalism. Indeed, given that first-personal phenomenal knowledge is distinct from its more objective counterpart, and given that this knowledge is portable—in the sense that it can be retained beyond the occasion of the known experiences, and the concepts involved can be employed in a variety of thoughts—the subjective physicalist, or anyone else for that matter, should acknowledge that there are phenomenal concepts. Nevertheless, subjective physicalism will differ from standard phenomenal concept views in the explanatory role it gives to such concepts. According to subjective physicalism it is simply a fact that there is something that it is like to instantiate certain physical states. Instantiating those states is sufficient for there being conscious experience—something that objective sciences cannot fully capture. Since instantiating these states is sufficient, phenomenal concepts are not necessary. The puzzling aspects of conscious experience are thus present before phenomenal concepts enter the picture. If this is wrong, and phenomenal concepts are necessary for conscious experience, it seems they are constitutive of that experience. In that case, they inherit the essential subjectivity of the experience and are not fully objectively explicable. So it seems that either phenomenal concepts are not explaining what needs explaining, or they are not themselves explicable.[16] Thus, although the subjective physicalist should acknowledge that phenomenal concepts exist, what is doing the work for the subjective physicalist is actually the more basic claim that there is something that it is like to instantiate certain physical states, and that it is only by instantiating those states that one can fully grasp them.

Subjective Physicalism and Mental Causation

It is probably clear that exclusive subjective physicalism bears more than a passing resemblance to property dualism. Both maintain that a complete physical science would be incomplete in that some properties would not be fully described, and both maintain that only by occupying certain states can an individual appreciate the lacunae left by physical theory. They differ, however, in that subjective physicalism maintains, whereas property dualism denies, that these qualitative states are completely metaphysically grounded in physical states.

Although subjective physicalism is not a form of dualism, it is tempting to think that it encounters the same problems. In particular, it seems likely that these new properties, discovered subjectively, will be epiphenomenal. The subjective physicalist has no problem, of course, with the exclusion arguments as they are traditionally stated (Kim 1998). Since the "subjective" properties are physical, their efficacy poses no problem for the causal closure, or even the causal completeness, of the physical.[17] The problem of exclusion, however, does not go away so easily.

The exclusion argument gains its force in part from the fact that no one feels comfortable making bets against the explanatory completeness of the physical. This is not a result of some abstract adoration of the physical, however. It is instead due to the explanatory success of the physical *sciences*. It therefore seems that the explanatory and causal closure of the physical is credible because of the apparent likelihood that the physically *describable* is explanatorily and causally closed. If so, the threat of epiphenomenalism threatens subjective physicalism no less than property dualism. Even if physics will never describe everything that is physical, as long as what it does describe takes care of itself causally, those undescribed subjective properties are out of a job. The uncomforting possibility of overdetermination aside, everything from arm-raisings to "ouch"-mutterings will be explained by the properties physics describes.

While this revised exclusion argument shows that merely being called "physical" does not redeem qualitative properties from causal irrelevance, it is important to recall that subjective physicalism is not simply a commitment to an idiosyncratic nomenclature. "Subjective" properties are called physical because they are necessitated by the physical. Therefore, the "objective" properties could not cause what they do without them, because they could not exist without them. Because of the necessary connection between these properties, it is perhaps best to say that when a subject is undergoing a conscious experience he occupies a state with two "aspects," a subjective aspect and an objective aspect. If so, we might want to say that it is the state that does the causing, not the aspects of the state.[18]

Still, can't we ask whether the state causes what it does in virtue of one property rather than another? If so, won't the issue simply reappear at this stage? While a full answer to this question involves issues outside of our scope, I suggest that in this context the "in virtue of" question is illegitimate. As a result, the question of causal competition between the objective and subjective properties cannot properly be raised. The reason is that causal explanation is not fine-grained enough to distinguish between necessarily coinstantiated properties. One can ask which of two coinstantiated properties are causally responsible for an effect if they are contingently coinstantiated, but one cannot really ask which of two necessarily coinstantiated properties cause a particular effect.

Two properties compete for causal relevance only if those properties are independent from one another. There are many different ways in which properties can be dependent on one another, and not all of them exempt the properties from competition.[19] Mutual metaphysical dependence does seem to be a relevant form of dependence. That is, the following claim seems highly plausible:

(NCNC)   For any properties F and G, if F and G are necessarily coextensive, they never compete for causal relevance.

NCNC (noncompetition of necessary coinstantiates) is plausible in large part because whenever we have coinstantiated properties and are inclined to think of one as the *real* cause, it is because we can ask which property would be sufficient for the effect if the properties failed to occur together. When a red brick breaks a window, the redness and the mass are coinstantiated, but we can ask whether the brick, were it a different color, would break the window. Here the question of which property is really responsible gains traction because of the separability of the properties. This is also why we can ask the property dualist whether the physical property that accompanies pain or the qualitative property of pain causes the "ouch." Even though it might be a matter of psycho-physical law that whenever there is one there is the other, the connection is not necessary, and we can therefore ask about possibilities where the laws are different and the pain occurs without the physical state or vice versa.

According to subjective physicalism, the subjectively discovered physical properties are necessarily coextensive with certain scientifically discoverable physical properties.[20] Thus there is no case where there is a pain without the neural state or vice versa. So how would we decide which property is responsible for pain-effects? It is not obvious that we can even make sense of the question.[21] Again, in cases where two properties are necessarily coextensive, it seems more natural to speak of the state, which includes both properties, as causing the effects.

Much more needs to be said about this matter, and I can hardly pretend to have closed the case here. What does seem to be clear, though, is that when it comes to mental causation there is a way out for the exclusive subjective physicalist that is not open to the property dualist. Dualism, by its very nature, runs into trouble with exclusion arguments—the mental properties are independent of the physical properties and as such they are apt to compete with them for causal roles. Subjective physicalism is a monist position precisely because it denies this sort of independence. If property independence is a condition for causal competition, therefore, subjective physicalism can avoid the problems of mental causation despite bearing some basic similarity to its dualistic cousin.

Conclusion

The metaphysical problems of qualia and consciousness are so intractable because it seems implausible that in this world of physical things our minds are the sole things that cannot be accounted for by physical laws, properties, and states of affairs. Nevertheless, it seems clear that in some sense physical sciences cannot account for what it is like to have conscious states. Subjective physicalism gets its foot in the door by pointing out that there are two senses in which things might be said to "account for" the mind: a metaphysical sense and an epistemic sense. Properties, relations, and objects account for things in a metaphysical sense, while theories account for things in an epistemic sense. According to subjective physicalism, this explains how we can consistently hold both of our strong intuitions about conscious experience. The physical features of the world account for conscious experience metaphysically by necessitating it. Physics, however, does not account for consciousness epistemically because there is an aspect of some physical states—the states that are also conscious states—that cannot be fully appreciated unless they are undergone.

As I mentioned at the beginning, subjective physicalism comes in two flavors: exclusive subjective physicalism, according to which a complete physics fails to describe all the properties in the world, and an inclusive version, which grants the descriptive completeness of physics but maintains that it nevertheless falls short epistemically. In this essay I have been defending exclusive subjective physicalism, but to many this will seem too close to property dualism. I have some sympathies with that concern, but I hope to have shown that even if exclusive subjective physicalism bears a close relationship to dualism, it stands a good chance of avoiding dualism's epiphenomenalist fate. Whichever view one takes, accepting the descriptive limitations of objective sciences seems far more attractive to seeing the world as mostly physical with a few spiritual sprinkles in the form of nonphysical qualia. Subjective physicalism has this in its favor, while still allowing that we gain a significant perspective on ourselves by occupying the states that we do.[22]

Notes

1. For the explanation and defense of exclusive subjective physicalism, see my forthcoming "The Ontology of Subjective Physicalism."

2. Alter (1998) also encourages this conclusion, as does Mandik (2001).

3. I defend this necessary condition in Howell 2007, but I think that it needs some modifications to be strictly correct. In particular, an objective theory of T-states should not require that one enter a state sufficiently similar to T in order to understand states of type T—this is to handle a range of "missing shade of blue"-like cases. "Sufficiently similar" obviously requires some legwork, but the necessary condition as stated seems adequate for our purposes here.

4. It is important to remember that subjectivity and objectivity are features of theories, points of view, or perspectives; they are not features of things or properties. In other words, subjectivity is a matter of how things are represented.

5. This problem is well discussed in Montero 1999, Crane and Mellor 1990, and others. Analyses that might prematurely close the gap between the objective and the physical include Wilson forthcoming and Melnyk 2003.

6. I defend supervenience definitions against counterexamples such as necessitarian emergentist dualism, as presented in Wilson 2005, elsewhere. See Howell forthcoming b.

7. This definition is inspired, in part, by one provided by Chalmers (1996: 39–40, 364).

8. As Jackson and Lewis do.

9. It would be a mistake to think that because the negative definition defines the relevant notion of the physical in terms of the mental that the physical is not ontologically prior. It seems plausible, though, that in this debate the relevant notion of the physical is not *conceptually* prior to the notion of the mental, in that our grasp of the nature of the latter helps us refine our understanding of the former.

10. Two notes on this definition. First, I intend "something" in NIP in the broadest possible sense, ranging over objects, properties, events, etc. Second, something is fundamental in this sense if and only if it is a basic posit that is not reducible to another posit. Negative definitions such as this are used by Papineau and Spurrett (1999) and Papineau (2002).

11. Subjective physicalism need not say that objective theories fail to provide a complete grasp of the world because they leave some properties undescribed. There is more on this—and the relationship between "aspects" and properties—in what is to come.

12. Some of the material in this section borrows from Howell 2007.

13. Though "missing shades of blue" surely happen in the musical realm.

14. Perhaps there is a sense of "expressibility" according to which the case described does not involve the expression of phenomenal content. It is not obvious that such a sense can be successfully fleshed out, but in any case, it seems far preferable to move away from this issue and focus on the underlying phenomenon—that understanding qualitative states requires actually undergoing them.

15. It is not always obvious why this is the case, however. If one were able, through sophisticated neural wiring, to apply one's phenomenal concept to someone else's experience, would one come to know what it's like to have that experience without actually having it?

16. On this count, subjective physicalism should agree with the dilemma that Chalmers (2006) poses for the phenomenal concept strategy.

17. The physical is causally closed if every physical event has a physical cause. It is causally complete if physical events have only physical causes. See Kim 2005.

18. I use "aspect" in a slightly different way in Howell forthcoming-a in that I do not take multiplicity of aspects to involve multiplicity of properties. This is one difference between the paths that lead one to inclusive versus exclusive subjective physicalism.

19. The question of competition and overdetermination is discussed much further by Bennett (2003), and the principle I offer here is one that is, as far as I can tell, harmonious with her account there.

20. I am assuming that there is necessary coextension, but on the face of it there is no reason a subjective physicalist could not acknowledge the multiple realizability of the subjective states. NCNC would not help this theory, but a very similar principle that seems equally plausible would.

21. Much more needs to be said about this, but I don't think the position I am taking depends on a counterfactual view of causation as opposed to a "generative

view" or something of the sort. The question as to which property is responsible for the energy transfer seems to be just as puzzling in cases of necessary coextension.

22. I wish to thank the National Endowment for the Humanities for their support during the "Mind and Metaphysics" summer seminar. Thanks to John Heil, Torin Alter, and the participants of that seminar, as well as Doug Ehring, Brad Thompson, and my colleagues at SMU.

References

Alter, T. 1998. A limited defense of the knowledge argument. *Philosophical Studies* 90: 35–56.

Alter, T., and S. Walter, eds. 2006. *Phenomenal Concepts and Phenomenal Knowledge.* Oxford: Oxford University Press.

Bennett, K. 2003. Why the exclusion problem seems intractable, and how, just maybe, to tract it. *Noûs* 37, 3: 471–497.

Block, N., O. Flanagan, and G. Güzeldere, eds. 1997. *The Nature of Consciousness.* Cambridge, Mass.: MIT Press/A Bradford Book.

Byrne, A. (2002) Something about Mary. *Grazer Philosophische Studien* 63: 123–140.

Chalmers, D. 1996. *The Conscious Mind.* Oxford: Oxford University Press.

Chalmers, D. 2006. Phenomenal concepts and the explanatory gap. In Alter and Walter 2006.

Churchland, Paul. 1985. Reduction, qualia, and the direct introspection of brain states. *Journal of Philosophy* 82: 8–28.

Crane, T., and D. H. Mellor. 1990. There is no question of physicalism. *Mind* 90: 185–206.

Crook, S., and C. Gillett. 2001. Why physics alone cannot define the "physical." *Canadian Journal of Philosophy* 31: 333–360.

Dowell, J. 2006. The physical: Empirical, not metaphysical. *Philosophical Studies* 131, 1: 25–60.

Hawthorne, J. 2002. Blocking definitions of materialism. *Philosophical Studies* 110, 2: 103–113.

Hellie, B. 2004. Inexpressible truths and the allure of the knowledge argument. In Ludlow, Nagasawa, and Stoljar 2004.

Howell, R. J. 2007. The knowledge argument and objectivity. *Philosophical Studies* 135, 2: 145–177.

Howell, R. J. Forthcoming-a. The ontology of subjective physicalism.

Howell, R. J. Forthcoming-b. Emergentism and supervenience physicalism.

Jackson, F. 1982. Epiphenomenal qualia. *Philosophical Quarterly* 32: 127.

Jackson, F. 1986. What Mary didn't know. *Journal of Philosophy* 83, 5: 291–295.

Jackson, F. 1998. *From Metaphysics to Ethics*. Oxford: Oxford University Press.

Kim, J. 1998. *Mind in a Physical World*. Cambridge, Mass.: MIT Press/A Bradford Book.

Kim, J. 2005. *Physicalism, or Something Near Enough*. Princeton: Princeton University Press.

Lewis, D. 1999a. *Papers in Metaphysics and Epistemology*. Cambridge: Cambridge University Press.

Lewis, D. 1999b. New work for a theory of universals. In Lewis 1999a.

Lewis, D. 1999c. What experience teaches. In Lewis 1999a.

Loar, B. 1997. Phenomenal states. In Block, Flanagan, and Güzeldere 1997.

Ludlow, P., Y. Nagasawa, and D. Stoljar, eds. 2004. *There's Something About Mary*. Cambridge, Mass.: MIT Press/A Bradford Book.

Mandik, P. 2001. Mental representation and the subjectivity of consciousness. *Philosophical Psychology* 14, 2: 179–202.

Melnyk, A. 1997. How to keep the "physical" in physicalism. *Journal of Philosophy* 94, 12: 622–637.

Melnyk, A. 2003. *A Physicalist Manifesto*. Cambridge: Cambridge University Press.

Montero, B. 1999. The body problem. *Noûs* 33, 2: 183–200.

Nagasawa, Y. 2002. The knowledge argument against dualism. *Theoria* 68: 205–233.

Nagel, Thomas. 1979a. What is it like to be a bat? In *Mortal Questions*. Cambridge: Cambridge University Press.

Nagel, Thomas. 1979b. Subjective and objective. In *Mortal Questions*. Cambridge: Cambridge University Press.

Nagel, Thomas. 1986. *The View from Nowhere*. Oxford: Oxford University Press.

Papineau, D. 2002. *Thinking About Consciousness*. Oxford: Oxford University Press.

Papineau, D., and D. Spurrett. 1999. A note on the completeness of physics. *Analysis* 59, 1: 25–29.

Wilson, J. 2005. Supervenience formulations of physicalism. *Noûs* 39: 426–459.

Wilson, J. 2006. On characterizing the physical. *Philosophical Studies* 131, 1: 61–99.

II Scientific Defenses

7 Color Qualities and the Physical World

C. L. Hardin

Color realists[1] and their adversaries will agree that the physical causes of color perception[2] are a heterogeneous lot. A perception of green can be brought about through a wide variety of physical mechanisms. These include blackbody emission, reflection, refraction, scattering, and polarization, to name only some. Two quite different underlying mechanisms may generate the same spectral power distribution (SPD) of visible light, and for a fixed set of viewing conditions and a specific observer under the same conditions of adaptation, the same SPD will be seen as the same color. But we must not suppose that the same perceived color betokens the same SPD. This is because there are only three kinds of color-relevant photoreceptors (cones) in the human retina. Objects producing two distinct SPDs that proportionally excite the three cone types under the same conditions will be seen as having the same color. This is the phenomenon of *metamerism*. Although it is rare in nature, metamerism is omnipresent in modern industrial societies; color photography and television rely on it. We are trichromatic beings who, because of our receptoral limitations, are able to match any colored light with three properly chosen basis lights. A tetrachromat might require four basis lights for color matches and thus be an unhappy consumer of our color telecasts.

Perceived colors are therefore two removes from the occurrent bases of the dispositions to see them. Many different mechanisms can produce the same SPD, and many different SPDs can cause us to see the same color. It is also important to note that animals with different receptoral sensitivities are unlikely to experience the same colors that we do under the same circumstances. It is little wonder that color categories have been described as "gerrymandered" and "anthropocentric."

The conditions of seeing have a substantial effect on just what colors are seen. Illumination is of course important. For a reflective sample, the SPD that arrives at the eye is the product of the surface spectral reflectance of the sample and the SPD of the illuminant. In the narrow-band illumination cast by a low-pressure sodium lamp in a parking lot, it becomes very difficult to distinguish cars by color because the stimulus returned from objects is spectrally impoverished compared to that from, say, daylight. What is less generally understood is that spectral differences in nominally "white" illuminants can produce significant shifts in color appearance of reflective samples, sometimes pushing the appearance of a surface over into another color category, for example, from a light blue to a beige. Even changes in the phase of daylight can affect the appearance of some materials strongly, despite the fact that the eye generally adapts well to shifts in the character of natural illuminants and objects. Architects sometimes exploit this effect. The granite of I. M. Pei's East Building of the National Gallery of Art in Washington, D.C., goes from gray to pink as the illumination shifts from diffuse daylight to direct sunlight. Given an object that shifts its color appearance markedly with changes in illuminant, especially with changes in natural illuminants, just what lighting conditions are required to show the object's *true* color?

Seeing requires contrast. A colored expanse without boundary or modulation rapidly begins to fade from view, to be replaced by a dark gray, the visual system's neutral state. If a visual target must be seen against a background, in what ways might we expect the background to affect the perceived color of the target? The general rule is that a background that is seen as coplanar with the target will drive the perceived color of the target in a direction that is complementary to the perceived color of the background. Thus a reddish background will make the target appear greenish, a dark background will make the target appear lighter, and so on. The effect can be dramatic. Surround an orange patch with a very bright background so that the patch-background combination occupies the entire field of view, and the patch will appear as a rich brown. Conversely, in bright light view a chocolate bar through a dark tube so that no other feature of the scene is visible, and the bar's color will appear to be orange. Pink, navy, olive, and, generally, all of the light and dark colors owe their being to achromatic contrast. This can be vividly seen in a color separation of a photograph with a wide range of colors. If the achromatic (black, white, and gray) information is removed, the chromatic information appears as a pale wash, with all of the light and dark colors missing. Even black is a contrast color. A grayscale in near darkness appears collapsed, with little differentiation of shades. Increase the illumination and the scale expands. Not only does white make its appearance at one end, black emerges at the other. Adding light increases blackness!

The lesson to be drawn from all of this is that there is no single background that will leave all perceived colors unaffected. However, by increasing the number and variety of color stimuli in a scene, we can minimize, though not eliminate, perturbations by neighboring color stimuli and attain relative stability of color appearance. This is because the eye-brain establishes color appearance by taking into account the relationships among all of the items in the field of view. The visual system calculates relative rather than absolute values of color information. In many cases, this means that a color patch viewed in isolation will look quite different from its appearance when seen as part of a complex field. But then the question arises once more: under what conditions do we see objects in their *true colors*?

We can now see that a color realist's appeal to "normal" or "standard" conditions to determine the "true" or "actual" colors of objects is mere hand-waving unless there is some clear reason for preferring one set of illumination or background conditions to another. So far, nobody who has held a realist position has been prepared to propose and defend such a set of conditions. What is to be said about the other half of the equation, the "normal" observer to whom philosophers so casually refer?

Simple considerations of biological variability would lead us to suppose that there must be some differences between observers in their response to chromatic stimuli. So the real issue is the extent of the variability and whether one can sensibly take a statistical average to arrive at a "standard" observer whose chromatic responses will be sufficiently close to those of actual observers. Indeed, for purposes of color matching, standard observers, such as the Commission International de l'Éclairage (CIE) 1932 Standard Observer, have been statistically constructed from experimental data drawn from real observers and proved very useful in commercial practice (Wyszecki and Stiles 1982: 173). However, there are strict limits to the validity of the CIE Standard Observer, one of which is that the Standard Observer's response tells us nothing whatever about color quality!

Let us examine some of the types of variability among observers. The first is, of course, so-called color blindness. In the strict sense, there are only two kinds of color blind persons: those who have lost color vision owing to a cerebral accident and have come to experience the world as only shades of gray, and *cone monochromats* who have but one cone type in their retinas. More common are *dichromats* who have two rather than the usual three types of cones. The most frequent type of dichromat has difficulty distinguishing reds from greens, especially when they are desaturated. Since such dichromats lack either the long-wave or the middle-wave cone types, it had been generally believed that they experience only blues and yellows. Recently, however, it has become apparent that many of them do experience reds and greens, albeit in restricted ranges (Wachtler, Dohrman, and Hertel 2002). For example, they report, as "normal" observers do, a reddish component in the short-wave end of the spectrum, which is predominantly blue. That people with just two cone types nevertheless experience all of the elementary colors is incompatible with the standard models of how the cones are connected to the opponent systems, and indeed suggests that other "deviant" connections may be biologically possible. For example, some of the people who respond behaviorally as the rest of us do might have their cones differently connected to their color-opponent systems, so that they have, for the same stimuli, a different chromatic response from most people (see Nida-Rümelin 1996). To put it another way, the door is at least slightly open for some form of spectral inversion. But this is, at the moment, pure speculation, of course.

What is not speculative is the substantial variety that is now known to exist in the eyes of trichromatic observers who are counted as "normal" by every standard test for color deficiency. Some of the differences lead to small but measurable differences in color discrimination. These include differences in the optical density of the lens, mostly due to aging, and in the genetically determined distribution and density of the macular pigment in the foveal region of the retina. Both of these lead to variations in the amount of short-wave light arriving at the retina and corresponding disagreements about the relative proportions of perceived green and perceived blue in a given stimulus.

Rather more striking is the recent discovery of large interpersonal differences in the relative number and absorption spectra of both the long-wave and the middle-wave photopigments (although often without impact on perceived color) (Neitz and Neitz 1998). Furthermore, variants of photopigments for the same cone type exist side-by-side with the retinas of certain people, typically women. These polymorphisms are genetically based, and the genes that code for them have been identified. Some of their perceptual effects have been carefully studied. For example, using an instrument called the anomaloscope, a standard instrument for diagnosing color deficiencies, color-normal observers are asked to match an orange test hemifield with a mixture hemifield of red and green primaries in which the observer can set the red–green ratio. For men, the distribution of ratios is bimodal, falling into two distinct groups, with approximately 60 percent of the observers in one group and 40 percent in the other. The distribution of ratios for women is unimodal, and broader than that for men. For an observer at one end of this range, the match set by an observer at the other end will look very reddish, while the observer at the other end of the range will see the match set by the first observer as very yellowish. Here we have a clear case of quantifiable, biologically based individual variations in color perceptions for normal observers under rigorously controlled conditions. No scientific sense can be attached to the claim that some of the observers are perceiving the color of the stimulus correctly and others not. And given the different character of the distributions for men and for women, as well as the bimodal male distribution, constructing an average has no useful statistical meaning.

The variations in normal color vision that we have so far considered are, for the most part, relatively small, though by no means insignificant. Let us now turn our attention to a level of visual processing that shows surprisingly large variations. The biological foundation of these variations is not well understood, but the phenomenology seems clear. In the nineteenth century, Ewald Hering (1964 [1920]) underlined the importance of the fact that of the many hues discernible by human eyes, exactly four are perceptually elemental. These *unique*, or *unitary* hues—red, yellow, green, and blue—appear to have no other hues as constituents. All of the other hues, such as orange, purple, lime, and turquoise, to name but a few, seem to be *binaries*, that is, blends of pairs of the elementary hues. In the mid-twentieth century, Sternheim and Boynton (1966) showed that the names of Hering's four elemental hues are both necessary and sufficient to describe all of the hues of the spectrum. They found that it is possible for observers to estimate the proportions of elemental hues in any spectral binary hue. If names for the elementary achromatic colors, black and white, are permitted, any color appearance can be characterized as a perceptual combination of at most two elemental hues plus black or white. Thus colors, as we perceive them, have a unitary-binary structure.

These phenomenological facts have consequences for the debate about color realism. In order to be orange, something must be both reddish and yellowish. On the other hand, although a something can be both reddish and bluish, or reddish and yellowish, it need not be in order to be red. If this unitary-binary structure is constitutive of the colors, no feature of the world outside of our skins that does not participate in this structure can be identical with a color. In particular, this structure does not seem to be implicit in classes of surface spectral reflectances, so they cannot be colors.

Defenders of colors as properties of the external world have responded to this criticism by conceding that colors are not natural kinds but rather anthropocentric properties. It is, they say, human visual systems that induce the required unitary-binary structure (Byrne and Hilbert 2003). Thus, any SPD that, under the appropriate conditions, causes the red–green opponent system to take a positive value while leaving the yellow–blue system in neutral balance is a unitary red, whereas a SPD that causes both opponent systems to assume positive values is orange. In this fashion, all SPDs are sorted into the appropriate classes.

The attentive reader will notice that this is just another variant in the "normal observer–standard conditions" gambit, and is therefore heir to all of its problems. Among other things, it supposes that there is an observer—perhaps a statistically constructable one—whose visual system can reasonably serve as the basis for making the required classification. In particular, it presupposes that all normal observers will locate their unique hues at approximately the same place in the spectrum, and, given a set of standard color chips under the same conditions, will agree on approximately the same chips as exemplifying those unique hues. This is by no means the case.

In fact, the differences are large enough to be shocking, as we shall now see. The stimulus locus for a perception of unique hue has been studied with a variety of techniques for many years. Every study with a reasonably large number of observers has found a wide distribution of unique hue stimuli among normal perceivers. Because the studies have used different experimental protocols, the mean results do not agree well across experiments; but substantial variability among observers within any given study is a constant. It is generally accepted that more "naturalistic" experiments using surface colors will reduce the amount of variance from one observer to another, so here are the results of some unique hue experiments with colored Munsell papers that were recently done by Kuehni (2001). He used a forty-step set, varying (according to Munsell) only in hue. The hues of the Munsell chips are approximately perceptually equispaced, so each chip is 1/40 of the complete hue circle. The figure shows the range of unique hue choices from experiments with two subject pools.

The male and female distributions are generally markedly different, and neither one approximates a Gaussian distribution for any of the hues. Even if the gender results are taken separately, no single chip will represent the unique hue choice of a majority of observers for a given hue category. The range of variability persists even when the choices of the least consistent observers are discarded. Furthermore, the unique hue choices of most individuals are very stable over time and highly repeatable.

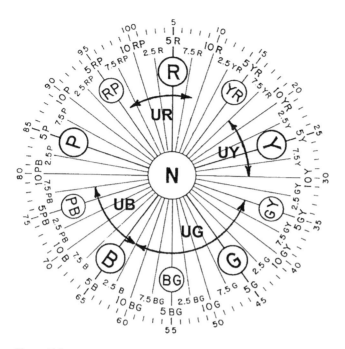

Figure 7.1
Individual variability in unique hue choices. Courtesy of Rolf Kuehni.

If the results for the four unique hue ranges are taken together, there fails to be consensus on 26 out of a total of the 40 chips composing the hue circle. That is to say, 65 percent of the hue circle is in dispute! Why has such an extensive disagreement escaped everyday notice? For one thing, people rarely have occasion to pick out unique hues in a carefully controlled situation. For another, people are remarkably insensitive to color nuances, changes, and differences unless the colors in question are juxtaposed both spatially and temporally. Our color memories are poor, even over the course of a minute. We pigeonhole colors into broad categories, label the categories along with a paradigmatic example that we do remember, and recall the colors largely on the basis of their verbal labels. Despite the very large numbers of color terms in use, very few of these terms are used with a high degree of consistency and consensus, and those that are apply only in limited regions of color space. The number of such terms in use among English-speaking adults ranges from eleven for many speakers to about forty that can be reliably employed by some color professionals.

When the facts about the variability of color perception among normal observers are pointed out to defenders of color realism, one common response is that there may be disagreements about particular, determinate colors, but there is certainly agreement about determinable colors. We can all agree, for instance, that a particular object is red. Well, yes and no. It is true that all of the normal observers will call most of the chips in the unique red range "red," most of the chips in the unique green range "green," and so on. But just how far does consensus go in color naming? Sturges and Whitfield (1995) examined color naming of a large sample of the Munsell color solid with responses from twenty subjects. Less than 25 percent of the chips were named with both consistency and consensus. If we consider just the hue dimension, we notice that the ranges for the judgments of unique hues and the consensus judgments for the four basic colors correspond pretty closely. But the consensus colors form islands in a sea of nonconsensual color naming. In particular, there is a pronounced gap in the hue range between the consensus green chips and the consensus blue chips that confirms the everyday observation that people commonly disagree about whether a particular color in this range is "really" green or "really" blue.

Should the realist content himself with the observation that all of us can agree that an object falling in this region is blue-or-green? The obvious rejoinder is that such an object falls under the determinables "bluish" and "greenish." This is perfectly true, but now we must ask whether we can generally agree of a given object whether or not it falls under a determinable such as "bluish." Take, for example, the Munsell chip 7.5G seen under the artificial daylight of Kuehni's second unique green experiment. Twenty-three observers judged it to be bluish, but fourteen observers judged it to be neither bluish nor yellowish, and six observers saw it as yellowish. It seems that we cannot secure agreement on the extension of this determinable, though each particular person can determine that extension with a high degree of reliability. The situation is no different if we ask observers to choose what they regard as the best examples of red, orange, purple, and so forth. Observers make their choices rather reliably, but with the same lack of consensus that one finds with choices of unique hues (Malkoc, Kay, and Webster 2006).

It is always open to the realist to see this as an epistemic problem. Perhaps, it has been suggested, people are like intelligent thermometers. Each of these thermometers reads a bit differently from the rest, but the fact that they cannot agree on the correct temperature does not entail that there is no such thing as the correct temperature. This is surely true; but the plausibility of the example depends on the fact that we know full well what constitutes temperature because we have a rich physical theory in which temperature plays a role, alternative means for measuring temperature, and a theory of thermometers that tells us under what conditions a thermometer will approximate the correct temperature and how close that approximation will be. None of this is present in the color case. Our sole access to colors is through our vision. We can, and do, know a great deal about surface spectral reflectances (SSRs), their causes, and their interactions with human vision. But only if we can determine which observers are to be regarded as canonical could we be able to establish which SSRs are to be identified with which colors. This is indeed an odd turn of events. One of the primary considerations fueling color realism has been the desire to do justice to the everyday intuition that colors are normally public and immediately accessible to view. Now it turns out that according to the realist, we cannot know which, if any, of us sees colors as they are.

There is a second motivation for color realism. Why, asks the color realist, has color vision evolved unless its job is to represent some property in the animal's environment? Is it not reasonable to regard the property that color experience represents as color? In response, we need to consider just what functions animal color vision serves. We can distinguish three principal types: discriminating an object from its background, identifying and reidentifying objects, and biological signaling. None of these functions requires that surface reflectances be represented in an absolute fashion. As is typically the case in vision, it is *relative* estimates that carry the load. Two animals with similar discriminative capabilities and similar categorization practices could perform these functions equally well in the same environment even though one was spectrally inverted with respect to the other. It is like painting by numbers. If contrasts are properly represented, what colorant is filled in for a given number is of little consequence. Color vision should be understood as a tool for carrying out the business of species survival rather than having some special business of its own.

A third motivation for color realism is that it promises to make life easier for materialistically inclined philosophers of mind. Sensory qualities are a nasty intrusion into a world whose basic ontology should include only entities and properties recognized by physical science. If colors "in" the mind are an embarrassment, then we must find some way of placing them "outside" the mind. A problem dodged is as good as a problem solved! Unfortunately, this stratagem is doomed to failure because of the multifaceted lack of correspondence between colors as we experience them and features of the physical world outside our bodies. We have already considered several instances of this, and there are many more to be had, including colors experienced as the result of stimulation by changing achromatic stimuli, by electromagnetic fields, and by mechanical pressure to the eye. And then there are nonlabile afterimages, such as those produced by the Bidwell disk and the long-lasting McCullough aftereffect, which involves the adaptation of cortical rather than retinal cells (Hardin 1993: 91–95).

One can see whole families of colors in the surface mode that cannot be realized by any material surface. Here is one example. Obtain an object with the most highly saturated red that can be produced. Under a bright light, stare for twenty seconds at a highly saturated piece of green material. Now shift your glance to the red patch, superimposing the afterimage onto the patch. The red patch will now appear substantially more saturated than it was before. Any patch, no mater how saturated, can in this way look even more saturated. By an analogous procedure, one can see colors that are "darker than dark," "lighter than light," and so on.

Much more remarkable are the "impossible" red–green and yellow–blue binary colors that come about as a result of filling-in retinally stabilized images, effectively bypassing the opponent color system. They were first produced by Crane and Piantanida (1983) in a series of experiments that gave ambiguous results because of imperfect techniques. Recently, improved methods have enabled Billock, Gleason, and Tsou (2001) to generate them reliably. They are "impossible" in the sense that no surface or light source could appear to be bluish yellow or reddish green. As Valtteri Arstila (2003) has pointed out, the fact that these hues can be realized in vision, but never be exemplified apart from nervous systems, means that a color ontology that regards colors as capable of existing apart from sentient organisms cannot be adequate.

It is clear that physics cannot do justice to the phenomenology of color. But is phenomenology to be the arbiter of what is and what is not an adequate theory of color? Consider a typical definition, commonly offered by color scientists, of color vision as the ability to represent spectral distributions irrespective of brightness. Many animals have such a capability, and it is not at all clear whether many of them have a phenomenology. Some human beings with brain damage can distinguish a boundary between two isoluminant stimuli that differ only in spectral composition despite being unable to pass any other color vision tests and not being aware of any chromatic colors. "Blindsight" patients can discriminate wavelength differences in their blind fields with remarkable accuracy provided that they are obliged to "guess." Some of them are even able in a two-alternative forced-choice experiment to guess whether a patch is red or green. Do any of these people see colors? Despite the standard definition, most of us would be inclined to say that they do not. They sense wavelength distributions and are able to categorize them. They do not have experience of color qualities (Stoerig 1993).

If it is color qualities that we wish to understand, phenomenology must be our arbiter of adequacy. To account for the phenomenology we require knowledge of the stimuli for the experience of color and the machinery by which the stimulus information is processed. About the first we know a great deal, and enough to understand what our knowledge can and cannot account for. About the second we know a great deal less, but enough to have at least a rough explanation of much of the phenomenology, with a reasonable expectation that the rest will become clear with plenty of time and good science.[3]

Notes

1. The color realist position I take as paradigmatic is that adopted by Byrne and Hilbert (2003).

2. The topics in color phenomenology and color science that are touched upon in this essay but not given specific citations here are discussed in greater detail in Hardin 1993.

3. I am grateful to Rolf Kuehni for his valuable comments.

References

Arstila, V. 2003. True colors, false theories. *Australasian Journal of Philosophy* 81: 41–50.

Billock, V. A., G. A. Gleason, and B. H. Tsou. 2001. Perception of forbidden colors in retinally stabilized equiluminant images: An indication of cortical opponency. *Journal of the Optical Society of America A* 18, 10: 2398–2403.

Byrne, A., and D. Hilbert. 2003. Color realism and color science. *Behavioral and Brain Sciences* 26, 1: 3–21.

Crane, H. D., and T. P. Piantanida. 1983. On seeing reddish green and yellowish blue. *Science* 221: 1078–1080.

Hardin, C. L. 1993. *Color for Philosophers: Unweaving the Rainbow*, expanded edition. Indianapolis, Ind.: Hackett.

Hering, E. 1964 [1920]. *Outlines of a Theory of the Light Sense*. Trans. L. Hurritch and D. Jameson. Cambridge, Mass.: Harvard University Press.

Kuehni, R. G. 2001. Determination of unique hues using Munsell color chips. *Color Research and Application* 26: 61–66.

Malkoc, G., P. Kay, and M. A. Webster. 2006. Variations in normal color vision. IV. Binary hues and hue scaling. *Journal of the Optical Society of America A* 22, 10: 2154–2168.

Neitz, M., and J. Neitz. 1998. Molecular genetics and the biological basis of color vision. In *Color Vision: Perspectives from Different Disciplines*, ed. W. G. K. Backhaus, R. Kliegl, and J. S. Werner, 101–119. Berlin: Walter de Gruyter.

Nida-Rümelin, M. 1996. Pseudonormal vision: An actual case of qualia inversion? *Philosophical Studies* 82: 145–157.

Sternheim, C. S., and R. M. Boynton. 1966. Uniqueness of perceived hues investigated with a continuous judgmental technique. *Journal of Experimental Psychology* 72, 5: 770–776.

Stoerig, P. 1993. Wavelength information processing *versus* color perception: Evidence from blindsight and color-blind sight. In *Color Vision: Perspectives from Different Disciplines*, ed. W. G. K. Backhaus, R. Kliegl, and J. S. Werner, 131–147. Berlin: Walter de Gruyter.

Sturges, J., and T. W. A. Whitfield. 1995. Locating basic colors in the munsell space. *Color Research and Application* 20, 6: 364–376.

Wachtler, T., U. Dohrman, and R. Hertel. 2002. Modelling color percepts of dichromats. *Vision Research* 44: 2843–2855.

Wyszecki, G., and W. S. Stiles. 1982. *Color Science: Concepts and Methods, Quantitative Data and Formulae*, 2nd edition. New York: John Wiley and Sons.

8 Heat, Temperature, and Phenomenal Concepts

Isabelle Peschard and Michel Bitbol

The so-called reduction of heat is recurrently mentioned in the discussions about the relations between phenomenal concepts (or properties) and physical concepts (or properties). We used to say that water was hot or cold, describing or expressing thereby the way it feels to us. Heat was then a phenomenal concept. The same phenomenon we describe now in terms of (mean) molecular kinetic energy (MKE). Now, "heat" refers to a physical property. This is meant to be an example of phenomenal and physical concepts referring to the same thing, a physical property. Or else, the reduction of temperature to MKE is meant to show that something that we know by (tactile) sensing can be the same thing as something we do not know by (tactile) sensing. This claimed identity between what the phenomenal report of experience and what the physical description of the world are about takes on an analogical function. As it happened there, it could happen somewhere else: the phenomenal description of experience could (at least in principle) be reduced to a physico-physiological description of neural activity. This claim, we shall contend, rests on conceptual confusions and equivocations. This point will be addressed in the second and third sections of the essay.

The epistemic function of the claimed identity between what the phenomenal concept of heat and what the physical concept of temperature refer to is not only analogical. It is also an assumption underlying certain experimental studies of the relation between phenomenal experience and neural activity. On that basis, the neural system is regarded as an instrument of detection of the properties of the world. Neural activity stands for something: it has a representational content that can be determined independently of phenomenal reports. That phenomenal reports are not in principle necessary to make sense of neural activity is essential to the reductionist project. The thrust of the fourth section will be to show that and why this assumption is empirically objectionable. Let's begin with a few points about experience and phenomenal concepts that will form our standpoint.

1   Perspectival Experience

By "phenomenal concepts" we will refer to concepts describing, sometimes merely expressing, the ways things appear, manifest themselves, in perceptual experience: the ways things seem to us.

There is no appearing without *awareness*. With phenomenal concepts we describe or express our awareness of our perceptual encounter with the world, how things or events look, feel, taste. If we call what phenomenal concepts refer to "qualia" of experience—describing an event as painful, an animal as frightening, honey as sweet—then qualia are directly introspectible in the sense that "one knows about one's own qualia noninferentially" (Kind 2001: 150).[1] If something happens to me without my realizing it, it is not a phenomenal experience. Should we even speak, then, of an experience in such a case?[2] If I suddenly realize that the dog is barking and think, looking at the clock, it must have been barking, as usual, for at least one hour, having the experience *now* of its barking is also having the experience of the difference between now and before, when I didn't have this experience. The case is slightly but significantly different if, driving on the highway while lost in thought, I suddenly realize that I missed the right exit—I suddenly have the image of the exit, and I realize that I did see it. This seems only slightly different from the previous case of the barking dog, for having this image of the exit seems highly contingent, and what happened to me earlier should be the same whether I happen to have this image or not. But the case is in fact significantly different, because having this image allows us to speak of the visual experience of the exit that I missed. Imagine someone saying "I realize that I have been hearing this dog for more than one hour but I do not remember hearing it." What could he or she mean?

Thus, taking the concept of experience in a Kantian rather than Aristotelian way,[3] we will say that there is no experience without *awareness* of an objectified something being experienced. In that sense, phenomenal experience is epistemic. But what about what happens to me before the moment where I realize that what I have been hearing in the background as I was working, and, as I realize as the same time, has been unnerving me increasingly, was the barking of the neighbor's dog? If I realize, at t_2, that I was hearing something at t_1, it must be that I was aware, at t_1, of something perceptual happening to me; I realize, at t_2, that I have been having a "hearing experience." If the concept of experience implies awareness, however, it shouldn't require reflective awareness, not at least as actual. But insofar as this awareness is intentional, it must allow the counterfactual statement to the effect that if I had been asked whether I could hear something then I would have realized it. There is something similar to this nonreflective awareness with the periphery of the visual field. The visual field is not restricted to what is in focus. Being able to move around, to notice suddenly that something happens on the side, a shape moving or the light changing, implies awareness of something, though not actual reflective awareness. But awareness of what? The question is pressing, but it is not so much about the awareness attached to phenomenal experience, that is, its being epistemic, as about the something this awareness is of, that is, about the representational character of phenomenal experience. Compared to what is in focus, the periphery of the visual field is certainly ill defined. But how much, or to what extent is it ill defined? "[A]ll round the periphery of your vision is an undoubtedly sensed region which is outside your ability to recognize" (Wright 2005: 74). Can it then be ill defined to the extent of being undefined, so that there would be no *representational* content? Let's postpone this "representational" issue for a brief moment and admit for now that there is no phenomenal experience without perceptual appearing.

Furthermore, there is no perceptual appearing without a *perceiver* to whom it appears. One's cognitive relation with the world originates in a physical encounter with the world, which involves one's body, particular, historical, and situated. Phenomenal reports describing or expressing our experience of the world—describing, that is, an interaction—are situated with respect to the condition of the interaction: we talk of how water feels to me, how honey tastes to me. One way to think about phenomenal reports being situated is to bring in the image of perspective. We may say that phenomenal language pertains to a perceptual perspective, on an object or an event—my tasting the honey, my feeling the water, relative to the conditions in which this perceptual event occurs. The notion of perspective is often used in support of the idea that a phenomenal fact or property and a physical fact or property could be one and the same even though it may be known, from different perspectives, under different descriptions (Lycan 2003). It is true that some objects or events can receive phenomenal and physical descriptions; but, as we will see, that does not provide any a priori support to the reductionist project.

The idea of perspective is not to be conflated with the idea of an enclosure, a separation from the world. Perception, though perspectival, is a direct access to the world. That there is something with which we interact, that perception is perspectival, implies that there is something that is being interacted with, something on which there is a perspective. We can think of the experience of warmth one has when putting one's hands in a cup of water as a perceptual perspective on water. That doesn't mean that we can conceive of water in general independent of the general possibility of perceptual perspectives on it. Being able to refer to water implies being able to learn the word, and that relies on certain possibilities of experience. But any particular "instance" of water doesn't need my experiencing it to be there.

Qualia are directly instrospectible, but phenomenal experience is a direct access to the world, that is, "phenomenal," as we'll use it, doesn't stand in contrast with "representational."[4] In perceptual experience, if certain things or states of things are perceived, apprehended in a certain way, insofar as a representation is characterized not only by what, but also by how it represents, then the content of perceptual experience is representational. The water is represented as warm, the dentist visit as painful, a strip-search as humiliating. The representational conception of phenomenal experience denies that there are aspects of experience, ways we see and feel the world, that cannot be interpreted as ways the world is represented (Dretske 2003), and denies that phenomenal experience has "'phenomenal' or 'qualitative' character that is not captured simply by saying what their representational content, if any, is" (Shoemaker 1994: 292) and which would be discovered thanks to a "sidelong glance" at something like a private sensation (Wittgenstein 1986: §274). That is, it is a claim for the transparency of phenomenal experience (Tye 2002).

But now imagine I am looking at an image on a screen, and it looks blurred. Suddenly I realize I am sitting too far away, that I need glasses. I put them on, and the image becomes distinct. How could the difference I am able to make between the two situations be a difference in representational content alone, since the image I look at on the screen is the same whether I wear my glasses or not? It must be that "[t]here are some phenomenal properties that really are attributable to experiences themselves" (Bach 1997: 467). It would have to be so, if "representational content" is taken to refer to what is represented independently of how it is represented. But the representational content is constituted not only by what is represented but also by how it is represented. The blurriness one experiences without one's glasses is not here a property of the object represented, but neither is it a property that should be ascribed to the experience itself. It is a property that the object is represented as having. The photograph of a block of ice (a sharply defined object) taken with an out-of-focus camera is blurry whereas the photograph of a cloud taken with a well-focused camera is not, even though they may look quite similar. Only the former is blurry, for only in that case the "fuzziness" the object is represented as having is not a property of the object being represented, that is, the sharply defined block of ice. An image shows an object in a blurry way when the object doesn't look the same as we know it looks when seen in what we know as "normal conditions"—and what is "not the same" here would have to be specified in terms of a descriptive contrast between fuzzy and sharp edges.

The same understanding of what it is for phenomenal experience to be representational can be applied to the experience of the periphery of the visual field. What is represented in the periphery of the visual field is not represented in the same way it is represented when it is in focus; the phenomenal experience is different, and the difference can be accounted for in terms of representational content. In fact, in the periphery the representational content is most often limited to shapes, lights, and movements. But to speak of the representational content of the experience of the periphery of the visual field doesn't require that we be able to identify what is represented in the same way as we would if it was represented in focus.

"Phenomenal" does not stand in contrast with "representational," but it does contrast with "physical" or "scientific."[5] A scientific description of water is free from perceptual dependencies. It is a description abstracted from experience, hence not perceptually perspectival. Not being situated with respect to perception doesn't preclude being situated some other way, though, for instance with respect to instrumental tools and practices, and thus being instrumentally perspectival.[6] The idea of perceptual perspective introduced here does not contrast with an "absolute conception of the world." The determination of the properties a scientific description assigns to objects abstracts from experience by appealing to experimental procedures and instrumental outcomes. But the conditions of possibility of this assignment are still rooted in experience in the sense that our having a sensation such as the sensation of heat is a condition of at least historical possibility of the development of thermometry.

Speaking of the qualia of experience and phenomenal language as pertaining to a certain way for things to appear, to a perspective, doesn't commit oneself to mental private "objects." Inner processes stand in need of external criteria. We learn to speak of our anxieties, pains, joys, "in the light of publicly observable symptoms" (Quine 1985: 5–6). But the acquisition of phenomenal language only begins with such general "symptoms." It develops, to a certain extent,[7] idiosyncratically, for it pertains to the grammar of phenomenal concepts (e.g., "Are *you* cold?,") that we can disagree on their conditions of application.[8] That doesn't commit us to any sort of antimaterialism. But contrary to what Quine claims, it is another matter to speak of the *reduction* of phenomenal language to neurophysical language, or of the *identification* of what is referred to by the former with what is referred to by the latter. The main reason for this is that, as pointed to by Quine for beliefs, for phenomenal experience too the external manifestations "vary drastically and unsystematically with the content . . . to be ascribed."

2   Reduction and Phenomenal Concepts

A reduction is primarily a relation between two forms of description, two languages. The general scheme of a reduction involves two vocabulary sets, and the possibility, in certain specified conditions, of replacing one language by the other. Ideally, where the reduction applies, the description of a phenomenon P given in the reduced language can be deduced a priori from the reducing language. But in practice, things are quite different. First, sometimes the replacement amounts to the elimination of the reduced descriptive terms. Second, when the new language (Tf) can be regarded as a more general descriptive instrument supplying the description provided in the first language (Tc), it is in particular conditions of application of Tf.[9] Third, in the most delicate cases, among which, in spite of its popularity, lies the case of the thermodynamics–statistical mechanics reduction relation (Hooker 1981: 47–48), the passage from Tf to Tc requires the introduction of an analogue Tc' such that, in certain conditions (limiting assumptions and boundary conditions),[10] Tf entails Tc' and Tc' is analogous to Tc.[11] That the deduction of Tc' (from Tf) is a reduction of Tc (to Tf) must then be warranted by correspondence rules, or "term-connecting assertions," relating their respective vocabulary. The restricted, idealist conditions of the deduction and the appeal to correspondence rules make it difficult to simply equate reduction with identification. Conceiving of these rules as statements of identity presents important epistemological advantages (Hooker 1981: 202–203). But whether it is always legitimate is a difficult question hinging on how the conditions for identity are to be specified.

All we can properly ask of a reducing theory, says Churchland (1985), is that the resources conjure up a set of properties whose nomological powers, roles, or features are systematic analogues of the powers, roles, or features of the set of properties postulated by the old theory. And if such a correspondence is achieved, the best explanation for this would be the identity of the properties that are referred to by the paired items. How would an analogue of "powers, roles, or features" be established? With concepts that have broadly functional or causal roles, the idea would be to show that the new description allows these roles to be filled. For instance, when the MKE rises the same effects occur as those that are associated with a rise in temperature.

Unfortunately, it is largely granted by the participants of the debate that phenomenal or mental concepts are not functional. They are recognitional, and as such they "lack any conceptual connections with concepts of other kinds, whether physical, functional or intentional" (Carruthers 2004: 155)— which doesn't mean that we don't have to learn, on the basis of external criteria, their conditions of application. That does not, however, according to Carruthers, rule out a reductive explanation of experience, for the facts or properties characterized purely recognitionally, from a first-person perspective, "also admit of third-personal characterization" (ibid.: 167).

The words used in phenomenal reports are sometimes used also to ascribe a phenomenal experience to someone else. But the "drastic and unsystematic" variability of criteria of ascription of mental state, the fact that identification of a state "depends heavily on symptoms *reported* by the patient" (Quine 1985, emphasis added), makes it very hard to see ascriptional language as anything like explanatory or functional. The ascriptional use is not autonomous with respect to the recognitional one. Patricia Churchland (1986: 303) claims that our folk psychology with its phenomenal language is a proto-scientific theory, just as folk physics once was, and there is no reason why it cannot become a mature science as well. But if an ascriptional use of phenomenal or mental concepts were to develop into something like an autonomous functional-psychological language, the question would remain of the relation between recognitional and ascriptional uses. If the ascriptional, in order to become functional, becomes independent of the recognitional, on what basis would one assert that the same word in the two languages refers to the same "thing"? Without a systematic connection between recognitional and functional languages, the reduction of the ascriptional to the functional-psychological is not an answer to the question of the reduction of the recognitional.

3 Sensation of Heat and Temperature

A classical objection to the mere possibility of establishing the identity between what phenomenal and neural descriptions are about appeals to the notion of *direct epistemic access*. What phenomenal concepts refer to is known directly, by introspection. The properties of neural activity are not known directly, by introspection; they are known through intersubjective investigations and measurements in terms that do not involve perceptual experience. The counterobjection seems easy, though: the notion of "being known directly" presents an intensional context where a mere difference in description can account for the difference in truth-value of the ascription of "being known directly." It is not necessary that something be known to have a certain property for it to have it. However, there is an antiphysicalist premise, as Loar (1990: 83) puts it, which even the physicalist should accept: phenomenal and physical-functional descriptions are cognitively independent. Loar adds that this cognitive independence doesn't imply the distinctness of what these descriptions are about (ibid.: 87). But what could be *in concreto* about the conditions of an assertion of identity?

Well, just look at the "reduction of heat," says the reductionist. We already have there such a case:

(1)   Warmth is identical with the mean level of the objects' microscopically embodied energies[12] (Churchland 1985: 18).

And as an argument against the objection of difference in epistemic access:

(2)   Temperature is known by me directly, by tactile sensing, whereas the mean molecular velocity is not; however, who could deny that for a body to have a certain temperature and to have a certain mean molecular velocity is one and the same thing? (ibid.: 20).

Don't we have, here, a case where a phenomenal description (viz., of the feeling of heat) turns out to refer to the same thing as a physical description?

Let's consider (1). If "being warm" is a phenomenal concept, it must be that being warm is feeling warm. There is no warmth, in the phenomenal sense, without the feeling of warmth, just as there is no pain without the feeling of pain. If you ask whether the water is warm enough to swim I will "try it out," with my foot, then the leg; it may feel different to me in each case, and different today from yesterday when I was so tired, even though for you it feels the same. The mean molecular velocity is a physical property whose determination has nothing to do with feelings and sensations. It has the value it has independent of my feeling anything. But then how can it have the same conditions of application as something like "being warm," which is completely, and necessarily, dependent on my feeling something?

There is an equivocation in "being warm," as there is one in "heat," as a physical quantity and as a "sensation of heat." "The reductive account of heat," writes Searle, "carves off the subjective sensations and defines heat as the kinetic energy of molecules' movements" (Searle 1998: 26). But Searle is twice wrong. The reduction doesn't carve off the subjective sensations because it relates physical concepts. What was reduced to kinetic energy was a thermodynamical variable which can be measured by using a thermometer. What was reduced is not a subjective quality, not even some admixture of subjective qualities and physical properties, but a previously objectified physical determination. Moreover, the elaboration of an objective, physical concept of heat didn't eliminate the phenomenal concept. When one speaks of a heat wave in contrast to a cold wave (note that this contrast between heat and cold doesn't exist in thermodynamics), the property that is referred to is phenomenal; the air is hot in the sense that it feels hot. It is only contingent that the temperature of the air during a heat wave is about 100° Fahrenheit. In the same way "being warm" can function as either a phenomenal or a physical description. Imagine a couple of biologists considering a test-tube of living cells that must be kept above a certain temperature. Asking "Do you think it is warm enough?" is not asking about someone's sensations. It is asking about the temperature, whether the biologist thinks it is high enough. Here anybody can simply find *the* answer by using a thermometer.

Of course the reductionist will insist that the words we use to express our experience, as happened with the word "heat," could be released from their subjective qualitative connotations and reduced to an objective description. But, again, the reduction of the concept of heat, or more precisely, the reduction of temperature, was the reduction of an objective large-scale property to an objective microscopic property, not the reduction of a phenomenal description. We still have, on the one hand, the phenomenal concept of heat ("heat wave" meaning that most people suffer from feeling hot), and on the other, the physical concept that has been reduced to another physical concept (the heat of a system meaning its energy). The reduction doesn't relate phenomenal and physical concepts.

Still, when the temperature varies the sensation I have varies, and in a predictable way. I can even sometimes say what the temperature is of the object I touch. There must be a correlation, and we want to make sense of it. Is it because of this correlation that Putnam (1992: 93) speaks of "heat (temperature)" as a secondary property, even though objective? Because it is a property that we can have a sensation of, namely, the sensation *of* heat? Do we have, as Churchland says, a tactile sensing of the temperature?

But within science, the conception of temperature and the ascription of a certain temperature are completely independent of any sensation anyone could have. And heat (temperature) is the same thing as MKE. So there is no more reason to call temperature a secondary property than there would be to call velocity, length, or duration secondary properties. If length and duration are not secondary properties, velocity is not either, and neither is heat (temperature). Speaking of "heat (temperature)" as a secondary property seems to be the result of a conceptual confusion.

In the present state of science, the relation between the physical concept of heat and the mean molecular velocity is such that their respective determinations are interdependent. But an object with a given temperature can feel different to different persons, or different to the same person depending on whether she is feverish, drunk, or touches it with the hand or the jaw. And one can suddenly feel hot or cold in connection with, for example, an emotive change of state. But if it is contingent that in the presence of heat (the scientific concept) we have the sensation of heat, what about the correlation? According to Kripke (1980: 132), given a certain sensation, sensation-of-heat, we identified a certain phenomenon as the property of heat because it is *able* to produce this sensation. When we have the kind of sensation we call "sensation-of-heat" (sensationh), we are not having the sensation *of* something, sensing a physical property, as if it were an object lying somewhere waiting to be stroked. What we feel is the water, the hot plate, the air, the cat. The correlation would result from this object's having a property "able to produce" the sensation.

But wait. Is this claim, that objects have a physical property able to produce (Searle speaks of "cause") a certain kind of sensation, an empirical one? Scientists developed experimental practices, in thermometry and thermodynamics, and achieved the conceptions of heat and temperature with no consideration for our sensations; these concepts have been defined in total independence from phenomenal concepts. "Being able to produce" or "cause" a sensation has no place whatsoever in the scientific conception of heat. Is it then a grammatical point? Imagine people eating together and one of them putting on his sweater; we usually do not expect any further explanation than "he is cold." And to the question "Why are you so cold?," an answer referring to the temperature would sound empty, since we are all submitted to the same without being cold; the question is "why are *you* so cold," with an implicit "when *we* are not," and calls for something personal, like "I am very sensitive to cold" or "I feel feverish."

We do have ordinary knowledge of a loose correlation, but no "process" of production or causation is needed to account for it. Science provides us with descriptions of how things change in terms of variation of physical parameters. We became able to describe the change of state of water in terms of the variation of a certain parameter, the temperature T, strictly correlated to the change of the state of the water. Long before we had this concept, we could already give a description of "the change of state of water," C—in terms of phenomenal difference, for instance, a difference in how it looks or feels. A phenomenal difference was hence already correlated to the change of state of the water, but too loosely for the taste of scientists. If a certain kind of sensation S is loosely correlated to C, and T strictly correlated to C, S had to be correlated to T, but it can only be a loose correlation. This loose correlation makes it possible for us to become able to *infer*, sometimes, the value of the temperature on the basis of our sensation, like someone can guess the mass of a box by lifting it. But being able to infer the value of the temperature from a phenomenal experience has nothing to do with "experiencing" or knowing "directly, by tactile sensing." The concept of temperature is autonomous with respect to experience, exactly in the same way as the MKE is. And if one is able to infer the value of the former, one can become able to infer the value of the latter as well. There is no epistemic access contrast. And rather than a case of reduction of the phenomenal to the physical, what we have is a case of *articulation* between phenomenal and physical concepts.

The reduction of thermodynamics to statistical mechanics provides no analogical support to the project of reduction of phenomenal to neuro-physical descriptions. The analogical argument fails. And we keep wondering how, if one admits the recognitional character of phenomenal concepts, and the "cognitive independence" of phenomenal and physico-functional concepts, the identity of what phenomenal and physico-functional concepts are about can be established. Certainly the best thing to do is to consider the experimental work devoted to this project.

4   Experimental Studies

How could one show the identity of what a phenomenal report and a neural description are about? Admittedly, a phenomenal experience is intentional; it is about something. As we saw, this aboutness is not only a "what," the water, but a "how," as warm, for instance. If one thinks about neural patterns as being characterized, identified, by merely physico-physiological parameters, the only relation one can establish seems to be a mere coexistence, cooccurrence, of a certain experience with a certain phenomenal content and a certain neural pattern. What the reductionist wants is an identity of the phenomenal state identified by its aboutness with a neural state, and a neural language that has sufficient descriptive power so as to make the phenomenal report merely optional for the description of our perceptual relation with the world. For that, the aboutness of the phenomenal state has to be, in one way or another, also a characteristic of the neural.

This points to a fundamental difference between a neural system and the physical systems we considered up to now, as having, say, a temperature. A neural system will be said to have, besides its physical (e.g., its firing rate) or physiological properties, representational properties, in the sense of being about something or having a representational content. This is philosophically daring—not that a physical object have a representational content, but that it have it on its own, by itself. It has this content not as the result of an intentional ascription, as in the case of a sign representing a bicycle path, or a painting representing a lake, but as the result of a natural process. An important question is then how the scientific experimenters find out what this representational content is, and whether there is room in it not only for the "what" but also for the "how" of experiential aboutness.

The neurobiological research program that seems the most promising to provide the expectations of the reductionist project with evidence is the work done on neural correlates of consciousness (NCC).[13] Chalmers (2000) proposes the following synthetic definition of an NCC: "A neural system N is a NCC if the state of N correlates directly with states of consciousness." At first sight, the notion of correlation rather looks like a betrayal of the reductionist hopes of evidence for identity. The reductionist needs a ground for the notion of identity that the mere notion of a correlate doesn't yield. A correlate, if it is something that is correlated, falls short of being identical with what it correlates with. But the notion of correlate may be misleading, downplaying the real ambition of the empirical research. In the case of visual experiences for instance, the search for NCCs, writes Chalmers, is the search for "the neural states that *determine* the specific contents of visual consciousness" (ibid., emphasis added). "Determine" sounds very different from merely "correlate."

However, without a condition on how the content of neural activity is identified, the identification would not yet be enough to support reductionism. To see why let's consider the experimental study that was conducted by Lutz et al. (2002) with the conclusion that "synchrony patterns *correlate* with ongoing conscious states during a simple visual task" (emphasis added). Several subjects are asked to press a button when they see a visual target appearing on a screen.[14] Before and after the task, the neural activity is recorded, as well as the phenomenal reports of the state of preparation, of attention, of how the perception of the form is experienced, with some surprise or not. The phenomenal reports lend themselves to a four-fold classification in terms of cognitive contexts. Each category corresponds to different patterns of neural synchronization identified by the experimenters at local and global scales; for instance they found that "local and long-range synchrony occurred at different frequencies before the stimulus depending on the degree of readiness reported by the subjects" (ibid.: 1588). An important upshot of this study concerned the variability of the neural activity of subjects submitted to identical tasks. Whereas this variability is generally "discarded by averaging techniques," the authors contend that, apprehended in terms of cognitive contexts, based on phenomenal reports, it becomes meaningful and allows a more differentiated analysis of neural activity. At the same time, the neural description induces more differentiated accounts of phenomenal experience.

This is an example of empirical study identifying neural correlates of phenomenal experience and ascribing content to them, in terms of "perception of something in a certain way." And yet, it doesn't contribute to the reductionist project; on the contrary. First, not only the identification of a correlate but also the determination of its content appeals to phenomenal report. Imagine that in order to determine something's MKE we had no other option than measuring the temperature; how could we then speak of a reduction? Second, this study aims to show that phenomenal reports not only cannot be done away with, but should be integrated in the scientific study of neural activity.

The kind of experiment that the reductionist project needs should have a procedure for determining the representational content of neural activity that doesn't appeal to the phenomenal description. And there seems to be such experimental work: for instance, the famous studies on the visual consciousness of monkeys.[15] A monkey M trained to react differently (action$_H$, action$_V$) to two different visual situations H and V (horizontal or vertical lines). For each situation, the scientist-observers record the neural activity of different areas of M's brain. They identify, both in the primary visual cortex and the inferotemporal cortex, distinct neurons, neurons$_H$ and neurons$_V$, as correlated to the presentation of H and V. It is known from human reports that if one is presented simultaneously with two different images, one to each eye, one will report a binocular rivalry, that is, seeing alternatively one and then the other. It is supposed that it should be the same for the monkey. Presented simultaneously with H and V to each eye, M produces alternatively action$_V$ and action$_H$.

What is "the neural system" determining the content of the experience of the monkey? In the primary visual cortex, the neural activity remains mainly correlated with the image that is presented: when the two images are presented, most of the neurons$_V$ and the neurons$_H$ respond, whereas M produces *alternatively* action$_H$ or action$_V$. The activity of these neurons doesn't seem therefore to reflect the content its phenomenal experience. By contrast, most of the neurons of the temporal cortex, identified before-hand as correlated with the presentation of a certain image I in a normal situation, respond in a binocular situation only when M produces the action associated with I. They are therefore good candidates for the status of neural correlate of the phenomenal experience of I, and would deter-mine the content of this experience since I is primarily their own repre-sentational content. What does this "I" stand for? Lines, butterfly, flower: whatever *the human observer* sees as being what M is confronted with and responds to.

In these experiments, the representational content of the neural system is specified by the correlation established by the scientist-observers between the visual situation, V, and the neural activity. This neural system correlates with the phenomenal experience of V insofar as it correlates with the "phenomenal report" (action$_V$) regarded as the expression of the per-ception of V. But there is a match in content only insofar as the observer defines the representational content of the neural activity according to how *he* describes the visual situation, and the representational content of the experience according to the same description. The phenomenal report doesn't seem necessary to define the representational content of the neural system only because it is assumed to be identical with the content of the phenomenal experience of the observer confronted with the same visual situation. The difference between action$_V$ and action$_H$ reveals a difference between the perception of situation$_V$ and situation$_H$; but what difference? Can't we imagine that, as happens in the work of Lutz et al. (2002), differ-ent (speaking) subjects could give different phenomenal reports of their experience? The experiment treats the phenomenal experience of M as a functional state, specified on the basis of the *effect* of a certain stimulation, "*input*"; but then, it contradicts the common assumption of the recogni-tional character of phenomenal description.

Treating the phenomenal experience as functional, with an input (which yields the representational content) specified by the observer, is ignoring the perspectival aspect of perceptual experience. Perceptual activ-

ity involves the whole body, as situated somewhere, in a particular relation with its environment: "the perceptual experience as of a vertical line
will represent the line as against a background and as occupying a certain
position in egocentric space, as occupying a certain spatial relation to *you*,
the embodied perceiver" (Noë and Thompson 2004: 12). If the representational content of a neural system is to be the same as the perceptual
experience it correlates with, then it should integrate the perceptual relation of the perceiver with this environment. What is at stake is the very
notion of representational content, and what is challenged is the underlying assumption about neural activity as a detector of features of the environment determined independently of the conditions of perception.

This assumption casts some light on how a phenomenal description
(of the experience of heat) could be regarded as reducible to both a statistical mechanical description of an external object and a neural description
of the activity of the brain. The external object and the neural activity are
indeed meant to have a property in common. The neural activity as we saw
is said to have a representational content, meant to be the property of an
external object. The neural system is viewed as an instrument of detection
and computation of the properties of external objects: "the senses show the
brain, otherwise blind, how things stand, 'out there,' both in the external
world and in its own distal body" (Akins 1996: 342). For instance, in the
case of peripheral thermoreception, according to the physicalist picture,
"like miniature biological thermometers, the receptors record the temperature of their immediate surround, its ups and downs. . . . The receptors, we
think, must react with a unique signal, one that correlates with a particular temperature state" (ibid.). The picture says that there must be a strict
correlation between the temperature and the reaction of the receptors. But
it is not *empirically* possible to make sense of the activity of the thermo-
system in these terms. For instance, in extreme temperatures, high or low,
the system reacts identically; so what does it "say" about the world? "That
must stop!" They are pain receptors. For the middle zone of temperature,
what happens with thermo-receptors depends on many things that have
no place in a scientific description of what happens outside. For instance,
how the system reacts depends on its initial state: imagine one hand in
water at 10° C, the other in water at 30° C, and then both in water at
40° C. The thermo-system reacts differently in the two hands, while the
state of the world, in scientific terms, is the same: 40° C. Moreover, what
happens with the thermo-receptors at the moment of the encounter with
the new medium is not the same as what happens after a while, although
the scientific description of this medium mentions no change. It is dif-

ferent also in different parts of the body, and it depends furthermore on how far the temperature is from the painful extremes. Accordingly, one can hardly make sense of what the thermo-system is doing in terms of the scientific description of the objects encountered; but it makes perfect sense in terms of the perspective of the perceiver on the world: the world is perceived from a certain state of the body and in terms of what matters to the body. And if one wants to ascribe a representational content, for that reason, it is not to the world scientifically described that one should turn, but to the perceiver.

Paradoxically the case of "heat" may have, finally, an analogical relevance regarding the relation between phenomenal and neural descriptions. It could have relevance not for a reduction (since if the concept of heat has been reduced it is as a physical concept), but for an articulation, as happens with the phenomenal concepts related to the sensation of heat and the physical concept of temperature. This is, in fact, the core of the conception defended by Varela (1997) of the naturalization of experience (Bitbol 2002; Peschard 2004): that of a scientific study of phenomenal experience aiming to bring together phenomenal reports and neural descriptions in an interactive and dynamical practice where each of them acts as an equal constraint on the other, thereby acquiring more differentiation.

Notes

1. The notion of direct introspectibility, as Kind (2001) aptly insists, doesn't imply other epistemic notions such as "infallibility," "incorrigibility," or "indubitability."

2. We thank Edmond Wright for his helpful comments and for encouraging us to develop this point.

3. Stevenson (2000: 284): "There is a wide, roughly Aristotelian, sense of the term 'experience' (or 'mental states') in which experiences can be ascribed to all creatures capable of sensation, emotional arousal, unconceptualized perception, and perception-guided activity. But we can distinguished a narrower, more distinctively Kantian use of 'experience' (his term was *Erfahrung*) which is distinctive of human beings. This involves the subject being able to apply concepts to represent states of affairs, to make perceptual judgment, and to evaluate the justification for such judgments."

4. Contrary to a conception of "qualia" as what in the "phenomenal character [of conscious experience] outruns representational content" (Block 1996: 20).

5. Hence the physical description of an object, of water, may change, ascribing it new physical properties, without the phenomenal description of the perceptual experience of water, and its representational content, being different.

6. The conception of scientific measurement as perspectival representation is developed, e.g., in Giere 2006.

7. To the extent that language is embedded in forms of life that involve cultural and biological common normalizing constraints.

8. Which is why the concepts of colors have such an ambiguous status between phenomenal and objective; "looking red" has a flexibility similar to "feeling warm," but "being red" involves normal conditions, contrary to "being warm."

9. For instance, Newtonian mechanics is an asymptotic limit of relativistic mechanics (for $1/c \to 0$), ray optics of wave optics (for $\lambda \to 0$) (Hooker 2004: 437–438).

10. E.g., the thermodynamic limit requires infinite numbers of molecules, large volumes, random motion, and ergodicity.

11. E.g., in Gibbs's version of statistical mechanics the analogues to thermodynamic functions are mean values of statistical parameters; the value of the temperature is given by the mean value of molecular kinetic energy.

12. A similar claim concerning pitch and oscillatory frequency is criticized in Crooks 2002.

13. See Metzinger 2000.

14. See also Peschard 2004: 400–403.

15. For detailed comments see, e.g., Chalmers 2000, and Noë and Thompson 2004.

References

Akins, K. 1996. Of sensory systems and the "aboutness" of mental states. *Journal of Philosophy* 93, 7: 337–372.

Bach, K. 1997. Engineering the mind. *Philosophy and Phenomenological Research* 57, 2: 459–468.

Bitbol, M. 2002. Science as if situation mattered. *Phenomenology and the Cognitive Sciences* 1: 181–224.

Block, N. 1996. Mental paint and mental latex. *Philosophical Issues* 7: 19–49.

Carruthers, P. 2004. Reductive explanation and the "explanatory gap." *Canadian Journal of Philosophy* 34, 2: 153–173.

Chalmers, D. What is a neural correlate of consciousness? In Metzinger 2000.

Churchland, P. 1985. reduction qualia and the direct introspection of brain states. *Journal of Philosophy* 82, 1: 8–28.

Churchland, P. S. 1986. *Neurophilosophy: Toward a Unified Science of the Mind-Brain.* Cambridge, Mass.: MIT Press/A Bradford Book.

Crooks, M. 2002. Intertheoretic identification and mind–brain reductionism. *Journal of Mind and Behavior* 23, 3: 193–222.

Dretske, F. 2003 Experience as representation. *Philosophical Issues* 13: 68–82.

Giere, R. 2006. *Scientific Perspectivism.* Chicago: University of Chicago Press.

Hooker, C. A. 2004. Asymptotics, reduction, and emergence. *British Journal of Philosophy* 55: 435–479.

Hooker, C. A. 1981. Towards a general theory of reduction. *Dialogue* 20: 38–59, 201–236.

Kind, A. 2001. Qualia realism. *Philosophical Studies* 104: 143–162.

Kripke, S. 1980. *Naming and Necessity.* Cambridge, Mass.: Harvard University Press.

Loar, B. 1990. Phenomenal states. *Philosophical Perspectives* 4: 81–108.

Lycan, W. G. 2003. Perspectival representation and the knowledge argument. In *Consciousness: New Philosophical Essays*, 384–395. Oxford: Oxford University Press.

Lutz, A., J.-P. Lachaux, J. Martinerie, and F. J. Varela. 2002. Guiding the study of brain dynamics by using first-person data. *PNAS* 99: 1586–1591.

Metzinger, T., ed. 2000. *Neural Correlates of Consciousness: Empirical and Conceptual Questions.* Cambridge, Mass.: MIT Press/A Bradford Book.

Noë, A., and E. Thompson. 2004. Are there neural correlates of consciousness? *Journal of Consciousness Studies* 11, 1: 3–28.

Peschard, I. 2004. La Réalité sans Représentation. La Théorie énactive de la Cognition et sa Légitimité Epistémologique. Thesis, l'Ecole Polytechnique, Paris.

Putnam, H. 1992. *Renewing Philosophy.* Cambridge, Mass.: Harvard University Press.

Quine, W. V. O. 1985. States of mind. *Journal of Philosophy* 82, 1: 5–8.

Searle, J. R. 1998. How to study consciousness scientifically. In *Toward a Science of Consciousness II*, ed. S. R. Hameroff, 15–29. Cambridge, Mass.: MIT Press/A Bradford Book.

Stevenson, L. 2000. Synthetic unities of experience. *Philosophy and Phenomenological Research* 60, 2: 281–305.

Shoemaker, S. 1994. Self-knowledge and "inner sense." Lecture III: The phenomenal character of experience. *Philosophy and Phenomenological Research* 54, 2: 291–314.

Tye, M. 2002. Representationalism and the transparency of experience. *Noûs* 36: 137–151.

Varela, F. 1997. The naturalization of phenomenology as the transcendence of nature: Searching for generative mutual constraints. *Alter: Revue de Phénoménologie* 5: 355–385.

Wittgenstein, L. 1986. *Philosophical Investigations.* Oxford: Clarendon Press.

Wright, E. 2005. *Narrative, Perception, Language, and Faith.* Basingstoke: Palgrave Macmillan.

9 A Process-oriented View of Qualia

Riccardo Manzotti

1 Galileo's Divide

At the root of the problem of qualia there could be an incorrect assumption, namely the separation between subject and object. This assumption lurks at the bottom of the philosophical analysis of qualia, and hinders the understanding of the nature of qualia. I will propose an alternative view, based on the concept of process, which appears capable of endorsing a realist view of qualia.

Although the notion of qualia is relatively recent in the philosophical debate (C. I. Lewis used the word for the first time in 1929), its conceptual origin can be traced back to the seventeenth century when the related notion of secondary qualities was developed. Most of the current literature on qualia (Block 1980; Jackson 1982; Levine 1983; Dennett 1988; Shoemaker 1990; Stubenberg 1998; Metzinger 2003) is inscribed inside the playground for the discussion that was defined in 1623 by Galileo Galilei's book *The Assayer*. In this text, which was one of the most profoundly influential books of the time, Galileo made a crucial step. He suggested that the "real" world is made only of quantitative aspects, and that all the other empirical aspects, like quality and form, are somehow created by the "living organism." It was an ontological claim with no empirical basis, heavy with metaphysical and ontological implications. He wrote (Galilei, *The Assayer*, 1623):

Therefore, I am inclined to think that these tastes, smells, colors, etc., with regard to the object in which they appear to reside, are nothing more than mere names, and exist only in the sensitive body; insomuch that when the living creature is removed all these qualities are carried off and annihilated; [. . .] if ears, tongues, and noses were removed, I am of the opinion that shape, quantity, and motion would remain, but there would be an end of smells, tastes, and sounds, which, abstractedly from the living creature, I take to be mere words.

This lengthy passage is the first outline of the modern theoretical frame-work in which the conscious mind is discussed. It contains: (1) the distinc-tion between primary and secondary properties (or "qualities," which is a misleading name); (2) the link between primary properties and quan-tity, and between secondary properties and quality; (3) the claim that the former are *real* while the latter are "mere words" that "exist only in the sensitive body." On the basis of an epistemological difference—what can be described by quantities and what cannot—Galileo put forward an onto-logical difference. This is the dualistic view. Nowadays, the role of the soul is taken by the brain (e.g., in Koch 2004).

To grasp the extent to which this standpoint has permeated our current scientific view, it is useful to quote a passage from a neuroscience text-book (Kandel, Schwartz, and Jessel 1995: 370) that closely mirrors Galileo's quote:

We receive electromagnetic waves of different frequencies but we perceive color: red, green, orange, blue or yellow. We receive pressure waves but we hear words and music. We come in contact with a myriad of chemical compounds dissolved in air or water but we experience smells and tastes.

Although the dichotomy between phenomenal and physical was sug-gested by the historical founder of the scientific method and has been carried on by many scientists, it is not, by any means, a scientific hypoth-esis. Recently, the neuroscientist M. R. Bennett and the philosopher P. M. S. Hacker observed that "[the previous hypothesis] is not an empirical claim or a scientific hypothesis, let alone a scientific theory that can be or has been confirmed experimentally. It is a *philosophical* or *conceptual* claim, which can be confirmed or disconfirmed only by conceptual investiga-tions" (Bennett and Hacker 2003: 129).

Galileo's definition of mental states is rather similar to more recent definitions of qualia. For instance, Frank Jackson defined qualia as "certain features of the bodily sensations especially, but also of certain perceptual experiences, which no amount of purely physical information includes" (Jackson 1982: 273). Another, common definition states that qualia are the "what it's like" character of mental states—the way it feels to have mental states such as pain, seeing red, smelling a rose, and the like. Along the same lines, Richard Gregory (1998) asks whether sensations are picked up by our sensors or created in our brains.

Following Galileo's seminal intuition, many authors, for example Daniel Dennett, have claimed that the only acceptable starting point is the physicalist, objective standpoint of science. It maintains that only objective entities belong to the physical world. Private, subjective, and first-person entities, by definition, cannot be reported or be the target of a reliable report. Furthermore, the neurological study of the brain does not show anything like subjective phenomenal experiences. Therefore, qualia were introduced to counterbalance the unsatisfactory phenomeno-logical score of physical ontology. Usually this low score is imputed to the dichotomy between physical and mental that is imperfectly mirrored in the dichotomy between objective and subjective—the former refers to an ontological gap, the latter to an epistemic one. Nevertheless, the notion of qualia has been heavily criticized by many authors, as it seems to intro-duce a very problematic subjective domain (Bennett and Hacker 2003).

This rather sparse introduction stresses one fact: the qualia debate rests on the assumption that there is a divide between the phenomenal and the physical or, at least, a divide between the subject and the object—a divide introduced by Galileo four hundred years ago. In the following, I will try to show that there is an alternative standpoint compatible with the physical stance that also addresses the issue of subjective phenomenal experiences.

2   A Realist Process-based View of Qualia

Like most of current philosophy of mind and neuroscience, the aforemen-tioned definitions of qualia are based on a substance-oriented ontology. By substance-oriented, I mean any ontology that is based on individuals or substances like objects, people, or representations. Such ontological schema often use terms like "properties," "mental states," and "sensa-tions," which refer to substance-like entities. The use of such terms leads to a separation between secondary and primary properties or, equivalently, to a separation between phenomenal and physical properties.

This often unquestioned and implicitly accepted separation entails the assumption that qualia correspond to properties different from those of the physical world or at least different from those of the external environ-ment. That is why many authors suggest that somehow the brain creates internally the qualia used to deal with external objects. And yet, as Alfred N. Whitehead observed, "Why should we perceive secondary qualities? It seems an extremely unfortunate arrangement that we should perceive a lot of things that are not there. Yet, this is what the theory of secondary qualities in fact comes to" (Whitehead 1920: 27). I have elsewhere started to address this issue (Manzotti 2006a,b) stressing the fact that it could be worthwhile to pursue some alternative framework.

Another relevant issue is the dichotomy between the representational and the phenomenal aspect of qualia. Some authors (e.g., Tye 1990) claim that all relevant properties of qualia are reducible to their representational role. When I see a red surface, my feeling could be reduced to the color that is represented by that mental state. On the contrary, other authors claim that there are aspects of qualia that cannot be reduced to their representational role. However, both claims depend on the assumption that the mental state (whether phenomenal or representational or both) is separate from the represented physical event.

According to this view, when I see a telescope, I have a mental state with a certain representational content. Furthermore, I have certain phenomenal experiences. This approach is based on the idea that the mental state—or, at least, its carrier—is separate from the external object. Once again we are dealing with the Galilean divide outlined in the previous section. On one side there is the external object with its supposed physical properties, on the other side there is the neural activity (with its physical properties) that is somehow (cor)related with the phenomenal properties. It is assumed that there is a separation between the object and the subject.

The following questions address the assumed separation between object and subject. Is it really possible to distinguish between what is represented in a mental state and the content of that mental state? If you ask me where is the red that I am seeing, I am not going to point at my brain, I am going to point at the external object. Let us postpone the analysis of cases of indirect perception (dreams, hallucinations, and afterimages) until a later section. In everyday perception, where would we locate qualia? We would locate them in the physical world.

However, this kind of naive realism introduces a set of difficulties. The main one is that the bearers of physical properties, namely physical objects, are separate from the body of the subject. Thus, the relation between the subject and such external entities is unclear, since it involves some kind of metaphysical relation between separate entities. Many authors have tried to formalize this intuition by developing various versions of externalism and realism. Suitable examples are neo-realism by Edwin Holt (Holt 1914) or externalism (Putnam 1975; Lycan 2001). But these versions of externalism are also based on the idea that there is a separation between what is perceived and the perceiver.

Consider this: in our brain, neural processes take place spanning time and space. These neural processes are physical and are the result of earlier physical processes that took place in the physical world. For instance, when I see a red ball, there is a physical process that begins from the surface of

the ball and hits the receptors of my eye. Then, the receptors trigger chemical reactions that propagate inside the brain through axons and dendrites.
From a causal and physical point of view, there is a continuous process
that progresses from the surface of the red ball to the activity of my brain.

There is no reason to separate what takes place in front of the eye,
and what takes place beyond. It is a continuous physical process. Instead
of considering the external object and the neural activity as two separate
entities, I suggest considering the whole physical process as beginning on
the external object and ending in the brain (Manzotti 2006a,b). According
to this view, phenomenal experience and external reality are two different
ways to describe the same process.

Consider the process of seeing a color. By means of the existence of
the brain and its neural structures, a complex set of physical conditions
becomes the origin of a complex process that ends in the brain whenever a color is recognized. There is neither a color in the wavelength nor
a color on the surface of the object. The latter case is shown by situations
where the perception of the color depends not only on the properties of
the surface but on more complex conditions. Finally, there is no color in
the brain in the neural activity as such. There are just chemical reactions.
But, if we consider the whole process (from the object to the inside of the
brain), we will find that this process has all the properties of our phenomenal experience.

The same rationale holds for sounds, smells, tastes, and even for more
complex phenomenal experiences such as those related with a face, a
pattern, a word, or a piece of music. They neither exist autonomously in
the world, nor are created inside the brain. They are processes partially
outside the brain and partially inside the brain. Thus the subject and the
object are not separate. On the contrary, they are two ways of describing
the same process. Qualia are neither inside the subject nor outside. Qualia
are processes taking place as a result of the external world as well as the
body and brain structures.

Consider the perception of a face as a whole; it is a distinct phenomenal experience different from that of the individual features. When a face
is recognized, a distinct phenomenal quale is experienced. A new quale
pops up. This is something that does not happen with subjects affected by
prosopoagnosia. But a face does not exist in isolation. It requires a proper
physical system, through which it is the cause of a physical process.

I recognize that the view presented here collapses the distinction
between sensation and perception. Each sensation is identical to a process
singling out a certain part of reality. The bare level of qualia is explained

as the lowest and most simple level of perception. Indeed, one could still distinguish between perception and sensation by defining qualia as those perceptions that cannot be further fragmented in lower-level perceptual contents. For instance, a face can be fragmented into facial features. A facial feature can be fragmented into shapes, colors, and lines. But a color cannot be further decomposed. Hence a color is considered to be a sensation. However, there is no such need to introduce a special ontological status that separates sensation and perception.

The standpoint presented here could be defined as an *externalist, realist, process-oriented* view of qualia. I would like to explain each of these features singly.

The view is an externalist one since the process corresponding to a quale is not completely inside the brain and the body of the subject. The process extends outside the body and spans over a longer time window than that occupied by neural processes alone. Qualia are spatially and temporally larger than the body. However, the view differs from other kinds of externalism because it does not assume that the external reality is separate and autonomous with respect to the activity in the brain. In other words, the red that I see is not in the ball if I am not looking at it. The red takes place, partially outside my body, whenever the process that ends in my brain, takes place. The red *is* that process both physical and phenomenal.

It is a realist view since there is no dualism involved. There is no separation between the representation and what is represented. There is identity between the two. What is perceived is neither a mental ink produced somehow by my brain nor a functional state supervening on my relation with the external world. Each quale is a physical process that singles out a part of reality. There is no longer a mental reality and a physical one, or a phenomenal content and a physical one. There is a process taking place. From a certain point of view, the position presented here is a realist one, since there is no longer a dichotomy between the representational–phenomenal and the physical world. However, the naive realist believes in a real world that is autonomous and external to the body, whereas I suggest that the world is a flow of processes partially shared by the subject (which is nothing more than that shared collection of processes).

Finally, it is a standpoint based on processes since it does not start from an ontology based on substances or individuals but rather based on a process ontology like those developed by authors like Alfred N. Whitehead or William James (James 1996 [1908]; Whitehead 1978 [1929]; Seibt 1997). A process-oriented ontology offers several advantages although it has been scarcely exploited.

In short, I suggest that a quale is a process that singles out a part of reality (a color, a shape, a smell) and that ends in the brain. According to this view a quale is neither internal to the brain nor located in an external and autonomous entity.

In perception, objects, events, or states of affairs take place as wholes, thereby being the cause of processes. Rainbows, faces, patterns, characters, words, constellations are suitable examples (Manzotti 2006a). Parts of reality, which would have remained separate, produce an effect as a whole, thereby becoming the cause of a process. It is interesting that a cause can be singled out of objects, events, and states of affairs scattered in time and not only in space.

For instance, a rainbow cannot be conceived without an observer. A rainbow is a process and thus requires the proper physical systems with which to interact. It can be shown that the proper physical system is a brain like that of a human. Where is the quale of the rainbow? Where is the rainbow? Where is the representation of the rainbow? Under the spell of a substance-oriented view, we had to struggle with three separate entities, trying to reconcile them together. Adopting the process view presented here, there is just one process, beginning in the cloud and ending in the beholder's brain. This process is a unity and can be described through three different perspectives: the phenomenal experience, the representation, and the rainbow itself.

Analogous rationales can be defended for colors, smells, objects, and more complex entities. The world is made of processes, not of substances. A word requires time to be uttered. A set of flashing lights is made of separate events; but they are a unity, since they are perceived as a whole and produce an effect as a whole. Interestingly enough, they are a unity spanning time and space. There are many suitable examples requiring time and thus existing only as processes: gestures, movements, fragments of music, words, and visual effects.

Is this view tenable? To defend it, I would like to make use of Daniel Dennett's famous list of the essential properties of qualia. It is a very strict list since it was introduced by Dennett in order to show that, in the end, "there are no qualia at all" (Dennett 1988). According to Dennett, there are four properties that are commonly ascribed to qualia. Qualia are: (i) ineffable (they cannot be communicated, or apprehended by any other means than direct experience); (ii) intrinsic (they are nonrelational properties, which do not change depending on the subject's relation to other things); (iii) private (all interpersonal comparisons of qualia are impossible); and

(iv) directly apprehensible in consciousness (to experience a quale is to know one experiences a quale).

The process I am suggesting here is ineffable, intrinsic, private, and directly apprehensible in consciousness. Furthermore, it is perfectly physical.

It is ineffable because it cannot be communicated by means of words or other third-person communication devices. If I want to communicate to Sara the taste of a certain wine, the only way is to make Sara reproduce the same process that took place when I tasted the wine. In other words, I cannot explain to Sara how the wine tastes. However, I can convince Sara to drink it and thus go through the same process that constituted my phenomenal experience. Of course, several conditions need to be satisfied. The substance that Sara drinks should be the same as the one I drank. Sara's body and brain should be reasonably similar to my own in order to allow the same process to be caused by the substance. If Sara were unable (owing to sensory or cultural differences) to interact in the same way with that wine, the same kind of process could not take place. Qualia cannot be communicated using words, but they can be reproduced.

It is intrinsic since each quale is a token process. In other words, the view does not commit to any kind of relational externalism such as that advocated by Putnam or Burge. Therefore it does not fall into the trap of the twin earth and similar thought experiments. Whenever a process that singles out whatever part of the world is called red (an extremely complex chain of causes and effects) takes place, it is "red" that takes place—phenomenal and physical red being two ways to refer to the same process. For the sake of argument, it is easy to show that a different cause would be a different process. For instance, if we had XYZ instead of H_2O, even if the high-level functional relation between the brain and the watery substance were the same, there would surely be different physical processes. Therefore it would be a different process and thus a different quale. So to speak, each quale is self-contained. However, new qualia can be derived by comparison with previous ones.

It is private. Every process takes place once and thus it cannot be shared. When Sara and I are observing a color, there are two separate processes taking place—one from the red object to my brain and another from the red object to her brain. Although they can be very similar, they are at least numerically different. They take place in different portions of space. The same rainbow cannot be seen by two different people, since each of them would single out a different rainbow owing to the fact that they necessarily occupy two different positions in space. Processes are necessarily private and yet physical. Consider the image you see in a mirror. Could it be shared? No, someone else would see a different reflection. Two people occupy different points in space and thus see different reflections.

Finally, the process is directly apprehensible in consciousness. There is no need to know anything else. Such a process is, at the same time, what is usually defined as a part of the world and the phenomenal experience of it—the two being different perspectives on the same process.

3   Representation by Means of Identity

A debated issue is whether qualia have a phenomenal aspect that is not exhausted by their representational role. In other words, when I see red, the felt redness either is simply a representation of the redness of the external surface, or it corresponds to some internal phenomenal redness. The approach presented here sidesteps the whole discussion by stressing a possible identity not only between the representational and the phenomenal, but between the phenomenal–representational and the physical. A somehow analogous position has been defended by Galen Strawson (Strawson 2003). I would like to carry on the same argument by suggesting a different solution to the old problem of representation—a solution that could also exhaust the phenomenal aspect of qualia.

A representation is normally conceived as something different from what is represented. For a representation is a re-presentation of something else, namely, the represented. Once again the assumption of the separation between entities is at work. However, authors like Edwin Holt have observed that "Nothing can represent a thing but that thing itself" (Holt 1914: 142) and that "A representation is always partially identical with that which it represents, and completely identical in all those features and respects in which it is a representations. In its more strictly logical aspect, every case of representation is a case of partial or complete identity between two systems" (ibid.: 143). According to the process view presented here, each phenomenal experience is identical with what it should represent. There is no longer a separation between the red represented and the representation of red. There is only a process, which can be seen either as the physical red or as the phenomenal one.

The whole notion of representation gets a twist and becomes more properly a notion of the presentation of some aspect of reality (a color, a smell, a complex set of features, a face). It is no longer a matter of re-presenting some aspect of reality in a separate physical system (in the brain or in the body). The suggested physical process is that aspect of reality which supposedly had to be re-presented in the brain. However, there is no longer a need to make such an assumption. The process is, at the same time, both the phenomenal red and the physical red. Therefore, the notion of representation is reduced to that of identity. To represent something is to be that something.

4   Difficult Cases Revisited

Any realist theory faces the apparently insurmountable counterexamples of situations like dreams, hallucinations, illusions, and afterimages. The counterexamples include all situations in which there seems to be no external "object" to be perceived. A caveat is needed here. In all the following examples I will try to point out a possible external cause (or collection of causes) of a phenomenal experience. This does not mean I claim that all our experience have a traditional object (like a chair or a car or a face) as their cause. It means that there is a set of physical events otherwise scattered in time and space that, by means of the neural structure of one's brain, are capable of producing a joint effect. For instance, one might occasionally pick out an edge, say, that momentarily reminded one of a familiar profile, but that does not imply that the profile was there in the chaos beforehand. Because an edge is producing an effect in a subject, that edge does exist. One can see "a face," even a completely unfamiliar one, in the foliage outside the window. Hence there is a certain pattern in the foliage that is the cause of one's neural activity. So although hallucinations can be entirely un-objectified, whereas we refer to traditional or conventional objects, they could still have a cause (or a set of causes) in the subject's past.

Some authors have suggested that an externalist view does not have to explain all cases of perception (for a comprehensive review see Hurley 2006). According to them, externalism does not need to characterize all mental states and hence has a lower burden of proof than internalism. Unfortunately a compromise between internalism and externalism could be rather dangerous, since it should support two different kinds of mental phenomena: one kind produced by means of external processes and another one by means of internal processes. How could we compare two phenomenally identical experiences if they were produced by different mechanisms? That is way, in my essay, I argue in defense of a radical form of externalism where all mental states (which I would not call states, but processes) fall under an externalist perspective. I will briefly address some of these situations to demonstrate that a process-oriented, external-ist-realist approach will overcome most of the problems.

4.1 Dreams

Last night, I dreamed of my grandmother, who died in 1985. During my dream I had qualia connected to her. How was this possible? A possible answer is that any phenomenal experience is continuous with a physical event. Any phenomenal experience is a process that ends in a brain. How long could this process last? During normal perception, it seems acceptable to take into account a process that spans time and space. Visual perception requires a time span ranging from approximately 10 ms to 200 ms. Is there any scientific evidence that constrains the maximum time length of a process? As far as I know, there is none. Therefore, I suggest that dreams are just cases of postponed perception. My dream of my grandmother would be nothing else than a perception of my grandmother that took many years instead of a few milliseconds to be completed.

The rationale is the following. In normal perception, phenomenal experience or qualia are processes that span from the external world to the neural activity inside the brain. Thus a quale is larger than the brain and longer than the neural activity encompassing the physical causal chain that began outside of the brain and the body of the subject. In a dream the time span is longer than usual—days, week, months, even years. Twenty years ago or so, a visual event with my grandmother took place. It produced effects in a very narrow time span and these effects were the end of processes that corresponded with my conscious perception of her at that time. Yet, it is still producing effects now. For instance, a recognizable effect is the fact that last night I dreamed of her. It was the end of a causal process that began twenty years ago and was able, owing to my brain structure, to produce an explicit effect now.

4.2 Afterimages

If I have a red afterimage as a result of a flashbulb going off, the spot I "see" in front of the photographer's face looks red, even though there is no such spot. There are different possible interpretations of this fact. A simple one suggests that my feeling of red is due to the instantiation of the same kind of neural activity that is normally elicited by a red objects. Thus, the phenomenal redness would be independent from the external world. Yet, another explanation is possible. Owing to the intensity of the flashbulb, my photoreceptors do not work in the usual way. Their sensitivity to a certain wavelength has been dramatically modified and reduced. As a result, I continue to be causally in relation with the flashing of the flashbulb. For instance, if the flash was so intense that for a few seconds I am completely blind, the result is that my brain is no longer causally connected with the surrounding environment. From a causal point of view, the state of my receptors is connected with the flash and not with the current scene in front of my eyes. That's why I have a feeling of red or white instead of having the qualia related with what is in front of my eyes.

There is also another kind of afterimage that is worthy of examination. Imagine staring at a cross in the middle of four squares of four different bright and saturated colors—let's say red, green, blue, and yellow. After ten seconds someone substitutes the four colored squares with a white surface. You will still see four squares for a while, and they will have the complementary colors of the original ones. A naive scientist could explain the phenomenon by saying that some neural activity elicited by the original colors is still going on and producing a phenomenal quale. I suggest an alternative explanation. For the sake of simplicity, let us consider only one of the squares—the red one. Staring at the cross you let an area of your retina be stimulated by a red light for ten seconds. As a result there was an adaptation of those receptors that are more sensitive to red light. When the white surface was shown, that area of the retina reacted in a different way to the white light than the other areas, namely, that area was less sensitive to the red component than to the green and blue ones. In that part of the visual field you were almost blind to red and not to green and blue. Since all components of the spectrum are contained in the white light, you saw a cyan square, which is the sum of green and blue. In sum, the afterimage was not inside your head. The afterimage was that part of the world that you were not blind to—namely the green and blue components of an area on a white surface.

From the point of view of phenomenal experience, there are two kinds of afterimages: those that correspond to a persistent perception and those that correspond to changes in the normal behavior of receptors. In the former case, the triggering event continues to be the origin of the process ending in the brain. In the latter case, we perceive something that is normally present in the environment and that is hidden to us by the normal behavior of our receptors.

4.3 Nonveridical Perception

When we look at a stick in a glass of water, we see the stick as if it were bent. Of course it is not. The quale we have does not have the right representational content. However, from the point of view presented here, there is one kind of process when we see the stick out of the water, and there is a different process when we see the stick bent in the water. It is no surprise that there is a different perception and a different phenomenal experience in each case. It is not simply a matter of looking different; the two situations correspond to two different processes. Once again, simply dropping a substance-oriented view of properties allows a reshaping of the traditional problems.

4.4 Phosphenes

If the visual cortex of a sighted subject is stimulated either by a strong mechanical blow or by direct electric stimulation, the subject reports having a visual phenomenal experience of sparkles of light called phosphenes. Where is the real light? Phosphenes seem to pose a real threat to the approach presented here.

A different explanation is the following. What takes places in the brain as a result of the stimulation of a visual area by a nonvisual stimulus (pressure on the eyeball, electricity, bumping) is related to a very long history of visual stimuli. As a result it maintains a causal continuity with these stimuli. On the other hand, what would be the perceived phenomenal content if the eyes were disconnected from visual stimuli from the very beginning and yet subjected to pressure? According to explanations analogous to the law of specific nerve energies, the perceived phenomenal contents should be visual phosphenes. On the other hand, according to the hypothesis of continuity with the external world, the phenomenal content should be of a tactile nature. The eyes should work as poor tactile receptors. Furthermore, if they were eventually exposed to light, by some technical or surgical means, they should elicit "tactile" phosphenes.

Interestingly, although the literature is rather poor on cases such as this (for a review see Senden 1932), there is the famous case reported by William Cheselden of a patient born blind who, after an operation that partially restored his sight, reported the first visual experiences as having a tactile phenomenal quality: "When he first saw [. . .] that he thought all Objects whatever touch'd his Eyes, (as he express'd it) as what he felt, did his Skin." Of course, more empirical data is necessary to draw a final conclusion.

4.5 Pink Elephants

I left one of the classic counterexamples for last. We can hallucinate or dream of a pink elephant or whatever has apparently never been part of our life. Although I have never seen a pink elephant, I have seen pink objects and I also have seen elephants. In normal perception the environment constrains the kind of combinations of processes that take place because of the brain. However, when I dream, my senses are shut and the proximal neighborhood does not produce effects in my brain. But what takes place in the brain is not independent of the past history of it; events that took place hours or years ago are still producing effects. Why not suppose that there are longer processes lasting for a longer span of time and ending in the brain when our senses are shut off? The case of the pink elephant could be explained by suggesting that a process originated by pink objects and a process originated by an elephant, originally spatially and temporally separate, merged into a longer process. In a similar way, we could explain situations like phantom limbs. Although the limb has been amputated, there are still physical processes that were originated by the limb. What takes place now is the effect of what happened before.

In dreams, we seem unable to dream of anything whose components were no part of our life thus far. For instance, people who are born blind are unable to dream of colors (Kerr and Domhoff 2004). Similarly, we are incapable of dreaming anything really exotic like an entirely new taste, a new smell, ultrasound, or infrared light. As far as I know, all mental imagery is a combination of actual physical events with which the subject had been in relation.

5 Conclusion

I have presented an externalist realist and process-oriented framework for qualia: a quale is a physical process spanning time and space, beginning in the environment and ending in the brain.

Traditionally, the brain, and possibly the body, has been conceived as separate from the environment. Although many authors stress the importance of embodiment and situatedness in order to develop certain neural structures, most do agree that—once the brain is formed through development—all the relevant properties are instantiated by what takes place inside the skull. Nevertheless, why should we consider the brain as a separate part of the environment? The brain is just a part of the physical world, and there are processes originating in the environment and ending inside it. From the point of view of such processes, the skin is not so important. On the contrary, the brain is the center of a whirlwind of processes extending in time and space.

References

Bennett, M. R., and P. M. S. Hacker. 2003. *Philosophical Foundations of Neuroscience.* Malden, Mass.: Blackwell.

Block, N. 1980. Are absent qualia impossible? *Philosophical Review* 89, 2: 257–274.

Dennett, D. C. 1988. Quining qualia. In *Consciousness in Contemporary Science*, ed. A. Marcel and E. Bisiach. Oxford: Oxford University Press.

Galilei, G. 1957 [1623]. *The Assayer.* Trans. D. Stillman. In *Discoveries and Opinions of Galileo.* New York: Doubleday.

Gregory, R. L. 1998. Brainy mind. *British Medical Journal* 317: 1693–1695.

Holt, E. B. 1914. *The Concept of Consciousness.* New York: Macmillan.

Hurley, S. L. 2006. Varieties of externalism. In *The Extended Mind*, ed. R. Menary. Aldershot: Ashgate.

Jackson, F. 1982. Epiphenomenal qualia. *Philosophical Quarterly* 32: 127–136.

James, W. 1996 [1908]. *A Pluralistic Universe.* Nebraska: The University of Nebraska Press.

Kandel, E. R., J. H. Schwartz, and T. M. Jessel. 1995. *Essentials of Neural Science and Behavior.* Stamford, Conn.: Appleton and Lange.

Kerr, N., and G. W. Domhoff. 2004. Do the blind literally "see" in their dreams? A critique of a recent claim that they do. *Dreaming* 14: 230–233.

Koch, C. 2004. *The Quest for Consciousness: A Neurobiological Approach.* Englewood, Colo.: Roberts.

Levine, J. 1983. Materialism and qualia: The explanatory gap. *Philosophical Quarterly* 64: 354–361.

Lycan, W. G. 2001. The case for phenomenal externalism. In *Philosophical Perspectives*, vol. 15: *Metaphysics*, ed. J. E. Tomberlin. Atascadero, Calif.: Ridgeview.

Manzotti, R. 2006a. A process view of conscious perception. *Journal of Consciousness Studies* 13, 6: 45–79.

Manzotti, R. 2006b. Consciousness and existence as a process. *Mind and Matter* 4, 1: 7–43.

Metzinger, T. 2003. *Being No One: The Self-Model Theory of Subjectivity.* Cambridge Mass.: MIT Press/A Bradford Book.

Putnam, H. 1975. *Mind, Language, and Reality.* Cambridge: Cambridge University Press.

Seibt, J. 1997. Existence in time: From substance to process. In *Perspectives on Time*, ed. J. Faye, 143–182. Dordrecht: Kluwer Academic.

Senden, V. 1932. *Raum und Gestaltauffassung bei operierten Blindgeborenen vor und nach der Operation* (Conception of space and gestalt in congenital blind children before and after surgery). Leipzig: Verlag Jd Ambrosus Barth.

Shoemaker, S. 1990. Qualities and qualia: What's in the mind? *Philosophy and Phenomenological Research* 50: 109–131.

Strawson, G. 2003. What is the relation between an experience, the subject of the experience, and the content of the experience? *Philosophical Issues* 13: 279–315.

Stubenberg, L. 1998. *Consciousness and Qualia*. Amsterdam: John Benjamins.

Tye, M. 1990. Representational theory of pains and their phenomenal character. *Philosophical Perspectives* 9: 223–239.

Whitehead, A. N. 1920. *Concept of Nature*. Cambridge: Cambridge University Press.

Whitehead, A. N. 1978 [1929]. *Process and Reality*. London: Free Press.

10   The Ontological Status of Qualia and Sensations: How They Fit into the Brain

John Smythies

It is widely believed today that neuroscience can explain most aspects of brain–mind functions except for qualia. These represent the tattered remnants of subjective experience that once loomed so largely in psychology. Indeed eliminative materialists deny that we have any experiences at all. Instead they claim that talk of "sensations," "experiences," "qualia," and the like are examples of the use of a worn-out vocabulary, and they recommend that we should introduce a new vocabulary that describes only states of the brain itself. However, many philosophers are unhappy at this sweeping use of Occam's razor and focus on "qualia" instead. "Qualia" may be defined as "what it's like" to have a particular experience. For example, it is held that the difference between a blue quale and a red quale is fundamentally intrinsic and cannot be fully accounted for only in terms of physical items such as differential wavelengths of light, or differential activation of neurons in the cortex.

However, I will argue in this essay that this approach focuses on the wrong issue. The real problem of conscious perception is the relation between our sensations themselves and their correlated brain states—in other words, not one of "what it is *like* to have a certain sensation" but "what it *is* to have a certain sensation."

One widely held error (see, e.g., Crick 1994) is the idea that we can only use data from neurophysiology to solve this problem. This ignores the large amount of existing relevant data in the field of introspectionist psychology accumulated by scientists such as Gregory (1981), Ramachandran and Blakeslee (1998), Cavanagh and Anstis (1991), Vernon (1962), and many others. It might seem obvious that any study of the nature of experience should start with a survey of what these scientists have discovered about our sensations and images that make up the body of conscious experience.

A brief summary of this body of data is as follows. "Objective" consciousness (that which an observer can introspect) consists of five sensory fields (with their attendant image fields) plus thoughts (Smythies 1999). Most prominent is the visual field. With our eyes closed in the dark, the visual field presents itself as a limited quasi-oval expanse of black in which a few afterimages may be present. On opening our eyes in the light, we find this dark expanse is replaced by an array of variously colored and shaped phenomenal objects that may or may not move. To account for this phenomenon most philosophers still adhere to the commonsense theory of naive or direct realism. This view states that phenomenal objects (contained in the visual field) are simply identical with physical objects (or at least with their surfaces) contained in the stimulus field. In other words the physiological mechanisms of perception function somewhat like a telescope (logically, not mechanically, of course), giving a direct view of the external physical objects being looked at. However, there is now abundant scientific evidence from clinical neurology, visual science, and neuroscience that this theory is totally false (see Schilder 1942 and Smythies 1994 for details). We now know that phenomenal objects are literally constructs of the representative mechanisms of perception, just as the images we see on our TV screens are constructed by a specific mechanism designed to do just that.

Recently some new experimental evidence has been obtained to underscore this opinion.

Everyone knows that the lens of the eye throws a topographic image of the stimulus field onto the retina. The retina converts this image into a spatiotemporal pattern of impulses in the optic nerve that projects to the lateral geniculate body where fresh neurons pass the message on to the visual cortex. Here a series of hierarchical parallel-distributed computational mechanisms find out (compute) what was in the input—that is, what is the content of the stimulus field. This information is expressed partly in an uncoded form mediated by a large number of topographic maps, and partly in a code mediated by vastly complicated patterns of various biophysical events (axon potentials ["spikes"], direct current oscillations, membrane potentials, etc.). The interesting feature of this computation is that color, shape, and movement are computed by three anatomically separate (though functionally interconnected) mechanisms. Finally, by some as yet undiscovered mechanism, these three separate processes are combined into the unitary phenomenal object that we experience in the visual field in which the color is inside the shape and both move together—where, as Pat Churchland (1986) describes it, "it all comes together." How this is done constitutes the so-called, and so far unsolved, binding problem in neuroscience.

One clue relating to this problem may come from studies of how human vision returns after damage to the occipital lobe (Schilder 1942; Gloning, Gloning, and Hoff 1968). This does not happen, as one might naively expect, by one's seeing first very fuzzy objects that gradually become clearer. Instead the normally invisible tripartite mechanism by which phenomenal objects are constructed becomes manifest. The first thing to return is an experience of pure motion (not object motion), usually rotary. Then the experience of light returns, but as a pure uniform Ganzfeld that covers the whole visual field. Later, space or film colors appear unattached to objects. At the same time fragments of objects become visible. Last, these fragments join up to form complete objects into which the space colors enter. This sequence suggests that the three mechanisms have differential rates of recovery from the injury. It seems to me that these data represent final nails in the coffin of direct realism. If, as direct realists believe, neural activity gives us "direct access" to external physical objects by a sort of logical equivalent to a telescopic mechanism, then there must be three such "telescopes," one for color, one for shape, and one for movement. This seems totally incoherent to me. In contrast, the representative theory has no difficulty with this data.

A second line of research that has thrown new and decisive light on this problem comes from the experimental establishment of the remarkable fact that we always perceive not what is actually "out there," but what the brain computes to be most probably "out there." In other words, our visual experience always contains a quantity of virtual reality. Until recently it was thought that the content of the visual field in waking hours derives entirely from the retina, so that we always see what is actually out there—the physical objects located in the stimulus field before us. Now we know that things are not that simple (Smythies and Ramachandran 1998). The first data came from research by Ramachandran and his colleagues into scotomata (Ramachandran and Blakeslee 1998: 96–104)—the small blind patches caused by brain injuries. It was discovered that these scotomata are not perceived as areas of nothing, but that the brain fills them in with sensations that it computes would most probably have been there if there had been no scotoma. Second, it was found that if the brain is presented with an input that it computes to be too improbable, it can override it and cause the subject to see something else that the brain computes to be more probable. A notable example of this is reported by Kovács et al. (1996). These workers took two photographs, one of a monkey's face and the second of a leafy tropical jungle. They converted these into two pastiches, each composed of portions of each photo so that in the location where one photo showed part of the monkey's face the other showed leafy jungle. Then each pastiche was shown separately to each retina so that retinal rivalry occurred. Under these circumstances, the subject did not see what was actually there—the two pastiches alternating—but rather a complete monkey face alternating with a complete leafy jungle. Clearly the brain had suppressed the improbable mixed pastiche in favor of what it was familiar with (and thus computed what was more probable). Many other experiments, based on stimuli such as moving plaid patterns, have shown this phenomenon where the perceptions of improbable patterns are suppressed by the brain and replaced with perceptions of what it computes to be more probable.

Other experiments (Kleiser, Seitz, and Krekelberg 2004) have shown that, during a saccade (rapid movement of the eye), information coming from the eye is suppressed and what we see is largely virtual reality created by the brain from memory. Kleiste, Seitz, and Krekelberg (2004) expressed it thus: "When you look into a mirror and move your eyes left to right, you will see that you cannot observe your own eye movements. This demonstrates the phenomenon of saccadic suppression: during saccadic eye movements, visual sensitivity is much reduced." In other words, "filling in" has a temporal as well as a spatial dimension that is based on a widespread network that includes the superior colliculus and parts of the thalamus.

Direct realism cannot account for this data either. It would obviously be absurd to claim that we see external objects directly when our eyes are still but indirectly when we execute a saccade.

The thesis that vision works much like television is supported by the many similarities that exist between digital TV compression technologies and how visual neural mechanisms operate that Max d'Oreye and I have drawn attention to (Smythies 2005), two of which I mention here.

1. Digital TV also computes color, shape, and movement of objects in scenes it is transmitting by three separate mechanisms.
2. Digital TV also uses virtual reality as a component of compression technology. TV engineers have found that sending every detail of every scene being televised over the bandwidth results in very clear pictures but at a high computational (i.e., financial) cost. Also they found that much of the information transmitted in this way turns out to be redundant. Quite satisfactory pictures can be obtained by constructing much of the final picture from the memory of the system coupled with predictions of the

most likely outcome of, for example, scene A, based on the system's previous experience of scene A and its previous outcomes. Another technique is to transmit only differences between successive frames. The art of TV compression technology is to find the optimum mix of these programs that yields the best picture at least cost.

In digital TV, the picture is built up by a computer activating pixels. In old-fashioned analog TV, the picture is built up by a simple scanning mechanism. The digital nature of brain activity suggests that the visual system in the brain is closer to the digital TV technology. Yet there is intriguing evidence that scanning may also be used. Grey Walter (1950) was the first to suggest that to discover the form of scan used in analog TV the thing to do is to illuminate the target with a flickering light instead of the usual steady one. If you do this geometrical patterns will occur on the screen whose form depends on the geometry of the scan being used and the temporal relation between the flicker and the scan. In human vision if you look at a flickering stroboscopic light (4–16 Hz) you will experience geometrical hallucinations in your visual field as predicted by the hypothesis. The detail of these patterns is also of interest (Smythies 1959/1960). They are composed mostly of parallel lines, grids, checkerboards, concentric circles, spirals, stars, and mazes. These are all derivable from the usual simple scan forms needed to cover a planar surface, for example, linear as in analog TV, maze-like as in digital TV (pixels), spiral as in Asdic, and star shaped. The origin of these patterns has not yet been established, but it is possible that Grey Walter's hypothesis is correct.

Philosophers have objected to the representative theory on several grounds. These include the claim that no such pictures ("phenomenal objects") that the theory describes as the final product of all this neurocomputation can be found in the brain. One answer to this objection may be that these pictures are not in the brain at all but are located in the mind. This theory—derived from Bertrand Russell (1948), C. D. Broad (1923), H. H. Price (1953), and myself (Smythies 1994)—basically suggests that a person's phenomenal space and physical space are geometrically and ontologically two different spaces, and that phenomenal space is occupied by organized mental events (sensations and images) that are only causally related to brain events. This theory differs fundamentally from Cartesian dualism. The latter selects extension in space as *the* criterion for distinguishing matter (*res extensa*) and mind (*res cogitans*). The new theory suggests selective location in different loci in a higher-dimensional space as *the* criterion for distinguishing matter (*res extensa*) from mind (a compound of *res cogitans* and another *res extensa*). Certain components of consciousness (e.g., thoughts) are not spatially extended, but other parts (e.g., visual and somatic sensations and images) are so extended in a region of their own (phenomenal) space. This theory has close links with brane theory in modern physics. (See Smythies 1994, 2003 for details.)

A second objection to the representative theory made by philosophers is that it leads to the dreaded homunculus and a fatal infinite regress. This argument originated with Descartes and was popularized by Gilbert Ryle (1949) and Francis Crick (1994). The objection states that if we posit an internal theater in which these images are presented then we have to posit a little green man inside the head looking at these pictures with his own brain inside which there must be another little green man, and so on. Fodor (1981) has pointed out that this argument is entirely spurious, as there is no reason to suppose that, because we need an image to see an object, we need another image to experience an image. It is a most obvious fact that we can observe by introspection phenomena like our own after-images and can decide without any qualms of doubt their properties such as color and shape, both at one instant in time and how these properties change over time, as they do. No little green men are involved in this operation. The same observation applies to ordinary sensations.

The demise of direct realism has an unfortunate effect on another widely held and equally spurious theory—the theory of mind–brain identity, commonly called the identity theory or IT. This theory is almost universally espoused by neuroscientists, but it is completely incompatible with the facts derived from psychological introspection. In the first place, our sensations, as we experience them, cannot be identical with the events in our brains that are related to them. If we claim such a relation of identity we are contravening Leibniz's Law of the Identity of Indiscernibles. Neurons A have one set of properties, whereas the sensations B they generate have quite a different set of properties revealed by introspective observation. Thus A cannot be identical to B. Also, the only thing the neuroscientific and neurological evidence shows is that neuronal activity in a person's brain is *correlated* with particular activity in that person's sensory fields. There is not one shred of evidence that indicates that this relationship is one of identity. The only relationship that fits the data and does not contravene Leibniz's Law is a causal one. Events in the visual brain *cause* correlated events to occur in quite a separate entity, that is, that person's visual field in his or her consciousness. The word "separate" here entails ontological independence as well as location in a different space. In other words, a person's complete system of causally connected visual representative mechanisms include the retina, the visual brain, *and* the visual field that is located *outside* the brain in a space of its own. The same system *mutatis mutandis* operates for the other senses. Identity theorists usually weasel out of this problem by the simultaneous and illegitimate use of the direct realist theory of perception. Crick (1994) says that the stimulus field is the same as the visual field. This is hardly possible on any theory not propped up by direct realism, because the stimulus field is occupied by physical objects light rays which form the *input* into the brain's neurocomputational mechanisms, whereas the visual field is the final result or *output* of these computations. It is obviously wrong to identify the input into a computer with the output from that computer, which, alas, is exactly what Crick does.

Note that the identity theory also has the following problem. The visual field we experience in consciousness consists of one single field in which the location of phenomenal objects corresponds topographically with the location of the external physical objects in the stimulus field that the phenomenal objects represent. Yet in the visual brain there are at least 30 different such topographic maps scattered throughout the system. How can one field be identical with >30 fields? Also, the visual field is not a *coded* representation of the stimulus field (like Morse code, for example)— it is an *uncoded* topographic representation (like the equally uncoded TV picture). The visual cortex contains coded visual information, as does the works of a TV set. But the final product in each is an uncoded pictorial representation.

So far this essay has concentrated on vision, but other senses are also relevant to the argument, especially somatic sensation. One of the most widely held misconceptions in modern science and philosophy relates to our experience of our own bodies. Hardly anyone even begins to doubt the naive commonsense view that the object that we directly experience in consciousness is the physical body itself. However, this idea is quite false. Clinical neurology has established beyond any possible doubt that we do not experience any events in our physical bodies (Schilder 1950; Smythies 1953). The object that we do experience—compounded of a mixture of various sensations from the skin (touch, temperature, pain, etc.), and our insides (pressure, stretch, pain, etc.) is called the "body image" in neurology. It is a product itself of the representative mechanisms of perception that include the brain. In no sense is the body image identical with the physical body (see Searle 1992). Instead it *represents* the physical body in consciousness. Usually it mirrors events in the physical body faithfully. At other times, as in the case of "phantom" limbs, it ceases to do so (see

Ramachandran and Blakeslee 1998 for details). If you ask a person where she thinks her brain is located in relation to the world that she experiences she will point automatically to the head that she experiences, and say "in here." But of course she would be wrong—the head that she experiences is really inside her mind.

References

Broad, C. D. 1923. *Scientific Thought*. London: Routledge and Kegan Paul.

Cavanagh, P., and S. Anstis. 1991. The contribution of color to motion in normal and color-deficient observers. *Vision Research* 31: 2109–2148.

Churchland, P. S. 1989. *Neurophilosophy*. Cambridge, Mass.: MIT Press/A Bradford Book.

Crick, F. 1994. *The Astonishing Hypothesis*. New York: Scribner.

Fodor, J. A. 1981. Imagistic representation. In *Imagery*, ed. Ned Block. Cambridge, Mass.: MIT Press/A Bradford Book.

Gloning, I., K. Gloning, and H. Hoff. 1968. Neuropsychological symptoms and syndromes in lesions of the occipital lobe and adjacent areas. In *Collection Neuropsychologica*, ed. H. Hécan. Paris: Gauthier-Villars.

Gregory, R. L. 1981. *Mind in Science*. London: Weidenfeld and Nicholson.

Kleiser, R., R. J. Seitz, and B. Krekelberg. 2004. Neural correlates of saccadic suppression in humans. *Current Biology* 14: R195–R201.

Kovács, I., T. V. Papathomas, M. Yang, and A. Fehér. 1996. When the brain changes its mind: Intraocular grouping during retinal rivalry. *Proceedings of the National Academy of Sciences USA* 93: 508–511.

Price, H. H. 1953. Survival and the idea of another world. *Proceedings of the Society for Psychical Research* 50: 1–25.

Ramachandran, V., and S. Blakeslee. 1998. *Phantoms in the Brain*. New York: Morrow.

Russell, B. 1948. *Human Knowledge: Its Scope and Limits*. London: Allen and Unwin.

Ryle, G. 1949. *The Concept of Mind*. London: Hutchinson.

Schilder, P. 1942. *Mind: Perception and Thought in Their Constructive Aspects*. New York: Columbia University Press.

Schilder, P. 1950. *The Image and Appearance of the Human Body*. New York: International Universities Press.

Searle, J. R. 1992. *The Rediscovery of the Mind*. Cambridge, Mass.: MIT Press/A Bradford Book.

Smythies, J. 1953. The experience and description of the human body. *Brain* 76: 132–145.

Smythies, J. 1959/1960. The stroboscopic phenomena. *British Journal of Psychology* 50: 106–116, 305–325; 51: 247–255.

Smythies, J. 1994. *The Walls of Plato's Cave*. Aldershot: Avebury.

Smythies, J. 1999. Consciousness: Some basic issues—A neurophilosophical perspective. *Consciousness and Cognition* 8: 164–172.

Smythies, J. 2003. Space, time, and consciousness. *Journal of Consciousness Studies* 10: 47–56.

Smythies, J. 2005. How the brain decides what we see. *Journal of the Royal Society of Medicine* 98: 18–20.

Smythies, J., and V. Ramachandran. 1998. An empirical refutation of the direct realist theory of perception. *Inquiry* 40: 437–438.

Vernon, M. D. 1962. *A Further Study of Visual Perception*. Cambridge: Cambridge University Press.

Walter, W. G. 1950. Features in the electrophysiology of mental mechanisms. In *Perspectives in Neuropsychiatry*, ed. D. Richer. London: H. K. Lewis.

III Attacks

11 The Churchlands' War on Qualia

Mark Crooks

Psychoneural identity theory with its variants has been elaborated since the 1950s to discredit sensory phenomenology (qualia) for philosophical realist and reductionist programs. Paul and Patricia Churchland's works are exemplary of such motivation. Paul Churchland's philosophizing of computational neuroscience attempts to resolve mental contents into vector coding and its transformations, yet what he describes is not phenomenology but rather psychology's sensory schema. Patricia Churchland admits there are few or no intertheoretic identities, and therefore no proper analogies from them to her projected psychology-to-neuroscience reduction. In this essay, I document their misrepresentations of perception's nature. The conclusion is that the doctrinaire denial of phenomenology by reductionist philosophy heretofore involves invalid and unsound arguments.

I do not think that the diversity of the opinions of the scholastics makes their philosophy difficult to refute. It is easy to overturn the foundations on which they all agree, and once that has been done, all their disagreements over detail will seem foolish.
—Descartes 1991 [1640]

1 Abstract Qualia

To explain or rather deny the mental phenomenology of cognition, desires, sensorimotor coordination, and emotive states as well as the phenomenal content of perception, Paul Churchland has interpreted computational neuroscience in a reductionist vein by extrapolating from computer modeling or neural-net simulations of the brain. From these are said to flow applications to traditional epistemological and ontological questions, including a vindication of the mind–brain identity thesis. It can be shown that, in addition to his reductionist program, Churchland has built the denial of phenomenology and the truth of philosophical realism into the axioms of his computational scheme, where such claims do not properly belong. His argued negation of phenomenal contents of perception constitutes the fallacy of irrelevant conclusion (*ignoratio elenchi*), because what he calls "phenomenology" is not what is so conceived and described within sensory psychology.

In his model of perception (P. M. Churchland 1995: 64), central neurons "buzzing furiously" that "light up" when triggered by stimuli compute the spatial locale, position, and trajectories of perceived objects. Such sensorial neurocomputations are then transformed into numerically coded vectors within a motor state-space that subserves behaviorally adaptive sensorimotor coordination (P. M. Churchland 1988, 1989, 1995; Churchland and Churchland 1997). There is no phenomenology manifest in such neural computation, nor could there be, as it has been axiomatically excluded from existence by his reductionist preconception. There are stimuli, and there are "sensations" (coordinates in abstract sensory state-space: P. M. Churchland 1989: 102–108; cf. Churchland and Churchland 1997: 169, 171), these being the sum total of perception's components. Motor and sensory state-spaces with their coordinates are themselves neurally implemented, so there are no existentially residual "nomological danglers" (Feigl 1967), that is, no nominally paranormal phenomenology. Below we will ascertain whither the phenomenology has been smuggled.

This "buzzing neuron" paradigm of perception is at variance with accepted psychology and indeed with itself, being internally inconsistent in its exclusion of sensory phenomena alongside its concurrent citation of them under other guises and terminology. For phenomenology reportage is employed within psychophysical experimentation from which, subsequently, is derived a tailored psychological construct requisite for hypothesizing neural substrates thereof (Horst 2005; Smythies 1994). Moreover, Churchland liberally cites these phenomenological descriptions as discriminated colors (1989: 103–105), ambiguous visual figure reversals (1995: 107–113), visual size constancies (1989: 261–262), and three-dimensional vision through a stereoscope (1995: 57–58). These sensory phenomena are adduced in face of the anomaly that, given his reductionist model's properly interpreted parameters of perception, such subjective "looks" of stimuli are nowhere to be found, for supposedly there exist only nonphenomenal vector numbers supervening on stimuli. If such phenomenal subjectivities of perception were not included in his original axiomatic prospectus for buzzing neurons *sans* phenomenology, how does one account for these qualia in its further elaboration?

Respecting the physical and phenomenological terms to be identified in philosophical reductionism, Churchland holds inconsistent views: "The tartness of one's lemonade turns out to be its high relative concentration of H+ ions" (1989: 30); yet contrarily, "The subjective taste [of fruits, including lemons] just *is* the activation pattern across the four types of tongue receptors, as re-represented downstream in one's taste cortex" (1995: 23). The second excerpt in fact correctly expresses the identity thesis within neuroscience regarding gustatory percepts, though we find its inherently hypothetical character stated dogmatically, which moreover constitutes a *petitio principii* as that identification is what Churchland purports to be determining. The first, incorrect expression of tartness's identification with hydrogen ions confounds a percept with its objective cause. The copula "is" in this context is properly construed as mere colloquial shorthand for "covaries with," signifying only psychophysical correspondence of the percept with its stimulus (see Wright 2005: 73–93). Churchland misconstrues phenomenology–stimulus correlations as intertheoretic identities, within an overarching intellectualized "naive" realism that would assimilate percepts to their material causation (Crooks 2002a,b; Kalat 2002; Smythies 2002).

A compound ontological character of physical plus phenomenal called "objective qualia" (P. M. Churchland 1989: 57) trenchantly illustrates Churchland's fictitious form of perception. These objective qualia are said to reside within the stimulus field and are the ostensible "objective phenomenal properties" to which our perceptual discriminations are keyed (ibid.: 56). Churchland, through his reductionist program and idiosyncratic scientific revisionism, assimilates somatic, visual, and auditory phenomenology to this construct of objective qualia ("external sensory qualities": Churchland and Churchland 1997: 169). Complementarily, he collectivizes "thoughts, sensations, desires, and emotions" (P. M. Churchland 1988: 13) under the rubric "subjective qualia" (P. M. Churchland 1989: 57).[1] Churchland identifies "subjective" sensations with coordinates of vector spaces that, in reality, constitute the computational substrate, not the identity, of phenomenal percepts (see below). Between the two extremes of these assimilations, inner and outer qualia conveniently vanish ontologically. This move is a reductionist transposition of Wittgenstein (1958: § 293): reductively "dividing through" sensations leaves no phenomenal remainder.[2]

Phenomenal properties so described, as tastes, colors, sounds, and warmth, are irreducibly subjective and necessarily resident in the central nervous system (CNS) if anywhere in the material universe, and nowhere within the domain of stimuli if physics, physiology, and psychophysics are to be trusted (see, e.g., Kalat 2002; Smythies 2002; Wright 1990). Identity theory proper holds that such phenomenology, despite its apparent exteriorized localization, must be domiciled in the brain, because that is where afferent projections from exteroceptors terminate. The objective phenomena Churchland describes, as light and sound waves, indeed constitute stimuli localized outside the brain; but their non-identical phenomenal representations are temporally subsequent to, and effects of, those proximal stimuli's sensory reception, transduction, and encoding.

What is most incongruous in the buzzing neuron model of perception is that, incomprehensibly, the sequence of perception has been reversed. Nominal objective qualia as phenomenal colors (in actuality, visual percepts phenomenally "out there," i.e., outside the somatic body image: Köhler 1971; Smythies 1953, 1954) are misconstrued as stimuli that generate, within the brain, vectorial coordinates of those putatively objective phenomenal properties. Properly construed, percepts are the phenomenal effect "in here" (within the brain) supervening on nervous stimulation whose input drives neurocomputation. It is not the case that percepts function as stimuli to generate vector coordinates of themselves. As there are no objective qualia, there is no vector representation of them either (see Crooks 2002a: 202).

Whether percepts are misidentified with their distal and proximal stimuli (see Beloff 1964; Lovejoy 1929; Wright 1993) or the visual field is mistaken as the stimulus field (see Smythies 1996), such errors of interpreting perception are diverse forms of naive realism inasmuch as phenomenology properly attributed to percipients is presumed existentially independent of their presence. Herein lies the answer to our immediate query: Churchland has unwittingly smuggled "objective" qualia from phenomenal existence by localizing them outside the observer, exteriorizing them and hence "denying and downplaying" (P. M. Churchland 1989: 237) any explanatory need for squaring their otherwise irreducible subjectivity with a presumed monopolistic material universe.

The Churchlands acknowledge transitional "phenomenological similarities" between colors (P. M. Churchland 1995: 26; Churchland and Churchland 1997: 166), but the context makes evident these are nonphenomenal neurocomputations. Such extreme liberality with the accepted semantics of philosophical and psychological terminology should alert us that nominal intertheoretic identifications, here, of color "sensations" with visual cortex, are being carried out not through legitimate conceptual or scientific analyses but rather by misleading fallacies of equivocation.

Simply put, Churchland has silently redefined "phenomenology" to mean his neurocomputations.

Naive realism is readily demonstrated in Churchland's schema of things (1989: 292). Incredibly, an ontologically incongruous inclusion of "color" alongside fundamental dimensions as length, mass, and time in physics would make objective color qualia independent of our perception by making them a fundamental constituent of material reality. There is no such entity as sentient-independent color qualia in the stimulus field of perception; Churchland has misidentified color percepts of visual cortex with their distal causation, that is, with surface efficiencies (Churchland and Churchland 1997: 163–164; Crooks 2002b; cf. Hardin 1993: 60–65). As color percepts are properly construed as arising from interacting physical and physiological parameters and are embedded within the phenomenal visual field of sensory consciousness, their very localization within the material world is what is in question by an informed mind–brain philosophy (Beloff 1964; Brain 1959; Dennett 1991; Köhler 1971; Lovejoy 1929; Smythies 1956, 1994). Phenomenal color, localized within a visual field whose spatial coordinates are not coterminous with the coordinates of either the brain or the stimulus field, is appropriately construed as a "derived" dimension and not at all on an ontological par with fundamental physical or physiological axes of measurement. Therefore it is a *petitio principii* to categorize such phenomenal content as having elementary physical dimensions treated within physics when those phenomenal contents' spatial dimensions (let alone qualia) relative to the material world are what is in question.

Moreover, phenomenal color is, both in psychology and philosophy, the paradigm of subjectivity in perception. Why then would Churchland paradoxically situate its ontology and localization with the ultimate objectivities such as length, mass, and time? Probably because if such an exemplar of phenomenology as color might be so situated, all other lesser species of heretical qualia might be similarly construed as, or eliminated by, their supposed objective material identities all the more plausibly.

Complicating such pseudoproblems, Churchland's "subjective" qualia such as taste sensations are in several locations (P. M. Churchland 1995; Churchland and Churchland 1997) identified with brain functions, but are also contrarily in other locations (P. M. Churchland 1979, 1989) existentially eliminated, identified with nothing. Overlooking this discrepancy and regarding only the eliminative materialism, to so uncompromisingly deny existence to deliverances of first person, inner sensorial experience "seems to be crazy . . . too insane to merit serious consideration"

(Searle 1992: 48). Acknowledging the gallery, Churchland posits ersatz neurocomputations in lieu of actual phenomenal content, calling them "phenomenology," "representations," "sensations," even "qualia," while heralding another imminent vindication of reductionist philosophy. This exemplifies what was said above: the denial of qualia has been incorporated into the axioms and terms of this neurocomputational philosophy by implicit redefinition and conceptual confounding. Thus by terminological devolution one simply retrieves what was built into the implicit semantics from the start. The only actual reduction involved therein is the improper substitution of terminology for concepts and phenomena to which they are not applicable and for which they were not devised. In other words, Churchland's systematic denials of qualia are transparent fallacies of ambiguity.

Churchland's neurally implemented vector spaces inclusive of sensation-coordinates are not in fact "phenomenological spaces" (Churchland and Churchland 1997: 167–170) and their sensations, respectively. They are psychology's sensory schemas, signifying neurocomputations integral with articulated memory and experience that operate on afferent input to produce the phenomenal contents of waking perception. As examples, there is a somatosensory schema generating the experiential body image (Brain 1950; Schilder 1950; Smythies 1953, 1994; Vernon 1962) and there are cognitive maps (Gregory 1981; Hochberg 1978) underlying the experiential visual field:

It appears that on the whole the class of situation grouped within a schema [perceptual archetype] is linked by some general framework which relates in turn to particular and appropriate courses of action. The most typical of schemata seem to be those which relate the position of the body to perceived spatial arrangements of objects in the environment. And these schemata are . . . laid down in accordance with the class of reactions which have been found by the child to be appropriate and effective in dealing with the spatial relations of objects to one another, and to his own position in space. (Vernon 1962: 13–14)

Schemas themselves may accordingly be characterized as vector spaces: "The schema is a neurophysiological disposition which may or may not enter consciousness, and which plays an essential part in perception and action, speech and thought. It is both physical and mental, and, when its neurological character is more fully understood, it may prove to be the bridge between body and mind" (Brain 1950: 139). Whether they realize it or not, Churchland and his colleagues (Bechtel and Abrahamsen 1991; Churchland and Sejnowski 1992) are delineating perceptual schema that generate the phenomenology of experiential consciousness, not usurp its proper ontological identity.[3] No one to my knowledge, philosopher, psychologist, or neuroscientist, has ever argued for the impossibility of sensory schemas being identified with or eliminated by their neural substrates. Rather, the published arguments pertain to a presumed nonidentity of brain with sensory phenomenology. Accordingly, much of Paul Churchland's corpus appears fallacious, directed at a straw man, arguing that cognitive neuroscience and connectionism bode ill for nonreductionist philosophical psychology. Charitably, he has established, if any conclusion, only that sensory schemas may in fact be numerically identical with their neural substrates. The contentious issue pertains to neural identification or otherwise of phenomenology, not schemas, and hence his arguments can still be faulted for *ignoratio elenchi*.[4]

Presumably, however, even that irrelevant conclusion is unsound, as Churchland's arguments incorporate his idiosyncratic buzzing neuron theory of perception, otherwise known as direct realism (see, e.g., Armstrong 1961, 1968; Byrne and Hilbert 2003; Kelley 1986; Sellars 1963; Smart 2002; cf. Smythies 1965, 2002), which inexplicably transmogrifies percepts into their stimuli. Churchland's ostensible scientific realism, regarding the nature of perception, is afforded little or no source citation and is demonstrably at variance with the consensual, elementary account of the physics and physiology of perception given within sensory psychology for almost two centuries (see, e.g., Boring 1942; Hochberg 1978; Mueller 1965). If intertheoretic identifications of spatiotemporally discontinuous sensory qualia and their stimuli are impossible, notwithstanding terminological redefinitions, Churchland's further analogical extrapolation to the identification of mind with brain has null inductive probability.

2   A Bumpy Reduction

Patricia Churchland's (1986) "neurophilosophy" and Churchland and Sejnowski's (1992) detailed computational neuroscience are tantamount to Paul Churchland's (1989, 1995) system in all essential respects, as the acknowledgments, citations, even identical illustrations from the 1992 text make clear.

Churchland and Sejnowski (e.g., 1992: 415) make only passing reference to theory reductions and concomitant identification of properties between those theories. The fuller account is given by P. S. Churchland (1986: chap. 7). In scientific progression, one theory is superseded by another because of its more comprehensive explanatory paradigm, its relative ontological simplicity, and its ability to subsume and make of the older construct a special, limiting case (P. S. Churchland 1986: 278–280). "Analogues" are correspondent constructs by which the principles and laws of the older theory are represented in the new; once this mapping has been suitably fashioned we may say the older has been "reduced" to its successor (ibid.: 282–283). If there obtain "close analogues" between the theories, we may pronounce the ontological identity of properties detailed in their respective theorizations (ibid.: 283–284).

Determining when the [analogue] fit is close enough to claim identities between properties of the old [supplanted theory] and those of the new is not a matter for formal criteria, and the decision is influenced by a variety of pragmatic and social considerations. The *whim of the central investigators*, the degree to which confusion will result from retention of the old terms, the desire to preserve or to break with past habits of thought, *the related opportunities for publicizing the theory, cadging grants, and attracting disciples all enter into the decisions concerning whether to claim [intertheoretic] identities* and therewith retention or whether to make the more radical claim of displacement [eliminative materialism]. In fact, I do not think it matters very much that we establish criteria for determining when the reduced and the reducing theory resemble each other sufficiently to herald identities of properties [!] . . . (Ibid.: 283–284, emphases added)

This frank, apparently inadvertent admission necessarily spells intellectual bankruptcy for so-called intertheoretic identities. The arbitrary, nebulous, indeed profoundly irrational criteria cited preclude any possible satisfactory and consensual objective determination of ostensible numerical identities of cross-theoretic properties, supposing any theory reductions actually carried out, past, present, and future.[5] That passage also intimates that standard heavy-handed flourishes of symbolic logic and schematic formulae of putative theory reductions (e.g., P. M. Churchland 1989; Hooker 1981; Nagel 1965) function essentially as window dressing to furnish an appearance of mathematical rigor and certainty to what is, according to Patricia Churchland, conditioned primarily by programmatic or even whimsical caprice. For it does not matter to what extent modeling of theory reduction partakes of clockwork logical formalisms. If identification claims comprise excrescences of academic grandstanding, fortuitous publicizing, "grant cadging," and grubbing for disciples, then the strict formalisms modeling those claims are belied and effectively negated by decidedly all-too-human motivations and foibles. It is not the formalisms per se that are inadequate; it is their incoherent and subjective application that provides the rub to any nominal theory reductions.[6]

Moreover, according to Churchland herself, few if any reductions have actually been demonstrated within science:

> There is not one example from the history of science that exactly fits the logical empiricist pattern of reduction, and some outstanding cases do not fit at all, force and bowdlerize how you will [1986: 281]. . . . Whenever the corrections to the old theory are anything more than relatively minor, it is always tendentious to claim that phenomena in the old theory are to be identified with phenomena in the reducing theory. (P. S. Churchland 1986: 282)

She then goes on to show there are few if any cases requiring less than "relatively minor corrections," Q.E.D. But if this is the case for logical empiricism, then the same goes *a fortiori* for the eliminativist epistemology held by the Churchlands (1979, 1986, 1989, 1997), though they appear not to recognize that their model of theory displacement, self-admittedly indebted to Thomas Kuhn's (1970) and Paul Feyerabend's (1988) philosophies of science, must necessarily undermine or overthrow the very identity claims they make. For the rigorous deduction of one theory from another, employing bridge principles, is what logical empiricists had banked on to establish the objectivity, coherence, and continuity of scientific progress and its unfolding theoretical superstructure. If that program were replaced by a posit of nominal intertheoretic identification predicated on the science models of Kuhn and Feyerabend, there emerges far greater discontinuity of "progression." (Indeed, the quotation from Churchland above on the absence of formal criteria for determination of presumed identities appears a direct reflection of Feyerabend's "anarchist" critique of science.)

This consequent interpretive shift away from logical empiricism's program renders any identification of properties between theories far more tenuous, hence lessening the plausibility for any claims of intertheoretic identification, emphatically including those of mind and brain, which are admittedly futuristic and analogical only. "There do not yet exist fleshed-out neurobiological theories with reductive pretensions, let alone reductive success, and to introduce neuroscientific fiction in the analysis stage [of intertheoretic identification] would only be confusing" (P. S. Churchland 1986: 279). By admitting much greater conceptual discontinuity within historical scientific progress, how can one then continue to unswervingly claim, as with logical empiricism, equivalence of analogues between theories and hence identification of their respective properties? The Churchlands have inconsistently retained logical empiricism's claims of identification of cross-theoretic properties while concurrently rejecting the premises on which those claims were based. If property identification as a corollary doctrine is original and implicated with logical empiricism, then once the latter is discarded, its brainchild should or could not be retained either.

This intellectual clangor is extenuated by Churchland (1986: 283–284) in her posit of a reductive spectrum covering "smooth to bumpy" cases. Examples such as mass within classical and relativistic physics (286–287) and genes within transmission and molecular genetics (284–285) are said to lie at the bumpy end of reduction, with imperfect or nonexistent reduction. Only optics as reduced to electromagnetic theory is said to be fairly smooth (280). All this is to leave aside those ubiquitous instances of total conceptual elimination of prior "analogues" as demonic possession and phlogiston (281), caloric (280), and impetus (289), cases in which no identity is claimed even by reductionists. When reservations are implied (281) concerning even that nominal exemplary reduction of optics, we necessarily are left wondering: supposing few if any passable analogues are available, hence no unambiguous identity of properties between theories, why would such an obviously non-explanatory interpretation of science be held so tenaciously?[7]

The reduction spectrum is simply an epicycle devised to explain away the lack of any discernible identification of cross-theoretic properties. For what appear to be relatively vague parallels across successive theories are alleged to be "really" intertheoretic identities at the bumpy end of that spectrum. Bumpy reductions are no reductions at all (per Churchland), at least respecting putative strict identities of properties, and all such adduced examples are relatively bumpy or incoherent.[8]

If there is merely one counterexample of a superseding scientific discovery that does not instantiate cross-theoretic property identification, then property identification is seen to be neither necessary nor sufficient to explain theory displacement. If indeed many such discoveries not only have no conceptual continuity with previous universes of discourse but also eliminate those prior *explicans* and their integral ontologies entirely, as the Churchlands maintain, we might plausibly generalize this (dare we?): *There are no intertheoretic identities at all.* These supposed identities should be construed as fictitious holdovers from logical empiricism, explanatorily superfluous for philosophy of science and hence violating parsimony of explanation. They have been inconsistently retained to the present, even when their axiomatically implicate logical empiricism was unceremoniously dropped. *This inconsistent retention occurred only because these ostensible identities have served as programmatic props to make plausible an eagerly anticipated analogical identification of qualia with neural properties* (cf. Crooks 2002b: 263).

If the only tentative candidates for hypothetical intertheoretic identity are to be had in such singular cases as that of optics' presumed reduction to electromagnetism, it seems more plausible and explanatorily justifiable to straightway deny any such sparse and tenuous identities, rather than "force and bowdlerize" (P. S. Churchland 1986: 281) the other multitudinous and more recalcitrant reductions into that ideal procrustean bed. This means that lone holdout of optics-to-electromagnetism would not constitute a genuine cross-theory reduction. This appears almost admitted by Churchland herself (ibid.), when adverting upon the "relatively little correction" required for optics' ostensible reduction. Yet on the next page we are informed that it is tendentious to claim intertheoretic identities when there is required anything more than "relatively minor corrections." This implies that optics, barely and at best, represents the sole validated instance of theory reduction, as it is said (ibid.) to be at the extreme smooth end of the reductive continuum. Most or all other nominal theory reductions with their integral property identities at any distance toward the bumpy end must then, by her interpretation, be tendentious and therefore untenable because they all require relatively major corrections, major relative to that singularly qualifying case of optics situated at the smooth end.

Thus by denying any intertheoretic identities at all, I am in effect denying but one alleged instance thereof! Paradoxically, with this unequivocal "blanket" (singular) denial of possible intertheoretic identities, I have done little more than quote and paraphrase one of their most articulate and committed advocates, Patricia Churchland, though having drawn a conclusion opposite to hers respecting the viability or actuality of intertheoretic identification. That she has not recognized such an obvious implication, nay explicit pronunciation, of her own analysis must be chalked up to cognitive dissonance engendered by her inconsistent retention-*cum*-repudiation of logical empiricism.[9]

The ultimate program served by all this supernumerary (if ingenious) philosophy of science is projected mind–brain identification, of qualia with brain states. If it can be established that other domains of science have effected empirically contingent identifications of properties across theories (e.g., Smart 1959, 1963; Hooker 1981), then reductionists may hopefully expect that folk or theoretical psychology will be reduced to their neuroscience analogues (P. M. Churchland 1979, 1988, 1989, 1995; P. S. Churchland 1986; Churchland and Churchland 1997). This intended projection neatly explains why the doctrine of scientific discovery *qua* property identification must be upheld in spite of its evident lack of confirming instances in historical progression, even though its implicate logical empiricism has already been relinquished by ultramodern reductionist philosophers.

If there is no plausible historical evidence that scientific discovery and supersession consist in the establishment of cross-theoretic identification of properties, then any presumed analogical extrapolation to projected mind–brain identification has no inductive probability. As there has not been any plausible identification of properties within the physical sciences, so none will be found between psychology and neuroscience.

Recapitulating: (a) there appear few if any actual intertheoretic identities admitted even by their proponents, and a number of these can be shown to be not identities at all but rather misidentified psychophysical correspondences (Crooks 2002a,b); this conclusion follows whether one's philosophy of science is defunct logical empiricism or (especially) one of its more formally relativistic successors. (b) Nonrational criteria are employed to determine even those few so promoted, despite the apparent mathematical rigor exhibited in models of reduction. (c) Any extrapolation from supposedly accepted identities within the physical sciences, so irrationally ascertained, must express only analogy, the weakest induction. Given that there are so few consensual candidates for identity claims, the inductive sample is extraordinarily small ($n = 1$ per Churchland or $n = 0$ per Hooker) and thus there is further diminution of probability to the vanishing point. (d) Besides, even supposing such identities from the physical sciences actually obtain, they could have application to the controversy between physicalism ("neurophilosophy") and dualism only at the cost of a *petitio principii,* as whether mind *is* a material (neural) organ, hence susceptible to analogies from physics, chemistry, *inter alia,* is precisely the controversial problematic (Crooks 2004: 115). (*Petitio:* "We rightly remain confident that chemical phenomena are nothing but the macrolevel reflection of the underlying quantum-physical phenomena. . . . As with chemical phenomena, so with psychological phenomena [neurally identified]": Churchland and Churchland 1997: 77.)

If the rejoinder to this reasoning were that such conceptual discontinuities exhibited in scientific progression only strengthen the argument for the eliminativist thesis, namely, that discarding the entire *explicans* and ontology of the eliminated theory vindicates the Churchlands' philosophy, this is yet another *petitio principii.* What is in question is whether there actually exists any such reduction spectrum with its posited gradations from smooth to bumpy reductions to complete elimination. If there is no such spectrum, the same goes *a fortiori* for any eliminativist wing thereupon. If the rigorous criteria of identification demanded by the logical empiricists are rejected, there is no longer any rationale for positing a *reduction* spectrum, which obtains whatever meaning it might have only on supposition of genuinely *identified* cross-theoretic properties, not spurious *eliminated* or dubious *bumpy* ones involving little or no reduction at all. Property elimination as privative foil is correlative to reductive identification and obtains meaning only by supposing those contrasting identities actually exist. And it is now being argued there are no such identities, hence no eliminative foil thereto. *This logic leads willy-nilly to the conclusion that mental properties including qualia will not be identified with or eliminated in favor of neural ones, because ex hypothesi neither property identification nor elimination has ever occurred historically or at least has not been demonstrated between any sciences.*

As with Paul Churchland's paradigm of sensory neurocomputation, axiomatically there should not exist phenomenology per se, as the model of perception that Patricia Churchland and Sejnowski (1992) share with him precludes its reality. There exist only stimuli and cell-assembly neuronal firings in registration therewith. Pictorial representations of those stimuli are explicitly rejected by their equation with programmatically outlawed "pictures in the head." We are embarrassed then to find that, again as with Paul Churchland, there is continuous and extensive citation of phenomenal percepts throughout their longish text. Indeed they acknowledge (1992: 13) with Horst (2005) and Smythies (1994) the indispensability of phenomenology reportage in psychophysical experimentation for the progress of neuroscience itself. Churchland and Sejnowski cite (1992), as manifestly existent, "phenomenology" (191), Mach bands (188), illusory depth via stereoscope (189), double visual images (190), false stereoscopic vision (195), illusory contours (219), phenomenal visual shifts during binocular rivalry (220), visual filling-in (230), and visual phi phenomena (326). "Presumably rehearsal, perhaps with the aid of *visual or auditory images,* keeps alive the processes that sustain working memory" (1992: 301, emphasis added).

All such "illusory" phenomenology, in other words nonveridical visual qualia, of course can exist only as percepts or "pictures" within the brain or "head" of a percipient undergoing such sensory experiences (cf. Wright 2005: 79–93), certainly not in the stimulus field of perception (supposing one is going to admit such percepts experiential presence at all). To cite this phenomenology as unproblematic and indeed theoretically utile is thus to undermine any concurrent programmatic asseverations of phenomenology denial. "You cannot [in psychophysics] throw out the phenomenology and keep the [metrical, statistical] data, because the data relate phenomenological properties to physical properties" (Horst 2005).[10] A facile rejoinder to this objection is that Churchland and Sejnowski, when speaking of "phenomenology," really mean "brain states and processes," a prospective intertheoretic identity that will be vindicated eventually by "completed" neurosciences (Churchland and Churchland 1997; Feigl 1967; Feyerabend 1963; Rorty 1965; Smart 1959, 1963). Accordingly, there would then be no inconsistency or improper semantics indulged by Churchland and Sejnowski's concurrent citation of phenomenology alongside its absence from their paradigm of perception (exclusively stimuli plus neurocomputations), as imagery, scotomata filling-in, and the Phi effect are presumed identical with brain structures and functions whose reality *is* entertained within their construct. Empirical data contrary to this averred identity might be adduced, for example, the ontological discrepancy of more than thirty visual maps in the brain contrasted with our singular and seamless phenomenal visual field (Smythies 1994). For my immediate purpose, though, it is sufficient to observe that Churchland and Sejnowski, following Paul Churchland, commit a streaming fallacy of equivocation by indiscriminately running together sensory schema functions (the "computational brain") with percepts, both called "phenomenology" or "representations." In other words, whatever witting psychoneural identity might be presupposed in their florid illustrations of phenomenal qualia, their unwitting identification of phenomenology is with schema neurocomputations, so that the conceptual and terminological confusion and consequent invalid argumentation exhibited in Paul Churchland's work are duplicated in their own.

Notes

1. "Subjective qualia" is a pleonasm, because all qualia are inherently subjective; "objective qualia" is oxymoronic for that same reason (cf. Wright 2005: 83).

2. P. M. Churchland (1985) argues that with introspection sufficiently informed by advanced neuroscience, we will be able to "directly introspect" brain straight through his subjective qualia. But this conjecture presupposes an equally "direct" perception by analogy: see Crooks 2007.

3. Psychology's sensory schemas and neural-net simulations as popularized by Churchland may be "intertheoretically identified" with the proviso that schemas tend to have been defined qualitatively whereas connectionism is expressly quan-

titative; e.g., a rat's learned negotiation of a T-maze treated behaviorally contrasted with the hypothetical modeling of its cognitive map by vector analysis.

4. That Churchland routinely emphasizes (1989, 1995, 1997) the phenomenon of prototype activation and abstractive capacities of neural-net simulations is immaterial to this argument. The relevant question is not whether he recognizes such prototypes are tantamount to psychology's schemas. The argument is that he does not recognize that phenomenology given in perception is not identical with any vector coordinates of those prototypical schemas. Specifically, he verbally and conceptually confounds phenomenal with vector "representations": "We can indeed give an illuminating physical account of the 'intrinsic' nature of our various sensory qualia. In short, they are activation vectors, one and all. . . . They must occur as part of the representational activity of a suitably recurrent [neural] network" (Churchland and Churchland 1997: 176). Churchland's "greedy" reductionism, i.e., "zeal to explain too much too fast" (Dennett 1995: 82) in oversimplified fashion, channels his theorizing into the misidentification of sensuous qualia with neurocomputations underlying their generation, spiriting qualia from mind toward brain functions or even ontological elimination—the greediest reduction of all.

5. It appears that philosophers, not scientists themselves, have made many of these claims of questionable intertheoretic identities, which are then cloaked with a mantle of misrepresented scientific authority. This consequently lends an aura of "heroic science" (Searle 1992) to philosophical reductionist reverse-engineering.

6. Am I here confounding the contexts of discovery and justification (committing the genetic fallacy)? No, because reductionists themselves have abandoned any justification of unequivocal theory reductions and property identifications via their junking of logical positivism—*there are no identities to justify* (see below).

7. The reason why the dogma of intertheoretic identification must be promulgated in spite of its lack of confirming instances is that the favored option of existentially eliminating mind by brain would have no meaning except as the terminus of incomplete identifications. Either there exists at least one such (manufactured) confirming identity (e.g., optics-to-electromagnetism) or identification is postulated as unattainable ideal, approached asymptotically. Either move establishes if only tenuously that counterpole complementary to (mental) property elimination, requisite for correlative *definiens*.

8. Churchland is following Hooker's (1981) "retention/replacement continuum." Hooker (1981: 45) places optics-to-electromagnetism near the retention end of his spectrum but contrarily also squarely in the middle (41, 42); while further (45), "the retention extreme . . . goes unoccupied"—i.e., there are no clear-cut intertheoretic identities, *contra* Churchland. He chides the logical empiricists as "rewriting theory and history [of science] in the positivist image" (41). A parallel criticism may be made of his and the Churchlands' reductionist constructions of scientific history

and theory, which, by happy coincidence, serve as paradigmatic object lessons for the anticipated, precisely analogical psychology-to-neuroscience reduction—the unmistakable design of their philosophy of science.

9. I suggest Churchland's implicit realization that intertheoretic reduction is untenable, combined with her understanding that that construct is yet *de rigueur* for projected psychology-to-neuroscience reduction, compelled her (1986: 283–284) to overcome this inconsistency by simply jettisoning all rational and formal criteria (following Feyerabend) for determination of identities and blithely claiming such identifications obtain even by wildly arbitrary fiat. No more desperate expedient might be conceived, save Dennett's construal of veridical phenomenology as "false belief" (Crooks 2003, 2004; cf. Smythies 2003; Wright 2003).

10. There is moreover a ubiquitous and convenient fallacy of equivocation perpetrated by most or all reductionist philosophers upon the word "illusory," epitomized by Dennett (1991). The term properly signifies existent (though nonveridical) phenomenal percepts with no stimulus "behind" them, whereas when reductionists typically use the term, they mean that there is no percept in the sensory field—two incommensurate semantics of "nothing there" (Crooks 2003).

References

Armstrong, D. M. 1961. *Perception of the Physical World*. London: Routledge and Kegan Paul.

Armstrong, D. M. 1968. *A Materialist Theory of the Mind*. London: Routledge and Kegan Paul.

Bechtel, W., and A. Abrahamsen. 1991. *Connectionism and the Mind*. Oxford: Basil Blackwell.

Beloff, J. 1964. *The Existence of Mind*. New York: Citadel.

Boring, E. G. 1942. *Sensation and Perception in the History of Experimental Psychology*. New York: Appleton-Century-Crofts.

Brain, R. 1950. The concept of the schema in neurology and psychiatry. In *Perspectives in Neuropsychiatry*, ed. D. Richter, 127–139. London: H. K. Lewis.

Brain, R. 1959. *The Nature of Experience*. London: Oxford University Press.

Byrne, A., and D. Hilbert. 2003. Color realism and color science. *Behavioral and Brain Sciences* 26: 3–64.

Churchland, P. M. 1979. *Scientific Realism and the Plasticity of Mind*. Cambridge: Cambridge University Press.

Churchland, P. M. 1985. Reduction, qualia, and the direct introspection of brain states. *Journal of Philosophy* 82: 8–28.

Churchland, P. M. 1988. *Matter and Consciousness*. Cambridge, Mass.: MIT Press/A Bradford Book.

Churchland, P. M. 1989. *A Neurocomputational Perspective*. Cambridge, Mass.: MIT Press/A Bradford Book.

Churchland, P. M. 1995. *The Engine of Reason, the Seat of the Soul*. Cambridge, Mass.: MIT Press/A Bradford Book.

Churchland, P. M., and P. S. Churchland. 1997. *On the Contrary*. Cambridge, Mass.: MIT Press/A Bradford Book.

Churchland, P. S. 1986. *Neurophilosophy*. Cambridge, Mass.: MIT Press/A Bradford Book.

Churchland, P. S., and T. J. Sejnowski. 1992. *The Computational Brain*. Cambridge, Mass.: MIT Press/A Bradford Book.

Crooks, M. 2002a. Intertheoretic identification and mind–brain reductionism. *Journal of Mind and Behavior* 23: 193–222.

Crooks, M. 2002b. Four rejoinders: A dialogue in continuation. *Journal of Mind and Behavior* 23: 249–277.

Crooks, M. 2003. Phenomenology *in absentia:* Dennett's philosophy of mind. *Journal of Theoretical and Philosophical Psychology* 23: 102–148.

Crooks, M. 2004. The last philosophical behaviorist: Content and consciousness explained away. *Journal of Theoretical and Philosophical Psychology* 24: 50–121.

Crooks, M. 2007. Introspecting brain. *Journal of Mind and Behavior* 28, 1: 45–76.

Dennett, D. 1991. *Consciousness Explained*. Boston: Little, Brown.

Dennett, D. 1995. *Darwin's Dangerous Idea*. New York: Simon and Schuster.

Descartes, R. 1991 [1640]. *The Philosophical Writings of Descartes*, vol. 3: *The Correspondence*. Trans. J. Cottingham, R. Stoothoff, D. Murdoch, and A. Kenny. Cambridge: Cambridge University Press.

Feigl, H. 1967. *The "Mental" and the "Physical."* Minneapolis: University of Minnesota Press. (Originally published 1958.)

Feyerabend, P. 1963. Materialism and the mind–body problem. *Review of Metaphysics* 17: 49–66.

Feyerabend, P. 1988. *Against Method*. London: Verso.

Hardin, C. L. 1993. *Color for Philosophers: Unweaving the Rainbow.* Indianapolis: Hackett.

Hochberg, J. E. 1978. *Perception.* Englewood Cliffs, N.J.: Prentice-Hall.

Hooker, C. A. 1981. Towards a general theory of reduction. *Dialogue* 20: 38–59, 201–236, 496–529.

Horst, S. 2005. Phenomenology and psychophysics. *Phenomenology and the Cognitive Sciences* 4: 1–21.

Gregory, R. L. 1981. *Mind in Science.* Cambridge: Cambridge University Press.

Kalat, J. 2002. Identism without objective qualia: Commentary on Crooks. *Journal of Mind and Behavior* 23: 233–238.

Kelley, D. 1986. *The Evidence of the Senses.* Baton Rouge: Louisiana State University Press.

Köhler, W. 1971. An old pseudoproblem. In *The Selected Papers of Wolfgang Köhler,* ed. M. Henle, 129–141. New York: Liveright. (Originally published 1929.)

Kuhn, T. 1970. *The Structure of Scientific Revolutions.* New York: New American Library.

Lovejoy, A. O. 1929. *The Revolt against Dualism.* LaSalle, Ill.: Open Court.

Mueller, C. G. 1965. *Sensory Psychology.* Englewood Cliffs, N.J.: Prentice-Hall.

Nagel, T. 1965. Physicalism. In *The Mind/Brain Identity Theory,* ed. C. V. Borst, 214–230. London: Macmillan.

Rorty, R. 1965. Mind–body identity, privacy, and categories. *Review of Metaphysics* 19: 24–54.

Schilder, P. 1950. *The Image and Appearance of the Human Body.* New York: International Universities Press.

Searle, J. 1992. *The Rediscovery of the Mind.* Cambridge, Mass.: MIT Press/A Bradford Book.

Sellars, W. 1963. *Science, Perception, and Reality.* New York: Routledge and Kegan Paul.

Smart, J. J. C. 1959. Sensations and brain processes. In *The Philosophy of Mind,* ed. V. C. Chappell, 160–172. Englewood Cliffs, N.J.: Prentice Hall.

Smart, J. J. C. 1963. *Philosophy and Scientific Realism.* London: Routledge and Kegan Paul.

Smart, J. J. C. 2002. The compatibility of direct realism with the scientific account of perception: Comment on Mark Crooks. *Journal of Mind and Behavior* 23: 239–244.

Smythies, J. R. 1953. The experience and description of the human body. *Brain* 76: 132–145.

Smythies, J. R. 1954. Analysis of projection. *British Journal for the Philosophy of Science* 5: 120–133.

Smythies, J. R. 1956. *Analysis of Perception.* New York: Humanities Press.

Smythies, J. R. 1965. The representative theory of perception. In *Brain and Mind,* ed. J. R. Smythies, 241–264. New York: Humanities Press.

Smythies, J. R. 1994. *The Walls of Plato's Cave.* Aldershot: Avebury.

Smythies, J. R. 1996. A note on the concept of the visual field in neurology, psychology, and visual neuroscience. *Perception* 25: 369–371.

Smythies, J. R. 2002. Comment on Crooks's "Intertheoretic identification and mind–brain reductionism." *Journal of Mind and Behavior* 23: 245–248.

Smythies, J. R. 2003. Commentary on Crooks. *Journal of Theoretical and Philosophical Psychology* 23: 149–156.

Vernon, M. D. 1962. *A Further Study of Visual Perception.* Cambridge: Cambridge University Press.

Wittgenstein, L. 1958. *Philosophical Investigations.* Trans. G. E. M. Anscombe. New York: Macmillan.

Wright, E. 1990. The new representationalism. *Journal for the Theory of Social Behavior* 20: 65–92.

Wright, E. 1993. The irony of perception. In *The New Representationalisms,* ed. E. Wright, 176–201. Aldershot: Avebury.

Wright, E. 2003. Dennett as illusionist. *Journal of Theoretical and Philosophical Psychology* 23: 157–167.

Wright, E. 2005. *Narrative, Perception, Language, and Faith.* New York: Palgrave Macmillan.

12 Why Frank Should Not Have Jilted Mary

Howard Robinson

1 How Jackson Has Changed His Opinion

As is now well known, Frank Jackson has abandoned the knowledge argument, of which he was the most famous protagonist. In this essay I want to investigate the reasons and rationale that he gives for this notorious *volte face*. The reasons I shall discuss are to be found in two papers, "Postscript on Qualia" (Jackson 1998) and "Mind and Illusion" (Jackson 2004). The outline of his overall argument, found mainly in the former, is as follows.[1]

A. Jackson's overall argument

1. If the knowledge argument (KA) is sound and physical closure (PC) is correct, then there are qualia which are epiphenomenal.
2. Epiphenomenalism about qualia is incoherent.

Therefore,

3. Either KA is not sound or PC is not correct (1, 2, modus tollens)
4. The success of science obliges us to believe that PC is correct.

Therefore,

5. KA is not sound. (3, 4 disjunctive syllogism)

The argument is valid. The premises are (1), (2) and (4). Premise (1) is plainly true if overdetermination is excluded, and I do not want any resistance to Jackson to rest on overdetermination; so I shall take (1) to be true. Premise (4) is something to which Jackson is committed by the form of his belief in science. He does not argue for it, but merely asserts it: "We know that our knowledge of what it is like to see red and feel pain has purely physical causes. We know, for example, that Mary's transition from not knowing what it is like to see red to knowing what it is like to see red will have a causal explanation in purely physical terms. (Dualist interactionism is false)" (Jackson 2004: 418). I do not share Jackson's faith in science as the true metaphysics, but this is not the point at which I wish to challenge his argument. If my challenge is successful, however, it will follow that his kind of scientific naturalism must be false.

The issue, on which Jackson has changed his opinion, is (2). In "Epiphenomenal Qualia," he had claimed that epiphenomenalism was respectable. His argument for abandoning epiphenominalism is as follows.

B. Argument for A(2)

1. Reference to any x involves causal influence from x to the referential act.

2. If x is epiphenomenal then it has no causal influence on anything, so *a fortiori*, not on any referential act.

Therefore,

3. If x is epiphenomenal then it is something to which we cannot refer. (1, 2, transitivity, hypothetical syllogism)

Therefore,

4. If qualia are epiphenomenal then they cannot be objects of reference. (3, universal instantiation)

5. Qualia (if they exist) are what we refer to by using our phenomenal concepts.

Therefore,

6. If qualia exist and are epiphenomenal then they can and cannot be objects of reference. (4, 5, conjunction)

Therefore,

7. Epiphenomenalism about qualia is incoherent. (6, reductio ad absurdum)

This argument is, I believe, sound. Jackson's defense of epiphenomenalism never was any good. We face, therefore, a straight choice between accepting physical closure and accepting the knowledge argument. The rejection of epiphenomenalism is not itself a direct attack on the knowledge argument, for that argument makes no appeal to epiphenomenalism. It is only that if you accept KA and PC then you are committed to epiphenomenalism. The title of Jackson's original paper—"Epiphenomenal Qualia" (1982)—was, in a sense, presumptuous, for he had not presented any argument to show that qualia are epiphenomenal, only that they exist and are not physical. It was a presumption that they must therefore be epiphenomenal. Jackson's rejection of the argument is not direct but, as one might put it, transcendental: it is a presupposition of the closure of physics that something must be wrong with the argument. This does not of itself tell us what is wrong with it. If it cannot be faulted, Jackson will be in an impasse. To take the matter further, therefore, it will be useful to remind ourselves of how the argument runs.

C. The knowledge argument

Mary has spent all her life in an environment in which she has lacked experience of chromatic colors, but she has achieved scientific perfection in her knowledge of the process of seeing, including its operation in those who do see such colors. The original intuition behind the argument can be expressed as follows.

1. Mary knows all those facts about chromatic vision that can in principle be expressed in the vocabulary of physical science.

2. Unlike those who have seen colors, Mary does not know what can be expressed as the phenomenal nature of chromatic color, or what it is like to seem to see chromatic color.

Therefore,

3. The phenomenal nature (etc.) of chromatic color in principle cannot be characterized in the vocabulary of physical science.

4. The nature of any physical thing, state, or property can be expressed in the vocabulary of physical science.

Therefore,

5. The phenomenal nature of (or what it is like to seem to see) chromatic color is not a physical thing, state, or property.

In this form, ignoring the character of Mary herself, the argument is not original to Jackson. His contribution comes in strengthening the intuition behind (2). Someone might deny (2) by insisting that someone with Mary's comprehensive knowledge could work out what the phenomenal nature of chromatic color must be. Jackson buttresses the intuition that she could not by imagining that she is released from her nonchromatic environment, and appealing to the thought that, as she first sees, for example, a red rose, it must come as a revelation to her that *that* is what (experiencing) red is like. Concentration on the moment of acquisition of the experience so far lacked is supposed to bring home the realization that, up to that point, a certain knowledge was lacking. By presenting the thought experiment wholly in the first person, in the sense of making the contrast not between Mary and others, but between Mary before and after having the crucial experience, we are supposed to feel for ourselves the reality of the difference. Now I must admit to not being convinced that this extra piece of dramatization adds much, because, given that one is not oneself Mary, imagining the contrast between Mary inside and outside her room is exactly the same imaginative situation and contrast as that between imagining her experience versus that of someone who sees normally: in both cases, it is one's own imagination of what the difference must be that is doing the job.

What is as plain as a pikestaff is that there is nothing about epiphenomenalism, interactionism, or physical closure employed directly in the argument itself. If the contrast between Mary and others, or between Mary before and after, is a genuine one, then property dualism is established and one must adjust one's views accordingly. If epiphenomenalism is not an available option, interactionism must replace the dogma of physical closure.

It is interesting to investigate at what point Jackson now rejects the argument; in my opinion, it is not wholly clear. There are two major strategies against the argument. One is to claim that the lack of experience is not lack of factual knowledge but lack of an ability. The other is to claim that Mary could, in principle, work out what the experience or experienced phenomenal quality was like and thus it is a failure of imagination on our part to see that she could. It is not clear to me which line Jackson is taking.

Jackson says (I have added the Roman numbering):

I now think that the puzzle posed by the Knowledge Argument is to explain why we have such a strong intuition that Mary learns something about how things are that outruns what can [be] deduced from the physical account of how things are. I suggest that the answer is the strikingly atypical nature of the way she acquires certain relational and functional information. . . . (i) The most plausible view for physicalists is that sensory experience is putative information about certain highly relational and functional properties of goings on *inside us* [emphasis added]. (ii) As it is often put nowadays, its very nature is representational: . . . (iii) sensory information is a quite unusually "quick and easy" way of acquiring highly relational and functional information. . . . Sensory experience in this regard is like the way we acquire information about intrinsic properties. . . . But, very obviously, it is not information about intrinsic physical nature, so the information Mary acquires presents itself as if it were information about more than the physical. (Jackson 1998: 419)

The key points in Jackson's explanation of the "illusion" of knowledge acquisition are that: (i) experience represents states that are (a) highly complexly relational and functional and (b) internal, so: (ii) such experience is purely representational. (iii) Experience does this in a "holistic" or "gestalt-like" way, so that the complex seems like a simple or intrinsic property. (iv) Because there is obviously no such physical property, it seems to be a nonphysical one.

This raises two points of contention. First is the adequacy of the purely representational account of the qualitative content of experience, which is enshrined in (i) and (ii). The second is the status of the claim that the unitary representation of a complex state of affairs presents itself as qualia-like (i.e., (iii)). I shall be principally concerned with the adequacy of representationalism. Jackson's claim in (iii) seems to me to have been adequately refuted by Alter (2007).

2 Pure Representationalism and Experience

It might not at first sight be wholly clear why anyone should think that representationalism in perception would avoid the knowledge argument. The recent use of the term "representationalism" in the philosophy of perception is likely to cause confusion. The traditional "representative theory of perception" is closely allied to the sense-datum theory and rests on the idea that there is, in perception, some introspectible vehicle that represents, but is not a part of, the external world. This invocation of an introspectible vehicle is absolutely the opposite of what modern representationalism asserts. Now the claim is that experience itself is, as it is put, wholly transparent. This, too, is not without ambiguity. Hume, in his failure to find either act or subject of perception, only ever discovering its object, treated experience as transparent, because nothing was introspectible except what it was of. But, for Hume, this object of experience was not a feature of the mind-independent, external world, but an impression or sense-datum. Transparency today signifies the idea that there is nothing introspectible in experience other than the external, physicalistically respectable objects that it is supposed to be of. This is often expressed by saying that experience is purely intentional. ("Intentional" and "representational" are in fact used more or less as synonyms.)

The way that representationalism is supposed to help the physicalist cope with Mary is, I think, as follows.

D. Jackson's positive account

1. When Mary leaves the room, she acquires a state the nature of which, *qua* experience, is wholly accounted for in terms of the properties it is of.

2. The properties it is of are physical properties.

Therefore,

3. When Mary leaves the room, she acquires a state the nature of which is wholly accounted for in terms of physical properties. (1, 2, identity)

4. Mary already has complete relevant knowledge about the nature of physical properties.

Therefore,

5. When Mary leaves the room she acquires a state the nature of which is wholly accounted for in terms of properties the nature of which she already completely knows. (3, 4, identity)

Therefore,

6. Mary does not learn about any new properties when she leaves the room. (5 and meaning of "new")

Therefore,

7. Her original total physical knowledge was not incomplete with respect to knowing the nature of experience. (6 and the principle that if nothing new needed, the old is complete)

We must look at the possible grounds for rejecting D. The premises are (1), (2), and (4). Premise (4) is ex hypothesis, so the argument focuses on (1) and (2). There are two paths for disputing (1). They are by claiming either or both of:

a. Representationalism about experience is not adequate as a complete account.

b. Representationalism is not, on its own, physicalistically respectable.

And one can dispute (2) by arguing:

c. The objects of perception, in the case of secondary qualities, are not physicalistically respectable.

The best way of considering these issues is to look closely at the nature of representationalism, and how it relates to physicalism. This will be our concern for the next four sections.

3   What Is Representationalism?

The notion of representation is part of the common currency of the contemporary debate on perception. Nevertheless, I find myself less than clear about what is involved in a state's being representational. I shall attempt to distinguish various propositions that might, on their own or in various combinations with each other, be thought of as representing the core idea of representationalism.

The weakest statement might be

1a. All experiences with phenomenal content *can be taken* as representing the world as being some way or another; that is, they can be taken as having an intentional object.

A slightly stronger version would be

1b. All experiences with phenomenal content *are naturally taken* as representing the world as being in some way or another; that is, they are naturally taken as having an intentional object.

Both (1a) and (1b) talk of phenomenal content being *taken as* representing the world, and this might suggest that the representational contribution is not intrinsic to the phenomenal content, but comes, for example, through interpretation. This might be thought to undermine the essential point of representationalism, because it suggests that there is something that is not essentially representational in itself, which is being interpreted as a representation. To avoid this limitation, one might suggest:

1c. All experiences with phenomenal content *naturally represent* the world as being some way or other; that is, they naturally present a certain object intentionally.

A sense-datum theorist might (though, for reasons I am about to present, need not) accept either (1a) or (1b); (1c) is, perhaps, therefore, the only version of (1) that a genuine representationalist could accept. (1c), however, does not present what one might call a complete representationalism, for although it says that all experiences with phenomenal content are representational, it does not say that every phenomenal aspect of the experience must be representational. This latter is necessary if representationalism is to present itself as an account of phenomenal content per se. This comprehensive version of representationalism can be stated in ways that combine with any version of (1), though, for the reasons I have given, only that which is modeled on (1c) is probably of interest. That version runs as follows:

2. There is no phenomenal aspect of experience that does not naturally represent the world as being some way or other.

This does not give us the full force of representationalism, however. Representationalists emphasize the transparency of experience. This means that the nature of experience comes entirely from the nature of its intentional object, not from the nature of the experiencing itself. This idea, though, is not entirely unambiguous, for it might be read as neutral on what contributes to the nature of the object, *qua* object of experience. For example, one could hold that the nature of the experience of seeing red is entirely a function of the nature of the redness of the thing perceived, but agree that secondary qualities such as red are what they are because of the way that objects interact with our sense organs. Insofar as the objective of the representationalist is to account for the nature of experience by reference to the nature of what it is of, such a compromised position is not adequate. What is needed is

3. There is nothing in the "act" of having an experience with phenomenal content, except what is contributed by the nature of the object, which nature is wholly independent of what it is like to experience it.

This is required to make it clear that the character of experience is entirely conceptually derivative from something external to and independent of experience itself.

Claim (3), however, would have been acceptable to Hume, because he believed that the "impressions" which were the objects of experience could, in principle, exist outside the mind. This strange doctrine is, of course, a consequence of his "bundle" theory of the mind, rather than of his account of consciousness. And is not clear whether or not an impression of red that were to float out of its mental bundle would then still constitute an experience, rather than an "unsensed sensibilium." These matters are all clarified from the representationalist and intentionalist perspective, without entering into discussion of these Humean niceties, by insisting that, because experience is essentially of its object, it is not itself characterized by instances of the properties attributed to the object. Hume's impressions, and all traditional "sense data," constitute the subjective contents of the experience, and are themselves instances of the basic sensible qualities the experiences are of. To avoid this, the representationalist must insist on the intentional inexistence of the object, as represented by

4. None of the subjective phenomenal contents of experience is an instance of the any of the properties the experience represents: for any F, such that the experience represents the world as being F, there is no instance of F constituting the content of the experience, other than that represented as being in the external world. The experience itself, and its subjective constitution, can only be characterized as being *of F*.

The purpose of representationalism, in this context at least, is to deny that individual experiences possess any features that they do not borrow from the world of which they are experiences. This has some initial plausibility for veridical perception, of which the content may seem to be things in the external world and their properties. But hallucinations and even what are traditionally called "illusions"—things not looking exactly as they really are—may seem to cause a problem. Their contents would not seem to be straightforwardly identifiable with features of the external world, and so would seem to constitute a challenge to the attempt to deny experience any ontological baggage that cannot be identified with physical reality. It is to overcome this problem that representationalists affirm

5. Insofar as the intentional object of an experience cannot be identified with an actual physical thing or state of affairs, it has no positive ontological status.

A representationalist with Jackson's physicalist ambitions must affirm

6. What it is to represent the world, including experientially, can be given a purely naturalist account.

Whether this adds anything to the other propositions, or whether they constitute such an account, might be an issue. We shall see that they do not, on their own, constitute a naturalistic account, but require to be set in the context of such a theory as Dretske's (1981) informationalism, or a purely functionalist account of consciousness and mind. This of itself might seem to leave problematic what representationalism itself contributes to the argument.[2]

If we take (1c) as defining the starting point for any intentionalist or representationalist theory of perception, it can be filled out or strengthened in the following ways. First, I think that (4) is essential if the contrast with a sense-datum theory is to made firm. Propositions (1c) and (4) together constitute an intentionalist theory of perceptual content, while leaving open the option that some phenomenal content might not be representational (and so not perceptual), but, as one might say, purely sensational. Provided that nothing that the naive realist would wish to impute to the external, physical world is included in the category of sensations, but is within the representational, these two propositions together are enough to satisfy someone who is an intentionalist about perception, but is not interested in deploying representationalism as part of a physicalist strategy. If the latter is the program, then (2) is necessary to bring all phenomenal content within its purview, and (3) is necessary to ensure that no phenomenal residue is contributed by the mind (as I explained above on introducing (3)). Proposition (5) is necessary to sweep up the contents of nonveridical experiences.

Because I am here concerned with the use made of representationalism by physicalists, I am not going to concentrate on (1c) and (4), except for the following important point: (1c) could be interpreted either as

1c'. All experiences with phenomenal content, taken individually, naturally represent the world as being some way or other;

or

1c''. All experiences with phenomenal content, taken as part of the general flow of experience, naturally represent the world as being some way or other.

The point of this distinction is as follows. If the property of being representational is an intrinsic feature of phenomenal content as such, then it ought to apply to each occurrence of such content in its own right. That is, (1c') ought to be true. But it seems to me that (1c'') is the only one that is plausible, and even that is plausible only given that the flow of experience has a certain structure. My reason for saying this can be brought out by considering the following case. Imagine someone born blind, who, because of internal activity in his brain, occasionally has experiences of a kind that we would recognize as being of flashes of color, and even colored shapes. These do not form any structure in their own right, nor do they correlate with any tactile or other sensory experiences. I can see no reason why the subject of these odd experiences should have any inclination to take them as representing any reality, either external or (as some philosophers want to say about bodily sensations) as apparently representing something going on in the body—presumably, in this case, the head. Representationalism as a whole ignores Hume's insight that the claim of experiences to be about the world depends essentially on the ordering and patterning of those experiences.[3] If they were wholly chaotic and fragmentary, there is no reason to believe that their qualitative nature would, of itself, point to anything beyond them.

Putting aside this general difficulty, from which representationalism suffers even when freed from the physicalist burden, I shall now consider problems facing (2), (3), and (5).

4   The Plausibility of (2)

The question of whether representationalism can be extended to all phenomenal content comes down, in the end, to the issue of whether sensations can all be treated representationally. Thanks to Ned Block, I think, this issue has focused on the question of whether the phenomenal content of orgasm can be wholly understood in perceptual and representational terms. He thinks that it cannot, for he thinks that it is clear that the experience contains something phenomenal that is not purely cognitive. Michael Tye (1995) disagrees. He says: "In this case, one undergoes sensory representations of certain physical changes in the genital region. These changes quickly undulate in their intensity. Furthermore, they are highly pleasing. They illicit an immediate and strong positive reaction" (Tye 1995: 118). Then he adds, presumably in case this seems too intellectualized an account: "It is important to stress . . . that the representations of bodily changes involved in orgasms are nonconceptual."

The issue is not whether Tye is right that one locates the sensations and associates them with certain bodily events. The issue is whether characterizing the sensations as being of those events, while understanding those events in a physicalist manner (that is, no irreducible secondary qualities present), entirely exhausts the experiential content of the sensation. The addition that they are "highly pleasing" only obfuscates the matter. Is this pleasingness itself a quality of the sensation, in which case an extra phenomenal residue has been imported? Or is it unpacked in the notion of a "strong positive reaction"; that is, is finding something pleasing only a matter of behavioral response? If it is the latter, then the experience of orgasm is being reduced to a nonconceptual cognition of bodily changes, plus a behavioral reaction of, for example, an "I want more" type. One must not be deceived into thinking that calling a representation "nonconceptual" somehow qualifies it as experiential. We shall see this more clearly when discussing Dretske's use of "analogue representation"—a close cousin of the nonconceptual—below. But, in the jargon of the informational theorist, mindless nature is full of "representations," and they are all nonconceptual and non-experiential.

What seems plain is that Tye's attempt to extend representationalism to brute sensations commits him to a radically reductive account of the experience itself. It is information inflow plus behavioral reaction. Representationalism, unless treated in this way, does not complete the job. It seems that (6) is required if representationalism is to do the work the physicalist asks of it.

5   Physicalism and (3)

Just how reductive (3) must be, if interpreted physicalistically, can be seen by considering how it relates to secondary qualities. Representationalism is a form of direct realism, allowing no intermediary entities.[4] The most natural form of direct realism for secondary qualities is what is often dubbed naive realism, which treats the phenomenal versions of those qualities as objective features of external objects. This runs into difficulty with physicalism in two ways. First, there is the fact that science has never found a place in the external world for the secondary qualities in their phenomenal form. This point is too obvious to need laboring. Second, and irrespective of the problem of secondary qualities, is the fact that it is a mistake to think that physicalism can accommodate the kind of *sui generis* awareness relation that nonreductive naive realism involves. The idea that naive realism is respectable from a physicalist viewpoint seems to rest on the mistake of thinking that physicalism is safe provided only that there are no subjective contents of awareness. This is plainly mistaken, however, because to postulate an irreducible awareness relation between perceiver and external world is to postulate something that is as inconsistent with the physicalist world picture as are subjective contents. The "torch beam" view of consciousness is antiphysicalist, whether it falls on something external and physical or internal and mental. The "transparency" of experience is not sufficient on its own to allow it to be an open empirical matter whether it is simply a state of the brain or not.

These two problems together mean that representationalism is helpful to the physicalist only if he can provide both a reductive account of secondary qualities and a reductive account of the perceptual relation (that is, condition (6)) in addition to the bare representationalism.

6   The Physicalist Need for (5)

To see how representationalism relates physicalism to perceptual experience, we can ask how representationalism is supposed to capture the particular "feel" of such experience without invoking anything that the physicalist cannot accept. How he might think it does this can be shown by examining the following two questions and answers.

Question 1. What gives experience its "feel"—its "what it's like"?
Answer to 1. Its intentional object—what it seems to be of.
Question 2. What specific ontology is involved with intentional objects?
Answer to 2. None, because either
(i) the intentional object = a physical object, or facet of the same, which covers the case of genuine (veridical?) perception;

or

(ii) the intentional object is a kind of non-entity, and so cannot be an ontological liability, which covers hallucination (and "illusion"?)

Propositions (i) and (ii) together constitute (5).

We have seen in discussing (3) some of the serious problems that face the physicalist, even for straightforward cases of perception, but I am concerned now with the case where the intentional object is not veridical and so cannot be simply identified with something external. As my way of stating (i) and (ii) shows, there is an ambiguity in the intentionalist position concerning whether the contrast is between perception and hallucination or between veridical perception and nonveridical perceptual experiences, where the latter category includes what was traditionally classified as "illusion," as well as hallucination. The arguments we are going to consider are all stated as concerning hallucination, but one should also bear in mind that there is, or may be, a parallel problem for the intentional objects of misperceptions (what, for example, is the ontological status of the blue involved in a white wall's looking blue, as well as the ontological status of the blue wall if one simply hallucinated such a wall).

I shall consider two strategies falling under (ii) for dealing with either or both of these cases. The first consists in claiming that intentional objects are abstract entities and that, as such, do not exist in the spatiotemporal world of objects, whether mental or physical. The second attempts to analyze the contents of hallucinations and nonveridical perceptions solely in terms of their indiscriminability from veridical perceptions, thereby avoiding invocation of their contents at all.

Dismissing the ontology of hallucination and the like on the grounds that it is abstract seems to be the line many representationalists take. The idea seems to be that, insofar as an experience is veridical, its intentional object is a thing, or facet of a thing, in the external world: and insofar as its intentional object is nonveridical, though phenomenologically quite real, any question of its ontological status can quite simply be dismissed.

Dretske, for example, explains the status of the contents of hallucination or misperceptions in the following way. He says that "the properties we are aware of in achieving this awareness (being universals) exist nowhere" (Dretske 1981: 160). He follows this up by saying: "Awareness of colors, shapes, and movements, when there is no external object that has the property one is aware of, is not, therefore, a violation of [the principle that experience involves no internal phenomenal properties]. A measuring instrument (a speedometer, for example) can (when malfunctioning) be 'aware of' (i.e., represent) a speed of 45 mph without any object's (inside

or outside the instrument) having this magnitude" (ibid.). The idea that
a malfunctioning speedometer and a hallucinating person both "hallucinate," in a similar enough sense for the analogy to be of any use in providing a physicalist model of hallucination, is bizarre enough. But it also
seems to carry the implication that crude analog representing devices do
actually experience what they represent—they just have rather limited
experiences. This seems to me to be a *reductio* of this approach.

Lycan's (1987) view is similar:

I take the view . . . that phenomenal individuals such as sense-data are intentional
inexistents *a la* Brentano and Meinong. It is, after all, no surprise to be told that
mental states have intentional objects that do not exist. So why should we not
suppose that after-images and other sense-data are intentional objects that do not
exist? If they do not exist then—*voila*—they do not exist; there are in reality no such
things. And that is why we can consistently admit that phenomenal-color properties qualify individuals without granting that there exist individuals that are the
bearers of phenomenal-color properties. (Lycan 1987: 88)

The cavalier attitude to intentional objects does indeed seem to be Jackson's
approach, as is shown by what Jackson says here:

Intentionalism means that no amount of tub-thumping assertion by dualists (including by myself in the past) that the *redness* of seeing red cannot be accommodated in
the austere physicalist picture carries any weight. That striking feature is a feature
of how things are represented to be, and if, as claimed by the tub thumpers, it is
transparently a feature that has no place in the physicalist picture, what follows is
that physicalists should deny that anything has that striking feature. And this is no
argument against physicalism. Physicalists can allow that people are sometimes in
states that represent that things have a non-physical property. Examples are people
who believe that there are fairies. What physicalists must deny is that such properties are instantiated. (Jackson 2004: 431)

There are at least three problems with this cavalier approach to intentional objects. First, to say that they are abstract and so not part of the
ontology of the empirical world leaves untouched the question of how,
for a physicalist, an abstract, immaterial entity is supposed to constitute
the content of a physical state: what is it for the brain to be aware of an
abstract object? Second, the emphasis on the possible non-existence of
intentional objects does not seem to be a fair account of the actual nature
of a mental state—absence is not what gives a state the phenomenological nature it has. (This sounds rather too reminiscent of Sartre's characterization of intentionality as "nothingness.") Third, the difference between
intellectual states and sensory ones is not given enough attention. The idea

that phenomenal redness might simply not exist, in the way that fairies do not exist, hardly seems adequate. You can stop believing in fairies, but you cannot stop things looking red. It is a bedrock fact that that is how things appear. Even the psychological event of someone's exercising his belief in fairies does not consist wholly in an absence. Something actual and real—say, saying some words to oneself—constitutes the phenomenology of it. The phenomenology of seeming to see something red must be constituted by something empirical and actual.

7   Martin's Theory of Hallucination

M. J. F. Martin (2004, 2006) proposes an account of hallucination that could be pressed into service at this point. With veridical-seeming hallucination in mind, Martin suggests that "At least when it comes to the mental characterization of hallucinatory experience, nothing more can be said than the relational and epistemological claim that it is indiscriminable from the [corresponding] perception" (2004: 72). He exemplifies this principle elsewhere: "For certain visual experiences as of a white picket fence, namely, causally matching hallucinations, there is no more to the phenomenal character of such experiences than that of being indiscriminable from corresponding visual perceptions of a white picket fence as what is" (2006: 369).

Like Dretske and Lycan above, Martin is trying to disembarrass himself of phenomenal content (or intentional objects) in the cases where it (they) cannot be identified with aspects of the external world. He does this, however, not by treating them as "abstract" and therefore lacking ontological "weight," but by saying that the nonveridical experiences which apparently possess such contents do so only indirectly, by being indiscriminable from experiences—veridical perceptions—that really do have such objects.

This way of characterizing hallucinations might remind one of J. J. C. Smart's treatment of afterimages: "The man who reports a yellowish orange after-image does so in effect as follows: 'What is going on in me is like what is going on in me when my eyes are open, the light is normal etc. etc. and there really is a yellowish-orange patch on the wall'" (1963: 94–95). Both Smart and Martin are trying to free themselves of nonveridical phenomenal contents by characterizing these delusive experiences simply and solely in terms of their likeness to proper perceptions, thereby, they believe, putting the burden of carrying the ontological weight of the content onto the perceptual case. Smart, however, recognizes and welcomes a consequence of this that Martin disavows.

Smart continues the above quotation: "In this sentence the word 'like' is meant to be used in such a way that something can be like itself. . . .With this sense of 'like' the above formula will do for a report that one is having a veridical sense datum too. Notice that the italicised words 'what is going on in me is like what is going on in me when . . .' are topic neutral." The consequence that Smart welcomes is that, if our introspective knowledge of the subjective character of nonveridical experiences is topic neutral, then our knowledge of the subjective character of genuine perceptions, which are subjectively like them, must also be topic neutral. And Martin's account of our introspective knowledge of the subjective character of hallucinations is topic neutral, for we know nothing about it except that it is indistinguishable from something else, namely the appropriate genuine perception. Martin, however, does not want to generalize this topic neutrality to our grasp on perceptual experiences. He is a naive realist, and what it is like for the subject to perceive an external object is a function of the accessible sensible features of the object he perceives. This creates an asymmetry between veridical and hallucinatory experiences of a kind that Smart avoids. The issue is whether this asymmetry makes phenomenological sense. Here is an argument to the conclusion that it does not.

Martin, I think, is committed to the following premise.

1. A subject, S, recognizes a veridical perception, x, as being phenomenologically the experience it is, from the sensible qualities that the object perceived presents, and appears to present, to him in that experience.

The following seems to me to be a necessary truth:

2. If someone, S, recognizes some object, state, event, etc., x, by its exhibiting or seeming to exhibit some feature F, then (i) anything y that seems to S indiscriminable from x must also seem to S to present F, and (ii) it is because it seems to present just that feature that it is indiscriminable by S from x.

From these it follows that

3. If a seeming veridical hallucination, x, had by S is indiscriminable by S from some veridical perception, y, that S recognizes as being a perception of some object that presents and seems to present sensible quality Q, then (i) the veridical-seeming hallucination x must seem to be of an object that presents Q, and (ii) it is because it seems to present an object with that feature that it is indiscriminable by S from y.

If the argument just presented is correct, then indiscriminability cannot be a primitive notion, when one of the indiscriminable things is recognized by some feature, but must then rest on indiscriminability in respect of that feature.[5] This is what (2) asserts. Martin recognizes this principle when the indiscriminable things are both real physical objects—his example is a real lemon and a very convincing soap lemon (Martin 2006: 386). But he denies that it applies when one of the experiences is hallucinatory. This seems to me to be totally implausible. First, I think we can assume that he does not deny (2i) and (3i): that is, he cannot deny that if two things are indiscriminable they must seem to present the same features and that this must apply to the hallucination—it could not be indiscriminable from the perception of the white fence if it did not seem to be of a white fence. So the pressure must come on clause (ii): it must be the case that a hallucination's seeming to be of a white fence is not be analyzed as its possessing an intentional or phenomenal object of a "white fence" kind, but that its having that object is to be analyzed in terms of its indiscriminability from a perception of such an object. This would seem to commit the hallucinatory subject to a swift unconscious inference of the form "this experience is just like one I would have seeing a white fence, so it must be an experience of seeming to see a white fence." This seems very bizarre, even if intelligible, and topsy-turvy. I say "even if intelligible" because I do not see how something could strike one as experientially similar to another experience, when the latter experience has a clear object, except by explicitly striking one as having an exactly similar object. Only if Smart is right, and all experiences, nonveridical and veridical, are introspectively neutral and free of positive character, could indiscriminability alone be the primitive feature.[6]

I conclude that Martin's attempt to avoid all kinds of reification of the objects of hallucinations by treating indiscriminability as a primitive fails.

8 Conclusion of the Argument So Far

Representationalism does not help physicalism unless: (i) it can cover all phenomenal properties, not just those that are naturally regarded as perceptual, and this is not plausible; (ii) it is associated with a reductive account of secondary qualities, and such accounts are not convincing; and (iii) it can provide an account of phenomenal contents in hallucinations and other cases of nonveridical experiences. So far, no account provided is plausible.

9   How Things Stand with the Knowledge Argument

Jackson's mistake in believing that representationalism can overcome the knowledge argument almost pales into insignificance, I believe, in comparison with his failure to appreciate the full force and generality of the argument. This failure is something he shares with most of those who discuss—at any rate, critically—this argument. The dialectical situation in which the knowledge argument is usually taken to be located is the following: it is accepted that physicalism gives an adequate account of nonconscious reality, which constitutes almost 100 percent of the universe, but struggles to accommodate certain features of mental life, namely the "what it's like" or qualia of certain conscious states. These latter constitute "the hard problem" for physicalism. The fact that they also constitute such a tiny part of the world is presented as a reason for thinking that they cannot plausibly be held to refute a unified physicalist account.

I think that this constitutes a radical misunderstanding of the dialectical situation. What the argument really brings out is that only experience of the appropriate kind can reveal the qualitative, as opposed to purely formal and structural, features of the world. The kind of thing that Mary did not know, generalized from color vision to all the other sensible qualities, is essential to any contentful conception of the world, and physicalism without it would lack any empirical content.

That this is the real outcome of the argument can be made plain by considering the role of those states described as qualia, or "what it is like," in forming our conception of the world. The assumption that such states concern only the nature of our subjective life ignores their role in forming our commonsense or naive conception of the external world—what Sellars famously called the "manifest image" of the world. "What it is like to see red" is essentially connected with our naive conception of what red things are like. For the naive realist, this connection between what it is like and our manifest image obtains because what it is like to see red is a function of the external, objective redness that the experience has as its object. For the representational realist (in the traditional sense of that term), it holds because our naive conception arises from the projection of the subjective content onto the external world. On either conception, what the world is like is simply the other side of the coin of what it is like to perceive it. This should come as no surprise to Jackson and other physicalists, because the equation of the subjective and objective poles of experience is the essence of the transparency of experience, which is essential to representationalism and to most of the physicalist strategies we have been discussing.

It is important that this applies to primary qualities as much as to secondary. The fact that it is easier to imagine experience like ours except that chromatic color is missing, than it is to imagine experience like ours without spatial features (if that is possible at all), does not affect the fact that an empirically contentful (as opposed, say, to a purely axiomatic) conception of space depends on visual or tactile or some other experience of a spatial field to give us a conception of what space might be empirically like, and that this is dependent on what it is like to perceive it in some particular way. Peter Strawson (1959) argued that a purely auditory universe would not be enough to generate a conception of space, however the sounds were managed and organized. Certainly, we can make prima facie sense of a mind with only auditory experience, where the sounds are organized in a way that certainly cannot sustain a conception of space. If such a mind were to be taught verbally all the proofs of geometry and of relativity theory, it seems clear that its resultant grasp on the nature of empirical space would be no better than Mary's on color. So, although the knowledge argument is most easily stated in terms of secondary qualities, which are seemingly easily relegated into the dustbin of the mind, the argument can be carried through for primary qualities that are fundamental to our conception of physical reality. Our conception of these is, at bottom, no more independent of what it is like to perceive them than is our conception of the secondary qualities.[7]

The correct way of looking at the knowledge argument is to see it as granting content to the physicalist hypothesis only for purposes of argument. "Even if we grant," it says, "that physicalism could cope with the rest of reality, it still cannot cope with what it is like to experience things." Once one recognizes the connection between what it is like to experience the world and what we can conceive the world we experience to be like, one can see that the knowledge argument cannot fail to be right, for if there were not some special kind of content that is revealed only in experience, then we could not have an empirically significant conception of the physical in the first place. So, if you are tempted to think that physicalism might somehow be able to defuse the intuition that Mary learns something substantive and new, you need only direct your attention to the way that any nonformal conception of the physical is dependent on the qualitative nature of reality as revealed uniquely in experience to see that this could not possibly be true. If, in general, the acquisition of experience did not teach something new, then a purely descriptive account of reality ought not to lack anything essential. In sum, the argument draws our attention to the fact that a physicalism that depends on a notion of the physical that is somehow independent of the nature of experience can only present us with a world that is so formal as to be empirically contentless.

This consequence might be taken as suggesting that the knowledge argument is set up in a way that is unfair to physicalism. It might seem to be unfair because it saddles the physicalist with having a purely descriptive account of reality, and surely he is not denied the resource of sense experience in forming his conception: something must have gone wrong in our understanding of what physicalism or materialism requires.

Nothing, however, has gone awry. Of course, the physicalist is allowed to rely on perception to explain the acquisition of particular information about the physical world. But he is not allowed to draw essentially on the subjective dimension of experience—on what it is like to experience the world—in forming his conception of the physical nature of the world, for his conception is one committed to the availability of a purely objective account of the world. Insofar as the qualitative content of our conception of the world—that part which goes beyond what can be wholly captured descriptively—is a reflection of "what experience is like," then it is a resource denied to the physicalist. This is the point at which traditional empiricism and physicalist realism as a metaphysical theory diverge.

This might not seem to be so, provided that the physicalist is a naive realist, for then the qualitative features of the world that give experience its character are public features of the world, not part of the subjective dimension. I cannot here discuss the flaws in naive realism, but the arguments above show that the naive realist cannot cope with nonveridical perception in a way that helps the physicalist.[8] Furthermore it seems to me that, even for veridical perception, naive realism does not help the physicalist, but only slightly relocates his problem. If the experience relation in which the naive realist stands to external qualities is to be one that gives him a grasp on the nature of those qualities quite different in kind from the comprehension that can come from the descriptive account provided by science—if it is to be, that is, a form of knowledge by acquaintance—then it must be a *sui generis* relation, not one that can be analyzed in physicalist (e.g., causal and functional) terms. But such a *sui generis* relation is no more acceptable to the physicalist than are subjective qualia.

These considerations show that all current attempts to reply to the knowledge argument miss the point. Jackson assumes that, within our physical picture, we have a perfectly clear notion of representation, and then argues that experience can be explained in terms of this. Loar (1990) and others claim that knowing "what it is like" is just a different way—a way that employs phenomenal concepts—of grasping the same facts as are presented using the concepts of neurology. Lewis (1988) and followers of the "abilities" account believe that what it is like can be explained in terms of abilities to respond and discriminate. All these philosophers assume that the physicalist account is entirely adequate in its treatment of physical phenomena, and try to show how experience can be accommodated within this frame. Those, like Levine (1983), who claim that there is an explanatory but not an ontological gap between the physical and mental, also must take it for granted that the concept of the physical is autonomously sound. Even philosophers like Nagel (1974) and Galen Strawson (1994) who think that we need a conceptual breakthrough in our understanding of matter before we can solve the mind–body problem, and even McGinn (1989) who thinks we are constitutionally incapable of making this breakthrough, think that we now have a contentful, if inadequate to the present task, conception of matter in its own right. But if what the knowledge argument brings out is that our understanding of the physical world presupposes something which can be captured only in the special nature of experience, then all these strategies must be hopeless, and classical physicalism is broken-backed from the start.[9]

Notes

1. References to these Jackson articles are to page numbers in Ludlow, Nagasawa, and Stoljar 2004.

2. That representationalism leaves Mary's problem untouched is one of the conclusions of Alter (2007).

3. Hume 1964: Bk. I, pt. 4, sect. ii, "Of Scepticism with Regard to the Senses."

4. A major debate has grown up around the question of whether representationalism (or intentionalism) is a form of direct or naive realism. See, e.g., Crane 2006 and Martin 2006. I cannot enter that debate now, but it seems to me that, as Jackson means and uses the notion of representation, it must be a form of direct realism.

5. This contrasts with the case often invoked by David Armstrong (see, e.g., Armstrong 1968) of chicken sexing, where the sexers recognize the sex of the chickens *without knowing what sensible feature they found their judgment upon.* They never recognize a feature as that by which they do it. Veridical perceivers in normal cases, on Martin's account, recognize quite clearly what sensible features they are judging about, yet the judgments of similarity in nonveridical cases are not founded.

6. The problem with Smart's theory is that it involves a radically externalist account of sensory content. All experiences are identified simply as "what I get when facing objects of type *F,*" but one cannot individuate experiences indirectly in this way,

because one only knows what objects are in the environment and hence what one is facing on the basis of what the experiences one is having are like. I argue this at length in Robinson 1994: 136ff.

7. I say "at bottom," because our conception of secondary qualities depends on experiences proper to one sense, whereas primary qualities can be accessed through different modes. Nevertheless, empirical, as opposed to formal, content requires a filling out in some qualitative way or other, and this is the relevant point here.

8. See Robinson 1994, especially chapter 6, for arguments against naive or direct realism.

9. Versions of this essay have been read to groups in Budapest, Belgrade, Oxford, and Liverpool, and I am grateful to many people for their comments. I am especially grateful to Tim Crane for discussions on intentionality and its relevance to the knowledge argument, and to my colleague Hanoch Ben-Yami, for discussion which gave rise to the main point in my final section.

References

Alter, T. 2007. Does representationalism undermine the knowledge argument? In *Phenomenal Concepts and Phenomenal Knowledge*, ed. T. Alter and S. Walter, 65–76. Oxford: Oxford University Press.

Armstrong, D. M. 1968. *A Materialist Theory of the Mind*. London: Routledge and Kegan Paul.

Crane, T. 2006. Is there a perceptual relation? In Gendler and Hawthorne 2006: 126–146.

Dretske, F. 1981. *Knowledge and the Flow of Information*. Cambridge, Mass.: MIT Press/ A Bradford Book.

Dretske, F. 2000. *Perception, Knowledge, and Belief: Selected Essays*. Cambridge: Cambridge University Press.

Gendler, T., and J. Hawthorne, eds. 2006. *Perceptual Experience*. Oxford: Clarendon Press.

Hume, D. 1964. *A Treatise of Human Nature*. Oxford: Clarendon Press. (Originally published 1739–40.)

Jackson, F. 1982. Epiphenomenal qualia. *Philosophical Quarterly* 32: 127–136.

Jackson, F. 1998. Postscript on qualia. In his *Mind, Method, and Conditionals*, 76–79. London: Routledge. Also in Ludlow, Nagasawa, and Stoljar 2004: 417–420.

Jackson, F. 2004. Mind and illusion. In Ludlow, Nagasawa, and Stoljar 2004: 421–442.

Levine, J. 1983. Materialism and qualia: The explanatory gap. *Pacific Philosophical Quarterly* 64: 354–361.

Lewis, D. 1988. What experience teaches. In *Proceedings of the Russellian Society* 13: 29–57. Also in Ludlow, Nagasawa, and Stoljar 2004: 77–103.

Loar, B. 1990. Phenomenal states (revised version). In *Philosophical Perspectives 4: Action Theory and the Philosophy of Mind*, ed. J. Tomberlin, 81–108. Atascadero, Calif.: Ridgeview. Excerpted in Ludlow, Nagasawa, and Stoljar 2004: 219–239.

Ludlow, P., Y. Nagasawa, and D. Stoljar, eds. 2004. *There's Something About Mary*. Cambridge, Mass.: MIT Press/A Bradford Book.

Lycan, W. 1987. *Consciousness*. Cambridge, Mass.: MIT Press/A Bradford Book.

Martin, M. J. M. 2004. The limits of self-awareness. *Philosophical Studies* 121: 37–89.

Martin, M. J. M. 2006. On being alienated. In Gendler and Hawthorne 2002: 354–410.

McGinn, C. 1989. Can we solve the mind–body problem? *Mind* 98, 391: 349–366.

Nagel, T. 1974. What is it like to be a bat? *Philosophical Review* 83: 435–450.

Robinson, H. 1994. *Perception*. London: Routledge.

Smart, J. J. C. 1963. *Philosophy and Scientific Realism*. London: Routledge and Kegan Paul.

Strawson, G. 1994. *Mental Reality*. Cambridge, Mass.: MIT Press/A Bradford Book.

Strawson, P. 1959. *Individuals*. London: Methuen.

Tye, M. 1995. *Ten Problems of Consciousness*. Cambridge, Mass.: MIT Press/A Bradford Book.

13 Phenomenal Knowledge without Experience

Torin Alter

Phenomenal knowledge usually comes from experience. For example, I know what it's like to see red because I have done so. Does knowing what it's like to have an experience with phenomenal character X require having an experience with X? No. A famous counterexample is Hume's missing shade of blue, in which one can extrapolate from phenomenally similar experiences (*A Treatise of Human Nature*, Bk. I, pt. I, sec. I).[1] One might think that a weaker version of the no-phenomenal-knowledge-without-experience thesis remains tenable, for example, that knowing what it's like to see in color requires having or having had color experiences. But this thesis also seems doubtful. Peter Unger (1966) devised plausible counterexamples over four decades ago, and since then others (e.g., Lewis 1988; Alter 1998; Stoljar 2005) have done the same. One could have phenomenal knowledge of color experiences without having such experiences. Indeed, one could have such knowledge without having experiences that are remotely like color experiences.

What is the significance of this observation for contemporary debates about consciousness and physicalism? Daniel Dennett (2007) and Pete Mandik (in press) suggest that it undermines the knowledge argument against physicalism.[2] That is because they take the claim that someone who has never seen in color could not know what it's like to see in color to be the basis of the knowledge argument's main epistemic premise: the premise that (roughly put) no amount of physical knowledge is sufficient for phenomenal knowledge of color experiences. If they are right, then this is not only a problem for antiphysicalists. Many physicalists (e.g., Loar 1990/1997; Papineau 2002, 2007) accept the knowledge argument's epistemic premise. Dennett's and Mandik's arguments threaten all versions of what David Chalmers (2003) calls *phenomenal realism*, the view that there are phenomenal properties, or qualia, that are not conceptually reducible to physical or functional properties.[3]

I will argue that this threat is illusory. Explaining why will clarify what is and is not at issue in discussions of the knowledge argument and phenomenal realism. The net result will be to strengthen the case for physically inexplicable qualia.[4,5]

1   The Knowledge Argument and the No-Experience-Necessary Response

The classic version of the knowledge argument is due to Frank Jackson (1982, 1986). It begins with his famous case of Mary, the super-scientist who is raised in a black-and-white room and has no color experiences. By watching lectures on black-and-white television, she learns all the physical information about seeing in color. This includes "everything in *completed* physics, chemistry, and neurophysiology, and all there is to know about the causal and relational facts consequent upon all this, including of course functional roles" (Jackson 1986: 291). Then she leaves the room and sees a red rose for the first time. Does she learn any truths? That is, does she gain any information? Intuitively, she does: she learns what it's like to see red.

Jackson takes this intuition to establish the knowledge argument's main epistemic premise, *the nondeducibility claim*: there are phenomenal truths that cannot be a priori deduced from the complete physical truth. He reasons that, if all phenomenal truths were a priori deducible from the complete physical truth, then Mary would learn no truths when she leaves the room; and so, because she does learn truths when she leaves, the nondeducibility claim is true. The knowledge argument's other main premise is the inference from the nondeducibility claim to the metaphysical conclusion that there are nonphysical phenomenal truths, truths that are not metaphysically necessitated by the complete physical truth. From that conclusion, most agree, the falsity of physicalism follows.[6]

Many phenomenal realists (e.g., Loar 1990/1997; Papineau 2002, 2007) reject the knowledge argument's inference from its epistemic premise to its metaphysical conclusion. These philosophers often argue that, when Mary leaves the room, she merely comes to represent information she already knew in new ways. But all phenomenal realists accept both the nondeducibility claim and the claim that Mary's new experiences provide her with information.[7]

Let us turn to the idea that seeing in color is required for knowing what it's like to see in color. Call that *the experience requirement* on phenomenal knowledge of color experiences.[8] Dennett and Mandik think the nondeducibility claim depends on the experience requirement. But this is not obvious. The nondeducibility claim does not seem to entail the experience requirement. Moreover, Jackson's argument for nondeducibility does not appear to invoke the requirement. His argument is that nondeducibility follows from the premise that Mary learns truths when she leaves the room despite her already knowing the complete physical truth. That reasoning does not appear to assume that the only way to know what it's like to see in color is to have color experiences. The intuition has the form "one cannot learn Q in way W," not "the only way to learn Q is in way W."

Why, then, do Dennett and Mandik think the nondeducibility claim depends on the experience requirement? Their reasoning could be summarized as follows:

The no-experience-necessary response The claim that Mary makes epistemic progress upon release would make perfect sense if having color experiences were required for knowing what it's like to have them. But if the experience requirement fails—if it is possible to know what it's like to see in color without having color experiences—then why couldn't Mary put herself in a state that allows her to figure out what it's like to see in color? If there is no logical bar to obtaining this phenomenal knowledge without seeing colors, then there is no reason why Mary could not obtain that knowledge by exploiting her comprehensive physical knowledge.

I will discuss three versions of this response: Dennett's, Mandik's, and another that I will construct. If my arguments are sound, then the no-experience-necessary response is fundamentally misguided and no version can succeed.

2 Dennett's Argument

2.1 RoboMary

Dennett develops his argument by varying the Mary case in ways intended to weaken the intuition that she gains knowledge when she leaves the room. The variation he emphasizes most is his Locked RoboMary case. RoboMary is a robot with the same physical knowledge as pre-release Mary. In one version of the case, she is equipped with a color-vision system. In another, she is "locked": her color-vision system—"the array of registers that transiently hold the codes for each pixel in Mary's visual field, whether seen or imagined" (Dennett 2007: 28)—is restricted to grayscale values. According to Dennett, being locked "doesn't faze her for a minute" (ibid.). This is because "she builds a model of herself and from the outside, just as she would if she were building a model of some other being's color vision, she figures out just how she would react in every possible color situation" (ibid.). He explains:

She obtains a ripe tomato and plunks it down in front of her black-and-white-cameras, obtaining some middling gray-scale values, which lead her into a variety of sequel states. . . . She looks at the (gray-appearing) tomato and reacts however she does, resulting in, say, thousands of temporary settings of her cognitive machinery. Call that voluminous state of her total response to the locked gray-tomato-viewing state A. . . . Then she compares state A with the state that her model of herself goes into . . . [namely] state B, the state she would have gone into if her color system hadn't been locked. RoboMary notes all the differences between state A . . . and state B . . . and . . . makes all the necessary adjustments and puts herself into state B. State B is, by definition, not an illicit state of color experience; it is the state that such an illicit state of color experience normally causes (in a being just exactly like her). But now she can know just what it's like for her to see a red tomato, because she has managed to put herself into just such a dispositional state. . . . (Ibid.)

There is no reason why Mary, while in the room, could not do what Locked RoboMary does. Recognizing this, Dennett contends, should weaken our faith in the intuitive judgment that Mary learns something when she leaves the black-and-white room.

2.2 The Problem with RoboMary

Dennett's case threatens the nondeducibility claim only if Locked RoboMary a priori deduces the phenomenology of seeing red from the physical truth. But she does not do that. Rather, she puts herself in a dispositional state that constitutes possessing such knowledge. This is little better than if she had simply unlocked her color-vision system. She uses her physical knowledge to produce the desired effect, but the way she uses that knowledge is not (or not only) a priori deduction. Therefore, her achievement does not threaten the nondeducibility claim.[9]

Sven Walter and I raised the foregoing objection to Dennett while his article was in draft. In response he writes, "I just don't see that this is what matters. . . . this objection presupposes an improbable and extravagant distinction between (pure?) deduction and other varieties of knowledgeable self-enlightenment" (Dennett 2007: 29). I take Dennett to mean that the distinction between a priori deducibility and other sorts of inferability is (a) deeply problematic or (b) not relevant to whether physicalism stands or falls. Let me address these charges in turn.

Regarding (a): the notion of a priori deducibility is a straightforward application of the notion of a priori knowledge to reasoning (the latter notion does raise nontrivial issues [Baehr 2006], but none seem particularly relevant here). Let me illustrate the basic idea with a simple example. Contrast two cases of coming to know that the sum of a trapezoid's angles is 360 degrees:

Case 1 You figure out the sum by constructing a proof from Euclid's axioms.

Case 2 A future neuroscientist time travels back to the present and describes a brain state characteristic of someone who knows the sum. She also gives you a device that can be used to put you in that state and explains that the device works only if you contemplate Euclid's axioms for a few seconds. You contemplate the axioms and use the device. It works.

In case 1 you a priori deduce geometrical information from Euclid's axioms. In case 2 you do not, even though the axioms figure essentially in the process you use to acquire that same information.

To see how the same distinction applies to phenomenal knowledge, consider Hume's missing shade of blue. There are different ways of moving from phenomenal knowledge of the surrounding shades to phenomenal knowledge of the missing shade, and only one qualifies as a priori deduction: deducing the missing-shade phenomenology by combining phenomenal information about the surrounding shades, without relying on other phenomenal information. Such an a priori deduction seems possible. But it remains intuitively plausible that Mary cannot deduce what it's like to see red by combining the information she acquires before leaving the room. The same is true of RoboMary. Although she figures out what it's like to see red, her reasoning involves more than a priori deduction from physical information. In this respect, her reasoning is more like case 2 than case 1.

Regarding (b), concerning the relevance to physicalism's truth or falsity of the distinction between a priori deducibility and other sorts of inferability: the distinction is relevant because physicalism requires a metaphysically necessary connection from underlying microphysical truths to all truths and, arguably, a corresponding relation of a priori deducibility is needed to ground that necessary connection (Chalmers 1996, 2004, forthcoming). To be sure, those claims raise hard issues. But those are not relevant here if Dennett wishes to do as he claims, which is to challenge the knowledge argument's epistemic premise. To challenge that premise just is to challenge a claim specifically about a priori deducibility (viz., the claim that there are phenomenal truths that cannot be a priori deduced from the complete physical truth). If Dennett wishes instead to challenge the inference from that premise to the metaphysical conclusion that there are nonphysical phenomenal truths (truths that are not metaphysically necessitated by the complete physical truth), then that is another story entirely—and it is hard to see how the RoboMary case even begins to threaten that inference.

Dennett presents the following argument apparently in defense of his skeptical views about a priori deducibility:

> Consider Rosemary, another of Mary's daughters, who is entirely normal and free to move around the colored world, and is otherwise her mother's equal in physical knowledge of color. Rosemary has a hard time imagining her mother's epistemic predicament. What must it be like, she wonders, not yet to know what it's like to see red? She is burdened, it seems, with *too much* knowledge. . . . This is, presumably, a psychological impediment to her imagination, but not an epistemological lack. (Dennett 2007: 30)

I assume that Dennett does not mean that Rosemary's knowledge *must* interfere with her ability to imagine her mother's epistemic predicament, but only that this can happen. The latter claim is plausible. But how does it show that the distinction between a priori deducibility and other kinds of inferability is problematic or irrelevant to physicalism? As far as I can tell, it does not.

Perhaps Dennett's idea is this: while RoboMary's inability to imagine in color prevents her from using one comparatively direct way of figuring out what it's like to see red, her inability need not place any limitation on her capacity for using reason to arrive at that knowledge; at best, any such limitation would be a contingent psychological impediment. But the problem is not that RoboMary's inability to imagine in color interferes with her ability to reason. The problem is rather that the method by which she obtains her phenomenal knowledge involves more than a priori deduction from physical information.[10]

Why does putting herself in state B enable RoboMary to know what it's like to see red? B is a dispositional and (let us assume) nonphenomenal state; there is nothing it's like to be in B. Nevertheless, B involves color phenomenology in that it contains the relevant phenomenal information. Therein lies the problem for Dennett's argument. By putting herself in a state that involves color phenomenology, RoboMary cheats. Pre-release Mary should be no less puzzled about B than she is about seeing red. If she lacks phenomenal information about seeing red, then she lacks the phenomenal information that B contains. If there are open epistemic possibilities about the nature of phenomenal redness that she cannot eliminate, then there are open epistemic possibilities about the content of B that she cannot eliminate. RoboMary comes by her phenomenal knowledge of color experience not by a priori deduction from physical information but rather by putting herself in a nonphenomenal dispositional state that contains the relevant phenomenal information.

The problems with the Locked RoboMary case are symptomatic of a more general difficulty with Dennett's strategy. If the states Mary, RoboMary, or another Mary counterpart puts herself in—states that enable her to deduce what it's like to see red—involve color phenomenology, then she cheats: she does not a priori deduce the phenomenology from physical information. In that case, her achievement fails to threaten the nondeducibility claim. If, however, the states she puts herself in do not involve color phenomenology, then it is hard to see how they would enable her to deduce the phenomenology. I see no way of modifying the RoboMary case to evade this dilemma.

3   Mandik's Argument

Mandik's version of the no-experience-necessary response consists mostly in showing how empirical considerations count against the thesis that knowing what it's like to see in color requires having color experiences. For example, he discusses a well-grounded prediction, based on a neural model of chromatic information processing, due to Paul Churchland (2005):

the differential fatiguing and recovery of opponent processing cells gives rise to afterimages with subjective hues and saturations that would never be seen on the reflective surfaces of objects. Such "chimerical colors" include shades of yellow exactly as dark as pitch-black and "hyperbolic orange, an orange that is more 'ostentatiously orange' than any (non-self-luminous) orange you have ever seen. . . ." (Mandik in press: 13)[11]

Mandik uses Churchland's prediction to construct his own variation of the Mary case. His case involves two characters. One is Larry, who has seen "all the typical colors a normally sighted adult has seen" (ibid.) but does not know the theory that predicts chimerical colors. The other is Hyperbolic Mary, who knows all the physical information that Mary knows, including the theory that predicts chimerical colors, and who has, like Larry, seen plenty of colors. Mandik notes that, upon experiencing chimerical colors for the first time, Larry will be more surprised than Hyperbolic Mary. He concludes: "If it is unreasonable to expect Larry to predict the possibility of hyperbolic orange, pitch-dark yellow, and the like, then it seems unreasonable to predict, on introspection and intuition alone, the impossibility of pre-experiential knowledge of what it is like to seen red" (ibid.: 14). Mandik may be right about this. The other considerations he discusses may also count against the thesis that "pre-experiential knowledge of what it is like to seen red" is impossible. But as I have noted, the knowledge argument depends on no such thesis. Thus, Mandik's strategy cannot succeed. If he could show that Hyperbolic Mary can a priori deduce the phenomenology of chimerical colors from physical information, then the knowledge argument would be in trouble. But he provides no reason to suspect that such an a priori deduction is possible.

4   Deviant Phenomenal Knowledge and the Indirect Argument

4.1   More Cases

Before turning to yet another version of the no-experience-necessary response, let me introduce some terminology and a few more cases. Phenomenal knowledge is *earned* if the experience requirement is satisfied. For example, since I have seen ripe tomatoes, my knowledge of what it's like to see red is earned, whereas RoboMary's phenomenal knowledge is not. To *access* phenomenal knowledge is to exercise closely related abilities, such as the ability to imagine, recognize, or remember relevant experiences. I access my phenomenal knowledge when I visualize a ripe tomato, stop at a traffic light, or have an episodic memory of seeing oxygenated blood. Phenomenal knowledge that is unearned, inaccessible, or both is *deviant*.

Now to the other cases. I begin with another case Dennett describes (which he attributes to Gabriel Love):

Swamp Mary   Just as standard Mary is about to be released from prison, still virginal regarding colors . . . a bolt of lightning rearranges her brain, putting it by Cosmic Coincidence into exactly the brain state she was just about to go into *after* first seeing a red rose. (Dennett 2007: 24)

As Dennett notes, the lightning bolt does not give Swamp Mary a hallucinatory experience of a red rose but rather "puts Swamp Mary's brain into the dispositional state, the competence state, that an experience of a red rose would have put her brain into had such an experience (hallucinatory or not) occurred" (ibid.). She has the equivalent of RoboMary's state B. In relevant respects, Swamp Mary's epistemic state closely resembles the state I am in while I neither see nor imagine red. I know what it's like to see red. Therefore, it seems reasonable to say the same of her. She has the same phenomenal knowledge that I have; the only difference is that hers, like RoboMary's, is unearned.[12]

Further cases of unearned phenomenal knowledge are not hard to devise. Unger imagines that scientists construct a man who is "cell-part for cell-part, cell for cell, nervous structure for nervous structure identical to" a man who both knows what it's like to see red and has come upon this knowledge in the ordinary way (Unger 1966: 50). Others (e.g., Lewis 1988; Alter 1998; Stoljar 2005) imagine cases in which surgeons operate on a person who has never seen red, creating brain structures similar to those found in the brains of people who have seen red. In all such cases, it is plausible that the subject knows what it's like to see red, despite never having done so.[13]

Regarding inaccessible phenomenal knowledge, consider:

Temporary Impairment John is epistemically just like pre-release Mary, except he has seen one color: red. Then a brain injury temporarily robs him of the abilities associated with this knowledge. He can no longer imagine red things, he would not recognize red objects as red if presented with them, and he has no memory of what it's like to see red. As the effects of his injury recede, he recovers these abilities. He does so without seeing red in the intervening time; his hospital room contains no red objects.

Temporary Impairment is modeled on cases of aphasia discussed by Noam Chomsky (1980, 1988). Aphasia is the loss of the ability to use and understand language. Do aphasia patients retain their knowledge of language despite losing the associated abilities? Chomsky argues that sometimes they do. Suppose Maria is raised as a monolingual Spanish speaker and becomes temporarily afflicted with aphasia. As the effects of her injury recede, she recovers the ability to speak Spanish, not Chinese or French. Why would this be unless her knowledge of Spanish was there all along? Our Temporary Impairment case lends itself to a similar analysis. John recovers the abilities associated with seeing red rather than green. Why would this be unless his phenomenal knowledge was there all along? Plausibly, John has inaccessible phenomenal knowledge.[14]

Combining Swamp Mary and Temporary Impairment gives us:

Temporarily Impaired Swamp Mary Before Swamp Mary leaves the room, she injures her brain. As a result, she is temporarily unable to exercise the abilities associated with seeing red. Like John, she eventually recovers those abilities without seeing red in the intervening time.

If, as I have argued, Swamp Mary and John know what it's like to see red, then Temporarily Impaired Swamp Mary does too. Her phenomenal knowledge is both unearned and inaccessible.

4.2 Is the Notion of Deviant Phenomenal Knowledge Coherent?

Before discussing the implications of these cases, let me discuss a couple of objections. Chomsky's argument, on which I model my argument for the possibility of inaccessible phenomenal knowledge, has been questioned. Anthony Kenny (1984) argues that linguistic knowledge cannot be detached from abilities in the way Chomsky's argument requires; in Kenny's view, Chomsky's notion of linguistic-knowledge-without-ability is incoherent. One might say the same about the notion of inaccessible phenomenal knowledge. Similarly, one might question the coherence of the notion of unearned phenomenal knowledge. And one might invoke a causal theory of knowledge to challenge the attribution of such knowledge to Swamp Mary and the other deviants whose states are caused by cosmic accidents.

Here such doubts may be set aside, for three reasons. First, regarding the last point, one might argue that a causal theory of knowledge is not appropriate for phenomenal knowledge—that such knowledge "does not consist in a causal relationship to experience, but in another sort of relationship entirely" (Chalmers 1996: 193). Also, the objection may not apply to Unger-style cases, in which the relevant dispositional states are created by neurosurgery rather than cosmic accident. Second, the possibilities of unearned and inaccessible phenomenal knowledge can only help the no-experience-necessary response. Rejecting these notions would decrease the chances of developing a successful version of that response. Third, the doubts may be partly terminological. In his response to Kenny, Chomsky emphasizes that, while impaired, Maria retains something that explains why she later recovers the ability to speak Spanish rather than Chinese or French. It is the possibility of such epistemic states, and not whether they should be described as knowledge, that is most central to his position. Similar considerations apply to deviant phenomenal knowledge. John has states that explain why he recovers the ability to recognize experiences of seeing red, rather than green. Swamp Mary has states that are strikingly similar to states Mary retains after seeing red and returning to the black-and-white room. Here these similarities, and not whether the states should be described as knowledge, are what matter most. I will continue to describe the states of our deviant subjects as knowledge, but essentially the same issues would arise if I refrained from doing so.

I have discussed the notion of inaccessible phenomenal knowledge elsewhere (Alter 2001). Laurence Nemirow criticizes it, writing "Under Alter's analysis, knowing what it's like to see red has been transformed from one thing into something quite different" (Nemirow 2007: 50). This is because phenomenal knowledge "is known for its immediacy" (ibid.) and inaccessible phenomenal knowledge would lack such immediacy. Nemirow concludes that the notion of inaccessible phenomenal knowledge "is a weird development—one that a proponent of phenomenal information should not welcome" (ibid.).

But even if phenomenal knowledge "is known for its immediacy," it does not follow that it can exist only if accessible, let alone immediately accessible. Perhaps the notion of inaccessible phenomenal knowledge seems odd because it is rarely considered. For example, most discussions of the Mary case focus on what happens as soon as she leaves the black-and-white room and becomes immersed in the world of color. But when we consider alternative scenarios, such as our temporary impairment cases, the notion may seem less bizarre. If phenomenal knowledge consists in (or includes) the possession of information, then presumably that information can be stored in the brain while not being accessed. In that case, why couldn't brain damage block access to that stored information? Far from a weird development, accepting the possibility of inaccessible phenomenal knowledge is a natural consequence of taking seriously the idea that phenomenal knowledge consists (at least in part) in the possession of information.

4.3   The Indirect Argument

In the cases discussed above, the knower acquires her deviant phenomenal knowledge by means other than a priori deduction. Therefore, these cases do not directly threaten the nondeducibility claim. However, they may seem to create an indirect threat. Consider the following argument:

1. The phenomenal information contained in the deviants' dispositional states is equivalent to that which Mary has after seeing a red rose and returning to the black-and-white room.
2. If the phenomenal information Mary has after seeing a red rose and returning to the black-and-white room is a priori deducible from physical information, then the phenomenal information she has while looking at the rose is a priori deducible from physical information.
3. The phenomenal information contained in the deviants' dispositional states is a priori deducible from physical information.
4. Therefore, the phenomenal information Mary has while looking at the rose is a priori deducible from physical information.

Call that *the indirect argument*. If it is sound, then Mary acquires no information upon leaving the black-and-white room and the nondeducibility claim and phenomenal realism are false.

The argument is valid. Its first two premises are plausible; let us grant them and focus on premise 3, the claim that the deviants' phenomenal knowledge is physically explicable. Why believe this premise? One might argue as follows:

Argument for premise 3   Consider Temporarily Impaired Swamp Mary. Her phenomenal knowledge exists in the form of dispositional states. These states are nonphenomenal; there is nothing it's like to be in them. They have never been triggered and, during her impairment, they cannot be triggered. William Robinson (1996) suggests that the reason phenomenal information is not physically explicable is that, unlike physical information, it lacks structural expression. This may seem plausible when one reflects on one's own experience of seeing red. One may wonder, "How could *this* be captured in merely structural terms?" But why think that Temporarily Impaired Swamp Mary's unearned, inaccessible phenomenal knowledge includes information that lacks structural expression? The way the lightning bolt endows her with phenomenal knowledge is, after all, by reconfiguring her brain. How could that process add more than structure? There is thus no reason to think that she has knowledge that eludes physical explication. Likewise for the other cases of deviant phenomenal knowledge.

This reasoning may seem cogent. Further, the objection I brought against Dennett's argument does not apply to the indirect argument. That objection was that the method by which RoboMary acquires her phenomenal knowledge of color experience is not a priori deduction. But in the indirect argument, there is no claim that the deviant characters do any a priori deduction. Rather, the claim is that from within the black-and-white room Mary can figure out everything there is to know about their dispositional states. It is Mary, not the deviants, who is said to do the a priori deduction. Finally, unlike Mandik's argument, the indirect argument challenges the nondeducibility claim, rather than the thesis that knowing what it's like to see in color requires having color experiences.

4.4   The Problem with the Indirect Argument

But the indirect argument fails. The problem concerns premise 3, the claim that the deviants' phenomenal knowledge is physically explicable. Suppose that, before leaving the room, Mary uses her black-and-white television apparatus to study Temporarily Impaired Swamp Mary. Mary asks herself, "What is the content of Temporarily Impaired Swamp Mary's phenomenal knowledge of seeing red?" Intuitively, Mary is in no position to answer that question. At least, she is no better positioned to answer that question than she is to answer the question, "What is it like to see red?" There are many epistemic possibilities that she cannot eliminate. As far as she knows, Temporarily Impaired Swamp Mary's phenomenal knowledge may concern phenomenal greenness rather than phenomenal redness. Mary will be equally perplexed about the content of the other deviants' phenomenal knowledge. Thus, on reflection, the reasons for doubting that ordinary phenomenal knowledge is physically explicable apply equally to deviant phenomenal knowledge.

What, then, of the argument for premise 3? It makes two errors. First, it assumes that brain structures cannot carry physically inexplicable information. But even nonphysicalists typically accept that phenomenal properties naturally supervene (supervene as a matter of contingent, natural law) on physical properties such as neural properties (Chalmers 1996). Given this natural supervenience thesis, there is no clear reason why restructuring a brain could not endow it with physically inexplicable phenomenal information.

Second, the argument for premise 3 assumes that the fact that the deviants' phenomenal knowledge exists in a dispositional form indicates that their knowledge is physically explicable. This is questionable. My earned, accessible phenomenal knowledge exists in a dispositional form while I am neither seeing nor imagining red. Yet my knowledge is no more a priori deducible from physical information than is the phenomenal knowledge I had an hour ago while looking at a red tomato. Why shouldn't we say the same about the deviants' phenomenal knowledge?

5 Phenomenal Concepts

5.1 The Objection from Conceptual Parity

I have argued that RoboMary and the other deviants know what it's like to see in color even if pre-release Mary does not. One might raise the following objection to my position:

Objection from conceptual parity If pre-release Mary does not know what it's like to see in color, then this is because she lacks the relevant phenomenal color concepts, namely, concepts that characterize phenomenal qualities as the qualities they are. But the deviants lack such concepts too. Because they have not had color experiences, they lack direct cognitive access to phenomenal color qualities, just as Mary does. Conceptually, pre-release Mary and the deviants are on a par. So, if pre-release Mary does not know what it's like to see in color, then neither do the deviants.[15]

But, arguably, the deviants do have phenomenal color concepts that pre-release Mary lacks. That they possess phenomenal color concepts follows from an assumption I defended in section 4 above: the assumption that the deviants know what it's like to see red. This view may also be confirmed by observing that pre-release Mary should be no less puzzled about the nature of Temporarily Impaired Swamp Mary's phenomenal red concept than she is about what it's like to see red. As far as pre-release Mary knows, Temporarily Impaired Swamp Mary's concept may pick out phenomenal greenness rather than phenomenal redness. The same point applies to the other deviants.

5.2 Phenomenal Concepts: Relational and Pure, Standing and Direct

Chalmers (2003) draws two distinctions that help to explicate the idea that the deviants have phenomenal concepts that pre-release Mary lacks. One is the distinction between pure and relational phenomenal concepts. The other is the distinction between direct and standing phenomenal concepts. I will explain these distinctions and then apply them to Mary and the deviants.

A pure phenomenal concept characterizes a phenomenal quality in terms of its intrinsic, phenomenal nature, that is, as the quality it is. A relational phenomenal concept characterizes a phenomenal quality in terms of a relation the quality bears to other things. For example, one might have a community relational concept, red_c: a concept that characterizes phenomenal redness as the phenomenal quality typically caused in normal subjects in one's community by their seeing paradigmatic red things. Or one might have a demonstrative relational concept, E, which picks out whatever phenomenal quality one is internally ostending ("*this* quality"). Pure phenomenal concepts are distinct from relational phenomenal concepts, even when they pick out one and the same phenomenal quality. To see this, consider a belief Mary forms when she first leaves the room and sees a red rose: the belief that seeing red things typically causes those in her community to have experiences with such-and-such phenomenal quality. Her "such-and-such phenomenal quality" concept, R, is a pure phenomenal concept of phenomenal redness. Her belief also involves red_c, which also picks out phenomenal redness. Her belief is cognitively significant, and this indicates that R and red_c are distinct concepts (Chalmers 2003: 225). Similar reasoning shows that R is distinct from any relational concept. E, red_r, and R pick out the same phenomenal quality, but only R is pure.

A *direct* phenomenal concept is "partly *constituted* by an underlying phenomenal quality" (Chalmers 2003: 235). Typically, one forms such concepts by "attend[ing] to the quality of an experience, and form[ing] a concept wholly based on the attention to the quality, 'taking up' the quality into the concept" (ibid.). Chalmers (ibid.: 240) remarks that, "The lifetime of a direct phenomenal concept is limited to the lifetime of the experience . . . that constitutes it." Right now, I see nothing red but I know what it's like to see red. Therefore, my knowledge does not involve a direct phenomenal concept. Instead, it involves what Chalmers calls a *standing* phenomenal concept. Standing phenomenal concepts "persist in a way that direct phenomenal concepts do not" (ibid.: 239). But standing phenomenal concepts may be pure: they may characterize a phenomenal quality not relationally but in terms of the quality's intrinsic, phenomenal nature. How is their content determined? Chalmers (ibid.) suggests that "their content is determined by some combination of (1) non-sensory phenomenal states of a cognitive sort, which bear a relevant relation to the original phenomenal quality in question—e.g. a faint Humean phenomenal 'idea' that is relevantly related to the original 'impression'; (2) dispositions to have such states; and (3) dispositions to recognize instances of the phenomenal quality in question."

Let us see how Chalmers' distinctions apply to Mary and the deviants. Before Mary leaves the black-and-white room, she has no pure phenomenal color concepts. By contrast, the deviants do have such concepts. Their pure concepts differ from those I form while looking at a red tomato: only mine are direct. But their standing concepts are pure. Consider Swamp Mary's standing concept of phenomenal redness. Although she has never seen red, she has a disposition to recognize phenomenal redness as the quality it is; this disposition determines her concept's content. The content of her standing concept should be no less puzzling to Mary than the content of my direct concept. As far as pre-release Mary knows, either might pick out phenomenal greenness rather than phenomenal redness.

Unlike Swamp Mary, John and Temporarily Impaired Swamp Mary would, while impaired, fail to recognize phenomenal redness as the quality it is. Does this imply that they lack the relevant recognitional disposition? No. As Mark Johnston (1992) points out, a fragile glass cup encased in packing material may retain its fragility—its disposition to shatter when dropped—even if the packing material prevents it from shattering when dropped. In such cases, a disposition is said to be *masked*. Our temporarily impaired deviants have the same recognitional dispositions as Swamp Mary, even though theirs are masked. Arguably, they have pure standing phenomenal redness concepts, even though they are temporarily unable to employ those concepts in their thinking. By contrast, pre-release Mary has only relational phenomenal color concepts. On reflection, the difference between Mary's epistemic situation and that of the deviants is striking.

6 Conclusion

Dennett writes: "Another unargued intuition exploited by the Mary intuition pump . . . is the idea that the 'phenomenality' or 'intrinsic phenomenal character' . . . cannot be constructed or derived out of lesser ingredients. Only actual experience (of color, for instance) can lead to the knowledge of what that experience is like" (Dennett 2007: 22). Here Dennett misconstrues the relationship between the Mary case and the claim that phenomenality "cannot be constructed or derived out of lesser ingredients": the case provides support for the claim, rather than the reverse. But put that aside; I wish to draw attention to a different point. The passage illustrates the most basic assumption behind the no-experience-necessary response: the assumption that the knowledge argument depends on theses such as "Only actual experience (of color, for instance) can lead to the knowledge of what that experience is like." As I have argued, that assumption is false. Associating the knowledge argument with such implausible theses makes the case for physically inexplicable qualia appear weaker than it is.[16]

Notes

1. Another counterexample: one might know about a complex phenomenal quality by knowing about its parts (Alter 2002: 52–53; Tye 1995: 227, n. 2). For example, someone who has seen red, white, and blue separately but never together may be able to deduce what it's like to see an American flag from a detailed description.

2. Derek Ball (unpublished) gives a related argument. He argues that (i) the knowledge argument requires assuming the existence of phenomenal concepts that satisfy something akin to what I call *the experience requirement* (see section 1) and (ii) there are no such concepts. My main criticisms of the no-experience-necessary response apply to (i), *mutatis mutandis*.

3. For brevity, when referring to physical or functional phenomena, I will henceforth leave off "or functional."

4. I use "physically explicable" to refer to information that is a priori deducible from the complete physical truth. On this usage, phenomenal realists who are physicalists accept that there is physically inexplicable information.

5. Explicit commitment to the thesis that knowing what it's like to see in color requires having color experiences may be rarer than Unger, Dennett, and others suggest. Unger (1966: 49, n. 2) cites three sources: Price 1962 (52, 53, 57–58); Russell 1948 (499); and Ryle 1949 (317). But on none of those pages is the thesis asserted or implied. Dennett quotes passages from Tye 1995 (167, 169) and Lycan 2003 (389) that seem to suggest the thesis. But later in his article (393), Lycan suggests that the thesis may be false. And in Tye 2000 (27), Tye implies that the thesis is false. Locke, Hume, and other early modern empiricists assert principles that seem to suggest the thesis. But as Unger (1966: 49) notes, these principles may be intended merely as contingent truths about human beings rather than necessary or conceptual truths.

6. This formulation of the knowledge argument is imprecise. For example, the deduction base mentioned in the epistemic premise should include all indexical information, such as the truths expressed by "I am *s*" and "Now is *t*" where *s* and *t* are descriptions specifying unique subjects and times. For a precise formulation (and forceful defense) of the argument, see Chalmers 2004. Jackson (2003, 2007) now rejects the argument. I criticize his basis for so doing in Alter 2007.

7. Despite its popularity, there are good reasons to think the conjunction of phenomenal realism and physicalism is unstable. See Chalmers 1996, 2004, forthcoming.

8. I focus on color experiences because of their role in the Mary case. What I say applies to other kinds of experience, *mutatis mutandis*.

9. Michael Beaton (2005) develops a related objection to Dennett's argument. But there are notable differences. In particular, Beaton assumes a version of the Lewis-Nemirow ability hypothesis (Lewis 1988; Nemirow 1990, 2007). I make no such assumption. Further, the ability hypothesis is incompatible with phenomenal realism.

10. Walter and I wrote (in correspondence with Dennett) that RoboMary *self-programs* herself into state B instead of a priori deducing the relevant information. In response Dennett (2007: 30) writes, "I didn't describe RoboMary as 'programming' herself. . . ." I regret the slip, but this terminological matter is incidental.

11. The final version of Mandik's article is pending as I write. But (in correspondence) he has confirmed the accuracy of my attributions. I quote from the version on his website: http://www.petemandik.com/philosophy/papers/nos.pdf.

12. Jackson (1998: 77) makes a similar point: "Seeing red and feeling pain impact on us, leaving a memory trace which sustains our knowledge of what it is like to see red and feel pain on the many occasions where we are neither seeing red nor feeling pain. This is why it was always a mistake to say that someone could not know what

seeing red and feeling pain [are] like unless they had actually experienced them: false 'memory' traces are enough."

13. In Alter 1998 (54, n. 15), I use such a case to raise the issue of whether phenomenal knowledge can be innate. There I do not attempt to resolve this issue. I would now suggest that innate phenomenal knowledge is unproblematic for the same reasons that unearned phenomenal knowledge is unproblematic. The idea that phenomenal knowledge could be produced by cosmic accident is not new. Unger (1966: 54) describes a case in which "the various parts of the duplicate person just ('by chance') came together." And Lewis (1988: 500) mentions the idea that phenomenal knowledge "could possibly be produced in you by magic."

14. In Alter 2001, I argue that the possibility of inaccessible phenomenal knowledge creates a problem for the Lewis-Nemirow view, based on their ability hypothesis, on which all Mary gains when she leaves the room are abilities, as opposed to physically inexplicable phenomenal information (Lewis 1988; Nemirow 1990, 2007). The Temporary Impairment case indicates that she gains something that can survive the loss of ability. Lewis and Nemirow could respond by revising their view and arguing that this something else consists in *proto*-abilities—mental states that normally underlie the relevant abilities but do not carry physically inexplicable phenomenal information. I reject a similar response in Alter 2001, but I now think it is probably adequate.

15. The idea that Mary's epistemic progress derives from her acquiring phenomenal color concepts suggests a natural response for the a priori physicalist (the physicalist who rejects the nondeducibility claim): although the phenomenal truth about color experiences can be a priori deduced from the complete physical truth, pre-release Mary cannot do the deduction because she lacks the requisite phenomenal concepts. See Tye 2000, Hellie 2004, Chalmers 2004, and Kirk 2005: 33–34. But Chalmers (2004) argues that she might not be able to deduce certain phenomenal truths even if she is given the relevant phenomenal concepts. For example, he writes, "once Mary has the relevant phenomenal concept, she will not automatically know whether or not *other* organisms (bats or Martians, say) are having experiences of the relevant sort, even given a complete physical description of them" (Chalmers 2004: 285).

16. For helpful suggestions, I thank David Chalmers, Amy Kind, Pete Mandik, Jennifer McKitrick, Yujin Nagasawa, and Stuart Rachels. This essay benefited from my participation in John Heil's 2006 NEH seminar, "Mind and Metaphysics."

References

Alter, T. 1998. A limited defense of the knowledge argument. *Philosophical Studies*, 90: 35-56.

Alter, T. 2001. Know-how, ability, and the ability hypothesis. *Theoria* 67: 229–239.

Alter, T. 2002. On two alleged conflicts between divine attributes. *Faith and Philosophy* 19: 47–57.

Alter, T. 2007. Does representationalism undermine the knowledge argument? In Alter and Walter 2007: 65–76.

Alter, T., and S. Walter, eds. 2007. *Phenomenal Knowledge and Phenomenal Concepts: New Essays on Consciousness and Physicalism*. New York: Oxford University Press.

Baehr, J. 2006. A priori and a posteriori. In *The Internet Encyclopedia of Philosophy*, ed. J. Fieser and B. Dowden. Available at http://www.iep.utm.edu/a/apriori.htm.

Ball, D. Unpublished. Physicalism and phenomenal concepts.

Beaton, M. 2005. What RoboDennett still doesn't know. *Journal of Consciousness Studies* 12: 3–25.

Chalmers, D. J. 1996. *The Conscious Mind: In Search of a Fundamental Theory*. New York: Oxford University Press.

Chalmers, D. J. 2003. The content and epistemology of phenomenal belief. In Smith and Jokic 2003: 220–272.

Chalmers, D. J. 2004. Phenomenal concepts and the knowledge argument. In Ludlow, Nagasawa, and Stoljar 2004: 269–298.

Chalmers, D. J. Forthcoming. The two-dimensional argument against materialism. In his *The Character of Consciousness*. New York: Oxford University Press.

Chomsky, N. 1980. *Rules and Representations*. New York: Columbia University Press.

Chomsky, N. 1988. Language and problems of knowledge. *Synthesis Philosophica* 5: 1–25. Reprinted in *The Philosophy of Language*, 4th edition, ed. A. Martinich, 558–577 (New York: Oxford University Press, 2001).

Churchland, P. 2005. Chimerical colors: Some novel predictions from cognitive neuroscience. *Philosophical Psychology* 18: 527–560.

Dennett, D. C. 2007. What RoboMary knows. In Alter and Walter 2007: 15–31.

Hellie, B. 2004. Inexpressible truths and the allure of the knowledge argument. In Ludlow, Nagasawa, and Stoljar 2004: 333–364.

Hume, D. 1964. *A Treatise of Human Nature*. Oxford: Clarendon Press. (Originally published 1739–40.)

Jackson, F. 1982. Epiphenomenal qualia. *Philosophical Quarterly* 32: 127–136.

Jackson, F. 1986. What Mary didn't know. *Journal of Philosophy* 83: 291–295.

Jackson, F. 1998. Postscript on qualia. In his *Mind, Method, and Conditionals: Selected Essays*, 76–79. New York: Routledge.

Jackson, F. 2003. Mind and illusion. In *Minds and Persons*, ed. A. O'Hear, 251–271. Cambridge: Cambridge University Press.

Jackson, F. 2007. The knowledge argument, diaphanousness, representationalism. In Alter and Walter 2007: 52–64.

Johnston, M. 1992. How to speak of the colors. *Philosophical Studies* 68: 221–263.

Kenny, A. 1984. *The Legacy of Wittgenstein*. Oxford: Basil Blackwell.

Kirk, R. 2005. *Zombies and Consciousness*. Oxford: Clarendon.

Lewis, D. 1988. What experience teaches. In *Proceedings of the Russellian Society*. Sydney: University of Sydney. Reprinted in Lycan 1990: 499–518.

Loar, B. 1990/1997. Phenomenal states. In *Philosophical Perspectives 4: Action Theory and Philosophy of Mind*, ed. J. Tomberlin, 81–108. Atascadero, Calif.: Ridgeview. Revised version in *The Nature of Consciousness: Philosophical Debates*, ed. N. Block, O. Flanagan, and G. Güzeldere, 597–616 (Cambridge, Mass.: MIT Press/A Bradford Book, 1997).

Ludlow, P., Y. Nagasawa, and D. Stoljar, eds. 2004. *There's Something About Mary: Essays on Phenomenal Consciousness and Frank Jackson's Knowledge Argument*. Cambridge, Mass.: MIT Press/A Bradford Book.

Lycan, W. G., ed. 1990. *Mind and Cognition: A Reader*. Cambridge: Basil Blackwell.

Lycan, W. G. 2003. Perspectival representation and the knowledge argument. In Smith and Jokic 2003: 382–395.

Mandik, P. In press. The neurophilosophy of subjectivity. In *Oxford Handbook of Philosophy and Neuroscience*, ed. J. Bickle. New York: Oxford University Press.

Nemirow, L. 2007. So *this* is what it's like: A defense of the ability hypothesis. In Alter and Walter 2007: 32–51.

Nemirow, L. 1990. Physicalism and the cognitive role of acquaintance. In Lycan 1990: 490–499.

Papineau, D. 2002. *Thinking about Consciousness*. New York: Oxford University Press.

Papineau, D. 2007. Phenomenal and perceptual concepts. In Alter and Walter 2007: 111–145.

Price, H. H. 1962. *Thinking and Experience*. Cambridge, Mass.: Harvard University Press.

Robinson, W. 1996. The hardness of the hard problem. *Journal of Consciousness Studies* 3: 14–25.

Russell, B. 1948. *Human Knowledge: Its Scope and Limits*. New York: Simon and Schuster.

Ryle, G. 1949. *The Concept of Mind*. London: Hutchinson.

Smith, Q., and A. Jokic, eds. 2003. *Consciousness: New Philosophical Essays*. Oxford: Oxford University Press.

Stoljar, D. 2005. Physicalism and phenomenal concepts. *Mind and Language* 20: 469–494.

Tye, M. 1995. *Ten Problems of Consciousness: A Representational Theory of the Phenomenal Mind*. Cambridge, Mass.: MIT Press/A Bradford Book.

Tye, M. 2000. *Consciousness, Color, and Content*. Cambridge, Mass.: MIT Press/A Bradford Book.

Unger, P. 1966. On experience and the development of the understanding. *American Philosophical Quarterly* 3: 48–56.

14   A Defense of Qualia in the Strong Sense

Barry Maund

1   Strong and Neutral (Minimalist) Senses of "Qualia"

The terms "phenomenal character," "qualitative character," and "qualia" are used in a variety of senses, sometimes as if they are equivalent or closely connected (e.g., qualia are features that comprise or contribute to the phenomenal character of experiences), and sometimes as applying to different aspects of experiences. It is not surprising therefore that there are often puzzling features to qualia discussions. Some theorists find them so obvious as to not require justification, while others reject them as if they belong to the powers of darkness. Nor is it surprising that there might be, as many theorists have pointed out, both weak or metaphysically neutral senses of qualia, and strong, metaphysically committed senses. Accordingly, any discussion of qualia that hopes to make progress needs to explain the terminology carefully.

It does seem that, at some level, there is little problem in understanding what qualia are, and of knowing that they exist. For example, each of us has a wide range of experiences of very different character: the taste of a ripe juicy peach, the smell of newly mown grass, the feel of soft velvet, the seeing of a setting sun: In each of these cases, I am the subject of a mental state with a distinctive subjective character. There is something it is like to for me to undergo each state, some phenomenology that it has.[1]

That is to say, there is something it is like for me to taste the juicy peach, to smell the newly cut grass, to feel the soft velvet, and so on. As Michael Tye points out, we can take it that the term "qualia," in this sense, applies to "the introspectively accessible, phenomenal aspects of our mental life," and that, in this neutral sense, "it is difficult to deny that there are qualia" (Tye 2003: 1).

We need to recognize, however, that there are at least two aspects to knowing what it is like to have a certain experience. One aspect concerns knowing what it is like to be a *subject* of an experience; another concerns the "phenomenal" or "qualitative" character of the experience. Joe Levine describes these two aspects as follows:

(1) there is something it is like *for me* to have this experience—this is the "subjectivity" of the experience;
(2) there is the qualitative character itself: "Qualitative character concerns the 'what' it's like for me: reddish or greenish, painful or pleasurable" (Levine 2001: 6–7).

Levine goes on to explain qualia in terms of this qualitative character of the experience. That is to say, qualia are those properties that constitute the qualitative character.

There is, however, a third aspect to the "subjective character" of experiencing—what we might term "a feel"—and some theorists associate qualia with this aspect. There are certain experiences where I know what it is to be a subject of the experience, but I am in no position to describe any qualitative character. This is the case, for example, with many acts of understanding: I can understand what you said when you asked "would you like some more tea?," but there need be no distinctive, intrinsic, or qualitative features to that experience of understanding. Indeed, it seems possible that there could be a range of intellectual experiences, for example, thoughts of a certain kind without sensuous or qualitative character. (It seems that they may have *a feel* to them, but a nonsensuous one.)

It would seem, therefore, that we can identify a certain (subjective) character that is distinctive of certain types of experience, a character that is usually termed "qualitative character," and what I shall call "phenomenal–qualitative character," and we can distinguish these types of experience from other types that do not have a phenomenal–qualitative character (they have a "feel"). Given that this is so, it is possible to specify a sense of "qualia" such that qualia are certain types of qualities: those qualities that constitute this phenomenal–qualitative character. However, we have, so far, specified "phenomenal–qualitative character," and hence, "qualia," only in a neutral, minimalist sense. We have left it open as to what its metaphysical status is.

There is, however, another, stronger sense of "qualia," and it is this sense that is understood (or at least, it ought to be) when people deny the existence of qualia. It is controversial in this sense whether qualia exist, not in the weaker, neutral sense. There are different conceptions of what this strong sense is. Daniel Dennett criticizes what I take to be a super-strong sense. I propose instead a more modest, but still strong conception:

Qualia are not only those qualities that constitute (or explain) phenomenal or qualitative character but, crucially, are qualities of a certain type: (a) they are introspectively accessible features of experiences; and (b) they are intrinsic, non-intentional features. In explaining this sense, we need to clarify what is meant by "intrinsic features." E. J. Lowe and Sydney Shoemaker interpret "intrinsic features of experience" as properties of *experiencing*, which, on the face of it, favors an adverbial theory of experience (Lowe 1995: 61; Shoemaker 1994: 29.) On another interpretation, the "intrinsic features" may be thought of as quality-instances presented in experience, presumably possessed by phenomenal items, for example, sensa or sense data, or fields. For the moment, I shall leave this question open. What is important is that both interpretations depend on drawing a contrast between two types of features experiences may have: an intentional or representational content and non-intentional, intrinsic features.

It should be noncontroversial that there is such a thing as the phenomenal–qualitative character to experiences, and with it, the existence of qualia, in a weak, neutral sense. What is a matter of dispute is whether there are qualia in the strong sense. There is a firm body of opposition, which holds that the phenomenal–qualitative character can be explained in terms of the intentional content of the experiences, and that there is no need for a stronger sense of qualia, for example, by Michael Tye, Gilbert Harman, Alex Byrne, Tim Crane, and many others. (There is a different version of intentionalism, that espoused by Austen Clark, but I shall ignore that complication.)

I shall argue, however, that if we examine some of the central arguments given for this position, intentionalism, we shall find that they do not establish the intended conclusion.

2   Can Qualia Vary without Variation in Intentional Content?

Qualia, in the strong sense, are non-intentional features of experience. As a result, it is commonly thought that the defender of qualia is committed to a certain view about the relation of the qualia to the intentional content of an experience. As Tye, for example, states:

(1)   *Qualia* are intrinsic features of experiences which can vary without any variation in the *intentional contents* of the experiences. (Tye 2003: 1)

A similar view is presented by Crane (2001a: 83). He allows that a person could believe in qualia but hold to a version of intentionalism, one that held that all mental states, including pains, bodily sensations, and perceptual experiences, were intentional, that is, had an intentional structure. Such a version is *weak intentionalism*: all mental states are intentional, but some have non-intentional conscious properties, qualia. Crane rejects this view in favor of strong intentionalism, which denies that there are any conscious, non-intentional aspects to experiences; but for our purposes, what is significant is that he says that the thesis of weak intentionalism can be equally expressed as the claim that the intentional nature of certain mental states does not exhaust their phenomenal character: two experiences could share their intentional nature and differ in their phenomenal character.

If the qualia hypothesis is committed to (1) above, then given the relation of qualia to phenomenal character, it would follow that the qualia hypothesis is committed to thesis (2):

(2)   Phenomenal character of experiences can vary without variation in intentional content.

It would seem, therefore, that the hypothesis would be disproved, if we could show that, for perceptual experiences (including pains) there is no difference in phenomenal character without difference in intentional content. Since it is just such a claim that Byrne (2001: 206–217), for example, seems to establish in his presentation of several thought experiments in his article in defense of intentionalism, qualia would seem to be under threat.

There are problems, however, with accepting (1) above, as it stands, as a characterization of the qualia theory's commitments. It holds only with respect to certain types of intentional content, and not, obviously, to the types of content presupposed by Byrne's thought experiments. Consider a typical account of perceptual experience, as presented, for example, by Alan Millar. According to Millar, "An experience of an F is one that satisfies two conditions: it is a F-type experience and it is such that it seems to the subject that an F is there" (Millar 2001: 1). An F-type experience is specified in terms of its typical causes: it is one that, roughly speaking, is an experience of the type that an F would yield under suitable conditions of normality. The second condition, which gives us the *content* of the experience, is satisfied if the experience is such that in the absence of countervailing considerations, its subject would believe that an F is there. (Note: this sense of "seems," though conceptual, is not an epistemic sense, but a phenomenological one.) The phenomenal character of the experience is spelled out with reference to experiences being F-type experiences, where the subject can only know what the phenomenal character is if she has the experience in question. (It is not necessary that she have the concept of F, either to have the experience or to know the phenomenal character.) If a qualia theorist appeals to Millar's account, then not only can she accept (1) as a commitment of the theory, she can show that (2) is true.

Nevertheless, the qualia theorist can maintain that thesis (1) is a commitment only to certain types of (conceptual) intentional content, and that there are special cases of intentional content to which it is not committed. For these special cases, thesis (2) is false. For example, take one of the standard formulations of the argument from illusion, an argument in favor of sense data, and thus for one form of qualia theory, and against naive realism. As Howard Robinson, for example, sets out the argument, perceptual experience obeys what is termed "the phenomenal principle" (PP):

(PP) Whenever something appears to a subject to possess a sensible quality, there is something of which the subject is aware and which does possess that quality (Robinson 1994: 57–58).

According to this theory, then, provided that the experience has content at all, we will not have difference in phenomenal character without difference of intentional content, expressed in terms of how the thing appears— at least for content with respect to sensible qualities.

There are other forms of qualia theories where whether thesis (1) or its denial is a commitment will depend on how the intentional content is specified. In particular, it is possible for the qualia—the non-intentional qualities—to contribute to (be part of) the intentional content (Maund 2006: 256–258). That is to say, the intentional content may be specified in terms of qualia. One way this can happen is described by "projective" theories of content, for perceptual experiences. On these accounts, qualities intrinsic to the experiences are "projected" into the content of the experience. If this is so, then the qualia cannot vary without variation in the intentional content (for at least some species of intentional content). Another possibility is that the content of the experience is specified in terms of intrinsic qualities of the experience itself. For example, the content could be specified in terms of a power to cause an experience of a certain type, one that is to be explained in terms of the presence of qualia. Yet another possibility is that the content is specified in terms of the power of an object to look a certain way—where that way of looking is explained in terms of the presence of qualia (Shoemaker 2000).

Consideration of this range of possibilities brings out an important point about the arguments of strong intentionalists against qualia. Most such intentionalists seem to me to work with too narrow a conception of perceptual experience—or at the very least, they fail to consider plausible alternatives to their own accounts. In particular, they fail to consider how a defender of qualia can combine his account with an intentionalist account of sense experience. One of the strongest of such accounts is that presented by Moreland Perkins (see Perkins 1983, but more especially Perkins 2005). On this account, perceptual experience has an intentionalist structure—it carries representational content—but that content is complex, containing nonconceptual and conceptual components. It contains a sensuous, nonconceptual representation—whose intrinsic properties are those characteristic of qualia—and a conceptual content. "For all forms of attentive (hence conscious) sense perception, every perception's representative content is of two integrated sorts: perceptually attributed nonconceptual sensuous content is fused with perceptually attributed conceptual content" (Perkins 2005: 207).

Perkins illustrates the account with the example of feeling a toothache, which, he persuasively argues, is a case of sense perception: perceiving a tooth. We perceive the tooth by perceiving its aching condition. As I perceive this aching, the pain appears to me as if it belongs to the tooth. In order for the pain to appear to me in this way, "I must perceptually attribute to the tooth the very pain that is sensuously present in my consciousness." As Perkins points out, one represents to oneself a sensuous quality as if it belongs to one's tooth "by the method of exemplifying this quality within one's sensory consciousness of the tooth" (ibid.: 205). Our felt pain can represent a tooth as trouble, but it can do so only when certain appropriate concepts—of a tooth and of a condition that needs to be changed or treated or fixed—are united with the pain within a complex perceptual representation (ibid.: 208). We have realistic representation of trouble in a tooth but only in virtue of misrepresentation—of the pain as if it is in the tooth.

To my mind, Perkins's account of pain is the best account that is faithful to the phenomenology of pain experience. It is this sort of account that I have attempted to extend to visual experience more generally, and to color experience in particular (see Maund 2003, 2006). For the moment, all that I insist on is that this sort of account is far more sophisticated than the sketchy accounts discussed by most strong intentionalists, who deny the existence of qualia in the strong sense.

Once we make this distinction between different types of content, we can easily see how Byrne's celebrated thought experiments on intentional content and phenomenal character lose their significance. For as I have argued, a defender of qualia can admit that phenomenal character is supervenient on intentional content—at least for certain types of intentional content.

Having said that, we need to recognize that there is a range of important cases in which the theorist is committed to thesis (1), or something similar. What's more important, with respect to such cases, there is good reason to think that both the thesis and its consequence, thesis (2), are true, and that as a result, intentionalism is false. There are, for example, experiences that have phenomenal–qualitative character, but do not have intentional content, at least of the right sort. There are visual experiences that have phenomenal character but no intentional content; for example, when my eyes are shut, particularly in a darkened room, then I have experiences of mottled gray type. They do not represent any state of affairs. Edmond Wright points to a range of experiences with such a character, for example, subjects' experiences of "hypnagogic" imagery when they go to sleep and "hypnopompic" imagery as they wake up (Wright 2005: 92).

There are other experiences that do have content, for example, they indicate the presence of a light in a certain direction, but this content is clearly different from the phenomenal character. A. D. Smith cites research with respect to patients who are described as having their sight restored by medical operations (Smith 2002: 140). Typically, these patients are not totally blind but did have visual experiences before the operation. Those experiences, however, only enable the subjects to perceive shades of light and darkness. With these subjects, the experiences, I claim, illustrate indirect realism rather than direct realism. With these subjects, we can conceive a situation in which the subjects' experiences should change so that the experience, with the same phenomenal character, should have a different content. In other words, with respect to these experiments, intentionalism of the strong variety fails.

3   Phenomenal Character and Transparency: The Three Explanatory Hypotheses

There is an important aspect to perceptual experience—the well-known "transparency," or "the diaphanous nature," of perceptual experience. As Crane points out, following J. J. Valberg (1992), when one introspects one's experience, one seems to discover no feature of the experience, but only features of independently existing objects: "One looks at the redness of a glass of wine, looking for non-intentional properties of experience, and all one finds is an apparent property of the wine: its redness" (Crane

2001a: 85). This feature of experience forms a substantial part of the argument many theorists present for intentionalism, and against theories that postulate sense data or qualia in the strong sense. My aim in this section, and the next, is to take this phenomenon—the transparency of perceptual experience—and turn it against the (strong) intentionalists. I shall argue that the phenomenon supports a different conclusion: that there exist qualia in the strong sense.

Michael Tye has provided one of the strongest and most detailed formulations of this argument from transparency (Tye 2000: 45–68). Tye explains the transparency of perceptual experiences as follows. First, he asks the reader to "focus your attention on the scene before your eyes and on how things look to you. You see various objects by seeing their facing surfaces." In seeing these surfaces, he adds,

> you are immediately and directly aware of a whole host of qualities. You experience these qualities as qualities of the surfaces. You do not experience any of these qualities as qualities of your experience. There are no qualities of the experience that one is aware of; one is simply aware of the qualities of the objects seen. The experience of seeing is transparent. (Tye 2000: 45)

Since you are not directly aware of any qualities of your inner experiences, your experience is transparent to you. But when you introspect, Tye argues, you are certainly aware of the *phenomenal character* of your visual experience. "Via introspection you are directly aware of a range of qualities that you experience as being qualities of surfaces at varying distances away and orientations; and thereby you are said to be aware of the phenomenal character of the experience" (ibid.). By being aware of the external qualities, you are aware of what it is like for you, and hence, of the phenomenal character.

Tye is right to draw our attention to the "transparency" or "diaphanous nature" of perceptual experience. In perceptual experience, I seem to be aware of qualities of certain objects, of experience, and not of the way of experiencing them. There seem to be three possible hypotheses open about the nature of these qualities (and the objects). They are: (1) qualities of physical objects themselves; (2) qualities of objects, specifiable in the content of experience; and (3) phenomenal qualities, that is, quality-instances or qualities of phenomenal items, presented in experiences. On the last hypothesis, the objects are phenomenal objects which we (mis)take for physical objects.

Tye dismisses the first hypothesis as unintelligible. This response, with respect to naive realism, is far too quick—as Michael Martin and A. D.

Smith have independently shown (Martin 2002; Smith 2002). The hypothesis may be false but it is not unintelligible. Take, for example, Tye's own description of the transparency of perceptual experience, when as he says, we see various objects by seeing their facing surfaces: "Intuitively, the surfaces you see directly are publicly observable physical surfaces. In seeing these surfaces, you are immediately and directly aware of a whole host of qualities. You may not be able to name or describe these qualities but they look to you to qualify the surfaces; you experience them as being qualities of the surfaces" (Tye 2000: 46). In his own terms, this is the intuitive view. Why is it wrong to think that these qualities are actually qualities of the surfaces? It seems to me that the sense-datum theorist was trying to capture the intuition that they are publicly observable qualities, while at the same time, reinterpreting that intuition.

More needs to be done, therefore, than Tye offers us, before we can dismiss naive realism. And following that, more needs to be done to rule out the sense-datum theory, or better, a theory that postulates qualia, in a suitable strong sense. It seems to me that what Tye calls "the familiar grounds" for dismissing the theory are not very good grounds at all (Maund 2003: 89–129). Moreover, those arguments were not aimed at showing that the sense-data theory was false, but rather that particular arguments for sense-data were defective. So, even if these counterarguments were effective, they don't show that sense data do not exist, and hence, they do not give reasons for excluding the sense-data hypothesis in this context, where it is put forward as an explanatory hypothesis. Crane, in an insightful historical essay, shows how much classical criticism of sense-data theories was flawed because of its misunderstanding both of the intentions of the sense-data theorists, and of the different ways the term "sense datum" was used. (Point of clarification: because of the ambiguities with the term "sense datum," I prefer the term "sensa." The term "qualia" can then be applied to the qualities of sensa. It should be borne in mind that Wilfred Sellars, the foe of "the Given," argues for the postulation of sensa [Sellars 1971].)

Martin has a different take on transparency from Tye, drawing a different consequence about the significance of the transparency claim. He reads it as providing the basis for an objection to the sense-datum account of experience (and as a result, to those accounts of experience in terms of phenomenal qualities in the strong sense): "The diaphanous character of experience would seem to indicate a lack of evidence for the existence of sense-data at a point where one would expect to find it. At the same time, introspection seems to reveal aspects of experience which a sense-datum account is ill-equipped to explain, but which can be explained in terms of an intentional theory" (Martin 2002: 378). This point is important for the strategy followed in Martin's paper, for he goes on to describe examples of other kinds of experiences which enable him to construct a parallel objection to the intentionalist theory. Martin's argument seems to be that just as the transparency phenomena provide an objection to the sense-datum theory, these other examples allow a parallel objection to be raised to the intentionalist theory. The outcome is said to leave the naive realist in a much stronger position than was at first thought.

It is important to recognize, however, that Tye does not defend the intentionalist theory in the way Martin describes. That is, he does not claim that the transparency phenomena present the basis for an objection to the sense-datum theory. On the contrary. What he argues is that this theory does provide one explanatory hypothesis for the transparency phenomena, but that it is a hypothesis that can be excluded on other grounds, ones he says are "all too familiar," that is, on grounds quite separate from those pertaining to the transparency phenomena. This point is important, for Martin's strategy would seem to work only for a theorist who adopts a different approach from that of Tye.

It is quite true that, on the sense-datum/sensa hypothesis, the phenomenology of our ordinary perceptual experiences is challenged. That phenomenology is not altogether rejected, however. The point about the sense-data theory is that its advocates claim that this theory makes the best sense of the phenomenology, that is to say, it captures more than any other theory does of the phenomenology that is compatible with what else we know. It saves as much as it is possible to save. The aim of the explanation is to explain the transparency within the framework of the phenomenology of the situation. It may not be possible to save everything about the phenomenology, but the aim is to preserve as much as it is possible to save, and to explain the errors, insofar as there is error.

4 Sensa and Intentional Content

Suppose that there are states with qualia—in the strong sense; indeed let us suppose that there are sense data, in the sense of sensa. Then the experience of sensing these sensa will have nonconceptual content, for they will be causally correlated in appropriate ways to corresponding physical qualities and states. Indeed they will carry all the same nonconceptual content as the brain states that underpin the qualia. The point is that the nonconceptual content will be based on the "structural isomorphism" between the inner state and the relevant input. (For a helpful discussion, see Wright 2006: 73–79.) Moreover, on the right version of the sensa theory, the sensa will have representational content, much in the way that a map of New York will represent states of that city. For on this theory, the sensa will be the sorts of states that a competent perceiver will have the capacity to use as a basis for recognizing the presence of the qualities of physical objects. On a theory such as that of Perkins (and Maund) they will form nonconceptual components of complex representational states.

So if we are trying to explain the transparency of perceptual experience, then intentionalism as such is not an alternative to sensa theories. The proper rival is a particular version, strong intentionalism or reductive intentionalism, which is spelled out in terms of certain kinds of content. Putting the point another way, if the phenomenal character of perceptual experiences, which we become aware of in introspection, is to be explained simply in terms of the content of the experience, that content will have to be specifiable in terms applicable to physical qualities of physical bodies. I propose to argue that there are strong reasons to think that such a condition cannot be satisfied and that the only viable form of intentionalism is one compatible with sensa theories.

To assess versions of intentionalism properly, we need to specify the properties contained in intentional content. It is plausible, for example, as Byrne states, that the content will be of the following sort: "There is a bulgy, red tomato on a billiard-table before me" (Byrne 2001: 202). Or, as Crane describes: "One looks at the redness of a glass of wine, looking for non-intentional properties of experience, and all one finds is an apparent property of the wine: its redness" (Crane 2001a: 85).

Let us concentrate on the property, *red*, that is said to be part of this content. A strong intentionalist is committed to holding that this property is a physical, objective quality of physical bodies. We have here a challenge for intentionalists: to provide a physicalist account of color. Strong intentionalists such as Tye and Byrne are confident that they can meet the challenge. If they cannot, their account is in trouble. I shall argue that they do not succeed.

Tye and fellow intentionalists, such as Byrne and Hilbert, endorse a version of reductive physicalism with respect to color—the view that colors are physical properties whose natures are discoverable by empirical investigation (Tye 2000; Byrne and Hilbert 2003). They argue that, in the case of surface colors, these properties are types of spectral reflectances, ones that meet certain conditions. This view, it is held, is consistent with the commonsense view about colors and, it is argued, shows how we can maintain the commonsense conception in the face of any factual claims made by color science—despite claims to the contrary.

The intuitive conception of color, Tye argues, is "one of mind-independent, illumination-independent properties" (Tye 2000: 148). However, this characterization of the commonsense conception omits certain other important features. The most important of these, as Hardin, Thompson, Maund, and others have pointed out, is that colors are of such a character that collectively they can be ordered into an array with a significant, distinctive "4 + 2" structure, that is, the structure based on the four unique colors blue, yellow, red, and green, with the two achromatic colors, black and white. If we take all of these features into account, the physicalistic reductionist account fails. The set of spectral reflectances simply do not stand together in the right kind of way.

Tye, and Byrne and Hilbert, have made a response. The physicalist account of color, they hold, can be adjusted so as to accommodate the facts raised by in this objection. The proposal draws on the model of opponent processing that Hardin describes as part of the explanation of why our experiences of color have the structure that they do (Hardin 1988). According to the model, chromatic color experience is the result of neuronal activity in two channels, one for green–red experience and the other for blue–yellow, where the channels are related to light-sensitive cones in the eye.[2] With this model, the distinctive 4 + 2 structure characteristic of the group of perceived colors can be understood as resulting from distinctive forms of opponent processing, in the relevant neural processes. The physicalist proposal that is offered as a counter to the objection raised by Hardin and others is as follows. We can specify a given color, say, unique red, by the following schema:

A surface is unique red iff it has one of the group of reflectances that, other things being equal, under normal viewing conditions, enables it to reflect light that produces opponent processing distinctive of the experience of pure red.

This schema can be modified for all other colors, and especially for binary colors such as orange, purple, turquoise, violet, and so on.

As it happens, there is a further problem that is fatal to the objectivist, reductionist approach to color, followed by Byrne and Hilbert, Tye, and others. As Hardin (2004) has argued, there is no non-arbitrary way of identifying the class of "normal" observers so that we can specify the right class of reflectances as the basis for unique red, or for any of the other colors. Among competent color perceivers, there is considerable statistical spread:

what one person identifies as a pure red (green, . . .) another will judge to be slightly blue, another slightly yellow, and so on. The reflectance profile for unique red (green . . .) will differ for different members of the "normal group."

The upshot of consideration of these problems is that the best attempt to produce a physicalistic account of color is that color is a relative property, a disposition to produce certain type of response in neural processes of certain kinds of perceivers. The property, that is to say, is relativized to kinds of perceivers.

The result, then, of this attempt is that the content of perceptual experiences is specified in terms of the disposition to induce certain sorts of response. There are two possible theories of what these neural processes might be. One is that they are the neural processes claimed (alleged) to be identical with the experiences themselves; the second is to take the relevant neural processes to be neural processes at an earlier stage of color-processing. Neither possibility is open to the intentionalist. The problem with the first possibility is that it violates the condition of transparency. We are asked to take it as given that the visual experiences reveal not qualities of the experiences but qualities of physical objects. If we accept the first possibility we are admitting that visual experiences do reveal features of the experiences themselves. The second possibility is hardly better. Admittedly, it does not commit us to saying that in introspecting our visual experiences we are aware of features of the experiences, but it commits us to saying that insofar as we are aware of the independently existing physical objects, we are not directly aware of their physical qualities; rather we are aware of them only indirectly, being aware more directly of our neural processes.

In view of these objections, the reductionist view of color as a perceiver-independent quality of physical objects fails. Accordingly, the intentionalist account of phenomenal character favored by Tye and Byrne fails.

There is a different form of strong intentionalism, one that Crane defends, which is also explicitly based on the phenomenon of transparency. According to Crane's version, the phenomenal character is fixed by a combination of the representational content and the intentional *mode*, and not by representational content alone, as on Tye's version. (By "mode" Crane means the form the intentional state takes, e.g., whether it is a case of believing, perceiving, supposing, understanding, etc.) According to Crane, "the intentional content of a pain might be something like this: my ankle hurts" (Crane 2001a: 86). Hurting, he adds, is therefore not just a matter of a part of one's body having an intrinsic property, but rather a matter of that body part and its properties apparently affecting oneself. Hurting thus has a relational structure: the content of the sensation is that one's ankle hurts, and the mode is feeling.

But this is far too quick. The content of typical pain states is not just that, say, my ankle is hurting, but that it is hurting in a special way: I feel a sharp pain in my side; I have a dull pain in my chest, a pulsating pain in my hand, a throbbing pain in my head, and so on. That is to say, pains don't just hurt: they throb, they pulsate, they are sharp in character. Accordingly, Crane cannot hope to account for all the phenomenal–qualitative character of pain states simply by appealing to the objective content—the ankle—and the mode, that is, the hurting (the feeling). There is the other aspect as well—the pulsating, throbbingness, dullness, sharpness, and so on.

Neither Tye's account of pain, nor that of Crane, compares favorably, I submit, to that presented by Perkins (see section 2), an account that accommodates strong qualia.

Conclusion

I have examined, and found wanting, several important ways on which strong intentionalism has been defended against qualia theories. I have suggested ways in which a proper qualia theory should be presented and defended. In particular, such a theory is better placed to explain the transparency of perceptual experience.

Notes

1. This quote is taken from Michael Tye's entry on "qualia" in the *Stanford Encyclopedia of Philosophy*.

2. In describing the model, I draw upon the description that Tye (2000: 160–165) offers.

References

Aydede, M., ed. 2005. *Pain: New Essays on Its Nature and the Methodology of Its Study*. Cambridge, Mass.: MIT Press/A Bradford Book.

Byrne, A. 2001. Intentionalism defended. *Philosophical Review* 110: 199–210.

Byrne, A., and D. Hilbert. 2003. Color realism and color science. *Behavioural and Brain Sciences* 26: 3–21.

Clark, A. 2000. *A Theory of Sentience*. Oxford: Oxford University Press.

Crane, T. 2001a. *Elements of Mind*. Oxford: Oxford University Press.

Crane, T. 2001b. The origins of qualia. In *History of the Mind–Body Problem*, ed. T. Crane and S. Patterson, 169–194. London: Routledge.

Crane, T., and S. Patterson, eds. 2000. *History of the Mind–Body Problem*. London: Routledge.

Hardin, C. L. 1988. *Color for Philosophers*. Indianapolis, Ind.: Hackett.

Hardin, C. L. 2003. A reflectance doth not a color make. *Journal of Philosophy* 100: 191–202.

Hardin, C. L. 2004. A green thought in a green shade. *Harvard Review of Philosophy* 12: 29–39.

Levine, J. 2001. *Purple Haze*. Oxford: Oxford University Press.

Lowe, E. J. 1995. *Locke on Human Understanding*. London: Routledge.

Martin, M. 2002. Transparency. *Mind and Language* 17: 376–425.

Matthen, M. 2005. *Seeing, Doing, and Knowing*. Oxford: Oxford University Press.

Maund, B. 2003. *Perception*. Chesham: Acumen.

Maund, B. 2006. The illusion theory of colour: An anti-realist theory. *Dialectica* 60: 245–268.

Millar, A. 1991. *Reasons and Experience*. Oxford: Oxford University Press.

Perkins, M. 1983. *Sensing the World*. Indianapolis, Ind.: Hackett.

Perkins, M. 2005. Pain perception. In Aydede 2005: 199–218.

Robinson, H. 1994. *Perception*. London: Routledge.

Sellars, W. 1971. Science, sense impressions, and sensa. *Review of Metaphysics* 23: 391–447.

Shoemaker, S. 1994. Phenomenal character. *Noûs* 28: 21–38.

Shoemaker, S. 2000. Introspection and phenomenal character. *Philosophical Topics* 28: 247–273.

Smith, A. D. 2002. *The Problem of Perception*. Cambridge, Mass.: Harvard University Press.

Thompson, E. 1995. *Colour Vision*. London: Routledge.

Tye, M. 2000. *Color, Content, and Consciousness*. Cambridge, Mass.: MIT Press/A Bradford Book.

Tye, M. 2003. Qualia. In *Stanford Encyclopedia of Philosophy*. Available at http://plato .stanford.edu/entries/qualia/.

Valberg, J. J. 1992. *The Puzzle of Experience*. Oxford: Clarendon Press.

Wright, E. L. 2005. *Narrative, Perception, Language, and Faith*. Basingstoke: Palgrave Macmillan.

15 How to Believe in Qualia

Amy Kind

Why should we believe that qualia exist? It would not be surprising if, when confronted with this question, the qualia realist were puzzled. "Look around you," she might say, "and then pause for just a moment and reflect on your experiences. Isn't there a redness to your experience of that soda can on your desk? And isn't there a sweetness to your experience as you take a sip from it? Surely your experiences have qualitative aspects—surely there is something your experiences are like." And thus, to many a qualia realist, the answer to the question posed above is simple. Why believe in qualia? Because our every experience reveals their existence.

Unfortunately, the matter cannot be resolved this easily. (If it could, then there would be no need to produce a collection of papers making the case for qualia.) The existence of qualia has long been under attack. Opponents of qualia typically fall into two camps. In the first camp, we have philosophers who admit that, at least on the face of it, the phenomenological data support the existence of qualia. By their lights, however, there are strong theoretical reasons that count against qualia (typically that they cannot be accommodated within a physicalist framework). These opponents thus have the task of explaining why we should disregard the phenomenology of our experience. They must convince us why we should *not* believe in qualia.

In the second camp, however, are philosophers who deny the phenomenological data. Qualia realists have it wrong, they say. In fact, our experience does not reveal the existence of any qualia, for our experience is *transparent*—when we attend to our experiences, our attention goes right through to their objects. Such philosophers typically take these considerations of transparency to support a representationalist view of consciousness according to which the qualitative content of experience supervenes on, or even reduces to, the intentional content of experience. But for our purposes, what's important is that these philosophers deny that we have any reasons to believe in qualia—or, at the very least, that if we do have any such reasons, they are not provided by our experience. These opponents of qualia thus shift the burden of argument to the qualia realist. It is the qualia realist's responsibility, they say, to convince us why we should believe in qualia.

This essay aims to do just that. As I will suggest, these philosophers in the second camp are mistaken—the phenomenological data do support the existence of qualia. I will not address those philosophers in the first camp, that is, I do not take up the question of how qualia can be accommodated in a physicalist, or even naturalist, account of the mind (though the argument may suggest that it needs to be). But by showing that experience does, after all, support the existence of qualia, I aim to show that qualia realism should be our default position.

1   The Transparency Thesis

The view that our experience is transparent is generally thought to trace back at least to G. E. Moore, who wrote, "When we try to introspect the sensation of blue, all we can see is the blue: the other element is as if it were diaphanous" (Moore 1903: 450). Although Moore subsequently qualifies this characterization of experience,[1] this remark has inspired many contemporary philosophers who present similar phenomenological descriptions. For example, consider the following passages from Michael Tye:

Focus your attention on a square that has been painted blue. Intuitively, you are directly aware of blueness and squareness as out there in the world away from you, as features of an external surface. Now shift your gaze inward and try to become aware of your experience itself, inside you, apart from its objects. Try to focus your attention on some intrinsic feature of the experience that distinguishes it from other experiences, something other than what it is an experience *of*. The task seems impossible: one's awareness seems always to slip through the experience to blueness and squareness, as instantiated together in an external object. In turning one's mind inward to attend to the experience, one seems to end up concentrating on what is outside again, on external features or properties. (Tye 1995: 30)[2]

If you are attending to how things *look* to you, as opposed to how they are independent of how they look, you are bringing to bear your faculty of introspection. But in so doing, you are not aware of any inner object or thing. The only objects of which you are aware are the external ones making up the scene before your eyes. Nor, to repeat, are you directly aware of any qualities of your experience. (Tye 2000: 46–47)

Likewise, consider Gilbert Harman's characterization of experience:

When Eloise sees a tree before her, the colors she experiences are all experienced as features of the tree and its surroundings. None of them are experienced as intrinsic features of her experience. Nor does she experience any features of anything as intrinsic features of her experiences. And that is true of you too. There is nothing special about Eloise's visual experience. When you see a tree, you do not experience any features as intrinsic features of your experience. Look at a tree and try to turn your attention to intrinsic features of your visual experience. I predict you will find that the only features there to turn your attention to will be features of the presented tree. . . . (Harman 1990: 39)

These passages support what I'll call the *transparency thesis*, that is, the claim that experience is transparent. Some philosophers who endorse considerations of transparency intend only a very weak claim, namely, that is *difficult* to attend directly to our experience, or that *typically* we don't attend directly to our experience. But I take it that philosophers like Harman and Tye want to endorse a stronger version of the claim. On their view, it is not simply difficult but *impossible* to attend directly to our experience. The only way to attend to our experience is by attending to the objects represented by that experience.[3] In what follows, I reserve the label "transparency thesis" for this strong claim.

As stated, even in this strong form, the transparency thesis is not itself a denial of the existence of qualia—or at least not straightforwardly so. In claiming that we cannot attend to qualia in attending to our experience, the transparency thesis remains silent on the question of whether qualia exist. But the transparency thesis nonetheless poses quite a threat to the qualia realist. First of all, we might plausibly suppose that any qualia worthy of the name must be introspectible, that is, introspectibility is essential to the nature of qualia.[4] If this is right, then the fact that the transparency thesis denies that qualia are available to introspection ends up being tantamount to a denial of their existence. But even if we were to accept that there could exist non-introspectible qualia, the transparency thesis would still have anti-qualia ramifications. For even if the transparency thesis is strictly speaking compatible with the existence of qualia, if qualia cannot be introspectively attended to then it looks like we no longer have any reason to believe that they exist. Insofar as our belief in qualia is driven by phenomenological considerations, our being deprived of those considerations leaves the belief entirely unjustified.[5]

Generally speaking, the main proponents of the transparency thesis are representationalists. In fact, many representationalists use the transparency thesis as support for their theory, claiming that representationalism offers the best explanation of the phenomenon of transparency. Tye, for example, claims that phenomenal content reduces to a special sort of intentional content.[6] According to Tye, this helps us see "why visual phenomenal character is not a quality of an experience to which we have direct access (representational content is not a quality of the thing that has representational content)" (Tye 2000: 48–49).

In what follows, I will not take up the question of whether the transparency thesis can help motivate representationalism. Rather, I would like to focus instead on the prior question of whether the transparency thesis is true. To some extent, this will require us to look at the relationship between transparency and representationalism, since the defense of the first thesis often goes hand in hand with the defense of the second. But my primary focus here will be on transparency, not representationalism. To my mind, the pro-qualia case against transparency has not yet been satisfactorily made in the literature. Granted, qualia realists have produced numerous cases of apparent counterexamples to the transparency thesis—and I find many of these cases quite compelling. But, as you might expect, such examples are by no means uncontroversial. More important, however, is that most of the cases that have generated discussion are unusual in various respects—involving illusions, blurriness, or other non-ideal circumstances. Thus, the transparency theorist can often blunt the force of such examples. Even if he concedes that transparency fails in these "exotic" cases, he can still maintain that transparency holds for the vast majority of our experiences.[7] And it is not very satisfying for the qualia realist to rest her belief in qualia on a few unusual cases.

This essay thus aims to advance the debate past a discussion of these exotic examples. Once we understand how the exotic cases get their purchase as counterexamples to the transparency thesis, we can use this understanding to think about the more mundane cases for which the transparency thesis is supposed to be obvious. Having seen that we attend to qualia in certain exotic cases, we are reminded how we attend to qualia in the mundane cases as well. In short, by seeing why the transparency thesis is false, we are reminded how, and why, to believe in qualia.

2 The Exotic

The first exotic case to consider comes from blurry vision.[8] Suppose that someone who needs reading glasses peruses the morning newspaper while wearing his glasses. He sees the front page headlines clearly and sharply. When he takes off his glasses, however, his perception changes—he now has a blurry experience of those same headlines. Of course, this phenomenon is not limited to those who need reading glasses. Someone with perfect vision may achieve the same effect by unfocusing her eyes while reading the paper. When someone takes off his reading glasses, or unfocuses her eyes, there is a difference experientially—a phenomenal difference. How should this difference be best described? Does it seem that the words themselves are blurry, that is, that the blurriness is on the newspaper page itself? Or does it seem that the experience itself is blurry? Many people have the strong intuition that attending to the blurriness is different from attending to the words on the page. So insofar as the blurriness feels like an aspect of one's experience rather than an aspect of the headlines themselves, the case of blurry vision presents a problem for the transparency thesis.

A related case comes from phosphene experiences, that is, the color sensations created by pressure on the eyeball when one's eyelids are closed (Wright 1981; Block 1996). In offering this example, Block suggests that the phosphene experiences do not seem to be representing anything; we don't take the experience to suggest that there are colored moving expanses *out there* somewhere. Likewise in attending to the phosphene experiences, we don't seem to be attending to the object of the experience (some colored expanse *out there*) but rather to the experiences themselves.

A third kind of case comes from considering afterimages (see, e.g., Boghossian and Velleman 1989). In general, afterimages occur subsequent to the removal of some original (usually intense) stimulus. When a camera flash goes off, you might experience an afterimage in front of the photographer's face.[9] If you stare intently at a bright light for a little while and then close your eyes, there will be a lingering glow in the darkness. And if you stare at a green dot for half a minute and then shift your attention to a bright white piece of paper, you will visually experience a red dot similar in size and location to the green dot you had been staring at. But in none of these cases does it seem as if the afterimage represents something that is really there. When you close your eyes after looking at the bright light, for example, you don't take the lingering glow to be on the inner surface of your eyelids. When you see the red afterimage against the white page, you don't take the redness to suggest the existence of a red dot on the page. As Block has suggested, afterimages "don't look as if they are really objects or as if they are really red. They look . . . illusory" (Block 1996: 32, ellipsis in original; see also Wright 1983: 57–58).

If the above descriptions of these cases are correct, they seem to pose a significant threat both to representationalism and to the transparency thesis. Each of these cases suggests that there can be phenomenal content that does not reduce to representational content—either because there is no representational content (as in the afterimage and the phosphene cases), or because there is a difference in phenomenal content that does not correspond to representational content (as in the case of blurry vision). The cases thus pose a problem for the representationalists. And each of these cases also suggests that we can attend directly to our experiences without attending to the objects of our experiences—either because there is no object of our experience (again, as in the afterimage and the phosphene cases), or because the experience comes apart from the object that it represents (as in the case of blurry vision). They thus pose a problem for the transparency thesis.

Much of the ink spilled in response to these cases has focused specifically on defusing the threat to representationalism. Tye, for example, claims that in cases of blurry vision there is indeed a representational difference that can account for the phenomenal difference. Less information is presented when one takes off one's glasses: "In seeing blurrily, one undergoes sensory representations that fail to specify just where the boundaries and contours lie" (Tye 2000: 80). In the phosphene and afterimage cases, Tye thinks that by distinguishing what the experience represents *conceptually* from what it represents *nonconceptually*, we can dissipate the threat to representationalism (ibid.: 81–82).

These responses, however, do not do anything to dissipate the threat to the transparency thesis.[10] As a general strategy, the representationalist responses suggest that the proponents of the exotic cases understate the representational richness of the experiences. There is more representational content there than we might have initially believed. But admitting this does nothing to change our original sense of the phenomenology of the experience. It still seems to us, when we are having a blurry experience, that we can focus on the blurriness itself, rather than on just what the blurriness is blurriness *of*. Our attention to an afterimage does not seem to be attention to some worldly content—we do not see "right through" the experience in this case. Even if we can be convinced that the blurry image, the phosphene experience, and the afterimage have representational content, that in itself does not convince us that they are transparent.

3   Between the Exotic and the Mundane

We see something similar by considering a set of cases that fall on the spectrum somewhere between the exotic cases considered in section 2 and the mundane cases for which the transparency thesis has the most force. Recall that the transparency thesis derives its primary support from mundane visual experiences of, say, seeing a tree. But having begun with visual experience, proponents of transparency typically move on to perceptual experience generally, and then even to nonperceptual experiences as well. Tye, for example, explicitly claims that transparency holds across sensory modalities: "[T]he qualities of which we are directly aware via introspection . . . are not qualities of the experiences of hearing, smelling, and tasting. Rather, they are qualities of public surfaces, sounds, odors, tastes, and so forth" (Tye 2000: 50). He also claims that transparency applies to bodily sensations, such as pains or itches. For the moment, let's grant the move from mundane visual cases to mundane cases in other perceptual modalities. Insofar as transparency is plausible for the mundane visual cases, it will be plausible for the mundane auditory cases, and similarly for the other perceptual modalities. Nonetheless, as we will see in this section, the plausibility of the transparency thesis becomes considerably more strained once we leave the perceptual realm.

One example frequently invoked in this context is the orgasm. As Block has forcefully argued (in, e.g., Block 1996: 33–34), it is difficult to specify what the representational content of an orgasm could be. All attempts seem to fall far short of capturing this phenomenally "impressive" experience. Similarly, if we think about introspecting an orgasm experience, it is difficult to see what it would mean to say that our experience is transparent. In attending to our experience, our attention goes right through to . . . to where? In the mundane visual case, when I introspect my experience of a tree, my attention is supposed to go right through to the tree. But what would be the analogue of the tree in this case? The only possible suggestion would be some bodily location, but this doesn't seem faithful to the phenomenology of orgasms. And even if in attending to the orgasm we must attend to a particular bodily location, that doesn't seem to be all that we're doing.

A similar point can be made by thinking about pains. Does introspecting an experience of pain amount solely to attending to a particular bodily location? Here the transparency theorist must answer affirmatively. But this is a very hard position to defend. Moreover, it is not adequately defended simply by claiming, as Tye does, that whenever you become introspectively aware of a painful sensation, "your attention goes to *wherever you feel the pain*" (Tye 2000: 50). This claim is much weaker than the claim that your attention to the pain *consists* in your attention to the bodily location. Opponents of transparency can grant that when, for example, I have a pain in my toe, in order to focus on the pain I will have to focus at least in part on my toe. But there is a difference between saying that introspecting an experience of pain *involves* or even *requires* attending to a particular bodily location and saying that *all that there is* to introspecting an experience of pain is attending to a particular bodily location. Even if the former, weaker claim is plausible, it's the latter, stronger claim that the transparency thesis requires.

It's worth noting, however, that the weaker claim too can be called into question. In at least some cases, it seems that we can introspect pain without attending to a particular bodily location where the pain is felt. With some kinds of throbbing headaches, for example, I can introspectively attend to the throbbing pain without my attention going through to a particular part of my head—or so it seems to me. Some headaches are confined to one side or another, other headaches do not even seem to be especially localized. Given that I lack any sense of "where" the headache is, it seems odd to claim that my attention is directed in any but the most general sense at a bodily location.[11]

The same point applies to certain kinds of toothaches. I was once in need of a root canal in a tooth in the lower right side of my mouth, but I didn't know which particular tooth was the problem. I was in pain— in intense pain, in fact—and yet I could not myself pinpoint the precise location of the pain—even when I probed each tooth with my tongue or my finger. Eventually, the dentist pinpointed the problem spot for me by whacking the decaying tooth with a dental instrument. (I don't recommend having your dentist do this.) But his doing so changed my introspective experience. Only after he whacked the relevant tooth could I "find" the pain, and thus, only after he whacked the relevant tooth could I attend to the pain by attending to the tooth.[12]

The plausibility of the transparency thesis erodes further when considering emotions and moods. Emotional transparency is supposed to be relatively unproblematic, especially in comparison with the transparency of moods, since emotions at least tend to be associated with bodily occurrences. As Tye notes, "the qualities of which one is directly aware in introspecting felt emotions are frequently localized in particular parts of the body and experienced as such" (Tye 2000: 51). Anger might involve an increased pulse rate, fear might involve a tingling sensation along one's neck or a queasiness in one's stomach, and so on. This point enables Tye to treat emotional transparency analogously to the transparency of pain and other sensations. When we introspect pain, our attention is supposed to go to wherever we feel the pain. Likewise, when we introspect emotion, our attention is supposed to go wherever we feel the emotion: introspecting anger involves attention to one's increased pulse rate, introspecting fear involves attention to one's queasy stomach, and so on.

Is this all it involves? For the transparency theorist, the answer must be "yes." When we introspect an emotional experience, our attention must go right through to some bodily quality or other.[13] But this seems even less plausible for the case of emotions than it did for the case of pains. The typically tight connection between pains and bodily locations lends plausibility to the claim that we attend to bodily locations when we introspectively attend to pains. As I suggested above, however, the transparency theorist needs to defend a stronger claim—that attention to pain *wholly consists* in attending to bodily locations—to show that experience is transparent. Since there is a much looser connection between emotions and bodily locations, it is harder to establish even the weak claim that we always attend to bodily locations when we introspectively attend to emotions. Matters are even worse for the transparency theorist when it comes to moods, where there is virtually no connection to bodily location. But even if Tye is right that the weak claim is true for emotions or moods, that would not be enough to show that our experience of emotions or moods is transparent.

4   The Mundane

At this point, it will be useful to distinguish explicitly four claims about experience that have been playing a role in our discussion. These claims split into two pairs. We can set out the claims as follows, letting "E" stand for an experience:

1. E has representational content.
2. The qualitative character of E consists wholly in its representational content (i.e., representationalism is true).
3. Attending to E involves attending to its representational content.
4. Attending to E consists wholly in attending to its representational content (i.e., the transparency thesis is true).[14]

Just as we should not confuse (1) with (2), we should not confuse (3) with (4). Moreover, just as (1) does not imply (2), (3) does not imply (4). Claim (1) is a necessary but not sufficient condition for (2), just as (3) is a necessary but not sufficient condition for (4). Finally, whatever the relationship between (2) and (4)—a question I am here setting aside—it is clear that the truth of (1) implies neither (3) nor a fortiori (4). On the other hand, however, the falsity of (1) implies the falsity of both (3) and (4). If an experience lacks representational content, then our introspective attention to it cannot consist even in part of attention to representational content. So (1) is a necessary but not sufficient condition for all three of the subsequent claims.

Now let's think about how the transparency theorist attempts to accommodate apparent counterexamples to his thesis such as the exotic cases of section 2 and the nonperceptual cases of section 3. The exotic experiences like blurry vision and afterimages that we considered in section 2 threaten (4) primarily because they do not typically seem to have any representational content; for these experiences, that is, (1) seems false. But to defuse the threat of these cases, it is not enough for the transparency theorist to defend (1), that is, to find some representational content that they might have. Since (1) is not a sufficient condition for (4), defending (1) is only the first step. Even if these experiences do have some representational content, we need to be convinced that in attending to these experiences what we are doing—and *all* that we are doing—is attending to that representational content. And here the transparency theorist does not seem to have much to say.

For at least some of the nonperceptual experiences considered in section 3, the transparency theorist is on the same shaky ground that he is on with respect to the exotic cases. When it comes to orgasms and moods, it is hard to identify any representational content of the experience, that is, (1) seems false. But even for the nonperceptual experiences that plausibly do have representational content—experiences like pains and emotions—the transparency theorist is not on solid ground. The considerations he advances to help us see that we are attending to the representational content when we are attending to those experiences do not go far enough. They do not show us that *all* we are attending to when we are attending to the experiences is the representational content of the experience. In other words, even if (3) is true of these experiences, we need to be convinced of something more. And here again the transparency theorist does not seem to have much to say.

With these lessons learned from consideration of the apparent counterexamples to the transparency thesis, we are ready now to turn back to the mundane cases with which the transparency theorist begins—the very cases that are supposed to motivate the transparency thesis. What I want to suggest is that our discussion of the apparent counterexamples to the transparency thesis opens up some new logical space for the opponents of the thesis to make a case against it. Once we see why transparency fails in the exotic cases, we can raise parallel questions about the mundane cases.

Upon reflection, even the supposedly paradigmatic examples of transparency no longer seem as obviously transparent as they initially may have.

Look at a tree, we are instructed, and we are asked to try to turn our attention to intrinsic features of our visual experience. Proponents of transparency predict that we will fail. The only features there for us to turn our attention to are features of the presented tree (Harman 1990: 39). Our attention will always slip through to the greenness, and so on, as instantiated in the tree (see Tye 1995: 30). Keeping in mind our discussion above of the various counterexamples to transparency, however, I think this prediction is now called into question.

First, recall our discussion of the introspection of pain. Pain experience was alleged to be transparent because we cannot introspect it without attention to the bodily location where the pain is felt. However, as I discussed above, this fact alone does not establish the transparency of pain experience. The fact we attend to bodily location in introspectively attending to pain, even essentially so, does not mean that this is all we do. Likewise, the fact that we attend to worldly objects in introspectively attending to our perceptual experiences of worldly objects, even essentially so, does not mean that this is all we do. Compare a visual experience of a tree with a pain in your toe. The fact that you cannot help but attend to the tree when introspecting your visual experience of it no more establishes the transparency of visual experience than the fact that you cannot help but attend to your toe when introspecting the pain in your toe.

This conceptual point helps to create logical space for the failure of transparency, even with respect to perceptual experience. But of course, mere logical space is not enough. When we introspect our visual experiences, if we do not, or cannot, find anything else to attend to, then it looks like the transparency thesis will be correct for these experiences.

Here is where the moral gleaned from the exotic cases comes into play. Those cases showed us that transparency fails for at least some visual experiences. Insofar as those cases showed us how our introspective attention comes apart from the representational content of the experience, we can apply the lessons to the mundane cases. Consider again your visual experience of a tree. How can you attend to that experience without attending to the tree itself? To try to focus your attention away from the tree itself, think about afterimages, and about what you attend to when you are introspectively attending to your experience of afterimages. Now, once again, try to focus on that same aspect of your experience in your experience of the tree. You might try the following. Look at a tree, focus on your experience, and then close your eyes and image the tree. Focus in on the greenness on your imaged experience. Now reopen your eyes, so that you're looking at the tree. I predict that you *will* find features there, other than features of the presented tree, on which to train your attention. In particular, you can continue to attend to the greenness that you were attending to while your eyes were closed.

If I am right about this, the problems for the transparency thesis extend beyond the exotic cases. Even mundane visual experience—the very kind of experience that was supposed to be a paradigm case of transparency—is not transparent. Interestingly, we are helped to understand what's going on in the introspection of mundane cases by better understanding what's going on in the introspection of the exotic cases. Our reflection on why the counterexamples are problematic for the transparency thesis—on what we attend to when we are attending to our exotic experiences—enables us also to see what we are attending to in mundane experience.

5 Conclusion

When we introspect our ordinary perceptual experiences, the world gets in the way. The presence of external objects—the representational content of our experience—threatens to crowd out the qualia. But that doesn't mean the qualia are not there. As I have suggested in this essay, we are reminded that the qualia are there in ordinary experience by thinking carefully about experiences that are more out of the ordinary. In these other cases, there is no external object crowding out the qualia, and we can thus more easily focus our attention directly on them. And having reminded ourselves what we do in these more exotic cases, we can gain a better understanding of what we do in the more mundane cases.

In particular, I contend that when we attend introspectively to our experience—whether exotic or mundane—we are attending at least in part to qualia. Our experience is not, in fact, transparent. And thus, based on the support of the phenomenological data, it seems that we have every reason—or at least, all the reason we initially thought we had—to believe in the existence of qualia.

Notes

1. The very next sentence (which, oddly, is often ignored) reads: "Yet it can be distinguished if we look attentively enough, and if we know that there is something to look for." See Kind 2003 for further discussion.

2. The quotation continues, "And this remains so, even if there really is no blue square in front of one—if, for example, one is subject to an illusion." As we will see in section 2, however, intuitions about transparency are much weaker with respect to illusions.

3. See Kind 2003, 2007, for further discussion of weak versus strong transparency.

4. See Kind 2001.

5. There might, however, be other (nonphenomenological) reasons to believe in qualia. See, e.g., Shoemaker 1994.

6. In particular, Tye thinks that the intentional content must be poised, abstract, and nonconceptual. This is what he calls his PANIC theory. See Tye 1995, 2000.

7. However, in Kind 2007, I deny that this sort of concessionary strategy saves representationalism.

8. See Block 1996; Boghossian and Velleman 1989; Wright 1975: 278.

9. It seems to me that this phenomenon was more dramatic in the "olden days" of actual flashbulbs. The flashes produced by today's digital cameras don't have quite the same effect.

10. For the purposes of this essay, I have set aside the question of the relationship between representationalism and the transparency thesis, but it's worth noting the following. If representationalism entails the transparency thesis, then showing that representationalism can accommodate the exotic cases would at least indirectly show that these cases do not pose a threat to the transparency thesis. But this alone would not help us to see where we went wrong in believing that we could attend directly to our experiences in the exotic cases.

11. Further support for this point might be derived from Ramachandran and Blakeslee's work on pain remapping (Ramachandran and Blakeslee 1999). In some amputees, touching one part of the body (such as the face) produces pain in the phantom limb.

12. For a different kind of example supporting this point, see Wright 1990: 3–14.

13. Strictly speaking, our attention need only go right through to some representational content or other, so if there were a plausible candidate for the representational content of emotions other than bodily states, the transparency theorist would not need to claim that attending to emotions involves attending to some bodily quality or other. Given the absence of a plausible alternative, however, the transparency theorist tends to interpret emotional experience along similar lines to pain experience, i.e., as representing states of the body.

14. Although (3) is weaker than (4), it does not correspond directly to what I have elsewhere called weak transparency (Kind 2003). Whereas strong transparency

claims that it is impossible to attend directly to our experience, weak transparency claims only that it is difficult (but not impossible) to do so. Nonetheless, if strong transparency turns out to be false, the truth of (3) might help to explain why weak transparency is true.

References

Block, N. 1996. Mental paint and mental latex. In *Philosophical Issues*, vol. 7: *Perception*, ed. E. Villanueva, 18–49. Atascadero, Calif.: Ridgeview.

Boghossian, P., and D. Velleman. 1989. Color as a secondary quality. *Mind* 98: 81–103.

Harman, G. 1990. The intrinsic quality of experience. In *Philosophical Perspectives*, vol. 4: *Action Theory and the Philosophy of Mind*, ed. J. Tomberlin, 31–52. Atascadero, Calif.: Ridgeview.

Kind, A. 2001. Qualia realism. *Philosophical Studies* 104: 143–162.

Kind, A. 2003. What's so transparent about transparency? *Philosophical Studies* 115: 225–244.

Kind, A. 2007. Restrictions on representationalism. *Philosophical Studies* 134, 3: 405–427.

Moore, G. E. 1903. The refutation of idealism. *Mind*, new series, 12: 433–453.

Ramachandran, V. S., and S. Blakeslee. 1999. *Phantoms in the Brain: Human Nature and the Architecture of the Mind*. London: Fourth Estate.

Shoemaker, S. 1994. Self-knowledge and "inner sense." *Philosophy and Phenomenological Research* 54: 249–314.

Tye, M. 1995. *Ten Problems of Consciousness*. Cambridge, Mass.: MIT Press/A Bradford Book.

Tye, M. 2000. *Consciousness, Color, and Content*. Cambridge, Mass.: MIT Press/A Bradford Book.

Wright, E. L. 1975. Perception: A new theory. *American Philosophical Quarterly* 14: 273–286.

Wright, E. L. 1981. Yet more on non-epistemic seeing. *Mind* 90: 586–591.

Wright, E. L. 1983. Inspecting images. *Philosophy* 58: 57–72.

Wright, E. L. 1990. Two more proofs of present qualia. *Theoria* 56: 3–22.

16 Transparency and the Unity of Experience

John O'Dea

The target of this essay is Michael Tye's theory of phenomenal unity. I will argue that Tye's theory is not consistent with clear facts about perceptual experience. My aim is not so much to arrive at a better account of the unity of experience, but rather to suggest that Tye's approach to the unity issue reveals an important problem with his version of the representational theory of mind itself. Tye's theory of phenomenal unity cannot account for the different ways that properties are linked together in perception. Further, the main reason for this is that the transparency thesis, one of the bedrocks of Tye's representationalism, is not itself consistent with one of these ways.

1 Tye's Representationalism

Tye is a representationalist, a view according to which phenomenal properties are intentional objects; they are the way external objects are represented in perception. To see red, on this view, is a matter of being in a perceptual state that represents part of the world as being red. The phenomenal quality associated with redness is a component of one's (perceptual) awareness of the redness of objects "out there" in the world. Being aware of the feeling of redness is nothing more than being perceptually aware of objects as red. There is no mental quality—in this sense no *qualia*—of which one need be aware; there are only qualities of the objects of perception.

The argument to which Tye continually returns is the argument from transparency (Tye 1995, 2000, forthcoming, and many other places), which goes like this: when you focus your attention on what your experience is of—on what it is that you are experiencing—you will simply notice in more detail the qualities of whatever it is that is the object of your experience. In particular, you will not become aware of any qualities of the experience itself distinct from its content. So, for example, were you to look at a blue sky and focus your attention on that experience, you would only become more aware of blueness (or perhaps a more complicated pattern of colors). It would not strike you that there is, in addition, a character of your experience that is over and above the blueness. Since the main reason for believing in nonrepresentational phenomenal character, or qualia, is our alleged direct awareness of it in experience, if there is no such direct awareness, as transparency suggests, then there is little reason to posit qualia.

2   The Problem, and Tye's Solution

It has been a commonplace within philosophy of mind to speak of visual experiences, auditory experiences, tactile experiences, and so on. But it is also widely believed that we are perceptually presented with a unified representation of the world. In two recent publications Tye attempts to clarify and then solve a problem that arises from the combination of these two ideas. The problem in a nutshell is this: how do we get *several* experiences to come together into *one* experience? Here is the way Tye describes the problem in his *Consciousness and Persons* (Tye 2003: 17–18):

> [A]ccording to the received view, if I am using all five of my senses at a given time, I undergo five different simultaneous perceptual experiences at that time, each with its own distinctive sense-specific phenomenal character. This generates one version of the problem of the unity of consciousness. How is it that if I am undergoing five different simultaneous perceptual experiences, it is phenomenologically as if I were undergoing one? How is it that the five experiences are phenomenologically unified?

In another paper, "The Problem of the Common Sensibles" (Tye forthcoming), Tye begins his solution by elaborating a point similar to Kant's famous dictum that a succession of experiences does not amount to an experience of succession. Tye's version is that the fact that one has an experience of hearing something and an experience of seeing that same thing does not mean that one has *an* experience of *seeing and hearing* it. This fact is important because if we start from the idea that each sense modality constitutes a different experience, we are faced with the problem of how those distinct experiences come together to form a unified perceptual encounter with the world. The best way to get around this problem, Tye (forthcoming) argues, is to deny altogether that there is such a thing as a "visual experience," or "auditory experience," and the like. Instead, there is an "experienced togetherness": "On this view, there really are no such entities as purely visual experiences or purely auditory experiences or purely olfactory experiences, etc. in normal, everyday consciousness. Where there is experienced togetherness across modalities, sense-specific experiences do not exist. They are figments of philosophers' and psychologists' imagination."

This view apparently defeats the problem of the senses for representationalism, because there is, in a sense, no such thing as the visual experience of a property—there is only a *perceptual* experience of shape, or color, or movement, and so on.

Tye's solution follows from his representationalism, according to which perceptual experience, including introspection thereof, does not include awareness of any *psychological* fact. Given this view of perceptual experience, the following chain of reasoning suggests itself (Tye 2003: 25): "If we are not aware of our experiences via introspection, we are not aware of them as unified. The unity relation is not given to us introspectively as a relation connecting experiences. Why, then, suppose that there is such a relation at all?" Furthermore, if we are not aware of our experiences via introspection, we are also not aware of them as *dis*unified. So, why suppose that there is any *need* for a unifying relation? This suggests a simpler scenario, namely (ibid.: 36):

Consider, for example, the case in which I experience a loud noise and a bright flash of light. The loudness *of the noise* is unified phenomenally with the brightness *of the flash*. Phenomenal unity is a relation between qualities *represented* in experience, not qualities *of* experiences.

Specifically, perceptual unity is a matter of simultaneously experienced perceptual qualities entering into to same *perceptual content*. The perceptual experience a normal perceiver undergoes has an enormously rich, multimodal representational content.

I think that this is not a convincing solution to the problem. In the next section I will give two related reasons to not be convinced by it. They have, I think, some interest beyond this particular context because they also present a challenge to the sort of representationalism Tye embraces.

3   The Gricean Epistemological Problem

In his 1962 paper, "Some Remarks on the Senses," H. P. Grice considers the proposition that the sense modalities are distinguished from one another by virtue of their respective contents. In the course of his rejection of this idea, he presents the following thought experiment. Imagine one is resting a coin in the outstretched palm of each hand. The coins feel the same size on one's palms, but when one gazes down at the coins, they *look* to be different sizes. A list of the properties that one is (directly) perceptually aware of in this case might look something like this: the coins are silver, the coins are cool, the coins are the same sizes, the coins are different sizes, the coin are round, and so on. The problem is that, contrary to the idea that content alone distinguishes the modalities, "there is nothing in [these] facts to tell us whether the coins *look* different in size but *feel* the same size, or alternatively *feel* different in size but *look* the same size" (Grice 1962: 136).

The problem that Grice thinks is brought out by this thought experiment is an *epistemological* one. The person looking at and feeling the coins *knows*, Grice is assuming, that the coins do indeed feel, but not look, the same size. But there is no way they *could* know that purely on the basis of the properties the coins seem to have. There must therefore be, so the logic goes, something *other* than those properties which carry the information on the basis of which a person comes to be aware of which modality is being employed in a particular case.

Note that the difficulty Grice brings out with the "two coins" thought experiment is in some respects a very general difficulty. For when we both see and touch the circularity of a coin, "circularity" does seem to enter twice into the contents of our experience. If we were to write the contents of both senses in a list it might look something like: silver, cold, circular, circular. The question immediately arises, How does one know which "circular" is felt and which is seen? There is no easier answer to this question than to the corresponding one in the "two coins" case, but it is not obviously less important, nor less clear that the person in this case *does know* which "circular" is seen and which felt.

But the question is also peculiar. It is misleading to say *simply* that "circular" appears twice on the list of properties perceived of a coin that is both seen and touched. When we describe the contents of a perceptual experience, we leave something out if we describe just the properties we are aware of and not also the connections between them. For example, to describe a visual experience of a red square as simply an experience of an object as red and as square is to miss out something crucial, namely that it is the redness that we are aware of that we are experiencing as square-shaped. It is not the case that we see an *object* which is square *and* which is red—it is the *squareness* which is red and the *redness* which is square. This link is constitutive of the experience itself. In the case of seeing and touching a coin, then, although "circular" is in the perceptual experience twice, it is there in two different *ways*: one perceives the object in one's hand as a *silver circle* and as a *cold circle*.

Why is this a problem for Tye? Well, it means that the apparent disunity brought about by the fact that we experience the world through different modalities is much more closely tied to the *contents* of experience than Tye supposes. The size of things that we see *and* feel are represented distinctly in experience, and yet we are not perceptually aware of things having *two* size properties. This disunity problem cannot be dissolved by denying that there are visual *experiences* distinct from tactile *experiences* in some strong phenomenal sense.

It cannot be solved this way because it is not created by the assumption that the different sense modalities instantiate phenomenally different experiences. Rather, it arises simply out of the attempt to accurately capture the *contents* of experience. What is worse, however, it may imply the falsity of representationalism as Tye defends it. And here we come to the second problem, which I will call the binding objection.

4 The Binding Objection

Here I will argue that Tye's view is false because it cannot account for the difference between intramodal and intermodal *binding*. To account for that difference, we need to allow that properties can be *doubly* represented, and that is inconsistent with the "experienced togetherness" that Tye proposes.

The process by which different properties in perception are represented as holding of the same object is generally known in psychology as "feature integration," and in the neurosciences as "binding." The problem—or rather *problems*—of discovering how this is achieved is generally known simply as "the binding problem." From the evidence currently available, it is fairly clear that it is achieved differently within a modality as compared with between modalities. For example, there is some evidence for "polymodal" neurons (or cortical areas) whose specific function is to integrate the different modalities, but virtually none for neurons whose function is to integrate representations of different features within a modality.

In addition, intramodal binding is more closely linked to attentional mechanisms than cross-modal binding. The most well-known illustration of this is the following sort of case: if one looks at an array of "+" signs, all of which are composed of a green horizontal line intersected by a blue vertical line except one, which is the other way around, the anomalous "+" sign will not be visible as such (that is, as anomalous) until one is actually looking attentively at it. In comparison, faced with a single green "+" sign surrounded by an array of entirely blue ones, one's attention will actually be *drawn* to the anomaly—the green "+" will "pop out." In contrast, cross-modal binding appears to take place outside of attention (Vroomen and De Gelder 2004), as does synesthetic binding (e.g., of colors to numerals in people with synesthesia; see Robertson 2003; Ramachandran and Hubbard 2001; Palmeri et al. 2002). This is illustrated in the former case by the fact that the so-called ventriloquist effect, where a sound is heard to be coming from (i.e., is bound to) the most likely *visible* source, can occur outside of attention, and in the latter case by the fact that synesthesia is also evident outside attention. Moreover, there is evidence that fewer attentional resources are available within a modality than across modalities, which suggests that insofar as the intramodal binding mechanism is also an attentional mechanism (as Treisman and Gelade [1980] propose), it cannot be *that* mechanism which is responsible for cross-modal binding.

Of most interest to me here, though, is the different (as they seem to me) *logical* structures of intra- and cross-modal binding.

Austen Clark (2001) argues that what is required for binding is that the features in question be taken to share a common *subject matter*. It requires that what is taken to be green is *the same thing as* what is taken to be vertical, or what have you. Or, alternatively, that "green" and "vertical" are true of the same *place*. Clark's purpose is to show that mere conjunction of representations is insufficient for binding (Tye would agree with this much). In addition, the representations must be taken as referring to the same sets of things, or the same coordinates in space.

This certainly seems true of cross-modal binding. However, in the case of intra-modal binding, something stronger seems to be needed. It is difficult to spell out precisely what that "something" is, but here is one way. W. V. O. Quine (quoted in Clark 2001: 12) objected to the idea that in the perception of a blue pebble, the binding of "blue" and "pebble" could be satisfied by the mere conjunction of those properties in perception, since the conjunction is satisfied by the perception of "a white pebble here, a blue flower there." Rather than conjunction, in order to correctly describe the *way* "blue" and "pebble" are conjoined in perception, we need an operation "requiring them to coincide or amply overlap. The blue must encompass the pebble."

Now there seems to me a substantial difference between the idea of coinciding and the idea of encompassing. In the case of the blue pebble, it seems apt to say that the blue encompasses the pebble—or perhaps even more aptly, that it *infuses* the pebble. Or, more strictly, that the blue infuses the pebble-*shape*; it is not the pebble merely, but in particular its *shape* which is blue—which is infused by blue. This contrasts markedly, it seems to me, with the situation in which, for example, the pebble drops to the ground and makes a clicking sound. In this case the *click* is heard to come from the pebble, and indeed to be made by a blue, pebble-shaped object. Unlike the color, however, the sound does not infuse the shape. Although the shape is, in perception, a *blue* shape, it is not—or not in anything like the same way—a *clicking* shape. This seems to be the crucial difference between the cases.[1] To describe it in an intuitive way, within one modality properties are bound to *each other*, whereas across modalities properties are bound to *the same object* (or, for that matter, location).

To illustrate this point in a different way, when one sees an object that is making a sound, one can imagine it losing all of its visible properties without affecting its audible properties. However, one cannot imagine an object losing all of its *color* properties (intended broadly to include brightness, etc), without affecting its visible *shape* properties; the shape of an object is simply *not visible* unless its color is visible. This tight relation may be asymmetric—it may be that color is visible without shape being visible—but it is a relation that simply doesn't hold across modalities.[2] Within vision, the visual representation of an object's shape does not merely have the same perceived *referent* as the representation of that object's color. In addition, one is tempted to say that the representation of the shape is *partly constituted by* the representation of the color. This is not true of the tactile representation of the object's shape. In this latter case, sameness of referent may well be sufficient to account for the link between the tactile representation of the shape of an object and the representation of that object's color.

If I am right about a sort of "infusing" relation holding between properties represented by one modality, but never intermodally, then it must be the case that within a perceptual experience a property can be represented twice. When I see a square and also touch it, the squareness that I *see* will be infused by the square's apparent color (at least) *and not its texture*, while the squareness that I *touch* will be infused by its apparent texture *and not its color*. These two instances of squareness falsify Tye's thesis of experienced togetherness, it seems to me, but this is simply to reiterate the conclusion of the first part of this essay.

The further problem, then, is this. If we accept that binding plays a part in the distinction between the senses, it is an interesting question whether what we are left with is still a version of representionalism. For although it does seem to be part of the *content* of perception that visible shapes are infused by color but not in the same way by temperature, within the object perceived there seems no way to draw this distinction. When I feel the shape of an object and thereby its temperature, and *see* the shape and thereby its color, nevertheless the object has only one shape, which in itself has neither temperature nor color. Although when I see an object making a noise, its shape is infused by the color but not by the sound, in reality the shape and the noise are as closely bound to one another as the shape and the color.

In other words, the differential binding of objects in perception is a *psychological fact* about the act of perception rather than a fact about the object perceived. However, according to standard accounts of representationalism, and certainly Tye's account, the content of the perception of an object consists of purported facts about the object itself *as opposed to* facts about the act of perception. The content of a perception depicts the world as being some way; but whether shape is more tightly bound to color than to sound, or the other way around, does not seem to alter the way the world is being represented *to be*.

This apparently psychological fact is part of what we are aware of when we are having a perceptual experience. This means that perceptual experience cannot be quite as transparent as Tye supposes, and if transparency is in trouble then Tye's representationalism is also in trouble, since the alleged fact of transparency is generally taken (it is so taken by Tye) to underwrite representationalism.

5 Conclusion

Tye's version of representationalism is quite a strong one, and I have given no argument here against the weaker versions—that is to say, versions that are consistent with a partial rejection of the transparency thesis. Some representationalists, for example, insist on a difference between the sense modalities that goes beyond any difference in the objects of the modalities.[3] On the other hand it is important to note that this objection to the transparency thesis does not involve any allusion to a nonrepresentational "what it feels like" quality in perceptual experience. It does not, therefore, give straightforward support to any version of antirepresentationalism centered around the supposed direct awareness of such a quality. There is obviously a strong connection between the contents of an experience and the way those contents are bound together in the experience in the way I have been discussing. The considerations put forward here do provide the basis of a case for qualia, but more theoretical work is required to bridge the gap between the apparent failure of complete transparency and the existence of qualia in any positive sense.

Notes

1. In this connection see also Wright 1990.

2. This should be distinguished from the phenomenon of "super-adding," whereby the perception of a very faint auditory stimulus is enhanced by an equally faint congruent visual stimulus, such as a point of light at the same location (cf. Lalanne and Lorenceau 2004). In these cases it is true that without the visual stimulus, the auditory stimulus would be too faint to be detected, but this is a mere causal relation rather than part of the structure of the respective representational contents. Incidentally the opposite effect has also been discovered; simultaneous incongruent visual and auditory stimuli (e.g., a faint "beep" on the left and a faint point of light on the right) are harder to detect than the same visual or auditory stimuli presented separately.

3. See Lycan 1996.

References

Clark, A. 2001. Some logical features of feature integration. In *Neural Coding of Perceptual Systems*, ed. W. Backhaus, 3–20. Hackensack, N.J.: World Scientific.

Grice, H. P. 1962. Some remarks about the senses. In *Analytical Philosophy*, first series, ed. R. J. Butler, 133–153. Oxford: Basil Blackwell.

Jackson, F. 2003. Mind and illusion. In *Minds and Persons*, ed. A. O'Hear, 251–271. Cambridge: Cambridge University Press.

Lalanne, C., and J. Lorenceau. 2004. Crossmodal integration for perception and action. *Journal of Physiology—Paris* 98: 265–279.

Lycan, W. 1996. *Consciousness and Experience*. Cambridge, Mass.: MIT Press/A Bradford Book.

Palmeri, T. J., R. Blake, R. Marois, M. A. Flanery, and W. Whetsell, Jr. 2002. The perceptual reality of synesthetic colors. *Proceedings of the National Academy of the Sciences USA* 99: 4127–4131.

Ramachandran, V. S., and E. M. Hubbard. 2001. Psychophysical investigations into the neural basis of synaesthesia. *Proceedings of the Royal Society London B* 268: 979–983.

Robertson, L. C. 2003. Binding, spatial attention, and perceptual awareness. *Nature Reviews: Neuroscience* 4 (Feb.): 93–102.

Treisman, A. M., and G. Gelade. 1980. A feature-integration theory of attention. *Cognitive Psychology* 12: 97–136.

Tye, M. 1995. *Ten Problems of Consciousness: A Representational Theory of the Phenomenal Mind.* Cambridge, Mass.: MIT Press/A Bradford Book.

Tye, M. 2000. *Consciousness, Color, and Content.* Cambridge, Mass.: MIT Press/A Bradford Book.

Tye, M. 2003. *Consciousness and Persons.* Cambridge, Mass.: MIT Press/A Bradford Book.

Tye, M. Forthcoming. The problem of common sensibles. In *Perception and Status of Secondary Qualities*, ed. R. Schumacher. Dordrecht: Kluwer.

Vroomen, J., and B. De Gelder. 2004. Perceptual effects of cross-modal stimulation: The cases of ventriloquism and the freezing phenomenon. In *Handbook of Multisensory Processes*, ed. G. Calvert, C. Spence, and B. E. Stein, 141–150. Cambridge, Mass.: MIT Press/A Bradford Book.

Wright, E. L. 1990. Two more proofs of present qualia. *Theoria* 56, 1–2: 3–22.

17 Phenomenal Character and the Transparency of Experience

Martine Nida-Rümelin

1 Phenomenal Character and Phenomenal Kinds

Although the term "qualia" occurs in the title of this book, I will avoid it in this essay. I prefer the following terms: "phenomenal character," "phenomenal differences," and "phenomenal kinds." Experiences have phenomenal character and they differ with respect to them. If two experiences are alike with respect to phenomenal character concerning a particular aspect then there is a phenomenal kind they both belong to. But if qualia are understood as in some sense "uninterpreted" and as fully determinate in the way it is to experience them (for the latter point see Clark 2005), then there is reason to doubt that for every phenomenal character there is a quale associated with that character. For instance, it is obvious that hearing a noise as coming from the right side is phenomenally different from hearing a noise as coming from the left side. Each of these kinds of experiences has a specific phenomenal character. But there is no fully determinate quale associated with each of these experiences, and the phenomenal character is partially determined by "interpretation." In this essay I will defend the view that phenomenal character is intrinsic (more precisely: that to have an experience with a specific phenomenal character is an intrinsic property of the experiencing subject), and I will not be concerned with the more restricted and theoretically more loaded notion of qualia.

To give an idea of the wide range of cases of phenomenal character I would like the reader to have in mind let me give a few examples. Listening to a piano piece played on a Steinway is phenomenally different from listening to the same piece played by the same person in precisely the same way on a Bösendorfer. Smelling a rose is phenomenally different from smelling basil. Seeing something as slightly reddish blue is phenomenally different from seeing it as pure blue. Feeling one's own leg without touching it and with closed eyes as being bent is phenomenally different from feeling it as being straight. Looking into the face of a person without recognizing her as one's childhood friend is phenomenally different from looking into the same face under otherwise identical conditions after the recognition. Thinking of someone with love is phenomenally different from thinking of someone with emotional indifference even if the thoughts involved have otherwise exactly the same content. Observing a running dog from the perspective of a human is surely phenomenally different in many ways from observing a running dog from the perspective of a dog.

2   Phenomenal Character and Veridicality Conditions

As some of the above examples illustrate, we do not have names for all differences in phenomenal character we are familiar with. We do not have names for all phenomenal kinds. Many phenomenal kinds can be referred to only through the content shared by experiences of the kind at issue. Members of some or even most phenomenal kinds share parts of their content necessarily. Let us call the content of a perceptual experience the conditions that must obtain for the experience to be veridical. If you wake up in the morning and feel your left leg bent via your sense of proprioception then you have an experience of a particular phenomenal kind. Other people may have experiences belonging to the same phenomenal kind. These experiences have a particular content characteristic of the phenomenal kind they belong to: they are veridical only if the left leg of the perceiver is in fact bent. It is highly plausible to assume that every experience with this specific phenomenal character necessarily has this particular content. (Siewert 1998 forcefully defends the claim that phenomenal character determines representational content in most cases.) Furthermore, we have no other way to refer to the phenomenal kind at issue than by reference to the content that is characteristic for experiences of this phenomenal kind: to pick out the specific phenomenal character of feeling one's own left leg bent we have to refer (as I just did) to the content of the experience. The intimate relation between phenomenal character and content just described does not exclude cases of misrepresentation and it does not exclude the possibility of experiences with phenomenal character but without representational content.

So there is an intimate relation at least in many cases between the phenomenal character of an experience and its content. Phenomenal characters often stand in a relation of metaphysical necessity to the content of the experience and phenomenal kinds can often be referred to only by reference to the content shared by experiences of the relevant kind. But some philosophers state a stronger connection. They claim that for an experience to have a specific phenomenal character is *nothing but* its having a particular content. This is, roughly, the representationalist view. According to representationalism with respect to phenomenal character, to have an experience of a particular phenomenal kind is nothing but to have an experience that represents the world in a particular way. According to that view there are no intrinsic phenomenal features. If we interpret representation in terms of veridicality conditions, then we arrive at a reduction of phenomenal kinds to kinds of experiences specified by their veridicality conditions. If the reasoning just sketched were correct, then the nature of a given phenomenal kind (the feature of experiences responsible for their membership in a particular phenomenal kind) could be fully described by reference to the associated conditions of veridicality. Such a reduction of phenomenal character to representational content seems attractive to many philosophers for well-known reasons: if the reduction is successful then it may seem easy to provide a materialist account of phenomenal character.

The present essay defends a nonreductionist view of phenomenal character. The nonreductionist claims that phenomenal differences between experiences cannot be reduced to differences in representational content. Phenomenal differences—even if they are closely linked by metaphysical necessity to differences in representational content in many or most cases—are nonetheless *intrinsic* differences in the way it feels to have the experience at issue. I will call this view *nonreductionism with respect to phenomenal character*. As I will use the term, the phenomenal nonreductionist is also a realist about phenomenal character. According to the nonreductionist in this sense, differences in phenomenal character are *real*, objective differences in the way it is like to have specific experiences. These differences concern the "subjective feel" of the experience; they concern what is phenomenally present in the experience for the subject at issue, but they are objective nonetheless. Facts about the way it feels to a subject to have a specific experience are facts about the real objective world.

The present essay will develop no positive arguments for the view that to have an experience of a specific phenomenal character is an intrinsic feature of the subject at issue. The purpose of the essay is to say why the so-called transparency of experience does not provide any counterevidence against the existence of phenomenal character.

3   The Argument from Transparency

Representationalism with respect to phenomenal kinds may sometimes be
motivated by the two insights formulated above: an insight about the way
we have to refer to phenomenal kinds in many cases (reference to phenomenal kinds by reference to content) and an insight about the intimate relation of metaphysical necessity between phenomenal kinds and content. But
there is a further common motivation: representationalists often argue for
their view by reference to what they call the transparency or diaphanousness of sensory experience. (For proponents of the transparency claim see
Harman 1990, Byrne 2006; for discussions of the claim see Siewert 2004,
Levine 2006: 272ff., Tye 2000: ch. 3, Jackson 2005: 322) A first approach
to the intuitive idea may be put for the case of colors as follows: in having
an experience of blueness while looking at an object, we see the object as
having a specific surface property, the property of being blue. We therefore
can characterize the phenomenal kind of blueness experiences by reference
to the property things appear to have in blueness experiences. It may be
tempting to conclude that therefore, to have a perception of the phenomenal kind at issue is to represent an object as having a specific objective
surface property. Furthermore, to represent an object as having a specific
objective surface property is to have an experience with specific veridicality
conditions: the experience is veridical with respect to the color aspect if and
only if the perceived object has the surface property that the experience at
issue represents it as having. This reasoning starts from a phenomenological observation and ends with an ontological reduction (or so it may seem)
of phenomenal kinds to kinds of experiences specified by veridicality conditions. I will call this reasoning the argument from transparency. For the
color case the argument may be summarized as follows:

C1. To have a visual experience of, for example, the phenomenal kind
designated by "experience of reddish blue" is to see the object as being
reddish blue. (Phenomenological claim)
C2. To see an object as being reddish blue is to visually represent the object
as being reddish blue. (Step from phenomenology to representation)
C3. To visually represent an object as being reddish blue is to have a visual
experience that is veridical with respect to color just in case the object is
reddish blue. (Step from representation to veridicality conditions)

Therefore:

R. To have a visual experience of the phenomenal kind designated by
"experience of reddish blue" is to have a visual experience that is veridical

with respect to color just in case the object is reddish blue. (Intended as a reductive claim about phenomenal kinds)

An analogous argument from transparency for the case of visual shape perception may be summarized as follows:

S1. To have a visual experience of, for example, the phenomenal kind designated by "circularity experience" is to see the object at issue as being circular. (Phenomenological claim)

S2. To see an object as being circular is to visually represent the object as being circular. (Step from phenomenology to representation)

S3. To visually represent an object as being circular is to have a visual experience that is veridical with respect to shape just in case the object is circular. (Step from representation to veridicality conditions)

Therefore:

R'. To have a visual experience of the phenomenal kind designated by "circularity experience" is to have a visual experience that is veridical with respect to shape just in case the object at issue is circular. (Intended as a reductive claim about phenomenal kinds)

I do not claim that every proponent of representationalism with respect to qualia may be understood as implicitly accepting the argument from transparency as formulated above. Some philosophers start with a claim of transparency that cannot be appropriately captured in the first premise. Others will object to the step from representation to veridicality conditions. There are different versions of the step from transparency to representationalism present in the literature. My hope is that some of the insights one may gain in thinking about the specific version of the transparency argument formulated above will carry over to other versions of the reasoning at issue.

I will argue that both arguments summarized above fail to support reductionism about phenomenal kinds and fail to undermine the view that phenomenal differences are differences in intrinsic qualitative features of experiences. But the two arguments fail in different ways and for different reasons.

4   A Closer Look at the So-Called Transparency of Experience

A short and common way to formulate the insight about the so-called transparency of experience with respect to color is to make the following two claims:

a. In color perception we are aware of an objective surface property of the perceived object (its color).

b. In color perception we are not aware of any intrinsic qualitative property of our own experience.

Claim (a) is a hybrid between a phenomenological claim and an ontological claim. On a certain reading (a) "points to" or expresses the undeniable phenomenological fact: colors appear to be on the surfaces of objects, we see them outside there on the thing perceived. In other words: in having a blueness experience we see the object at issue as being blue. However, claim (a) goes beyond this phenomenological assertion. First, if we move from appearance talk to talk about "being aware *of*" we move to a *de re* description of the experience at issue. We leave the phenomenological level and enter the ontological level: we state a relation between the experiencing subject and some other entity. It is quite clear that phenomenology alone is incapable of supporting any such *de re* description. Second, (a) asserts that the property the experiencing subject is aware of is an objective property of objects. But again, phenomenology cannot support the claim that the properties to which we stand in the relation of being aware (in color experiences) are objective properties. Colors appear to be properties *of objects*, but it is doubtful that they also appear to be *objective* in any more substantial sense. But even if the properties that objects appear to have in color experience seem to be objective, it does not follow that there are objective properties we are aware of in color experience. It is often claimed that the transparency of experience is a phenomenological fact. If we take this claim seriously then we need to separate the phenomenological and the ontological elements in the claim of transparency and stick to the phenomenological elements while skipping the ontological elements. We should then replace (a) by the more cautious and purely phenomenological assertion:

a*. In color experience things appear to have certain surface properties.

Many philosophers seem to think that the claim (a) (in color experience we are aware of objective surface properties) implies (b) (in color experience we are not aware of intrinsic qualitative properties of our own experiences). But (a) does not in fact imply or support (b), and there is reason to reject (b). To see this, consider the following example.

Violetta looks at a uniformly colored surface in front of her. She wonders whether she thereby has an experience of pure blue or rather of a slightly reddish blue. She finally realizes, after some reflection, that the color she experiences is a blue with a very slight red component.

A first question: is Violetta's insight an insight about the property the thing appears to have in her experience, or is it an insight about the phenomenal character of her own experience? Quite obviously we should say this: Violetta's insight is an insight about both. There is no opposition between the two alternatives. Her judgment is a judgment about the property the surface appears to have in her experience, and it is at the same time a judgment about the phenomenal character of her own color experience. There are no two judgments involved, since every difference in the property a thing appears to have in color experience constitutes a difference in the phenomenal character of the color experience, and vice versa (see Nida-Rümelin 2006: sect. 2). Second question: What is Violetta attending to in her reflection? Is she attending to the surface outside there and to the properties the surface appears to have in her experience, or is she attending to some intrinsic feature of her own experience? The answer is: she is attending to both simultaneously. She is attending to the color the surface appears to have, and she is thereby attending to a phenomenal feature of her experience which consists in seeing something as having that particular color. There is no opposition between the two possibilities. Also, it would be a mistake to think that Violetta thereby manages to direct her attention in two different directions. It is sometimes said that when we try to attend to the phenomenal character of our own experiences we inevitably find ourselves attending to the features of objects. This is correct in many cases, and it is surely correct in the case of color in this sense: when we try to attend to the phenomenal character of our color experiences we find ourselves attending to the colors that things appear to have in the experience. But attending to the apparent colors does not constitute a failure in the attempt to attend to the phenomenal character of the experience—as some seem to suggest. Attending to the color a thing appears to have in one's experience *is* to attend to the phenomenal character of the experience.

These points are quite obvious but not sufficiently appreciated in the present debate. This may in part be due to mistaken metaphors induced by common terminology. When reflecting on the phenomenal character of our own experiences we are not looking inside. We are not perceiving what is going on in our brain or looking into some inner space. "Introspection" is a term that should be avoided for that reason. "Phenomenological reflection" is more appropriate to Violetta's activity. Second, the phenomenal characters we are able to detect should not be thought of as some "inner paint"; Block's (2003) term "mental paint" is misleading. There are no experiences understood as perceptible individual things that we discover by somehow "looking into ourselves." We can distinguish different qualitative ways it is like to be in a state by being in that state. We make these distinctions by carefully attending to the way we experience that state. But carefully attending to the way it is to experience something is not to look in some mysterious manner into one's own body or brain or some other inner space in order to observe some quasi-painted entities. (For similar remarks about so-called introspection see Siewert 2004: 24).

Let us call the combination of (a) and (b) the *radical transparency claim*. According to the diagnosis here proposed, proponents of the radical transparency claim make two related mistakes: first, they fail to distinguish the radical transparency claim from the mere phenomenological assertion formulated here as (a*). Second, they fail to see that in being aware of the properties things appear to have in our experiences we are aware of intrinsic phenomenal features of our experiences. (Thus they fail to see that (a) does not imply (b).) I suspect that the latter mistake is in part due to bad metaphors nourished by terms like "introspection" and "mental paint." These metaphors create a mistaken picture of the view that the proponent of intrinsic phenomenal properties is trying to defend.

5   Colors as Mere Appearance Properties

To introduce the discussion of the transparency argument below, I will now present a view about the nature of colors. According to this view colors are mere appearance properties, in a sense that will be explained. The basic idea may be put like this. To be blue is nothing over and above having the following property: subjects who see the object veridically with respect to the aspect called color have a visual experience of the phenomenal kind designated by "blueness experience." The proposal implies that you see the color of a blue object veridically if and only if you have the phenomenal kind of experiences designated by "blueness experience," and it adds to this the substantial ontological claim: for an object to be blue consists in the fulfillment of this condition. The proposal is compatible with (in a sense even implies) the well-known intuition that colors reveal their nature in experience: the property you see or rather seem to see instantiated in an object that appears blue to you is the property of looking *this* way to every subject who sees the object veridically with respect to color. At the same time, the account is compatible with an illusion theory about color vision. Suppose we accept the plausible claim that different visual systems (leading to different phenomenal kinds of color experiences at the sight of the same object under the same external conditions) are equally well equipped to present the world veridically to the perceiver. This is to say that the surface properties of an object cannot determine which phenomenal kind of color experience an arbitrary subject must have in order to see the object veridically (see Hardin 2004). It follows almost directly that no objects ever instantiate a property such that to see the object veridically with respect to that property requires having a color experience of some specific phenomenal kind. So, on the account just given, strictly speaking, colors are never instantiated. (This additional claim will play no role in the following argument. For more on the illusion theory, see Maund 2006.)

The account of the nature of colors proposed here can be stated more precisely like this:

The nature of colors as appearance properties
Colors are *mere* appearance properties in the following sense: For every color C there is a corresponding phenomenal kind K_C such that to have color C is nothing but having a property P that fulfills the following condition:

(VER) A perception is veridical in virtue of the object's having P just in case the perception belongs to the phenomenal kind K_C.

In the following section I will use this account of colors to give an answer to the transparency argument for the case of color vision. The transparency argument for the perception of shapes will require a different response, since shapes are not mere appearance properties. As in the case of colors, it is plausible to assume for the case of shapes that there is a necessary connection between veridicality conditions and phenomenal kinds that may be stated as follows for the case of circularity: A subject sees a circular object veridically with respect to its shape if and only if the subject has a visual experience of the kind designated by "circularity experience." However, in contrast to the color case, to be circular does not consist in the fulfillment of this condition, nor is it part of the nature of being circular. To be circular is to be spatially arranged in a specific way. What it is to be circular can be specified without reference to kinds of phenomenal states, whereas we need to refer to kinds of phenomenal states if we wish to explain the nature of colors.

An objection against this account of colors that will come to mind quite quickly is to suspect that the proposal is circular in a vicious way. On the one hand, the nature of colors has been explained by reference to blueness experiences: to be blue is to be veridically perceived with respect to color exactly by those who have a blueness experience. On the other hand, the nature of experiences of blueness has been explained by reference to being blue: to have a blueness experience in one's perception is to see something as being blue (compare C1). But this objection can be answered: neither of the two claims is intended or should be interpreted as a reductive ontological analysis. We can explain what it is to have an experience of blueness by reference to the property of being blue, and we can explain what it is to be blue by reference to the property of having an experience of blueness. However, neither of the properties thus explained is ontologically more fundamental than the other. This relation of "being at the same ontological level" is reflected in the conceptual realm: in order to understand what it is to be blue we need to understand what it is to have an experience of blueness, but in order to understand what it is to have an experience of blueness we need to understand what it is to see something as being blue. Thus neither of the two concepts involved (the concept of being blue and the concept of being an experience of blueness) is ontologically more fundamental than the other. But there is a conceptual interdependence: it is impossible to understand one of them without understanding the other.

6 Why the Argument from Transparency Goes Wrong for the Case of Color Perception

I will argue in this section that the argument from transparency has only true premises in the case of color. Since the argument is also valid, I accept the conclusion. More precisely, the discussion will lead to the following view about the transparency argument concerning colors: (C1) is correct, (C2) is true if representation is interpreted as proposed in (C3), and (C3) is acceptable for the proponent of nonreductionism with respect to intrinsic phenomenal character who accepts in addition the view of color sketched in the preceding section. However, the truth of (C2) and (C3) is due to the special status of colors as mere appearance properties. But this account of color also undermines the intended interpretation of the conclusion of the argument. The account of colors proposed implies that the conclusion cannot be read as a successful ontological reduction of the phenomenal to the representational and that the conclusion is therefore compatible with the nonreductionist view of the phenomenal that it is supposed to reject.

The first premise of the argument was:

C1. To have a visual experience of, for example, the phenomenal kind designated by "experience of reddish blue" is to see the object as being reddish blue.

Premise (C1) states that there is a one-to-one correspondence between phenomenal kinds of color experiences and apparent properties. If Violetta sees an object as being slightly reddish blue and Celeste sees it as being pure blue, then the object appears to have a property in Violetta's experience that is different from the property it appears to have in Celeste's experience. Also, if the property the object appears to have in Violetta's color experience is different from the property it appears to have in Celeste's color experience then the two color experiences belong to different phenomenal kinds. This premise seems undeniable to me. Phenomenal differences with respect to color are differences with respect to the specific property things appear to have in the experience.

What about the second premise, (C2)? Representation is accounted for in many different ways in the literature. What should be said about (C2) depends on the account of representation presupposed. But let us consider (C2) presupposing the account of representation formulated in (C3). Instead of looking at premises (C2) and (C3) in isolation we may now have a look at the result obtained when (C2) and (C3) are combined (i.e., when the account of representation in terms of veridicality conditions given in (C3) is inserted in (C2)). We thus get the following claim:

C2-3. To see an object as being reddish blue is to have an experience that is veridical with respect to color just in case the object is reddish blue.

If we apply the proposed claim about the nature of colors to this claim we can replace every occurrence of "being reddish blue" by the expression "having the property of being seen veridically with respect to color exactly by those who have an experience of reddish blue" (this is a simplified version of the precise formulation in section 5, but the simplification does no harm). We thus get the following assertion:

A. To see an object as having the property of being seen veridically exactly by those who have an experience of reddish blue is to have an experience that is veridical just in case the object has the property of being seen veridically exactly by those who have an experience of reddish blue.

Let us try to understand the intuitive content of this complex assertion. Suppose that you see an object as reddish blue. According to the proposed account of colors, this is to see the object as having the property of looking like *this* to any subject who is capable of seeing the color of the object veridically. Claim (A) states that to see an object as having this property is nothing over and above having an experience that would be veridical if the object really had the property of being perceived veridically with respect to color exactly by those who see the object like *this*. As far as I can see there is no reason to reject this thesis from the point of view of the nonreductionist about phenomenal kinds. Claim (A) is in no conflict with the basic intuition the nonreductionist defends: experiences of reddish blue are characterized by an intrinsic phenomenal feature. This intrinsic phenomenal feature recurs in the above explanation of what it is to see an object as reddish blue.

We have seen why the nonreductionist about phenomenal kinds who accepts the account of colors proposed can accept all premises of the transparency argument for color vision. (Note, however, that the acceptability of the second premise depends on presupposing the third premise.) To see why the result of the argument does not undermine a position that combines these two claims, we only have to reapply the reasoning of the previous paragraph. According to the proposed view about colors, the result of the transparency argument

R. To have a visual experience of the phenomenal kind designated by "experience of reddish blue" is to have a visual experience that is veridical with respect to color just in case the object is reddish blue

is no ontological reduction of the phenomenal. According to the account of colors as mere appearance properties we can replace "is reddish blue" by "has the property of being seen veridically exactly by those who have a reddish blue experience." So again reference to the same phenomenal kind occurs in the explanation of what it is to have an experience of the phenomenal kind at issue. This is no objection against (R). The circularity is not vicious if we do not read the explanation as reductive. But it is, of course, an objection to the idea that (R) reduces the phenomenal to the representational. To the contrary, (R) is perfectly compatible with the nonreductionist view that to have an experience of reddish blue is to have an experience with a specific intrinsic qualitative feature.

8 Why the Argument from Transparency Goes Wrong for the Case of Shape Perception

The kind of answer just given to the transparency argument for the case of colors is not available for the case of shapes. The answer was based on an account of colors as mere appearance properties; shapes are not mere appearance properties in the sense explained.

Thus the nonreductionist needs to give a different answer. In this case, the result of the argument (R') is unacceptable for the nonreductionist. (R') makes no reference to phenomenal kinds and therefore does express an ontological reduction of the phenomenal to the representational.

The acceptance of the combination of premises (C2) and (C3) in the color case was motivated by an account of colors as mere appearance properties. Since shape properties are not mere appearance properties there is no parallel intuitive motivation for accepting the corresponding premises (S2) and (S3) in the shape case. In addition, there is intuitive reason for the nonreductionist about phenomenal kinds in shape perception to reject the two premises. Let us again directly consider the result we obtain if we combine the relevant premises (S2) and (S3):

S2-3. To see an object as being circular is to have a visual experience that is veridical with respect to shape just in case the object is circular.

(S2-3) should not be confused with the weaker claim, which states the corresponding relation of equivalence by metaphysical necessity. The nonreductionist has no reason to deny that the following equivalence is metaphysically necessary: A subject has a visual circularity experience if and only if the visual experience at issue is veridical with respect to shape just in case the object at issue is circular. The nonreductionist can accept that the phenomenal character of circularity experiences determines their corresponding veridicality conditions, and he or she need not object to the opposite (even though less obvious) implication. But the nonreductionist has to insist that having a circularity experience of does not *consist* in having an experience that would be veridical just in case the object was circular. An argument for the negation of (S2-3) could appeal to the insight that you cannot grasp what it is to have a circularity experience unless you have formed—on the basis of your own visual experiences—a phenomenal concept of that phenomenal kind. If the ontological analysis proposed in (S2-3) were correct, then it would be possible—in contradiction to the claim just formulated—to grasp the nature of visual experiences of circularity without having formed an appropriate phenomenal concept. (For the notion of grasping at issue, see Nida-Rümelin 2006b.)

9 A More Fundamental Mistake: Leaving Out the Subject of Experience

So far I have discussed an argument for the claim that phenomenal kinds of certain visual experiences can be reduced to kinds of visual experiences characterized by their representational content. Many philosophers are interested in the reduction of the phenomenal to the representational in the context of a broader project: they wish to develop a materialist account of consciousness. Many seem to think—on both sides of the divide between materialists and nonmaterialists—that the problem of consciousness is the problem of phenomenal consciousness, and that the problem of phenomenal consciousness would be solved if we were able to reduce phenomenal kinds to representational kinds in the sense given in the result of the transparency argument. But this common assumption is mistaken. The transparency argument, if successful, supports a materialist solution to what one may call the problem of individuation of phenomenal kinds. But a materialist solution to the problem of individuation of phenomenal kinds is far from a materialist solution to the problem of consciousness.

The problem of the individuation of phenomenal kinds is captured in the following question: what is it that makes an experience an experience of a specific phenomenal kind? If the feature of an experience that makes it an experience of a given phenomenal kind can be described in terms that make reference only to entities acceptable to the materialist, then there is a materialist solution to the problem of the individuation of phenomenal kinds. A materialist solution to the problem of the individuation of phenomenal kinds is not automatically a solution to the problem of consciousness for a simple technical reason: a solution to the problem of the individuation of phenomenal kinds may be completely silent about the nature of experiences. It need only say what makes an experience one of a specific phenomenal kind; it need not say anything about what makes an event an experience. Experiences do, however, necessarily involve a subject of experience. There can be no experience of blueness without there being a subject who sees something as being blue in that experience. Therefore: no account of experiences can be given without an account of experiencing subjects. The more fundamental philosophical issue about the ontological nature of experiencing subjects must therefore be addressed in any philosophical account of the nature of experiences. It follows that a materialist solution to the individuation of phenomenal kinds based on the reduction of the phenomenal to the representational is far from solving the problem of consciousness.

But this simple point is not commonly appreciated. We need to understand why this is so. What are the background assumptions that make it difficult or impossible to acknowledge this quite obvious point? I suspect that we can answer this question at least partially as follows. The following assumptions are implicitly accepted or considered as obvious by many:

1. A materialist solution to the problem of consciousness would be attained if we had a satisfying materialist answer to the following question: what

makes it the case that a given physical process (e.g., a brain process) has phenomenal character?

2. To have phenomenal character is to have some specific phenomenal character.

3. A materialist solution to the problem of individuation of phenomenal states would be a general materialist account of what it is for a physical process to have some given specific phenomenal character.

It follows from (3) (given (2)) that a materialist solution to the problem of individuation of phenomenal kinds would provide a materialist answer to the question: what makes it the case that a given physical process (e.g., a brain process) has phenomenal character? With (1) we arrive at the conclusion: a materialist solution to the problem of individuation of phenomenal kinds is a solution to the problem of consciousness.

The mistake in this reasoning, I claim, is induced by the locution "a physical process P has phenomenal character C." This common terminology invites a mistaken picture that makes it easy to overlook the subject of experience involved. If we accept, as we should, that there is no experience without someone who experiences, and that issues about phenomenal character are always issues about how it is *for some given experiencing subject* to have a given experience, then we have to replace the short formulation "the physical process P has phenomenal character C" by the more complicated expression which explicitly mentions the subject involved: "the physical process P gives rise to the fact that the experiencing subject at issue has an experience of the phenomenal character C." With this reformulation in mind we can see what goes wrong in the above reasoning. We can accept (1) if "to have phenomenal character" is appropriately replaced. (We may reasonably doubt that phenomenal consciousness is the only problem about consciousness, but I skip this issue here.) Premise (2) is undeniable. However, premise (3) is unacceptable: as argued above, a materialist answer to the problem of the individuation of phenomenal kinds does *not* constitute a general materialist account of what it is for a physical process to have some given specific phenomenal character (since the answer is silent about the nature of subjects of experience).

These considerations show that a solution to the problem of the individuation of phenomenal kinds does not solve the problem of consciousness. The contrary idea rests on a cognitive illusion produced by a widespread unfortunate terminology. It thus turns out that the central theme of the present essay—the controversy about the reduction of phenomenal kinds to representational kinds—although surely of some theoretical interest, is much less relevant to our understanding of the nature of consciousness than it is common to assume in the present debate.

References

Block, N. 2003. Mental paint. In *Reflections and Replies: Essays on the Philosophy of Tyler Burge*, ed. M. Hahn and B. Ramberg. Cambridge, Mass.: MIT Press/A Bradford Book.

Byrne, A. 2006. Color and the mind–body problem. *Dialectica* 60, 3: 223–234.

Clark, A., 2005. Painfulness is not a quale. In *Pain: New Essays on Its Nature and the Methodology of Its Study*, ed. Murat Aydede, 177–197. Cambridge, Mass.: MIT Press/A Bradford Book.

Hardin, C. L. 2004. A green thought in a green shade. *Harvard Review of Philosophy* 12: 29–39.

Harman, G. 1990. The intrinsic quality of experience. In *Philosophical Perspectives*, vol. 4: *Action Theory and Philosophy of Mind*, ed. James Tomberlin, 31–52. Atascadero, Calif.: Ridgeview.

Jackson, F. 2005. Consciousness. In *The Oxford Handbook of Contemporary Philosophy*, ed. F. Jackson and M. Smith, 310–333. New York: Oxford University Press.

Levine, J. 2006. Color and color experience: Colors and ways of appearing. *Dialectica* 60, 3: 269–282.

Maund, J. B. 2006. The illusory theory of colours: An anti-realist theory. *Dialectica* 60, 3: 245–268.

Nida-Rümelin, M. 2006. A puzzle about colors. *Dialectica* 60, 3: 321–336.

Nida-Rümelin, M. 2007. Grasping phenomenal properties. In *Phenomenal Knowledge and Phenomenal Concepts*, ed. T. Alter and S. Walter. New York: Oxford University Press.

Tye, M. 2000. *Consciousness, Color, and Content*. Cambridge, Mass.: MIT Press/A Bradford Book.

Siewert, C. 1998. *The Significance of Consciousness*. Princeton: Princeton University Press.

Siewert, C. 2004. Is experience transparent? *Philosophical Studies* 117: 15–41.

Diana Raffman

Representationalist solutions to the qualia problem are motivated by two
fundamental ideas: first, that having an experience consists in tokening a
mental representation; second, that all one is aware of in having an experience is the intentional content of that representation.[1] In particular, one is
not aware of any intrinsic features of the representational vehicle itself. For
example, when you visually experience a red object, you are aware only of
the redness of the object, not any redness or red quale of your experience.
You are aware of outer red without being aware of inner red. According
to the representationalist, the phenomenal character of your experience
is just (an element of) the intentional content of your representation. In
effect, inner red just is outer red.

For her part, the defender of qualia, or anyway the defender of qualia
who will figure in the present discussion, grants that experiencing a red
object involves mentally representing it, and that when you have such an
experience you are aware of its intentional content. But she denies that
that intentional content exhausts your awareness. The defender of qualia
(call her "Phen") contends that your mental vehicle is itself *mentally* or
phenomenally red, and that in addition to the outer redness of the object,
you are aware of this inner redness, the intrinsic phenomenal character of
your representational vehicle. Thus, *contra* the representationalist, you are
not aware of the content of your representation without being aware of its
intrinsic features.

In this essay I will argue that although the representationalist (call him
"Rep") has told a credible materialist story of how a perceptual experience
represents, that is, how it gets and carries its intentional content (say, by
causally covarying with a property in the world), he has not yet explained
how we can be *aware* of that content without being aware of intrinsic
features of the experience. It is essential that Rep do this, for the qualia
problem is at bottom an intuitive problem; it is fed by deep-seated "first-

person" intuitions about the character of human perceptual experience. Hence the materialist who would resolve it must do some justice to those intuitions, or at least provide a plausible diagnosis of them or a plausible reconstruction, in materialist terms, of the notion of qualia.[2] In particular, Rep must *explain*, in the sense of enabling us to understand, how you can be aware of the content of your experience without being aware of inner intrinsic properties of it. I will argue that he has not yet explained this, and so has not yet solved the qualia problem.[3] (Another explanatory gap.)

In what follows, the part of Rep will often be played by Michael Tye, a leading proponent of the representational view and author of a well-developed and influential version of it (e.g., 1995, 2000).

1

How does Rep suppose that you can be aware of the intentional content of your experience without being aware of intrinsic features of your representational vehicle? The fact that an experience is a representation cannot by itself ensure this result. After all, an ordinary color photograph of ripe apples represents red, but it exemplifies the color, and awareness of its intentional content seems to require awareness of its intrinsic vehicular redness. (Of course, the red in the photograph is external, not mental or phenomenal. I will come back to this point, and say more about pictures, later on.) Alternatively, maybe the way your mental representation gets its content fixed is supposed to ensure that it does not (mentally) exemplify what it represents. For instance, maybe a causal covariational or tracking account of content fixation is supposed to ensure such a result. But that can't be right either, since the color photograph too could have its content fixed by a tracking relation. *How content gets fixed, and how one gains awareness of that content, are two different questions.*

Perhaps something about the character of your mental vehicle itself enables awareness of its content without awareness of its intrinsic properties. The same content may be represented in different ways, or by different vehicle "formats" or under different "modes of presentation." For instance, perhaps your vehicle for red is a mental word "RED" that affords awareness of the color in a manner analogous to that of the public word "red": the word "red," unlike the color photograph, affords awareness of its intentional content without needing to exemplify—without needing to *be*—red. Or perhaps your mental vehicle for red affords awareness of the color in the manner of a demonstrative term like "this," or in the manner of a notational representation like a musical score. Or maybe it does so in the manner of an analog but non-red representation like a graph or a map or a hand gesture. These do not exhaust the possibilities.

Tye opts for the view that your mental vehicle for red is a mental word "RED."[4] He even supposes that your vehicle for a particular determinate shade of red, for example red_{19}, is a mental predicate "RED_{19}." If Tye is right, and if representation by a mental word is relevantly analogous to representation by a public word, then your mental vehicle for red_{19} affords you awareness of its intentional content without awareness of its intrinsic features. In that case I think Phen should concede that Rep has explained, has made intuitively comprehensible, how one can be aware of outer red (red_{19}) without being aware of inner red (RED_{19}).

I want to reemphasize the requirements of intuitive plausibility and comprehensibility on any candidate solution to the qualia problem. Because the qualia problem is an intuitive problem, Rep must explain, in the sense of enabling us to understand, how you can be aware of the content of your experience without being aware of inner intrinsic properties. To the extent that the experience of a red_{19} surface can plausibly be thought to consist in the tokening of a mental predicate, I claim, Rep has discharged this obligation. So the question is: how plausible is the idea that experiencing red_{19} consists in tokening a mental predicate "RED_{19}"?

Elsewhere (Raffman 1995) I have discussed some negative empirical evidence. Just for example, if you consciously represented red_{19} by tokening "RED_{19}," then *ceteris paribus* you should have little difficulty learning to recognize the shade on sight. But as Tye himself acknowledges, the limited "grain" of perceptual memory makes recognition impossible. Perhaps we should also expect reaction-time evidence: if your experience of red_{19} consisted in tokening a mental "RED_{19}" and your experience of (e.g.) red_{190} consisted in tokening "RED_{190}," then maybe perceptual integration should take longer in the latter case; in other words, you should be able to see red_{19} faster than you can see red_{190}. But that seems incredible.[5]

At present, though, I want to set aside these empirical considerations and focus on a different, largely intuitive line of reasoning. Tye is quick to point out that although you consciously represent red_{19} with a mental predicate "RED_{19}," you don't have a concept of red_{19}:

[T]he representational content of visual experience is extremely rich. It operates on a number of different levels and it goes far beyond any concepts the creature may have. Consider, for example, the representation of hue. . . . The fact that a patch of surface is represented in my experience as having a certain hue, red_{19}, say, does not demand that I have the concept red_{19}. For I certainly cannot recognize that hue as such when it comes again. (Tye 2000: 74)[6]

Understood: we are not talking about conceptual representations. But this only makes Tye's view more mysterious. It's one thing to suppose that your conceptual representation of red_{19} is a mental word, quite another to suppose that your *perceptual* representation is a word. Tye says that you experience the surface "as having a certain hue, red_{19}." Perhaps he is right, in the merely *de re* sense that red_{19} is the color you experience the surface as having, rather than, say, red_{18} or red_{20}. But the latter claim concerns only the content of your representation, whereas our present question concerns its format or mode of presentation—how the content is represented. And plainly you do not experience the surface under the mode of presentation red_{19} (*a fortiori* under *having the hue red_{19}*).

Let me be clear. Of course I do not question that a mental "RED_{19}" would represent the shade. But in the present context the term "represent" is ambiguous between what might be called its "weak" and "strong" senses. Let us say that to weakly represent something is just to have or carry that content, whereas to strongly represent something is to carry and *afford awareness of* that content. I am contending that a mental predicate could weakly represent red_{19} but not strongly represent it. My evidence is the implausibility of supposing that when you consciously experience a red_{19} surface, you are aware of it, you experience it, *as red_{19}*. You, or some subpersonal part of you, may represent red_{19} with a mental predicate somewhere in the course of perceptual processing, but not in your conscious representation or experience of the shade.

How then *do* you experience the red_{19} surface? I suggest that, in the first instance, you experience it as *looking like this:* ■. (Here and throughout the essay I must ask the reader to imagine that the patch is a brilliant, central red—say, the red on the Union Jack. Constraints on publishing being what they are, the patch could not be printed in red ink.)[7] Red_{19} things look a certain way. Which way? This way, i.e. , the way this patch looks: ■. This way of describing things is common in ordinary speech. For example, if I tell you that a hat I saw at the store is ochre, you might well ask "Ochre? What does that look like?" I might reply that the hat looks, or is, brownish yellow; but better, I might show you an ochre fabric swatch and say "It looks like this" (ostending the swatch). The point is even clearer if I tell you that the hat has a certain determinate color, for instance $ochre_{32}$. As Tye notes, given the limits of human perceptual memory, my only recourse in such a case is to show you a sample of the color: it looks like this (here I ostend an $ochre_{32}$ swatch). Similarly, we say that two objects look the same or look different in color, that a pair of pants looks black in incandescent light but blue in the sun, that red looks more like orange than like yellow.

This talk of *how things look* or *what things look like* in respect of color is a familiar, ordinary way of talking, and, importantly, one that is innocent of any implications about qualia. To say that a surface looks like this: ■ is to say nothing one way or the other about awareness of an inner intrinsic quality (mental red$_{19}$).[8] So Rep can hardly object. Indeed Tye himself often talks this way. For example:

> The representationalist . . . should hold that the phenomenal character of Ted's experience of chip *M* is indeed different from that of Alice's experience of *M*. *M* looks a certain shade—call that shade *S*—to Ted and it also looks a certain shade—call it *S'*—to Alice. *M* looks the same shade as the mixture of lights to Ted, but the mixture of lights looks a different shade (*S''*) to Alice (that of another chip). (Tye 2000: 91)

My discussion here will lean heavily on this notion of the visual appearances or "looks" of things.

Perhaps, in response, Tye would try to pull apart the question of mode of presentation from the question of vehicular format. Perhaps he would grant that you experience the surface as looking like this: ■, but maintain that experiencing it that way consists in tokening a mental predicate "RED$_{19}$." Is such a view plausible? The question can be made more pressing. Doesn't it seem intuitively right to say that the surface's looking a certain way, *viz.*, like this: ■, just consists in your having a certain visual experience of it? On Rep's view, that is to say that the surface's looking like this: ■ consists in your tokening a certain mental representation of it. Note: Rep isn't claiming merely that the surface looks like this: ■ *because* you token "RED$_{19}$," or *when* you token "RED$_{19}$." He is claiming that the surface's looking like this: ■ *consists in*—just is—your tokening "RED$_{19}$." Hence the question becomes: how plausible is it to suppose that the surface's looking like this: ■ consists in your tokening a mental predicate "RED$_{19}$"? Surely not very. A mental predicate doesn't seem to be the sort of vehicle that could present a "look" or visual appearance. Predicates—public, mental, or otherwise—don't show us how things look. They aren't the right format. At the very least, we do not yet understand how a mental predicate could do this, any more than we understand how a public predicate could do it. I do not say that such a view is false—only that it does not provide the sort of intuitive explanation necessary to resolve the qualia problem.

The same defect seems to handicap any vehicle that affords awareness of its content in the manner of a word. For example, could the tokening of a mental "THIS" or "THIS SHADE" (not: "THIS: ■" or "THIS SHADE: ■") constitute something's looking like this: ■? (Imagine the Union Jack.) How could the tokening of a *word* constitute a *look*? Alternatively, could red$_{19}$ be represented in your visual experience by an element of a formal notational system like, say, a mental musical notation, or a logical calculus, or a programming language? It seems to me that we have no grasp at all—Rep has given us no grasp—on the idea that the tokening of any of these kinds of mental representation could serve to present the look or visual appearance of a red_{19} surface.[9] No doubt the trouble with these vehicle types has to do with their being "digital," "disjoint," "discrete," "differentiated," "syntactically structured," and the like, rather than "analog" or "dense" or "undifferentiated" or "presentational" or "imagistic" or "pictorial." Getting straight what these terms mean, and why mental words and notations (among others) are not plausible candidates to constitute our experiences of perceptual values like red_{19}, is an important task. I am not going to undertake it here, however. Here my goal is just to show that Rep has not yet explained how a mental word or notation could do the job he requires of it.

Perhaps Rep will say that I am demanding too much analogy between mental and public representations, and that mental words and notations and the like differ from public ones precisely in ways that enable their tokenings to constitute the looks or visual appearances of things. For example, Rep might contend that the mental word "RED_{19}" differs from the public word "red_{19}" precisely in ways that enable tokens of the former to constitute your visual experiences of red_{19} surfaces as looking like this: ■. But of course he cannot simply *assert* this; he cannot just stipulate that there is a (hitherto unknown!) kind of mental representational vehicle that has all and only the properties his theory requires—namely it constitutes red_{19}'s looking like this: ■, but does so without in any sense exemplifying the shade. Stipulating *that* would barely move from stipulating a priori that we are not aware of inner intrinsic qualities, and so would effectively beg the question against Phen. To solve the qualia problem, Rep must specify the pertinent differences between mental and public representations and explain how, in virtue of those differences, the mental ones can function in the special way he requires. Apart from such an explanation, the claim that they do function in that special way is ad hoc. We don't understand it, and we have no reason to believe it.

2

If our perceptual experience doesn't consist in tokening mental words or notations, what other kinds of representational vehicle might fill the bill for Rep? I am going to discuss several others, but I don't want to be coy. In fact I think we are hard pressed to see how a patch of red_{19} surface could be presented to us in experience, *as looking like this:* ■, by any vehicle other than some sort of image or picture—something like a mental red_{19} patch.

Could a mental red_{19} patch serve Rep's theoretical purposes? Could its tokening constitute our awareness of a red_{19} surface without requiring awareness of its intrinsic properties? To do this, of course, a mental patch could not represent in the manner of a public color picture. In his classic defense of representationalism, Gilbert Harman speculates that visual experience may involve "some sort of picture of the environment" (1990: 36), but he warns that the analogy is limited:

In the case of a painting Eloise can be aware of those features of the painting that are responsible for its being a painting of a unicorn. That is, she can turn her attention to the pattern of the paint on the canvas by virtue of which the painting represents a unicorn. But in the case of her visual experience of a tree, I want to say that she is not aware of, as it were, the mental paint by virtue of which her experience is an experience of seeing a tree. She is aware only of the intentional or relational features of her experience, not of its intrinsic nonintentional features. (Ibid.: 39)

But now how is Eloise supposed to do this? Apart from some intuitively adequate explanation of how one can be aware of the determinate color content of a picture without being aware of the picture's intrinsic features, we do not yet understand how Eloise could be aware only of intentional features of her experience. When Harman writes "I want to say . . . ," he is stipulating, not explaining.

It is worth noting that some of Harman's examples appear to undercut his own view. For example, he writes that it is "very important to distinguish between the properties of a represented object and the properties of a representation of that object. Clearly, these properties can be very different. The unicorn is pictured as having four legs and a single horn. The painting of the unicorn does not have four legs and a single horn. The painting is flat and covered with paint. The unicorn is not pictured as flat or covered with paint" (ibid.: 35). Well, the painting may not have legs, but it *is* white; and the unicorn may not be pictured as flat, but it *is* pictured as partly horn-shaped. What seems to matter is not whether the painting has legs or a horn but whether, like the unicorn, it has parts that are visibly leg-shaped or horn-shaped. And it does. Similarly, a typical painting of a red_{19} apple is painted in red_{19} paint, and it looks red_{19}.

Of course, there are more kinds of pictures than ordinary color pictures. Might a mental picture of red_{19} afford awareness of the shade in the manner of some other kind of picture—one that doesn't exemplify red_{19}?

Naturally I cannot canvass every kind of pictorial vehicle Rep might try, but I want to examine two sorts of pictures that seem to me indicative.

Consider a pointillist still life of ripe apples, whose surface appears red_{19} from a distance of five or six feet, but which close examination reveals to be a mass of tiny specks of $black_3$ and $yellow_8$. As is familiar to philosophers of art, such a case suggests that at least some pictures represent what they represent not by exemplifying it but (roughly) by giving rise to a visual experience relevantly similar to the experience that would be brought about by looking at it.[10] In particular, the pointillist still life affords awareness of the red_{19} of the apples insofar as looking at the painting gives rise to a color experience relevantly similar to the color experience that would be brought about by looking at red_{19} apples.[11]

Could a mental picture of red_{19} afford awareness of the shade in a manner analogous to that of the pointillist painting? I don't think so; for even if the still life does not exemplify what it represents, still the painting—the vehicle itself—is an object of awareness.[12] The "intrinsically" $black_3$ and $yellow_8$ canvas represents the red_{19} of the apples by itself looking like this: ■. To put the point another way, your being aware of the painting's determinate color content, namely, red_{19}, essentially involves (consists in?) the painting's looking to you the way red_{19} things look. Hence Rep's purposes would not be served by supposing that your mental picture of red_{19} represents the shade in analogous fashion.

Alternatively, perhaps your mental picture represents in the manner of a "nonrealistic" analog vehicle. For example, in a famous passage from *Languages of Art*, Nelson Goodman writes that

whether a denoting symbol is [a picture] depends not upon whether it resembles what it denotes but upon its own relationships to other symbols in a given scheme. A scheme is [pictorial] only insofar as it is dense; and a symbol is a [picture] only if it belongs to a scheme dense throughout or to a dense part of a partially dense scheme. . . . [In a picture,] every difference in every pictorial respect makes a difference [to what is represented]. (1968: 226–227)

Vastly simplified, Goodman's view is that a picture represents what it represents by varying systematically and continuously with it, so that any difference in the picture signifies a corresponding difference in the thing represented. For example, given the convention that shades of red are to be represented by a scheme of black lines on a canvas, the shades are *pictured* by the lines insofar as any relevant difference in the lines represents a corresponding difference in the shades. Suppose length of line represents redness of shade—the longer the line, the redder the shade. Then any difference in length represents a difference in redness. As Goodman might put it, variation in length is an *analog* of variation in redness.

I think Goodman is wrong about pictures, but we needn't get into that issue here. Right or wrong, he introduces a possibility Rep will want to consider, namely, that your experience represents determinate colors with analog but apparently non-exemplifying mental vehicles modeled on (e.g.) the scheme of lines just described. Would such vehicles serve Rep's purpose? Again, I don't think so. For one thing, we might expect to see some reaction-time differences: maybe perceptual integration for shades represented by relatively longer lines should take longer than perceptual integration for shades represented by relatively shorter lines, so that (implausibly) seeing a nearly pure red should take longer than seeing, say, an orangey red.

But set the latter problem aside, and consider again the public scheme of lines on a canvas as described above. What do those lines strongly represent? Because of the perceptual memory limitations mentioned earlier, the public lines could not in fact afford you awareness of their determinate color contents, that is, awareness of the shades they (weakly) represent. Apart from consulting a chart showing the relevant length-shade correlations, you could not be aware of the specific shade represented by a given line. Even supposing, implausibly, that you could learn to recognize by eye, say, fifteen different lengths of lines, you still wouldn't be able to remember the determinate shades they represent; consequently you could not learn the length–shade correlations needed for awareness of the shade represented by a given line. If that's right, then the public scheme of lines could not strongly represent shades of red. Whatever content you could be aware of in the lines is impoverished compared to the content you could be aware of in (e.g.) an ordinary color picture of the same shades of red. Thus Rep's purposes would not be well served by supposing that your mental vehicles for determinate shades represent them in the manner of a scheme of lines.

We can say more. What content *could* you be made aware of by the public scheme of lines? As far as I can see, the lines do strongly represent the pattern of variation in the shades: you could be made aware that one shade is just *this* much less red than another, that a certain series of shades becomes steadily redder at just *this* rate of change, and so on. When I say "just this much less red" and "just this rate of change," I mean "this determinate amount less red" or "this determinate rate of change." In other words, the latter contents, like the shades of color in a public picture, are *determinate* contents of the scheme of lines: they are the finest-grained contents, the finest-grained differences, we can discriminate. (Recall that every difference in the lengths of the lines signifies a corresponding difference in the redness of the shades represented.) And my present point is that these contents, the contents of which you could be aware in the lines, are *exemplified* by them: the lines represent the pattern of variation in the shades by themselves exemplifying that pattern.[13] Thus your awareness of the pattern of variation of the shades would consist in awareness of the analogous pattern in the line lengths. Like ordinary color pictures, the lines exemplify what they strongly represent; the pattern of variation in the line lengths *pictures* the pattern of variation in the shades. Hence your awareness of their content would require awareness of their intrinsic properties.[14]

As I said before, there are various kinds of pictures to which Rep might appeal in defending his view, and a decisive case against him will require examination of them all. Furthermore, the philosophical literature contains many analyses of pictorial representation, one or more of which might suit Rep's purposes better than the analysis proposed here in terms of a vehicle's exemplification of what it strongly represents.[15] However, I think our discussion of ordinary color pictures, the pointillist canvas, and the scheme of lines provides a good indication of the sorts of challenges Rep is likely to face. So far, he has not explained, in the sense of enabling us to understand, how your awareness of the determinate color content of an experiential representation could proceed without awareness of its intrinsic features.

In sum, Rep appears to need a mental vehicle that works like a picture in presenting how red_{19} looks, but like a predicate (or other word or notation) in representing the shade without exemplifying it. Can there be such a vehicle? A word-picture? A description-depiction? I don't know. (We have no examples to go by.) What I do know is that, at present, we have no idea how such a vehicle would work.

3

I will conclude by considering some potential responses on Rep's behalf.

(1) One might suppose that Rep is not obliged to explain how you can be aware of outer red without being aware of inner red, since *by its nature* a mental representation, unlike a public one, does not require awareness of its intrinsic features for awareness of its content.[16] Consider, such a respondent might say, that in order to be aware of the content of a public

word, you must do at least two things: you must identify the vehicle, that is, identify which word it is, and you must associate the vehicle with the right content. Call these two tasks together, "figuring out" the word. For example, when you hear or read the public word "dog" you must somehow identify it and associate it with the right content. And doing that requires awareness of its intrinsic features (e.g., how it looks or sounds, how many letters it has). However, there would seem to be no analogous sense in which you must figure out your mental word "DOG," if such there be, when you see or think about a dog. You don't need to identify your own mental representations or figure out what they mean; you just *have* them. Hence you don't need to be aware of any of their intrinsic features.

The thought that mental vehicles don't need to be figured out is surely right; when you token your mental representation of red_{19} you don't need to identify it or associate it with the right perceptual content. Nevertheless, you do need to be *aware* of its content. And Phen's objection to Rep concerns the nature of that awareness. She claims that Rep has not explained how you can be aware of the content of your mental representation of red_{19} without being aware of its intrinsic quality.

(2) At least one representationalist has replied (in conversation) that there *could be* a representation of the sort Rep's view requires; and that is all Rep needs to say. Presumably the objector means that it is psychologically possible that there be a mental vehicle that strongly represents red_{19} without exemplifying it; otherwise his reply is irrelevant to the qualia problem. The qualia problem is a problem about actual, real-time perceptual experience. Even thus construed, however, the reply is a nonstarter. For unless and until Rep supplies an explanation of the sort we have been asking for, we can't tell whether such a representation *is* psychologically possible. Indeed, for reasons I mentioned at the end of section 2, we can't even tell whether the requisite sort of "word-picture" is metaphysically possible.

(3) Perhaps Rep will say that the tokening of a mental picture of red_{19} is just a matter of, say, having certain cells activated in a two-dimensional matrix in your visual buffer,[17] so that no awareness of inner red_{19} need be involved. While this "design level" account of mental picturing may be true as far as it goes, it is couched in the wrong terms for resolving the qualia problem. In particular, it does nothing to show how awareness of the content of a mental picture proceeds without awareness of its intrinsic properties. To put the point another way, Rep has not shown how awareness of the content of the relevant activation pattern could proceed without awareness of the pattern's intrinsic phenomenal properties.

Again, Rep cannot simply *assert* that a mental picture "doesn't work that way"—that unlike a public picture or other analog symbol, a mental picture does not require awareness of its intrinsic features for awareness of its content. If a mental picture "doesn't work that way," then how exactly does it work? Apart from an (intuitively acceptable) explanation of how a mental picture strongly represents without requiring awareness of its intrinsic features, such an assertion by Rep amounts to the ad hoc introduction of a new kind of vehicle that does all and only what his theory requires.

(4) Maybe Rep will insist that although your mental representation of red_{19} in some sense resembles or bears an analog relationship to red_{19}, it does not represent the shade *by* resembling it.[18] His idea would be that your representation is to be understood on the model of the word "red_{19}" where it happens to be printed in red_{19} ink. Like the $redness_{19}$ of the linguistic vehicle, the $redness_{19}$ of your mental vehicle is representationally idle; hence in neither case need awareness of content involve awareness of properties intrinsic to the vehicle. The trouble with this reply is that if the $redness_{19}$ of your mental vehicle is representationally idle, then we are left, as in the case of a mental predicate, with no account of how the tokening of the vehicle could constitute the visual appearance or look of the surface.

(5) Finally, at least one representationalist has responded that being aware of red_{19} is just a matter of *having* or *tokening* a mental picture (or other analog representation) of red_{19}, and need involve no awareness of intrinsic features of the picture. I hope it is clear by now that such a response simply begs the question. Phen grants from the start that you have or token a mental representation (word, picture, or otherwise) of red_{19}. So in effect, this response simply asserts that awareness of red_{19} can be had without awareness of intrinsic features of the mental picture that one has or tokens. That is just what Phen questions, and what Rep has not yet explained.

Notes

1. A mental representation that satisfies certain other conditions, of course; I am simplifying enormously. Michael Tye elaborates:

Phenomenal content . . . is content that is appropriately poised for use by the cognitive system, content that is abstract and nonconceptual. I call this the PANIC theory of phenomenal character: phenomenal character is one and the same as Poised Abstract Nonconceptual Intentional Content. (1995: 137)

To undergo a state with a certain felt or phenomenal quality is to be the subject of a state that represents a certain external quality (by being appropriately causally connected with it in optimal conditions) and that is poised for use in the formation of beliefs and/or desires. (Ibid.: 162–163)

2. On the other hand, Phen is not entitled to run an endless open question argument against Rep ("Yes, but have you captured the qualia?"). Just how much Rep is obliged to do to make Phen happy, just how much she can legitimately demand in the way of intuitive satisfaction, is itself a disputed matter. The main point of this essay will be that Phen is entitled to, but has not received, an explanation of how we can be aware of outer red without being aware of inner red.

3. For some other criticisms of representationalism, see, e.g., Block 1998 and 2003, Pautz 2006, Macpherson 2005.

4. See, e.g., Tye 1995: 122–123. He has also made this claim in personal correspondence.

5. It's worth emphasizing that in mind–brain theory construction, you don't get representational formats for free. You need evidence to justify proposing that a given vehicle is (e.g.) "propositional" or imagistic or maplike, etc. This is of course a central tenet of functionalism, and it protects functional theories from a charge of triviality.

6. I first made this point in Raffman 1995. Tye usually speaks of hues, but I will use the more ordinary terms "color" and "shade." Strictly speaking, hue is the chromatic dimension of the three-dimensional property of color, but I will ignore that technical notion here.

7. Although I finally decided to rely on the reader's imagination, I am much indebted to Edmond Wright for his efforts to secure a red patch, and for later providing me with a number of references in the literature to black qualia or phenomenal characters. See, e.g., Locke (*Essay*, II, viii, 2), W. Russell Brain (*Mind, Perception, and Science* [Oxford: Blackwell, 1951: 10]), and C. L. Hardin (*Color for Philosophers: Unweaving the Rainbow* [Indianapolis: Hackett, 1986: 24]). See also Wright's and Brown's contributions to this volume.

8. I say more about "looks" in Raffman 2005.

9. Here, for the sake of argument, is a way to think about the present question that materialists will deem regressive. Red_{19} objects present a certain visual appearance or "look" in respect of color. When looked at they look like this: ■. This visual appearance is not identical to any feature of the surface of the object. Rather, it is constructed by the mind–brain in response to certain causal interactions with the surface and the light. The situation may reasonably be described as one in which the viewer's mind–brain (visual system) presents the viewer (conscious awareness) with this appearance. And it is utterly mysterious how any verbal representation could play such a presenting role.

10. See, e.g., Schier 1986.

11. One might argue that inasmuch as the canvas looks red_{19} to normal observers under at least some normal conditions, it does exemplify red_{19}, at least under those conditions. I set this idea aside here.

12. Can we say that the painting *appears* to exemplify what it represents? I don't know the answer.

13. Even Goodman must acknowledge this "resemblance" between lines and shades, for it is surely the source of whatever plausibility accrues to the idea that the former could picture the latter.

14. Joe Levine has suggested to me that since length, unlike color, is not a phenomenal property of an (external) object, an awareness of inner line lengths would be less problematic for Rep, i.e., less likely to generate the qualia problem, than an awareness of inner colors. Insofar as I understand this thought it seems to me mistaken; but the mistake shows the need for a clarification. Strictly speaking, the (public) lines strongly represent variation in shade by way of analogous variation in their apparent or phenomenal lengths. Just as small differences in wavelength are indiscriminable, so are small differences in length; and only discriminable differences in wavelength or line length, i.e., phenomenal differences, differences of which we can be aware, can represent anything in the strong sense of "represent." I said above that "any difference in length (of the public lines) represents a difference in redness." Given the distinction between weak and strong senses of "represent," I should say instead that where strong representation is concerned, any discriminable or phenomenal difference in length represents a difference in redness. Hence awareness of variation in shade consists in awareness of variation in phenomenal length. Awareness of mental line lengths can then be understood on this model, and seems on a par with awareness of mental colors.

15. See, e.g., Wollheim 1980, Schier 1986, Peacocke 1987, Walton 1990, Hopkins 1995.

16. Levine suggested this line of reply to me (personal correspondence).

17. Cf., e.g., Tye 1995: 138–140.

18. David Papineau and Michael Tye have suggested such a reply (in conversation).

References

Block, N. 1998. Is experience just representing? *Philosophy and Phenomenological Research* 58: 663–670.

Block, N. 2003. Mental paint. In *Reflections and Replies: Essays on the Philosophy of Tyler Burge*, ed. M. Hahn and B. Ramberg, 165–200. Cambridge, Mass.: MIT Press/A Bradford Book.

Brain, W. Russell. 1951. *Mind, Perception, and Science.* Oxford: Blackwell.

Goodman, N. 1968. *Languages of Art.* Indianapolis, Ind.: Bobbs-Merrill.

Hardin, C. L. 1986. *Color for Philosophers: Unweaving the Rainbow.* Indianapolis, Ind.: Hackett.

Harman, G. 1990. The intrinsic quality of experience. In *Philosophical Perspectives,* vol. 4: *Action Theory and Philosophy of Mind,* ed. J. Tomberlin, 31–52. Atascadero, Calif.: Ridgeview.

Hopkins, R. 1995. Explaining depiction. *Philosophical Review* 104, 3: 425–455.

Macpherson, F. 2005. Colour inversion problems for representationalism. *Philosophy and Phenomenological Research* 70, 1: 127–152.

Pautz, A. 2006. Sensory awareness is not a wide physical relation: an empirical argument against externalist intentionalism. *Noûs* 40, 2: 205–240.

Peacocke, C. 1987. Depiction. *Philosophical Review* 96, 3: 383–410.

Raffman, D. 1995. On the persistence of phenomenology. In *Conscious Experience,* ed. T. Metzinger, 293–308. Paderborn: Schöningh Verlag.

Raffman, D. 2005. Even zombies can be surprised: Reply to Graham and Horgan. *Philosophical Studies* 122: 189–202.

Schier, F. 1986. *Deeper Into Pictures.* Cambridge: Cambridge University Press.

Tye, M. 1995. *Ten Problems of Consciousness.* Cambridge, Mass.: MIT Press/A Bradford Book.

Tye, M. 2000. *Consciousness, Color, and Content.* Cambridge, Mass.: MIT Press/A Bradford Book.

Walton, K. 1990. *Mimesis as Make-Believe.* Cambridge, Mass.: Harvard University Press.

Wollheim, R. 1980. *Painting as an Art.* New York: Cambridge University Press.

19 Why Transparency Is Unethical

Edmond Wright

A fool sees not the same tree that the wise man sees.
—William Blake

1 Introduction

The argument here will centrally constitute an ethical criticism of the transparency thesis. If this seems surprising, one needs reminding that there is no doubt that profound ethical issues underlie the debate. Diagnosis of the malady of "qualiaphilia" finds as symptoms, (i) its much-touted challenge to common sense, the Berkeleian eccentricity betrayed by apparently claiming that human access to the real is indirect. For this, it is considered by some that Dr. Johnson's kicking of the stone still produces cures. More seriously, however, (ii) qualiaphiles, if it is the case that within their theory contact with the real is considered to be out of reach, are presumed therefore to be infected by association with relativism and solipsism. It puts them in the same ward with postmodernists and other such skeptics in the modern scene. Both the righteously minded among philosophers and the tough-minded among physicalists are tempted to reject the proposal out of hand, the former for its rendering eternal verities dubious, particularly truth and objectivity, and the latter for its determinedly trying to smuggle occult entities into science. John McDowell, as an example of the former, says that anyone who argues for sensing being a "bare presence," that is, brute evidence of the real, intruding between our recognition of things and persons, is threatening "to dislodge our grip on the requirement that empirical thinking be under constraint from the world itself" (McDowell 1994: 42); and, of the latter, Daniel Dennett views his opponents as "crowds of theorists transfixed by an illusion" (Dennett 1991: 39).

There is also a tendency to make the facile equation of sense-datum theory with qualia theory, so that a mere mention of objections to the former is taken to be a sufficient dismissal of the latter; see, for example, the stance of Michael Tye, who dismisses sense-datum theory, and by implication indirect realism generally, "for a host of familiar reasons"—which he does not specify, and later, when he does mention actual objections, he unprofessionally takes for granted that no refutations of the speckled-hen and privacy objections have ever been attempted (Tye 2000: 45–46, 112; for refutations see, e.g., Fitzgerald 1977: 107; Perkins 1983: 302–304; Wright 1983: 71–72; Robinson 1994: 91–118). John McDowell's favored way with indirect realism is to stress its implausibility, finding the whole notion "unintelligible" and "mysterious," sometimes arguing as if its being a mystery to him were sufficient proof of its non-existence. To take an example—"we cannot make sense of thought's bearing on the world in terms of an interaction between spontaneity and receptivity" (McDowell 1994: 139); it is fair to ask who are the "we" who cannot make sense of it.

2 "Differential Correlation"

I am going to begin the argument with a return to one of the objections: the oldest—indeed, the most antiquated—since it was first mooted by Hermann Lotze (Lotze 1884: 492–493) is that of the impossibility-of-pictures-in-the-brain (through its resulting in a vicious regress). More than 123 years later this is still confidently paraded as comically ruining the indirect realist case: witness Kevin O'Regan and Alva Noë among the most recent (O'Regan and Noë 2001: sect. 6, vii): they are under the impression that "misguided" qualiaphiles are still arguing for "red neurons in the brain."[1] One would assume from their confidence that they are convinced that this objection sets down both sense-datum theory and qualia theory in the chronicle of philosophical defeats. However, the battlefield of the debate is not cleared of their enemies, not even of all proponents of sense-datum theory, the reason being that *not all sense-datum theorists did argue that there was a pictorial reproduction of external colour and shape in the brain.* Because of this, Ned Block ought not to have adopted Gilbert Harman's term "mental paint." Although intended as a coat-trailing gesture, it was still misleading (Harman 1990: 39; Block 2003: 8).

Roy Wood Sellars, the father of Wilfrid Sellars, held the view that the only resemblance between what arrived at the sensory organs and what appeared in the brain was that of a "differential correlation" (R. W. Sellars 1922: 37). This is not a difficult notion: such a differential correlation is a matter of *proportional variations matching across two utterly dissimilar processes.* Consider the soundtrack down the side of a cinema-film: the variations in the width of this white strip match the sounds the audience hears, but it is obvious that there is no other resemblance.

Within qualia theory, to use vision as illustrative, the case is the same with the input to the eyes and the phenomenal realization in the brain. As Stephen Palmer recently described it, there is a "structural isomorphism" between input and phenomenon (Palmer 1999). This implies that there is no similarity between input and phenomenon other than causally covarying relations (to frequency, intensity, spatial distributions, etc.), Sellars père's "differential correlations." There is therefore no further claim whatsoever that there is a *pictorial* similarity between the input to the eyes and the phenomenal response, for that is ruled out. What is in the brain is not a picture even though it is a phenomenon, for visual phenomena are *not pictures*. Colors, stereoscopic depth, intensities, and distributions featured within that "depth" bear only causally traceable covariation to what caused them. Furthermore, that covariation is not direct: James J. Gibson and others have told us how there is a great deal of involuntary modification of the input to produce what have—up to now—resulted in evolutionary advantages (e.g., edge-enhancement, night vision, movement detection, etc.; Gibson 1968; Marr 1982). Both Descartes and Locke thought that the inner "sign" might have no resemblance to light (Meyering 1989: 82; Locke, *Essay*, II, viii, 7; see also Alroy 1995).

Here it can be deduced that there cannot be a pictorial similarity between input and phenomenon for an associated reason: within the terms of the theory, *actual pictures in the real are not colored*, nor are neurons. Neither do three-dimensional pictures and stereo-holograms have sensed depth (since only a visual system of two eyes together with neural structures in a brain can bring such a sense of depth into existence).

So the real is both colorless and devoid of *stereoscopic* depth, even though we operate indirectly with correlations in the distributions of color and the sensed "depth." It is surprising that real space does not possess that sense of depth we experience with our two eyes (or with our body image or our two ears). In any case, sensed stereoscopic depth disappears with distance because the difference in perspective angle of the two eyes on which the stereoscopic-depth experience depends is not great enough to work over miles. Ask yourself, too, what it is a one-eyed man loses, for he still has some indirect access to real space.

We also can experience stereoscopic depth without what Tye would call veridical input. I possess a set of children's books from the 1920s (the "Joy Street" books) and there is a repeating pattern on their covers. If I do the kind of controlled squint Helmholtz encourages us to practice (Helmholtz

1901: 249) when I am looking at these books so that the pattern moves to refix itself over its repetition (that is, the right eye's field and the left eye's field move to being one step out in the pattern of their normal match), a whole series of depth irregularities appears over the cover of the book, lumps and hollows that have resulted from the fact that the repeats in the pattern were not exactly the same. That I can thus learn this veridical fact of inaccuracy in the repeats of the pattern from inspecting what Tye would call an illusion is already *an empirical disproof of transparency*: from what appears to be *one* item in my visual field I can thus learn about *two* items. Helmholtz pointed this out over a hundred years ago with regard to the police practice in his time of placing in a stereoscope suspect banknotes side by side with genuine ones; the forgeries showed up because of the stereoscopic distortions (Helmholtz 1901: 252). So I can "transparently" look at *one* "object" and find out about *two*, an impossibility in Tye's theory.

So, *pace* O'Regan and Noë, red does exist in the brain, but neither do we need eyes to experience it, nor are the neurons red to normal sight since the real is colorless. Red is an experience going on inside them and *it does not characterize a surface there*. So we can happily agree with Norton Nelkin without inconsistency that "phenomena are not like photographs" (Nelkin 1996: 39).

At this point someone who recalls the earlier pro-qualia volume might protest that this dismissal of O'Regan and Noë's claim is exactly the same as what was said about Daniel Dennett and there being no yellow and black in the brain (Wright 1993b: 178–179). Why then am I repeating it? Because none of our opponents seems to have regarded the argument as worth refuting, which I regard as a measure of their failure to comprehend what is being argued for. Dennett is still locked onto the notion of qualiaphiles arguing for pictures in the brain (Dennett 2006: 66). Gilbert Ryle, like Dennett, convinced of the vicious regress of spectators in the endless array of "Cartesian Theaters" could not get his head round Hobbes's idea that neither was color seen with eyes (but directly experienced), nor are those portions of the brain that produce the experience of color themselves externally colored, as color is not a quality of surfaces at all: "But you will say, by what sense shall we take notice of sense? I answer, by sense itself" (Hobbes 1839: 389). Ryle protested that "in effect it explained the having of sensations as the *not* having of sensations" (Ryle 1949: 215). The argument is still being produced as conclusive by Mohan Matthen (Matthen 2005: 329). However, A. J. Ayer in a rejoinder correctly identified this objection as "very weak" as it betrayed an inability to detach the notion of eyes, indeed any sensory organ, from the neural sensory experience (Ayer 1957: 107). Eyes respond to a limited set of *colorless* light-waves, not to *neural* color, and, as Dennett himself correctly said in the quotation above, there are no light-waves in the brain—and, as he *incorrectly* said, it is "pitch-black" in the skull (Dennett 1991: 28; Dennett, by the same token, shows himself ignorant of the fact that blackness is itself a positive sensory phenomenon [see Locke, *Essay*, II, viii, 2]). In addition, the phenomenon as a real display can show dreams, mental imagery, afterimages, phosphenes, hallucinations, the "fortification" zigzags of migraine sufferers—just as a TV screen can show videos, cartoons, interference patterns, as well as live shows, *without ceasing to exist* (this is a point Helmholtz was at pains to make about visual experience [Helmholtz 1964: 164]).

It is worth adding at this point that Dennett and his allies can no longer reject the analogy of a TV screen for the neural display because no pictorial resemblance is being claimed, merely a neural matrix or raster (useless to eyes) that responds with differential correlations to the input. Furthermore, as I argued some time ago (Wright 1981), a phosphene induced by an electrical probe in the brain can be excited by all kinds of causes in the form of differential correlations, for example, by its being connected to a microphone, or even a pressure-pad under a mat at a door, so that the one experiencing it can reliably tell us when someone is waiting at the door—which would indeed be a bizarre example of "transparency"! But one need not go in for brain probes to obtain the same result: just use a Smythies TV-Hood.[2]

3   The Non-epistemic Nature of the Differential Correlations

If anyone is still unhappy with the television analogy, he or she should consider carefully how the differential correlation argument suitably limits the "ground" of the metaphor, as I. A. Richards would call it (Richards 1936: 96ff.). All that is being claimed is an indirect causal path (that allows for all kinds of automatic predisplay adjustments, just as the TV allows for contrast, color, and brightness settings) transmitting differential correlations between camera/eye and screen/inner display—but there is *neither a pictorial resemblance nor any necessity for inner eyes to be looking at an inner screen*. The metaphor is trimmed of these objectionable aspects. If opponents still try to protest without further argument, they are either betraying ignorance or merely blustering.

A second similarity lies in the following consideration. An electronics engineer could, if pressed, give us a determinate account of the changes in the states of the phosphor cells on the TV screen. Note that this would be a precise punctiform list of the condition of the screen, but it would make no reference whatever to "what" we perceived on it. Describing the screen by the entities one sees thereon and by the state of the phosphor cells are obviously on different empirical levels. The screen is thus not in the least "ineffable" at this "field-determinate" level, though it may be, as we shall see in the next paragraph, at the "object-determinate" level. Hence, it cannot be ruled out that the display in the brain or at least a small part of it might one day yield to a precise punctiform description by a neurophysiologist, so there is nothing necessarily ineffable about it. Dennett uses a supposed ineffability as a device to prove an inner display impossible (Dennett 1991: 382–383). Our visual experience, furthermore, is not of the nature of a punctiform list, as it is for the robots Dennett describes (Dennett 1998: 141–152), but of a *field* from which we choose at the behest of our motivation, even when we choose for fun, as in seeing faces in the fire. How could you—or a robot—detect the ambiguity *needful for fun* in a such a list?

There is also a third permissible similarity between a TV screen and the inner display. If a TV screen was upside down in a darkened room and only a portion of it was visible, and you did not know that it was a TV screen, you would not be able to identify, as we say, "what" was on it. It might be showing a night-vision scene, one using an infrared camera, in which only the distribution of heat of was being tracked in green; it might be merely interference on the screen, or some portion of a surreal advertisement, or a screen-saver, or a cartoon. The same is true of our sensory experience: whatever someone better apprised of the context might say, the field itself in its present immediacy contains no clues to what we would call the objective causes. This reveals that it is no more than bare evidence, the "bare presence" which McDowell rejects, requiring either the pain–pleasure regime to enforce a sorting, or the memory of earlier such sortings to provide contextual clues to interpretation, or an updating via the provision of them from someone else. What has been called "the autonomy thesis," the radical non-epistemicity of all sensing at all times, is thus far from implausible (*pace* José Luis Bermudez 1995).

Those who propose a "sensorimotor" theory of perception forget, as Piaget, the first user of the term, did not, that a regime over a period of time of the adjustment of *motivated* choices is needed (O'Regan and Noë 2001; Piaget 1955). A child does not learn of the dangers of touching a hot radiator at the first unpleasant encounter: perhaps at the first pain she might only remember with fear all ribbed surfaces; subsequent reminders will refine that judgment. So the sensory experience considered by itself, detached from all motivated memory interpretation, is devoid of meaning, a fortiori, of any given indication of what it originated from, hence "non-epistemic." This is exactly what gives us the power to move our percepts flexibly over the field, the most important *evolutionary* advantage that qualia bestow, allowing "the object" to be a selection that remains alterable, a selection from the real whether useful or inadequate. It is evolutionary in two senses: (1) in providing a species advantage, *because of* (2), its being evolutionary in the structure of developmental process it supplies.

Moreover, the field is entirely involuntary, and as brute as what causes it, as Locke insisted (*Essay*, II, ii, 2). "The eye it cannot choose but see" (William Wordsworth, "Expostulation and Reply," line 17). One can therefore say that, sensations, strictly speaking, are *not mental*. Qualia are therefore *physical*, a strange form of the physical no doubt, but one that can neither be denied scientific investigation nor consigned to a dualist mental substance. We know that the visual field can exist apart from perception as in the case of agnosics, those who, as a result of brain injury, have lost the power to select from what they "see" perfectly well. This is the view of Aquinas, that the senses in themselves were not part of the mind: "sense is a power to undergo, not to initiate change" (Kenny 1993: 34). I would add that we cannot "initiate change" unless we *mind*—I prefer it as a verb (on the vital element of motivation in perception, see McDougall 1911: 81–159). It is even not impossible that some unhappy mutation could be born without any neural connections between the motivation module, the sensory fields, and the memory: such a creature would be quite unable to recognize anything, would not be conscious, but the sensing could still be of high vividness. Qualia being nonmental is a significant fact leading to the reasonable hunch that, in the future, they could be investigated by science. One can therefore qualify Franz Brentano's claim that the mark of the mental is intentionality, "direction upon an object" (Brentano 1973, 77–100). By this analysis, there can be no intentionality, indeed, no consciousness, until the motivation module (initially pain and pleasure) is operating upon the sensory fields to place memories marked with fear or desire into memory. It is the "directing upon" that is critical, and, since more than one observer is involved, what "the" object is cannot be regarded as given (on this see below, pp. 350–352). The motivation module, its pains and pleasures, however vivid, also would not be mental, not conscious, without connection to the sensory fields and memory. Using Ned Block's terms, one could say that one cannot have "access-consciousness" without "phenomenal consciousness" (Block 1995).

We can, of course, open and close our eyes, choose the direction of our glance, and so on, but that does not make visual awareness cease. For example, instead of there being "a blank" when we close our eyes as O'Regan and Noë unscientifically say (O'Regan and Noë 2001: 944), we experience (i) the effect of light through the eyelids; (ii) some after-images (which may not be identified—as they were not by O'Regan and Noë, even though, as Helmholtz noted a hundred years ago they overlay all our seeing all the time); and, (iii) if one is a good visile, as Daniel Dennett is plainly not, perhaps the mental image of a pretty girl turning around and saying, visually and aurally, "I love you!"—and, some people, as well, can imagine her hand in theirs as well as smell her perfume.

Mental imagery is unusual in being sometimes voluntary, sometimes not, but, even with the voluntary sequences, there remains the non-epistemic base. A proof of this can be found in the aural imagery of some expert musicians, who can, like Mozart, hear whole pieces in full orchestration.[3] A common experience of theirs is to discover in a well-known piece aspects they had not noticed before, such as a modulation from key to key they had not identified, perhaps because it was triggered by an instrument they had not singled out before from the *iconic* evidence. If they could not do this, they would certainly not be able to compose from their mental imagery, which, in a work being newly composed, would be entirely unfamiliar to them. I myself can hear entirely new orchestrated music in my head, sometimes quite involuntarily, but, not being musically trained, I cannot recognize the keys, harmonies, or rhythms in order to write the music down—which, as you can imagine, is peculiarly frustrating. The non-epistemic precedes the epistemic.

Another way of putting it is to say that to sense is not to know. Roy Wood Sellars's remark that "Being is one thing: knowledge is quite another sort of thing" (Sellars 1919: 407) applies to our sensory experiences as it does to all other things referred to by science. Gerald Edelman and Giulio Tononi have pointed out that "nobody expects that a scientific description of a hurricane will *be* or *cause* a hurricane. Why, then, should we not apply exactly the same standards to consciousness?" (Edelman and Tononi 2000: 127). Knowledge of sensing does not constitute it. It just so happens that we ourselves are what is referred to in the consciousness case, and not in the hurricane case, nor in the case of any other scientific referent (W. S. Robinson [2004: 187–188] makes the same point). To speak of a "phenomenal concept" does not imply that phenomena are basically conceptual. Even the phenomena taken up into concepts are not wholly defined by them.

Another empirical proof, completely ignored by those for whom all vision is of recognizable entities, is that hallucinations *need not be of objects at all*. Hypnagogic imagery, experienced by many as they fall asleep, can be as random as a screen-saver (and may even have a similar purpose). I commonly experience such phantasmagoric and chaotic imagery before falling asleep; it is often changing so rapidly that my perceptual system is defeated and I cannot even play at finding "faces-in-the-fire." It changes as strangely as the current Citroen advertisement for their C4 car, in which a lightbulb is slowly but smoothly transformed into the car: one cannot identify the intervening stages as any*thing*. Qualiaphobes always confine themselves to discussing *objectified* hallucinations, such as Macbeth's dagger, but their approach, being insufficiently general in ignoring the non-objectified ones, skews the argument in favor of objective transparency from the start (as typical, see Smart 1959; Dilman 1967; Evans 1982: 200; Dennett 1986 [1969]: 136ff; Tye 1995: 107).[4]

There have been attempts recently to use the phenomenon of "change-blindness" to create an argument that qualia, being "incorrigible," can exist out of notice (Dennett 2006: 82–88). However, the present argument *for* qualia makes no claim for "incorrigibility" since the fields, as non-epistemic, can exist without any "correction" being performed. As a youth I used, in a very simple way, to defeat the local newspaper's "Find the Difference" competition (they printed two photographs side by side and asked us to discover the differences). I used to squint so that the two photographs were superimposed on each other: the differences showed up clearly as *flickering regions*. When I squint the "Joy Street" book-cover pattern into false superimposition, the same phenomenon occurs, in that in one place by a cross there is a flickering dot. This epistemically alerted me to the fact that the pattern did not match in this respect—and, hey presto!—there was a small ink blot on the cross to the right but not on the one to the left. I might ask who else doing such a squint would be aware of that flickering dot's *epistemic* import—not in the least "transparent"! The non-epistemic precedes the epistemic.

Long before Paul Boghossian and David Velleman (1989), and Michael Tye (2000: 79–83), I, though unmentioned by them, was the first to draw attention to the blurry image problem and to suggest a solution (Wright 1975: 278). I pointed out that "ineffability" did not apply to the matrix of the display itself, the field-determinate level, but only to the object-determinate level where we operate together in trying to arrive at the best current mutual interpretation. As I put it, whether what is being seen is a cloud of steam perfectly in focus or a snowball seen through misted spectacles is a decision that can only be made with contextual memory-clues to assist us; the bare evidence is virtually the same in both cases.

So, faced with bare evidence, we are, like all animals, forced by our motivational system to place our guesses at relevance into memory and tab them there with fear or desire, which are motivations for future action— are *all* ribbed things dangerously hot and thus to be avoided? As human beings, of course, we have the advantage of language to allow us, we hope, to transfer our interpretations to others to save them having to suffer unnecessary deprivations and pains, and having to pursue satisfactions only by the hit-and-miss procedure raw nature has provided us with at the animal level. The non-epistemic allows us this evolutionary flexibility in perception: Locke's "white paper" never goes away (Locke, *Essay*, II, I, 2). One could say that his metaphor misled him for he believed that "writing" on it removed its "blankness"—a closer analogy than "white paper" would be one of those child's toys with a gray screen under clear plastic on which one can draw endlessly. And language, therefore, is all about the conveying of transformations, in the hope that this will speed up the plodding progress of our animal sensorimotor system. Language, thus, inevitably forms the topic of the next stage of the argument.

4   The Idealization of Reciprocity

In jokes, stories, and games, including the language-game, the trick— and I do mean "trick"—is to perceive another interpretation of the same evidence, that is, to bring another clue from memory to bear upon the sensory presentation. Consider this interchange between two bird-watchers engaged in a bird-count, which can be taken as a paradigm of the informative statement:

A: That bird in that tree you just counted.
B: Well, what about it?
A: It was two-and-a-bit leaves.

It seems that B should not really have been so confident in her use of the singular pronoun "it." What is noteworthy here is that A used the singular form "that bird"—to get B's attention fixed on a fuzzy region of their own non-epistemic evidence. At the beginning of a statement these two engaged in dialogue have assumed that they have selected the same *singular* entity from the real continuum. But this mutual assumption of singularity was really only something in the nature of a *catalyst* in the process of transmitting information, for at the end of the statement the "entity" was not the same for B as it had been before. It had not even preserved its singularity, but B had nevertheless been updated by A about her perception of the world by the provision of a rival memory-clue that transformed her perceiving. As Dinnaga, a sixth-century Indian Buddhist sage, put it, "Even 'this' can be a case of mistaken identity" (Matilal 1986: 332). McDowell cannot therefore found objectivity on "that shade" (McDowell 1994: 56–57), nor can Frank Jackson find security in the "thus-and-so" (Jackson 2007: 62). *What is perceived is not all that is sensed, nor could it be.* As Herbert Dreyfus has said, "Things are never given to us as fully determinate" (Dreyfus 2002: 399), and one can add that "demonstrative concepts" are tied to different sensings for each observer.

This has been argued to be the core of any informative statement (Wright 2005: 121–188; see this reference for a full account). The two participants begin by assuming the *singularity* of "the entity" in view—yet this assumption is no more than that, an assumption, a taking-for-granted, which is useful nevertheless in bringing two differing perceptions into enough of an overlap on the real to allow the updating to go through, just as in a joke. But this is no surprise, for the phrasal verb "to take for granted" contains the same indication of suggesting a tentative hypothesis.

The reason is that "to take for" means *to accept one thing* as if *it were another* (e.g., "It was so foggy I *took* him *for* his brother"); and "granted" means *allowed, permitted, exposed to no expectation of opposition of will and desire from the other.* So "to take for granted" means *to accept an illusion of real agreement as a perfect agreement, an apparent blending of motivation with another as a perfect fusing,* as if no violent disagreement were possible in the future. And what is this illusory agreement the illusion of which is to be temporarily ignored?—that a *single* object, the same for both, is before the agents concerned—and they are concerned agents, that is, driven by motivations. So, in order to obtain a rough-and-ready mutual fix on a portion of the real, a *partial* overlapping of their differing selections, they have to behave *as if* they have a *perfect* one. My own way of describing this trick by which we get a rough mutual grasp on the Real has been to say "It is by a PRETENCE of *complete* success that we *partially* capture THE REAL" (Wright 1978: 538).

This idea is not a new one. It has been called "the idealization of reciprocity" by the sociologist Alfred Schutz, although the same basic notion can be found in the work of others.[5] It is noteworthy that C. D. Broad, the most eminent of the sense-datum theorists, as well as acknowledging the place of motivation in perception, was also inclined to see objects as "defined by Postulates" (*sic*) (Broad 1937: 219–220; see also the prescient F.

C. S. Schiller 1902: 91–104). But note that it involves not just one person's postulate.

If I might take up here David Chalmers's new notion of an "Edenic" perception (Chalmers 2006) to show how it dovetails with what I have argued in my recent book (Wright 2005: chs. 4 and 6): he suggests that "To characterize the phenomenology of an experience, it is often helpful to characterize the sort of world in which that experience would be perfectly veridical" (Chalmers 2006: 116). He is tempted to call it the "basic sort of phenomenal intentionality" (ibid.: 84), even though we all have to deal with "imperfect" perception. The explanation lies in the fact that two people cannot make a statement unless speaker and hearer begin by "helpfully characterizing" their actually differing referents *as if* they were perfectly, "Edenically" singular (in the logical subject of that statement) so that the hearer can be brought to realize (by means of the logical predicate of that statement) that his own referent had been "imperfect." In no other way can an updating be carried through.

Finally, since that "singularity" is no more than a catalyst, we do not need to believe in it; for it is quite otiose in our ontology, however valuable it is in communication—a paring away of the unnecessary with that Razor with which William of Ockham has provided us. This economy has no bearing whatever on the *existence* of the region of the real from which the selections are being made. One can ask "Which is the more frugal ontological position?—to believe in a prodigality of timeless singular entities beyond our understanding or to operate with singularity as a linguistic tool that can be picked up and laid down and picked up again as a set of useful running hypotheses?" As against McDowell, one does not thereby lose "a constraint" from the real: the very fact that one person can alter another's percepts, whether or not that alteration is successful, is a proof of the existence of and non-epistemic nature of the sensory fields of both observers, since it allows a play with percepts (even, as we have just seen with their very singularity). It also proves that *objectivity* can never be equated with *existence*. As philosophers of the late nineteenth century would have said, the "What" (existence) always escapes the "That" (knowledge) (see Royce 1976 [1899]: I, 49–52).

For the indirect realist it provides a helpful disproof of the accusation of solipsism for this view—since another mind can invade one's own perception of oneself, even change it traumatically; witness the scenario of the man at the keyhole graphically imagined by Jean-Paul Sartre 1969: 259ff.). Of course, the real with its varying lumps and viscosities goes on tolerating many of our tentative mutual choices, but, even so, the gap between our differences in sensing and perceiving cannot be bridged. When Gareth Evans tried to find an analogy for an indirect-realist setup, he used that of a guided submarine (equipped with camera and automatic prostheses), and suggested that the person in charge could "play" at being the submarine device (Evans 1982: 166). What he did not add, as he should have done, was that to match the human case there should be two such devices, steered by two different people: the two persons guiding would then have had to negotiate about "what" they saw and "what" they did, a situation that I have already explored in my own bomb-defusers analogy (Wright 2005: 96–102): the structure of play is precisely what results.

There is another element of philosophical support here: as we saw earlier, the senses are not mental, so they are actually the reverse of a "veil of sensation"; their "bare presence" is precisely what keeps us in unavoidable and intimate contact, not only with the external real, but with an internal real since they are *real in themselves*. Sensations, being in our brain, are parts of our body, not part of the self, so this is another reason why solipsism is impossible. It must be added, however, that it is pleasure and pain, selecting sensory gestalts and placing them in memory marked with fear and desire, that provide the womb in which the self begins and grows, for it is perceiving, driven by motivation, in which the mental does come into play, beginning with distinguishing an "I" from a "not-I," neither of which is more than a viable identification.

We have seen, then, that the brute nature of our differing sensory fields is evidence of their existence, and of the existence of the real continuum which has causal effects on them: whereas the doubled nature of all mutual identifications is proof that "objectivity" is radically hypothetical, deriving all its aura, partly from our luck with existence so far, partly from the delusions of habit, but more from the *faith* with which we sustain it across the fact of the differences in our access to it (for a more detailed account of this ontology, together with the corresponding weakness of direct realism, see Wright 2005: 70–120).

What we call objectivity thus emerges, one hopes, as a result of mutual teaching (from speakers) and learning (in hearers), with the "entity," be it thing, person, or self, as an "Edenic" idealization never wholly attained because of the inescapable relativity across persons of concept and sensation (Chalmers 2006: 75–85; Cussins 1990: 428–437). The vital implication here is that any statement whatsoever (other than a lie)[6] depends on an act of *mutual trust*, for hearers are acting on the assumption that the change of meaning will be to their motivational advantage. Speaker and hearer are engaged in an adjustment of the relation of language to the world, and their trust in that assumption therefore involves the expectation that the new meaning will contribute to the advance ultimately toward some future felicity (even enemies making statements to each other depend on a minimal trust). Janet Levin, an opponent of qualia, indirectly acknowledges this when she links rationality to trust in the other (Levin 2007: 107). Nevertheless, however sincere both parties may be, each does understand the words differently, and yet, though they indirectly acknowledge that fact in the "taking-for-granted," they are not aware of what that difference is or whether it will be of any significance later as to what matters to them. One cannot therefore begin a theory of perception with the conviction that *singular* material objects precede the perception of them, as in Mohan Matthen's recent book (Matthen 2005), nor with the conviction that intentionality can be defined as "direction upon an object" if an object is *believed* to have a preexisting singular sameness for all observers.

In opposition to Robert Brandom's (1994) claim that all should be made publicly "explicit," the claim here is that *what is implicit for each cannot all be explicit for both*. At the very moment that "in all good faith," as we say, we declare our sincerity and integrity, saying that we have ignored all but the negligible, what cannot be ruled out is that what is concealed from both in that neglect is what might produce a moral divergence later. So the aim of their mutual hope can never be other than a project without an objective end, a hypothesis without belief in its realization—thus a dramatic, indeed fictive, act within the ongoing language game.

The two parameters of relativity, sensory and perceptual, across persons, imply that unexpected outcomes of sincere agreements cannot be ruled out. An *agree*ment is, after all, an assumption that mutual purposes are relevantly identical, that no frustration will ensue, but that is exactly what cannot be guaranteed. The supposedly agreed "truth" thus is secondary to the original "troth" (it is not without significance that the word "truth" derives etymologically from the word "troth"). Not only that, but in a comic or tragic situation, the troth is ethically secondary to the quality of the love that the two parties have for each other, for the resulting emergence of the mismatch may only be resolvable by sacrifice on the part of one or both.

That this is an alarming possibility leads many into being blind to the very act of trust involved in speaking, to the point where they superstitiously project their own understanding as a fact and not a mutual, *provisional* assumption. A philosophical implication is that anyone who is tempted to take the singularity of entities, either of their own selfhood, other selves, or any external entity as a given, objective, impersonal fact—

and not, as it is, a provisional experiment in the coordination of two differing selections out of the undoubted real—is being *superstitious*.

That this accusation includes both idealists and hard-headed positivists may come as something of a salutary surprise to them. When Robert Kirk said to me (personal communication), "You're not going to tell me that that is not the sun up there!" (a plain invitation to share "transparency"), I reply, "All you are doing is *exhorting me to share the basic trust of language with you*, and I will, for unless we treated our *co*reference as a perfectly singular reference, I could never update you about the Real, such as now by saying that, strictly speaking, that bright source of light is not the sun, for the actual sun is invisible some degrees further down the sky."

I have been myself updated in this argument by Ulrike Hanraths (personal communication), a German writer on ethics, who draws attention to the opening part of what Kirk said, namely, "You are not going to tell me that . . ." What this manifestly implies, in her view, is that he is saying that no statement can be made by me that can disturb our mutual faith in the singularity of our perceptual identification, which amounts to Kirk refusing to hear an updating of his understanding (or proffer one of his own), thus *demanding a virtual prohibition of our speaking at all*. I gratefully add that it is an unconscious attempt at an assertion of the basic faith (a grasping of the catalyst), but one obviously self-contradictory since, in banning all predication (in refusing to use the catalyst as one), it denies the risk that an updating from a trusted other may produce, for risk is something all true faiths accept (on this omnipresent risk, see F. C. S. Schiller 1929: 47). One cannot set up an injunction against the transformation of what it is we all share faith about. To ignore the risk entails a denial of trust in the other. The actual state of the case is that all "entities," including that of the self, are maintained as cooperative, though tentative, choices from the real by this hidden faith—to quote the poet Edwin Muir, "Faith made the whole," that is, our commonsense "world," everyday "reality." That is what we trust others to do and which others trust us to do, *without knowing the possible outcomes*. It is what *sharing* knowledge amounts to. If a mutual faith has been and should be the basis of all our knowledge, no wonder Berkeley claimed that "God" sustained all our "objective" identifications, and, further, that most religions claim that "God" has created all "things," or that Chalmers should ask whether God has created his "Edenic world" (Chalmers 2006: 79). One can see that even creationism has a distorted truth inside it.

Therefore, when G. E. Moore held up his two hands and said that there was one thing he was transparently, "diaphanously," certain of was that those were his hands, his reiteration of the transparently obvious was no more than a veiled assertion of this common faith that sustains all our "objectivities" (Moore 1966: 144). It is significant that, like Kirk, he did not raise the question of the sensory and perceptual differences between himself and his audience as regards those hands—for example, (a) that they were not feeling those hands; (b) that they were hardly aware of their idiosyncratic features; (c) that, as he held them up, they saw a different side of them than he did, and so on—which points to a neglect of the extent and limitations of the intersubjective overlap. His hands were only considered to be impersonal facts because he and they preferred to be unaware of their differences as a support of their trust in each other, and there was little likelihood of a surprising discovery of cross-purposes about those hands at that merely illustrative moment.

Look now at the reasons for the temptation to be certain that together we see and refer to the same "singular" things:

(1) We have the mistaken idea that singular objectivity entails existence, when all it shows is that, yes, it is chosen from existence, but each person is choosing *differently* at the very moment that they have to pretend that they have chosen the *same* portion as everyone else. How insidiously easy, then, is it to move from the employment of what is only one half of a linguistic method (for the other half of any informative statement is an attempt to subvert that "agreement") to ignore that ever-present ambiguity and be convinced that all is as we each currently conceptualize it. There, it seems, in all its bland facticity, is the "single" thing or self before us—who could doubt "its" existence as exactly the same for all of us? We say things like "There can't be confusion in the real, can there?" or, with Ruth Millikan, "The original or most immediate objects of reference are not before the mind but in the natural world" (Millikan 1998: 67). Wilfrid Sellars said that there are not any objects, only "an ongoing tissue of goings-on": it is better to put it thus, that the notion of "Edenic" objects works very well within our commonly maintained "reality" (mutually sorted out from that "ongoing tissue" of the real), but there are not any *singular* ones (W. Sellars 1981: II, 57); otherwise we could never update each other about "them."

(2) It is deeply disconcerting to think the other does not understand what one is saying at the very moment that an act of trust is being performed. It looks like suspicion of the other, though in actuality it is an acknowledgment of the other's genuine difference from oneself. This is one reason why philosophers such as John McDowell and Bill Brewer stress "the way things are" apart from individual perspectives, for it is a way of discount-

ing the sensory and perceptual differences between persons (McDowell 1994: 26; Brewer 1999: 201). It is also the reason why McDowell and Tye seem to believe that merely expressing their disbelief in qualia amounts to a powerful argument: Tye says that it is "totally implausible that visual experience is systematically misleading in this way" (Tye 2000: 46).

(3) It is consoling to our narcissism and our fear to believe that the agreement reached will be exactly as we have ourselves understood it. It hides the ever-present threat of the Real's contingencies, both in the world of things, in the other, and in our own self. It is difficult to face up to this endemic *risk*.

(4) The language game has in entirely hypothetical view the impossible perfect union of word and world, and, for the narcissist, that union is taken to be a real promise, that life does in reality hold out the full satisfaction of "one's" desire as conceived of in the present, the oneness of that stale self being guaranteed as unchangeable by the misconstruction of what the trust of language involves.

(5) It is reassuring and flattering to think that one's own understanding is blessed by a "public" one, which is again the equivalent of being convinced that our words and the world are at one. It leads to *both* the extreme conservative *and* the extreme anarchist twisting the idealization of reciprocity, which must allow the risk of faith, into a guarantee of their prejudice.

(6) Many people, for all sorts of personal reasons, are unable to remain in a state of doubt. Like the child who cries when he is "taken prisoner" in a war game, or someone who is embarrassed when asked to act on a stage, a person who is troubled by the constant challenges of living her "identity" gets lost in a fearful obsession with certainty. Such persons cannot play the language game, finding that the movement from interpretation to interpretation shakes their too rigid sense of self. It is often said, mistakenly, that the neurotic are "insecure": on the contrary, *they are too secure*, since "identity" is no more a given than any other singularity—it is "in play" in both senses of that phrase, *loose* and *make-believe*, and play implies risk.

(7) And, since the transformation involved in every informative statement is a make-believe in real actual progress, and since its performance therefore really involves paradoxical behaviors, the rationalist mind can only wince away in distaste from such "illogical" requirements. Acting is altogether suspect from the viewpoint of the puritan logician, since it raises questions about reliance on singular identity. He sees something devilish about the "skeptical dissenter" who puts forward such aesthetic nonsense.

All of these reasons have the same timid, even cowardly, impulse behind them. Under the cloak of asserting a blameless objectivity, *it is avoiding the risk that attends all faith.* It is the very acceptance of risk that characterizes a proper faith; the affectation of absolute certainty, superstition. It is the superstitious who are being inconsistent, for, since we "only talk about the problematic," they are admitting to the risk in their very engaging in language (F. C. S. Schiller 1929: 87–88). We do not talk about what we think we know we agree on, the only exception being if we are concerned to assure ourselves that the other has taken the point of some earlier communication—which still amounts to a "problematic" case. To hold to "transparency" therefore constitutes an illicit turning of the idealization of reciprocity into a rigid *non*-agreement.

So, the motto is not "In reason we trust"—for that is only an exhortation, like Kirk's and Brandom's, to join in the common faith—but *"In trust we reason,"* that is, it is within faith that we talk to each other. This implies that all our reasonings, our laws, our promises, our words, our objectivities, our very selves, are embraced within the measure and kind of trust that we have in each other. Every familiar thing that you have been taught to recognize (look around you now) is upheld by the faith that has been passed on to us by our forebears, by "God" who "created" them all, as so many of our forebears put it. And this faith has to acknowledge the perhaps terrible risk of our implicit understanding not turning out to be the same as that of those we love, when existence breaks through the familiar objectivity—and, for the self, this should be acknowledged as discovering "self-deception." This is why one has not to say merely that troth comes before truth, but love before troth. What one had neglected to mention before the real sprang its surprise might call for a completely unexpected degree of sacrifice. One then might discover that one's own trust has been inadequate all along. The fact that both the extreme conservative and the extreme anarchist demand sacrifice of their followers, though not of themselves, is a hideous distortion of this moral preparedness, as well as a half-acknowledgment of the risk.

Kant was half-aware that faith underpinned our identifications: "I have therefore found it necessary to deny *knowledge* to make room for *faith*" (*Critique of Pure Reason*, B xxx, his emphases), but, hampered by the individualistic rationalism he had not thoroughly shaken off, he did not make the move to the *intersubjective* nature of language, and the strictly illogical transformations in which it deals. There are no singular *Dinge-an-Sich* except as those mutually imagined catalysts which enable us, we hope, to shift each other, joke-like, story-like, from one stage of knowledge of the real to the next. Neither, with reference to our present concern, can there thus be any "transparent" entities that reveal themselves to us.

So any argument that begins with the assurance that our "taking-for-granted" guarantees the unshakable singularity of all we perceive is being *superstitious*. One finds some repeating the mantra that "we have to take for granted that particulars and persons exist" without their realizing what they have actually said—"we have 'to *take for* granted.'" Take R. J. Hirst, one of the first to attack sense-datum theory, who asks us to join in the "publicity assumption"—he means the "commonsense" publicity of objects and persons—without realizing that he has used the word "assumption" (Hirst 1959: 303; for other examples, see note 7).[7] The superstitious are precisely those who cannot face not only the risk of living at all, but the risk that even our own self can turn uncanny on us—what we *took* ourselves *for* is no longer inhabitable. The superstitious, in clinging to a fixed singularity, are actually *ignoring* the risk-laden, non-epistemic existent that lies unknown within every identification, even of the self.

This ethical critique applies equally to Tye's form of representationalism, to that of any qualia theorist who adheres to a object-causal theory of perception (Grice 1967; Fumerton 1985; Chalmers 2006: 94), to the phenomenologist who relies on Husserl's preexisting "determinable x" (Woodruff Smith 1989), to Frank Jackson who, formerly, tried to defend qualia as essentially a matter of knowing and, recently, as wholly representational (Jackson 1982, 2007), and to an epistemologist like Saul Kripke, who, unintentionally ironically, called the act of naming an entity a "baptism," thus betraying an unconscious admission of the part imagination (or myth) *plays* in naming (Kripke 1980: 96–97). Tye has recently attempted to found an understanding of the self on a given "unity," but this is the same superstitious move to bestow permanence upon the singularity of any entity, and the self is no exception (Tye 2003). *Such a view disguises the intersubjectivity in all subjectivities.* To believe in the objective "transparency" of perceptions, even of the self, is to be ignorant of the nature of the game in which we are engaged, and thus to be lacking in faith, to be fearful of the disagreements that will inevitably challenge those catalyst-presuppositions we cling to as confirming thing and self, and, in particular, to fear the sacrifices that they may require of us.

There has to be a "principle of hope" (Bloch 1986), but this must be coupled with the full awareness that the ideal can never be other than *imagined together* in a faith that accepts risk. With Josiah Royce and C. D. Broad we must see that "Eden" of objectivity as "defined by Postulates" (Royce 1958 [1885]: 298; Broad 1937: 219–220). The Chalmersian "Edenic world" in which there is a final match between perception and sensation, word and world, is the ever-unrealizable goal which human beings, forever constrained—and liberated—by their otherness, must intersubjectively, paradoxically, ludically, strive for together.

So, borrowing from Hume, equally concerned to banish superstition (*Enquiry*, 12, iii), we can close as he did, and say, "If we take in hand any volume, of divinity, of epistemology, philosophy of mind, or school metaphysics, for instance; let us ask *Does it commence with the conviction—and not with faith—that singular entities predate our selection of them?* Yes. *Does it base all its arguments on the immediacy of the perception of those singular entities?* Yes. *Does it therefore confuse objectivity with existence?* Yes. Commit it then to the flames: for it can contain nothing but sophistry and illusion."

Notes

1. Ned Block could be regarded as cheekily trailing his coat when he writes of "mental paint" and "mental oil." It certainly riles the opposition but whether it is the best tactic is questionable (Block 2003).

2. See Smythies 1951: 39ff.; Mackie 1976: 44–45. A Smythies TV-Hood, of course, can interchange sound-wave and light-wave input so it can preserve useful differential correlations *across sensory modalities* without any objective resemblances whatever (see further Wright 1993).

3. Mozart, having heard once a choral work in the Vatican, one that was not generally published, was able several weeks later in Vienna to write it down from his mental image of it, which he could not have done had he not been able to hear it in the form of a mental image. I myself, through having played some favorite works on record countless times, am able to hear them through at will. I often entertain myself on a boring journey listening, say, to Sibelius's *En Saga* or Vaughan Williams's Fifth Symphony. I don't need an iPod. Furthermore, since I can hear these and other pieces at various tempos as I choose, my experience is an empirical disproof of Dennett's unwise declaration that no one could speed up or slow down a mental image (Dennett 1978: 168). Incidentally, I discussed this ability of mine in an article in 1983, but no one has referred to it. Do they take it that I have invented this empirical evidence? (Wright 1983: 67). Oliver Sacks' father had the same ability.

4. Tye actually defines hallucination by reference to an identified object: "an *F* image is an image *that represents that something as F*" (Tye 1995: 107). See also Crane 2006: 139–140, and Martin 2006: 357–408.

5. This idea can also be found in the works of philosophers Friedrich Nietzsche (1968: 289, 307); William James (1977 [1907]: 139, 333–334, 433, 449–461); Fritz Mauthner (1923: II, 117); Josiah Royce (1976 [1899]: I, 73, 586); Roy Wood Sellars

(1969 [1916]: 57); C. I. Lewis (1929 [1916]: 21); F. C. S. Schiller (1902: 103–104; 1929: 163–1664, 223; and Humberto R. Maturana and Francisco J. Varela (1980: 32–33); the linguists Alexander Bryan Johnson (1968 [1828]: 72); and Sir Alan Gardiner (1932: 80); the psychologist Hermann von Helmholtz (1977: 140–142); the sociologist Alfred Schutz (1962: 3–47); the social theorist Theodor Adorno (1973: 14); and the psycholinguist Ragnar Rommetveit (1978: 31).

6. Even a liar may convey truth without knowing it; see Wright 2005: 144.

7. For examples, see Evans 1982: 40–41; Blackburn 1984: 20; Grayling 1985: 3, 12–13; Ben Ze'ev 1989: 537; Davidson 1984: 196; Heller 1990, xi; Van Inwagen, 1990: 6; Hoffman and Rosencrantz 1997: 151; O'Regan and Noë 2001: sect. 6, vii; Williams 2002: 53; and, for good measure, two psychologists, Wilcox and Katz 1984. The reader can no doubt find more.

References

Adorno, T. W. 1973. *Negative Dialectics*. Trans. E. B. Ashton. New York: Continuum.

Alroy, D. 1995. Inner light. *Synthese* 104, 1: 147–160.

Ayer, A. J. 1957. *The Problem of Knowledge*. Harmondsworth: Penguin Books.

Ben Ze'ev, A. 1989. Explaining the subject–object relation in perception. *Social Research* 56: 511–514.

Bermudez, J. L. 1995. Nonconceptual content: From perceptual experience to sub-personal computational states. *Mind and Language* 10, 4: 333–369.

Blackburn, S. 1984. *Spreading the Word: Groundings in the Philosophy of Language*. Oxford: Clarendon Press.

Bloch, E. 1986 [1959]. *The Principle of Hope*, 3 vols. Trans. N. Plaice, S. Plaice, and P. Knight. Oxford: Basil Blackwell.

Block, N. 1995. On a confusion about a function of consciousness. *Behavioral and Brain Sciences* 18: 227–247.

Block, N. 2003. Mental paint. In *Reflections and Replies: Essays on the Philosophy of Tyler Burge*, ed. Martin Hahn and Bjorn Ramberg. Cambridge, Mass.: MIT Press/A Bradford Book.

Boghossian, P., and D. J. Velleman. 1989. Colour as a secondary quality. *Mind* 98: 81–103.

Brain, W. R. 1951. *Mind, Perception, and Science*. Oxford: Basil Blackwell.

Brandom, R. B. 1994. *Making It Explicit: Reasoning, Representing, and Discursive Commitment*. Cambridge, Mass.: Harvard University Press.

Brentano, F. 1973 [1874]. *Psychology from an Empirical Standpoint*. Trans. A. C. Rancurello, D. B. Terrell, and L. L. McAlister. London and New York: Routledge.

Brewer, W. 1999. *Perception and Reason*. Oxford: Clarendon Press.

Broad, C. D. 1937. *The Mind and Its Place in Nature*. London: Kegan Paul, Trench, Trubner.

Chalmers, D. 2006. Perception and the Fall from Eden. In *Perceptual Experience*, ed. T. S. Gendler and J. Hawthorne, 49–125. Oxford: Clarendon Press.

Crane, T. 2006. Is there a perceptual relation? In *Perceptual Experience*, ed. T. S. Gendler and J. Hawthorne, 126–146. Oxford: Clarendon Press.

Cussins, A. 1990. The connectionist construction of concepts. In *The Philosophy of Artificial Intelligence*, ed. M. Boden, 368–440. Oxford: Oxford University Press.

Davidson, D. 1984. On the very idea of a conceptual scheme. In *Enquiries into Truth and Interpretation*, 183–198. Oxford: Oxford University Press.

Dennett, D. C. 1978. *Brainstorms: Philosophical Essays on Mind and Psychology*. Hassocks: Harvester Press. Republished 1981, Cambridge, Mass.: MIT Press/A Bradford Book.

Dennett, D. C. 1986 [1969]. *Content and Consciousness*. London, Boston, and Henley: Routledge and Kegan Paul.

Dennett, D. C. 1991. *Consciousness Explained*. London: Penguin Books.

Dennett, D. C. 1998. *Brainchildren: Essays on Designing Minds*. Cambridge, Mass.: MIT Press/A Bradford Book.

Dennett, D. C. 2006. *Sweet Dreams: Philosophical Obstacles to a Science of Consciousness*. Cambridge, Mass.: MIT Press/A Bradford Book.

Dilman, I. 1967. Imagination. *Proceedings of the Aristotelian Society*, supp. vol., 41: 19–36.

Dreyfus, H. L. 2002. Samuel Todes's account of non-conceptual perceptual knowledge and its relation to thought. *Ratio* 15, 4: 392–409.

Edelman, G. M. 1992. *Bright Air, Brilliant Fire*. London: Allen Lane, Penguin Press.

Edelman, G. M., and G. Tononi. 2000. *Consciousness: How Matter Becomes Imagination*. London: Allen Lane.

Evans, G. 1982. *The Varieties of Reference*. Oxford: Clarendon Press.

Fitzgerald, P. 1977. Review of Frank Jackson, *Perception*. In *International Philosophical Quarterly* 19, 1: 103–113.

Fumerton, R. A. 1985. *Metaphysical and Epistemological Problems of Perception*. Lincoln: University of Nebraska Press.

Gardiner, Sir A. 1932. *The Theory of Speech and Language*. Oxford: Clarendon Press.

Gibson, J. J. 1968. *The Senses Considered as Perceptual Systems*. London: Allen and Unwin.

Grayling, A. C. 1985. *The Refutation of Scepticism*. London: Duckworth.

Grice, H. P. 1967. The Causal Theory of Perception. In *The Philosophy of Perception*, ed. G. J. Warnock, 85–112. Oxford: Oxford University Press.

Harman, G. 1990. The intrinsic quality of experience. In *Philosophical Perspectives* vol. 4: *Action Theory and Philosophy of Mind*, ed. J. Tomberlin, 31–52. Atascadero, Calif.: Ridgeview.

Heller, M. 1990. *The Ontology of Physical Objects*. Cambridge: Cambridge University Press.

Helmholtz, H. von. 1901. *Popular Lectures on Scientific Subjects: First Series*. London: Longmans Green.

Helmholtz, H. von. 1964. Unconscious conclusions. In *Visual Perception: The Nineteenth Century*, ed. W. Dember, 163–170. New York and London: John Wiley.

Helmholtz, H. von. 1977. *Epistemological Writings*. Ed. Robert S. Cohen and Yehuda Elkana. Dordrecht: D. Reidel.

Hirst, R. J. 1959. *The Problems of Perception*. London: George Allen and Unwin.

Hobbes, T. 1839. *Elements of Philosophy, The First Section: Concerning Body*. Trans. Sir Bart W. Molesworth. London: John Bohn.

Hoffman, J., and G. S. Rosencrantz. 1997. *Substance: Its Nature and Existence*. London and New York: Routledge.

Jackson, F. 1982. Epiphenomenal qualia. *Philosophical Quarterly* 82: 127–136.

Jackson, F. 2007. The knowledge argument, diaphanousness, representationalism. In *Phenomenal Concepts and Phenomenal Knowledge: New Essays on Consciousness and Physicalism*, ed. T. Alter and S. Walter, 52–64. Oxford and New York: Oxford University Press.

James, W. 1977 [1907]. *The Writings of William James: A Comprehensive Edition*. Ed. John J. McDermott. Chicago: Chicago University Press.

Johnson, A. B. 1968 [1828]. *A Treatise on Language*. Ed. David Rynin. New York: Dover.

Kenny, A. 1993. *Aquinas on Mind*. London: Routledge.

Kripke, S. 1980. *Naming and Necessity*. Cambridge, Mass.: Harvard University Press.

Levin, J. 2007. What is a phenomenal concept? In *Phenomenal Concepts and Phenomenal Knowledge: New Essays on Consciousness and Physicalism*, ed. T. Alter and S. Walter, 87–110. Oxford and New York: Oxford University Press.

Lewis, C. I. 1929 [1916]. *Mind and the World-Order: Outline of a Theory of Knowledge*. New York: Charles Scribner.

Lotze, H. 1884. *Metaphysic in Three Books: Ontology, Cosmology, and Psychology*. Oxford: Clarendon Press.

Mackie, J. L. 1976. *Problems from Locke*. Oxford: Clarendon Press.

Marr, D. H. 1982. *Vision*. San Francisco: W. H. Freeman.

Martin, M. G. F. 2006. On being alienated. In *Perceptual Experience*, ed. T. S. Gendler and J. Hawthorne, 354–410. Oxford: Clarendon Press.

Matilal, B. K. 1986. *Perception: An Essay on Classical Indian Theories of Knowledge*. Oxford: Clarendon Press.

Matthen, M. 2005. *Seeing, Doing, and Knowing: A Philosophical Theory of Sense Perception*. Oxford: Clarendon Press.

Maturana, H. R., and F. J. Varela. 1980. *Autopoesis and Cognition: The Realization of the Living*. Dordrecht: D. Reidel.

Mauthner, F. 1923 [1901–1902]. *Beiträge zu einer Kritik der Sprache*, 3 vols. Leipzig: Meiner.

McDougall, W. 1911. *Physiological Psychology*. London: J. M. Dent.

McDowell, J. 1994. *Mind and World*. Cambridge, Mass.: Harvard University Press.

Meyering, T. C. 1989. *Historical Roots of Cognitive Science*. Dordrecht: Kluwer Academic.

Millikan, R. G. 1998. How we make our ideas clear: Empiricist epistemology for empirical concepts. The Tenth Annual Patrick Romanell Lecture. *Proceedings and Addresses of the American Philosophical Association* (November): 65–79.

Moore, G. E. 1966 [1959]. Proof of an external world. In *Philosophical Papers*, 126–148. New York: Collier.

Nelkin, N. 1996. *Consciousness and the Origins of Thought*. Cambridge: Cambridge University Press.

Nietzsche, F. 1968. *The Will to Power*. New York: Vintage Books.

O'Regan, K., and A. Noë. 2001. A sensorimotor account of vision and visual consciousness. *Behavioural and Brain Sciences* 24, 5: 939–1011.

Palmer, S. E. 1999. Color, consciousness, and the isomorphism constraint. *Behavioural and Brain Sciences* 22: 935–944.

Perkins, M. 1983. *Sensing the World*. Indianapolis, Ind.: Hackett.

Piaget, J. 1955. *The Child's Construction of Reality*. London: Routledge and Kegan Paul.

Richards, I. A. 1936. *The Philosophy of Rhetoric*. London and New York: Oxford University Press.

Robinson, H. 1994. *Perception*. London and New York: Routledge.

Robinson, W. S. 2004. *Understanding Phenomenal Consciousness*. Cambridge: Cambridge University Press.

Rommetveit, R. (1978) On negative rationalism in scholarly studies of verbal communication and dynamic residuals in the construction of human intersubjectivity. In *The Social Contexts of Method*, ed. Michael Brenner, P. Marsh, and Marilyn Brenner, 16–32. London: Croom Helm.

Royce, J. 1958 [1885]. *The Religious Aspect of Philosophy: A Critique of the Bases of Conduct and Faith*. New York: Harper and Brothers.

Royce, J. 1976 [1899]. *The World and the Individual. First and Second Series*. Gloucester, Mass.: Peter Smith.

Ryle, G. 1949. *The Concept of Mind*. London: Hutchinson.

Sartre, J.-P. 1969. *Being and Nothingness*. Trans. Hazel E. Barnes. London: Methuen.

Schiller, F. C. S. 1902. Axioms as postulates. In *Personal Idealism*, ed. H. Sturt, 47–133. London: Macmillan.

Schiller, F. C. S. 1929. *Logic for Use: An Introduction to the Voluntarist Theory of Knowledge*. London: G. Bell.

Schutz, A. 1962. *Collected Papers*, vol. I: *The Problem of Social Reality*. The Hague: Martinus Nijhoff.

Sellars, R. W. 1919. The epistemology of evolutionary naturalism. *Mind* 28, 112: 407–426.

Sellars, R. W. 1922. *Evolutionary Naturalism*. Chicago: Open Court.

Sellars, R. W. 1969 [1916]. *Critical Realism: A Study of the Nature and Conditions of Knowledge*. New York: Russell and Russell.

Sellars, W. 1981. Naturalism and process. *Monist* 64, 1: 37–65. (No. II of The Carus Lectures.)

Smart, J. J. C. 1959. Sensations and brain processes. *Philosophical Review* 68: 141–156.

Smythies, J. R. 1951. *Analysis of Perception*. London: Routledge and Kegan Paul.

Smythies, J. R. 1994. *The Walls of Plato's Cave: The Science and Philosophy of Brain, Consciousness, and Perception*. Aldershot: Avebury.

Tye, M. 1995. *Ten Problems of Consciousness: A Representational Theory of the Phenomenal Mind*. Cambridge, Mass.: MIT Press/A Bradford Book.

Tye, M. 2000. *Consciousness, Color, and Content*. Cambridge, Mass.: MIT Press/A Bradford Book.

Tye, M. 2003. *Consciousness and Persons: Unity and Identity*. Cambridge, Mass.: MIT Press/A Bradford Book.

van Inwagen, P. 1990. *Material Beings*. Ithaca, N.Y.: Cornell University Press.

Wilcox, S., and S. Katz. 1984. Can indirect realism be demonstrated in the psychological laboratory? *Philosophy of the Social Sciences* 14: 149–157.

Williams, B. 2002. *Truth and Truthfulness: An Essay in Genealogy*. Princeton: Princeton University Press.

Woodruff Smith, D 1989. *The Circle of Acquaintance: Perception, Consciousness, and Empathy*. Dordrecht: Kluwer Academic.

Wright, E. L. 1975. Perception: A new theory. *American Philosophical Quarterly* 14, 4: 273–286.

Wright, E. L. 1978. Sociology and the irony model. *Sociology* 12, 3: 523–543.

Wright. E. L. 1981. Yet more on non-epistemic seeing. *Mind* 90: 586–591.

Wright, E. L. 1983. Inspecting images. *Philosophy* 58: 51–72.

Wright, E. L. 1993a. More qualia-trouble for functionalism: J. R. Smythies TV-Hood Analogy. *Synthese* 97, 3: 1–18.

Wright, E. L. 1993b. The irony of perception. In *New Representationalisms: Essays in the Philosophy of Perception*, ed. E. L. Wright, 176–201. Aldershot: Avebury.

Wright, E. L. 2004. The defence of qualia. Available at http://www.cus.cam.ac.uk/~elw33/articles/qualia.html/.

Wright, E. L. 2006. *Narrative, Perception, Language, and Faith*. Basingstoke: Palgrave Macmillan.

Contributors

Michel Bitbol was born in 1954. He is currently Directeur de Recherche at the Centre National de la Recherche Scientifique, in Paris (France), based at the CREA (Centre de Recherche en Epistémologie Appliquée), Paris. He also teaches the philosophy of modern physics to graduate students at the University Panthéon-Sorbonne. He was educated at several universities in Paris, where he received his M.D. in 1980, his Ph.D. in physics in 1985, and his Habilitation in philosophy in 1997. He worked as a research scientist in biophysics from 1978 to 1990. From 1990 onwards, he turned to the philosophy of physics. He edited texts by Erwin Schroedinger, and published a book entitled *Schroedinger's Philosophy of Quantum Mechanics* (Kluwer, 1996). He also published two books in French on quantum mechanics and on realism in science, in 1996 and 1998. More recently, he has focused on the relations between the philosophy of quantum mechanics and the philosophy of mind, working in close collaboration with F. Varela. He published a book in French in 2000 and some subsequent papers on that topic. He is recipient of an award from the Academie des sciences morales et politiques (in 1997) for his work in the philosophy of quantum mechanics.

Harold I. Brown is Professor Emeritus of Philosophy at Northern Illinois University; author of three books: *Perception, Theory, and Commitment: The New Philosophy of Science* (Chicago University Press, 1979), *Observation and Objectivity* (Oxford University Press, 1987), and *Rationality* (Routledge, 1988), and more than fifty articles. He has received research support from NEH and NSF, has been a member of the Governing Board of the Philosophy of Science Association, and currently serves on the Editorial Board of *Philosophy of Science*.

Mark Crooks studied philosophy and psychology at Michigan State University. His previous papers include "Intertheoretic Identification and Mind-Brain Reductionism"; "Four Rejoinders: A Dialogue in

Continuation" (*Journal of Mind and Behavior*, where he is assessing editor); "Phenomenology in absentia: Dennett's Philosophy of Mind"; "The Last Philosophical Behaviorist: Content and Consciousness Explained Away" (*Journal of Theoretical and Philosophical Psychology*); and the forthcoming "On Direct Introspection of Brain States."

George Graham is the A. C. Reid Professor of Philosophy at Wake Forest University in North Carolina. Until 2003, he taught at the University of Alabama at Birmingham. His research focuses on the philosophy of mind and the philosophy of psychiatry. Among the nine books that he has published or helped to publish is the *Oxford Textbook of Philosophy and Psychiatry* (Oxford University Press, 2006). He is at work, along with Terence Horgan and John Tienson, on a book on phenomenal intentionality. His authored or coauthored papers have appeared in a wide variety of professional journals, such as *Noûs, American Philosophical Quarterly, Synthèse*, and the *International Review of Psychiatry*.

C. L. Hardin is Emeritus Professor of Philosophy at Syracuse University. His book *Color for Philosophers* (Hackett, 1986) has become a classic in the philosophy of perception; it won the Johnsonian Prize in the same year. He has also edited with Luisa Maffi *Color Categories in Thought and Language* (Cambridge University Press, 1997), and published over forty articles in learned journals, as well as being a distinguished invitee to lecture at a wide range of colloquia and conferences.

Terence Horgan is professor of philosophy at the University of Arizona. He works in philosophy of mind, metaphysics, philosophy of language, metaethics, and epistemology. He has published numerous articles in these areas, often coauthored. He is coauthor (with John Tienson) of *Connectionism and the Philosophy of Psychology* (MIT Press, 1996), and (with Matjaž Potrč) of *Austere Realism: Contextual Semantics Meets Minimal Ontology* (MIT Press, 2008). He is at work, along with George Graham and John Tienson, on a book on phenomenal intentionality.

Amy Kind is Associate Professor of Philosophy and Associate Dean of the Faculty at Claremont McKenna College, where she has been a member of the faculty since receiving her Ph.D. from UCLA in 1997. Her research in philosophy of mind proceeds primarily on two fronts. One project concerns the imagination, in particular, trying to get clear about its nature and its role in modal epistemology. In her paper, "Putting the Image Back in Imagination," she defends an image-based account of sensory imagination. Her second project concerns phenomenal consciousness, where she has recently published several papers arguing against representation-alism and in favor of a realist view about qualia. In addition to these two projects, she has also written on personal identity, self-knowledge, and introspection. Her work has appeared in leading philosophical journals such as *Philosophy and Phenomenological Research, Philosophical Studies,* and *Philosophical Quarterly.*

E. J. Lowe is Professor of Philosophy at the University of Durham, U.K. His publications include: *Locke on Human Understanding* (Routledge, 1995), *Subjects of Experience* (Cambridge University Press, 1996), *The Possibility of Metaphysics* (Oxford University Press, 1998), and *An Introduction to the Philosophy of Mind* (Cambridge University Press, 2000).

Riccardo Manzotti is Assistant Professor of Psychology at the IULM University, Milan, Italy. He obtained a degree in electronic engineering (1994), a degree in philosophy (2004), and a Ph.D. in Robotics (2001). He focuses his research on the nature of phenomenal experience, how it emerges from physical processes, and how it is related to the conscious subject. He believes that in order to understand the nature of phenom-enal experience we need to adopt a process-oriented view. He has pub-lished several papers on consciousness, perception, artificial intelligence, and artificial consciousness. He is joint editor of *Artificial Consciousness* (Imprint Academic, U.K., 2007), and the author of *Coscienza e realtà* (Il Mulino, 2001).

Barry Maund is Associate Professor in Philosophy at The University of Western Australia. He is the author of two books: *Colours: The Nature and Representation* (Cambridge University Press, 1995) and *Perception* (Acumen, 2003). He is the author of the entry "Color" in the *Stanford Encyclopedia of Philosophy* (1997/2002) and many articles on philosophy of perception, philosophy of mind, and philosophy of science.

Martine Nida-Rümelin is professor for philosophy at the University of Fribourg in Switzerland. Her main research interests lie within the philoso-phy of mind. She has published in particular on phenomenal conscious-ness and identity across time of conscious individuals. In her book *Der Blick von Innen* (Suhrkamp, 2006) she develops a nonreductionist view with respect to transtemporal identity of conscious individuals (English transla-tion in preparation). She has published a series of articles on phenomenal states, beliefs about phenomenal states, and concepts of phenomenal states (see her paper "What Mary Couldn't Know," reprinted in *There's Something About Mary*, edited by Peter Ludlow, Yujin Nagasawa and Daniel Stoljar

(MIT Press, 2004). In her recent article "Grasping Phenomenal Properties" (in the collection *Phenomenal Knowledge and Phenomenal Concepts* edited by Torin Alter and Sven Walter, Oxford University Press, 2007), she uses her account of phenomenal concepts for an argument in favor of property dualism. In her contribution to the volume *Contemporary Debates in the Philosophy of Mind* (edited by Brian MacLaughlin and Jonathan Cohen, Blackwell, forthcoming) she argues for a dualist version of emergentism. A book presenting her views on phenomenal consciousness (*Thoughts about Qualia*, Oxford University Press) is in preparation.

John O'Dea took his Ph.D. in philosophy in 2002 from Monash University, Melbourne, Australia, before spending three years as a postdoctoral fellow at the Australian National University in Canberra. He is currently on a postdoctoral fellowship at the University of Tokyo. His publications mainly concern representationalist theories of experience and the philosophical problem of the distinction between the senses.

Isabelle Peschard was born in 1968. She received, in 1995, a Ph.D. in fluid mechanics, with a dissertation on unstable behavior and chaotic evolution in coupled oscillator complex systems. She then turned to philosophy of science studies at the University Panthéon-Sorbonne in Paris and became especially interested in the dynamical tools used to address different classical questions in philosophy of mind. At present, she is finishing a dissertation which aims to criticize and challenge the representationalist framework in both the philosophical and scientific conceptions of cognition. She proposes to articulate a Wittgensteinean grammatical critique of philosophies of knowledge with the scientific enactive theory of cognition, developed by F. Varela, so as to allow a scientific study of cognitive processes able to account for the lived experience of knowledge.

Matjaž Potrč is professor of philosophy at the University Ljubljana, Slovenia. He has written and edited numerous books, published many papers, and is the founder of the international journal *Acta analytica*. He studied in Paris with Jacques Lacan, in Munich with Wolfgang Stegmüller, and was a Fulbright fellow in Memphis with Terry Horgan. Together with Mark Lance and Vojko Strahovnik he is coeditor of *Challenging Moral Particularism*, to be published with Routledge. Continuous collaboration with Horgan has resulted, among other things, in the book *Austere Realism*, which is being published by MIT Press.

Diana Raffman is Professor of Philosophy at the University of Toronto. Her primary research is in the philosophy of mind, cognitive science, and philosophy of language. She was formerly a professional musician and is the author of a book, *Language, Music, and Mind* (MIT Press, 1993), and several articles on consciousness and perception. She has also published papers on vagueness and is currently completing a book on vagueness entitled *Vagueness without Paradox*, in which she advances a new theory of vagueness and solution to the sorites paradox. Her research for this book included two psychological experiments on color discrimination and categorization.

Howard Robinson is Professor of Philosophy at Central European University, Budapest, Honorary Visiting Professor at the University Of York, and Honorary Research Fellow at the University of Liverpool. He is author of *Matter and Sense* (Cambridge University Press, 1982) and *Perception* (Routledge, 1994, 2001), editor of the Oxford World Classics edition of Berkeley, and editor or coeditor of collections on the philosophy of mind, ancient philosophy, and Berkeley.

William S. Robinson is Professor of Philosophy at Iowa State University who has published in several areas of philosophy of mind and philosophy of artificial intelligence. Recent work on consciousness includes the entry on epiphenomenalism in the *Stanford Encyclopedia of Philosophy* (1999) and "Jackson's Apostasy" (*Philosophical Studies*, 2002). His book, *Understanding Phenomenal Consciousness,* was published by Cambridge University Press in April, 2004.

John Smythies is a neuropsychiatrist, neuroscientist, and neurophilosopher. He obtained his medical degree at Cambridge, and a post-graduate M.D. (neuroanatomy) and M.Sc. (psychology) from the same university, as well as an M.Sc. in philosophy and anthropology from the University of British Columbia. He is a Fellow of the Royal College of Physicians of London. He held the posts of Reader in Psychiatry at the University of Edinburgh (1961–1973) and C. B. Ireland Professor of Psychiatric Research at the University of Alabama at Birmingham (1973–1988). Currently he is Director of Neurochemistry at the Center for Brain and Cognition, UCSD, and Senior Research Fellow at the Institute of Neurology, UCL, Queen Square, London. He was President of the International Society of Psychoneurocrinology from 1970–1974, Consultant in Psychopharmacology to WHO from 1964–1968, and Editor of the *International Review of Neurobiology* from 1956–1988. He has published over 200 papers and 14 books in the area of basic and clinical neuroscience, neurophilosophy, and neurotheology. His recent books include *The Walls of Plato's Cave* (1994), *The Dynamic Neuron* (2002), and *Trial of God* (2006). He was elected a member of the Athenaeum in 1968.

Edmond Wright holds degrees in English and philosophy and a doctorate in philosophy. He is a member of the Board of Social Theory of the International Sociological Association, and was sometime a Fellow at the Swedish Collegium for the Advanced Study of the Social Sciences, Uppsala. He has edited *The Ironic Discourse* (*Poetics Today*, 4, 1983), *New Representationalisms: Essays in the Philosophy of Perception* (Avebury, 1993), *Faith and the Real* (*Paragraph*, 24, 2001), and coedited with his wife Elizabeth *The Zizek Reader*, and is author of *Narrative, Perception, Language, and Faith* (Macmillan, 2006). Over sixty articles of his have appeared in philosophical journals. He has also published two volumes of poetry.

Index